1995

VALUES BASED PLANNING
FOR QUALITY EDUCATION

HOW TO ORDER THIS BOOK

BY PHONE: 800-233-9936 or 717-291-5609, 8AM–5PM Eastern Time

BY FAX: 717-295-4538

BY MAIL: Order Department
Technomic Publishing Company, Inc.
851 New Holland Avenue, Box 3535
Lancaster, PA 17604, U.S.A.

BY CREDIT CARD: American Express, VISA, MasterCard

PERMISSION TO PHOTOCOPY–POLICY STATEMENT

Mildred L. Burns, Ph.D.

VALUES BASED PLANNING FOR QUALITY EDUCATION

TECHNOMIC
PUBLISHING CO., INC.
LANCASTER · BASEL

Values Based Planning for Quality Education
a TECHNOMIC publication

Published in the Western Hemisphere by
Technomic Publishing Company, Inc.
851 New Holland Avenue, Box 3535
Lancaster, Pennsylvania 17604 U.S.A.

Distributed in the Rest of the World by
Technomic Publishing AG
Missionsstrasse 44
CH-4055 Basel, Switzerland

Printed in the United States of America
10 9 8 7 6 5 4 3 2 1

Main entry under title:
Values Based Planning for Quality Education

A Technomic Publishing Company book
Bibliography: p. 473
Includes index p. 495

Library of Congress Catalog Card No. 95-60606
ISBN No. 1-56676-284-7

To the memory of
Asa and Alice
who valued the past and built for the future
and to
Jeri and Larry,
the future

CONTENTS

Chapter 4. Paradigms and Metaphors   111

Chapter 5. Planning Metaphors and Definitions   155

Chapter 6. Models and Systems of Planning   183

Chapter 7. Dynamics of Participation   229

SECTION III: BUILDING A PLAN BASED IN VALUES

Chapter 8. Logic and Planning   279

TO "make the education system better" is the rallying cry of present-day educators and the public. For some, the reasons and results desired are to be found at the national level, in national economic competition. For others, they are to be found at the personal level with good jobs and high standards of living. For still others, they are to be found in increasing humanity and an expanding world family. Both what a quality education is and how to achieve it are subjects of intense debate.

This book does not offer prescriptions or formulae to address these profoundly important issues. Indeed, it makes the assumption that there are no formulae—there can be no prescriptions. Quality has to do with the individual child, individual teacher, school, and community.

A major proposition of the book is that a broad perspective on values and sets of values offers more potential for growth and development than a narrow perspective on national standards and national curricula. Therefore, the book reviews basic *sources* of different points of view — different patterns of thinking, feeling, and believing.

A second major proposition is that being knowledgeable about many different patterns of thinking and different sets of beliefs about education contributes to that desirable broad perspective. The emphasis in the book is on how to examine different ideas and patterns of thinking to understand them, to recognize their implications, and to make them usable as bases for choice and action.

The third major proposition of the book is that planning is the fundamental process that enables educational leadership, points the direction to valued outcomes, and proposes reasonable means to achieve the results desired. It is assumed that there is no such thing as "goal-free" planning, that such a phrase is an oxymoron, but it is equally assumed that all planning is hypothesis making and that, therefore, all plans are tentative, subject to future realities.

The book proposes that ideas, theories, and models are tools that can help maintain harmony between vision, action, and personal values. The exercises are presented to assist educators and concerned stakeholders to "read" abstract theories or models into the language of the school and classroom, the language of everyday choice and action.

Therefore, the hope is that the book will be useful to leaders at the school level—administrators, teachers, and community members, as well as to students of planning. It is hoped that the book will be useful in two ways—by moving toward a broader perspective on and understanding of values as sources of different ways of thinking and by developing greater skill in use of tools and techniques for applying new ideas to everyday projects and programs for the school. The heart of the philosophy of planning proposed throughout the book is best expressed in the Values-Based Planning System presented in Section III.

To try to acknowledge the debts one owes for the development of a book is an almost impossible task. First, of course, is the debt I owe to all of those scholars whose work has contributed directly or indirectly to the ideas and the substance of this book. Second, an equal debt is owed to all of the students whose questions, challenges, and contributions have forced me to think more clearly and who have added richness and depth to ideas I have presented to them. This debt of gratitude is particularly strong in the case of the 1994 class of master's students who have diligently worked every exercise and have studied and critiqued all ideas and propositions presented.

I must give special thanks to all of the professors at Stanford with whom I studied and worked. Three professors in particular woke up a sleeping mind: N. L. Gage, my thesis advisor and a practical humanist; W. R. Odell, an administrator with a wide angle lens; and L. G. Thomas, philosopher, who forced me to answer my own questions.

I also want to express my appreciation to colleagues at McGill. Professors Ratna Ghosh, Jing Lin, and Clermont Barnabé have constantly battled out ideas with me and offered insightful comments on parts of the present manuscript. Special thanks are due to Dr. Jean Huntley-Maynard, a former student and a friend, who has engaged me in a continuing debate about issues, theories, propositions, and models, and who has spent many hours critiquing and proofreading drafts of the manuscript.

Finally, my most sincere thanks go to two colleagues in Western Canada who read and critiqued major portions of the manuscript, Professors Erwin Miklos of the University of Alberta and Kevin Wilson of the University of Saskatchewan. Both gave valuable feedback on many of the points being developed. Their comments and suggestions were particularly valuable in developing the line of thought and presentation.

THE primary consideration of this book is planning for quality education and determining how the focus on values can be maintained while creating a practical plan. The book is based on the assumption that the meaning of "quality education" comes from beliefs about a "good life," about what should be learned, and about how we learn. Tools useful for planning quality education, particularly at the school level, are described, and practice exercises in the use of such tools are presented. It is intended that the book should be useful for all educational leaders – administrators, teachers, community activists.

It is well known that the ways we think, our habits of thinking and believing learned from our culture, education, and life experiences affect every choice and action. Therefore, to talk about "quality education" or about planning and planning tools for quality education, the sources of our habits of believing and of the "ways we think," must be considered.

This book proposes that every choice and action and every educational plan arises from and *expresses* the deepest, perhaps subconscious, patterns of our beliefs and values. One important aim of the book is to provide tools or techniques for recognizing different patterns of beliefs, ways of viewing the world in general, and education in particular, and for making the patterns themselves available as useful tools for planning and action.

Section I discusses planning as an organizational process and proposes that planning is the key process through which educational leadership is fulfilled. Chapter 1 relates planning to quality education and illustrates some distinctions between planning and decision making. Chapter 2 discusses different ways that planning has been described in the literature: as problem solving, decision making, and system analysis. Differences among these processes are proposed and are related to specific functions that each fulfills for the organization. Models proposing the interactive relationships of administrative processes and organizational functions are presented.

Section II defines *tools* as the term is used in this book, and it proposes three types of planning tools: holistic, process, and management systems tools. It emphasizes that ideas, beliefs, and values are basic tools for educational planning but that, to be *tools,* they must be chosen consciously from sets of ideas and used under appropriate circumstances.

This section proposes that deep structures of beliefs and values provide the holistic meanings that we apply to every hope for the future and to every choice and action. Those deep structures exist at several levels. The deepest are one's beliefs about the meaning of life itself: What is existence? What is reality? What is knowing? and What is learning? For most people, these beliefs are expressed in practical terms, but they act as a philosophy of life and education. These two propositions establish the rationale for Chapters 3 through 7, which present different *sets* of ideas about planning, organizations, education, leadership, and participation as they relate to educational choice and action.

Chapter 3 briefly reviews four philosophical systems and provides exercises for considering whether particular actions, methods, and choices come from well-known philosophical systems. It discusses some of the impact these four systems have had on education.

Chapter 4 considers some examples of general patterns of thinking that have shaped not only research and theory in particular domains of educational endeavor, but have also had tremendous influence on practice. It is generally agreed that these patterns, or "world views" called paradigms, arise out of philosophical orientations and provide perspectives on, or world views of, such domains as organizations, administration, leadership, teaching effects, and learning.

It is proposed that recognizing and understanding the different frames of reference is an important first step toward making patterns of thinking available for conscious use in planning for education. In this chapter, as in all others, the aim is to provide techniques for linking general ideas (theories, paradigms, models) to real situations—*to make ideas more readily available as tools for planning, choice, and action.*

Chapter 5 moves even more closely toward the particular. It presents different perspectives on organizations, administration, and planning as they are expressed in metaphors and definitions.

Chapter 6 discusses models and systems of planning as their orientation has changed since the early twentieth century. It is proposed that three processes are involved in planning, as in all educational activity: conceptual (the use of ideas), norming (the use of expectations and customs), and the dynamics of participation (modes of involvement). Each of these three sets of processes varies along a continuum from an orientation toward the organization and its aims or needs to an orientation toward the individual within the organization.

Although all three vary along this continuum of orientation for choice and action, they are described differently. Conceptual processes are customarily modeled in step-by-step patterns that are linear in nature. Norming processes are more frequently described within classes or categories of expectations and customs. These two sets of processes are discussed in Chapter 6.

Chapter 7 proposes that the processes involved in the dynamics of participation cannot be modeled in the linear patterns of conceptual processes or in categories or classes as norms. It proposes that the processes of participation are interactive, interpersonal, and interdependent. The reality of participation is that it originates and is controlled as much by individual members as by administrators. Planning within groups can become developmental. One effective system for participative planning in groups is described.

Section III presents the Values-Based Planning System developed and used by the author. This system can be considered the heart of the book. All of the bases of thinking in Chapters 1 through 7 lead up to this system. They provide the sources of all plans and can help focus this planning system, or any planning system, on values and quality education.

Chapter 8 presents the logic base of planning. It defines planning as hypothesis making and provides exercises to relate goals and options to the IF↔THEN basis of hypotheses. Each step in the Values-Based Planning System is described and illustrated in Chapters 9 and 10.

Some readers may wish to begin with Section III, the "how to do it" chapters. Students using this book as a guide to better planning for their schools are expected to carry forward at the same time, both the background thinking put forward in Chapters 1 through 7 and building a plan based in values as described in Section III.

Chapter 8 discusses forms of logic and how they are applicable to planning. It proposes that any planning system is a map of the logic of a completed plan but not necessarily of the order in which thinking proceeds. Thinking customarily begins with *action,* not with a *goal,* but the Values-Based Planning System proposes that all steps in the logic of a plan must be thought through for values to become the basis for action.

Chapter 9 presents the first stage in the logic of a plan, the meaning of success. It is emphasized that describing goals and objectives is seldom the first step in planning, but clarifying the meaning of success is fundamental to good planning. *It is the meaning of success that grounds any plan firmly in values.*

Chapter 10 takes the process of planning through Stages Two, Three, and Four. Stage Two is unique to the Values-Based Planning System. It requires the planners to set a value cost on the potential project *before* choosing the specific project to be implemented. This stage of planning is related to "environmental scanning," as proposed in much of the strategic planning literature. It asks the planners to estimate time and effort (resources) that can be committed to the particular outcome desired, the value to be focused on in perspective of the total commitments, aims, and purposes of the school or system.

Stage Three presents techniques for analyzing the probability of success and the feasibility of alternative strategies or proposals. Stage Four, planning the action, is most familiar to educators. Techniques for task analysis and resource allocation planning are presented.

Section IV describes process tools and management systems tools that have been found useful for particular purposes in education. Chapter 11 describes tools and techniques that have been used to identify goals for education, needs of special groups, or directions the education system should take under changing circumstances. Management by objectives (MBO) is discussed as an overall management system focused on clarifying objectives and aims.

Chapter 12 describes common tools for resource and for cost/benefit analysis. Tools for analysis and coordination of tasks, such as PERT and CPM, and the SPEC system are described. Types of budgeting systems are presented as tools for resource use, planning, and control. Their usefulness as analytical planning tools is compared in terms of the types of information they provide to planners.

Chapter 13 summarizes the ideas presented in the book and reviews the aims set out for the book. The plan of the book is illustrated below.

This format emphasizes that Sections II and III parallel to each other. As with planning itself, many readers will be comfortable to go from Section I directly to action (Section III) and return to reasoning and the bases of thinking (Section II).

Section I: Planning: A Skill for Leaders

CH. 1: Planning and Quality Education
CH. 2: Planning and Related Processes

Section II: Values Bases of Planning	Section III: Building a Plan Based in Values
CH. 3: Philosophy and Planning	CH. 8: Logic and Planning
CH. 4: Paradigms and Metaphors	CH. 9: The Meaning of Success
CH. 5: Metaphors and Definitions	CH. 10: Value Cost, Choice, and Action
CH 6: Models and Systems of Planning	
CH. 7: Dynamics of Participation	

Section IV: Tools Useful for Specific Purposes

CH. 11: Vision and Perspective
CH. 12: Task Analysis and Resource Use
CH. 13: Summary and Conclusion

PLANNING: A SKILL FOR LEADERS

IT might well be proposed that human achievement could be recorded in the history of processes developed to make it possible for people to work comfortably in groups toward some end or purpose. Among these many processes (including, among many others, communicating, decision making, supervising, motivating, and coordinating), planning is recognized as one of the most vital. Planning is the process that consciously and intentionally looks to the future for the most desirable outcomes of action, and tries to create the best means to achieve those outcomes.

Whether planning should focus on the distant ideal future or on the immediate critical present has been debated. Whether educational "planning" is even possible or useful has also been debated. This book takes the position that planning is inevitable, so it behooves us to make it as productive and as useful as possible, to make every effort to orient it toward ends we value. This can be done most effectively if planners are conscious of their own value systems and are knowledgeable about the many different value systems that may be brought to the education table.

Section I presents the perspective on planning developed in this book. It proposes that planning is the process that looks at both the future and the present and concerns itself with bringing the desired future into being today. A plan points to the direction considered desirable and proposes reasonable and feasible means for moving effectively toward the desired results. Because leadership is also a matter of "where we are going" (the direction the group shall take), it is proposed that planning is the key process that supports leadership in any organization, and it is the key process through which quality education is defined and comes into perspective.

Everyone in an organization makes plans for the organization

1

(whether formally or informally, whether legitimately or not); it follows, therefore, that everyone is to some degree, or at some level, a leader in the organization. Becoming better planners can enable members to have greater impact on choice and action. *Good planning helps make good leaders.* Thus, planning is particularly critical because the dramatic changes foreseen for the twenty-first century are rapidly approaching.

Many tools have been developed to help educational planners be logical and systematic in their work. These include models, systems, and descriptions of various steps in planning. Other tools provide techniques for thinking differently—nonlogic, or visionary, creative thinking. To learn to use these tools to create the quality of learning and achievement we aim for is the focus of study for planning.

Beyond using such technical tools well, however, the study of planning must concern itself with the sources of our beliefs about what quality education means and with the differences that may exist in any community. It is readily accepted that mature social behavior requires one to dress and act appropriately for the particular situation. It is also a common proposition of leadership literature that one should vary one's style of leadership according to various contingency factors.

It is a basic assumption of this book that, by recognizing different patterns of beliefs about education, administrators and all educators can learn to use the patterns that fit the circumstances and can learn to use the patterns themselves as tools for planning. Therefore, Section II considers the different patterns of beliefs and perspectives that have produced different visions of quality education.

CHAPTER 1

Planning and Quality Education

To plan is to assert faith in the future.

INTRODUCTION

WE take it as an article of faith that any action that has a "reason for being," that has purpose, is to some degree *planned*. In fact, purpose could be seen as the defining characteristic of planning because it frames planning in the contexts of values held, future orientation, and intention or will. It is particularly important to accept this perspective in the case of planning for quality education. Will plans support the values held for education and fulfill the purposes for which the education system has been established and is supported and maintained by the various publics it serves?

We assume, too, that purposes are conscious or unconscious expressions of values. They are values made intentional through goals, objectives, and proposed action. The ends or outcomes we value in life often come into conflict with each other. We value both justice and mercy. As Portia made movingly clear in *The Merchant of Venice,* which of those intentions will prevail may not be easily resolved. We value equality of opportunity *and* the right to pursue personal advancement; "unto the least of these" *and* "I did it my way"; better roads, education, and health services *and* lower taxes. The values people hold for education compete with other values they hold—for safety or comfort, for example, or for self-expression and pleasure, even for "titles, power, and pelf."[1] Purpose puts will, commitment, and resources at the disposal of particular values.

In financial matters, the term *value* is understood in quantitative

---

[1]Sir Walter Scott, "The Lay of the Last Minstrel." *Pelf* is from ancient French: money, wealth, perhaps ill-gotten gains.

terms. It implies a cost/benefit ratio—the worth of a thing under varying market conditions. In behavioral studies, the terms $\underline{a}$ *value* and *values* are understood in qualitative terms. They imply principles upon which choices are made and actions are based. A person with "high principles" and a person who has "good values" mean much the same thing in common discourse. They describe a person who acts consistently on the bases of moral and ethical precepts.

The values we hold for education generally have to do with the quality of learning that is achieved and the quality of life that exists during and after the period of formal education. Throughout Sections I and II, the terms *values* and *a value* are used with that qualitative meaning, implying moral, ethical, and professional principles as bases of choice and action. In Chapter 10, "Value Cost, Choice, and Action," *value cost* is used with cost/benefit implications. *Cost* is quantified in terms of time and other resources used, and *benefit* is quantified in terms of measures of success.

Values are close to the heart of education systems. Beliefs about and hopes for life are central to our thinking when it comes to our children. We universally have high hopes for our children's lives and futures; however, it is a realistic fact that different people, in different periods, hold different beliefs about what a "good life" is and what will bring it about. This fact is part of what creates the complexity of determining direction, goals, programs, curricula, policies, and practices in modern education systems. What *is* quality education; in what direction *should* the system be headed?

Planning is the conscious effort to deal with such complexities, to define *quality* by clarifying values to be aimed for and to point the way to quality in education by proposing reasonable means to achieve those values. Techniques for thinking through complexities to create a reasonable proposal for action have been developed. These "thinking tools," many of which have been invented to promote better planning and decision making, provide methods for creating links between values, quality education, and action.

EMPHASIS IN THE LITERATURE

Planning was recognized early as a key factor in good management or successful administration; it was one of the five factors named by

Fayol (1949), for example. However, when one examines the organizational and administrative literature related to education, one finds little emphasis placed on planning and discovers that the tone of discussions about planning is often negative. Compared with decision making, for example, planning holds a low priority in published textbooks, research reports, and presentations of theoretical or practical discussions of administration. An ERIC search covering all publications to 1982 produced 5239 titles under educational decision making and only 573 under planning. The totals for the period 1979 to 1982 were 407 and 175, respectively.

Equally revealing is an analysis of thirty-five texts and references on school administration published between 1960 and 1985 to determine the relative emphasis on four topics considered particularly relevant to the school system's ability to move effectively toward quality education: decision making, leadership, planning, and values. Three indicators were used: a count of all listings in the table of contents and index, number of pages allocated to the topic at each listing, and total number of works cited in which the particular concept occurred in the title. Figure 1.1 shows the relative emphasis on each of the four topics.

It is clear that through the mid-1980s, planning and values received much less emphasis in the literature than did decision making or leadership. Indeed, decision making was commonly accepted as the heart of administration. Even more unfortunate is the tone in which planning has been presented. Commonly held views are expressed in such statements as, ''Planning is often viewed as a luxury which few administrators can afford'' (Sergiovanni and Carver, 1980, 285), or ''When planning is most needed, it is least feasible'' (Friedmann, 1973). Propositions about ''goal-free'' planning and the ''garbage can'' metaphor of the organization also imply that planning is misdirected or hardly worth the effort.

It is my position that all four concerns are basic to directing the school system toward quality education. I propose that planning and decision making are parallel processes, contributing equally to the direction an organization takes, and that both processes arise from and express the values that take priority under particular circumstances. Planning as a process supports the function of leadership in an organization and permits adaptability to changing conditions. Decision making supports the function of legislation, or regulation and norming, and thus contributes to the stability or predictability of action and operation.

More recently, planning is receiving increased attention. This may be

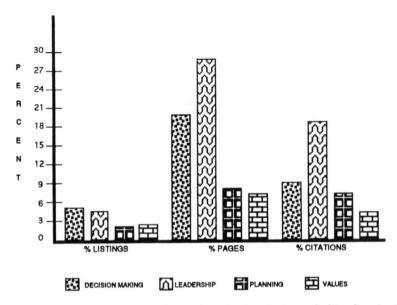

Figure 1.1. Relative emphasis on four topics related to the issue of taking direction in education. From thirty-five educational administration textbooks, 1960–1985. (Based on Table 1, Burns, 1985, 2.)

due in part to the emphasis on strategic planning in the literature of private sector management; however, other more fundamental factors are involved in education. Changes taking place in the meaning of work have brought about changes in the dynamics of administration. Electronic technologies make information so quickly available that administrators are pressured for better informed, more immediate, and broader based generation of ideas, plans, and decisions. A more mature, better educated, and culturally diverse work force demands consideration of multiple interests. Unstable social conditions, scarce resources, and competing demands for those resources have forced attention onto priorities.

The result of such changes is increased emphasis on planning in the public sector and particularly in education. However, the complexities of the present have forced planning attention onto the social and political processes that are involved in determining directions and "best means." The emphasis has turned from analytical and technical processes emphasized in that large body of decision-making literature to strategies, negotiating, involvement, policy-making, and communication [see, for example, Freire (1985), Lewis (1986), Beneviste (1989), Murphy (1990), Carlson and Awkerman (1991), Kaufman and Herman (1991), and Shashkin and Walberg (1993)].

Decision-making literature did, of course, address the two dimensions, sociopolitical and conceptual. Participation in decision making and models of decision making form two large, separate sectors of the body of administrative literature. The question of how to plan well for an organization incorporates the same two dimensions, the social process dimension and the conceptual process dimension. The literature of planning has drawn heavily on the literature of decision making.

Planning involves choices. Choices are made at every step in creating a plan, so the two processes are integrally related. It is our view, however, that they do not serve the same function in the system and that the process emphasis employed differs. It is proposed that planning emphasizes conceptual processes (though sociopolitical processes are also critical). Planning *conceptualizes* values and hypothesizes means to achieve those values. Decision making emphasizes sociopolitical processes (though conceptual processes are involved). Decision making *confirms* values and one or more of the hypotheses proposed.

Similarities among Process Descriptions

The study of organizations and groups and of organizational or group action can be frustrating for several reasons. One difficulty lies in identifying the boundaries of the specific behavioral phenomena to study, such as planning, decision making, problem solving, and systems analysis. Another lies in the lack of a commonly accepted conceptual terminology for these phenomena. In everyday action, we are reasonably clear about when we are planning, making decisions, solving problems, or analyzing the system. Common usage assigns different names to these related phenomena, even though it is extremely difficult to distinguish among them in action terms. They do not take place in isolation; the *set* of processes works interactively to fulfill purposes.

However, definitions and descriptions in the literature cannot make easy distinctions. Even a cursory examination of any set of descriptions of planning, decision making, problem solving, systems analysis, and change strategies reveals commonalities. The steps to be taken in each of these processes or the actions identified as elements of each are much the same. An analysis of thirty-two descriptions of related processes revealed that the steps or actions most commonly included, regardless of which specific process was being described, are the following (Burns, 1978a, 5):

(*1*) (Identification) (clarification) of (needs) (goals) (problems) (objectives)

(*2*) (Documentation) (getting information)

(*3*) Identification of alternative (strategies) (tools) (methods)

(*4*) (Listing advantages and disadvantages of each set of alternatives) (analyzing alternatives)

(*5*) Deciding on action

(*6*) Arranging for (implementation) (test) (execution)

(*7*) Determining performance effectiveness

I propose that this set of activities incorporates the several administrative processes that provide guidance and direction for the education system. I believe that each process, planning, decision making, systems analysis, and problem solving makes its own particular contribution to the overall guidance and direction of the education system. I assume that these processes are not separable or discrete and cannot take place in isolation from each other; however, they are seen in common sense terms as somehow different from each other. It can be profitable for further study of administration in general and planning in particular to accept the hypothesis that identifiably different phenomena exist and to attempt to clarify each in terms of its contribution to the system and the technologies and skills involved.

In the next two sections, there is consideration of the two administrative processes, planning and decision making, because they have been so closely related in the literature. Indeed, planning is often defined as an element of, or step in, the decision-making process. Some distinctions will be drawn between them, and a case example is presented that illustrates those distinctions.

Planning

If there is, as we have seen above, so much similarity in the descriptions of the processes of planning and decision making, is it possible to distinguish between them except by arbitrary definition? A plan may come into effect because a decision is made, but, in common discourse, plans and decisions are not thought of in the same terms. A plan is inherently a prototype, a test of a set of "things" and relationships among those things, that, it is predicted (hypothesized), will result in a particular outcome, a particular thing, action, or event. A plan is a test, in miniature or in brief, of a set of proposed choices. Generally prepared for decision makers, a plan presents, in some form established by relevant conventions, a simulation or model considering hypothesized relationships between the proposed choices and the outcome.

The everyday language we use to speak about planning and decision making gives evidence that we think of them differently. We say, for example, "We *are* planning," but more often, "we *will* decide" or "we *have* decided." That is, planning is thought of as an activity over time, while decision making is thought of as at a point in time. A plan proposes a course of action; a decision either confirms or denies it. A decision is ultimately either "yes" or "no," an end point in any consideration that leads directly to action.

Planners have, of course, made choices; choice making has taken place throughout the process of planning. These are choices to test, in simulation, the possible effects of one factor upon others and upon the whole. They are not decisions that bind implementers to action. The choice to design an open-area school or a school in connected pods and the choices of particular elements for either design are not binding on the public for action or on the public dollar. Different architects propose different designs and different plans, and competition between designs is accepted practice in such major projects.

The decision to accept one proposed design and the decisions to use specific materials, methods, and techniques as construction proceeds are binding. The fact that decisions, or choices, have been made during the planning period does not obviate the fact that the plan that develops is a model, a set of hypothesized relationships, a set of *proposed* choices, not a set of decisions for action.

Eisenhower's proposed battle plan for the final attack on Berlin in World War II was very different from Montgomery's battle plan for the same operation. Because of his perceptions of the situation, Eisenhower's plan rested on the design principle, the strategy, of "encircle and contain." The plan proposed by Montgomery, arising out of different perceptions of the same situation, was based on the principle "thrust and divide." Both plans hypothesized the same outcome, victory, but they proposed different sets of actions and relationships among groups of men and materiel[2] (Ryan, 1966, 199 – 203).

Eisenhower's plan was implemented and, while ultimately successful, was found to be inadequate operationally in certain respects. The same would have been true if Montgomery's plan had been implemented. A plan is not fixed, unchangeable. It is tentative, based on predicted conditions and hypothesized relationships. It is subject to modification to meet real conditions as they arise. A battle plan, a blueprint, an outline, a design, all are simulations, conceptual models developed for the purpose of proposing hypothesized lines of action and subjecting those hypotheses to testing and review prior to decision and also during action.

The psychology that builds up around a set of hypotheses is different from that which surrounds a set of decisions. In their impact, they differ. When someone says, "I think thus and so would work," the reaction is almost automatically to test the proposal mentally. Discussion and debate may ensue; change and modification may result. When someone says, "I have decided that we will do thus and so," the reaction may be mental debate, but there is less opening provided for discussion and modification.

In its form, a plan, or conceptual model, is both general (abstract) and specific (concrete). The process of planning requires both analysis and synthesis; the whole must be made specific through its parts, and the parts must compose the desired whole. A plan moves from the abstract to the concrete in two directions: in the direction of describing the desired outcome in terms of criteria and standards of success and in the direction of specifying elements of the whole, tasks necessary for operation or action and resources to be provided. The whole, the concept, should be revealed as clearly through the objectives ↔ actions relationships as through the objectives ↔ standards relationships specified. Figure 1.2 illustrates the two-directional characters of planning.

All planning proceeds in much the same pattern. What is often called "rational" planning generally requires that the "model" or plan should be developed in some concrete form, and that the relationships assumed between ends and means should be clearly specified. Thus, a more careful testing of hypothesized relationships is possible; however, even if the rationality of a plan has not been carefully tested by the planners,

---

[2]*Materiel* is the military term for "all material things of an army except personnel."

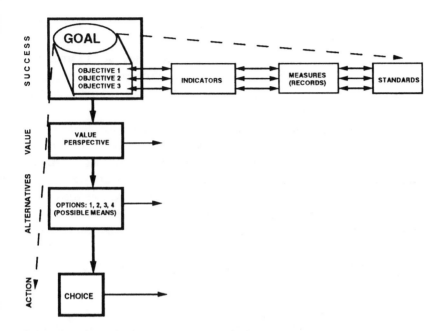

Figure 1.2. *Planning moves from abstract to concrete, or from general to specific, in two directions: toward standards of success and toward action.*

planning is essentially rational in nature. By nature, any plan proposes a means to an end.

Planning, then, is the *process* of preparing a conceptual model of a thing, an action, or an event. It is one of two processes that affect, in fundamental ways, the direction an organization or group takes. The other is decision making. The two processes determine direction; they balance each other. Planning points out direction, and decision making establishes a chosen direction for group action. They should take place in harmony with each other. Planning without decisions destroys enthusiasm and motivation; decisions without planning are potentially dangerous.

Decision Making

Definitions of decision making are relatively consistent, there being general agreement that it involves making choices among alternatives. Discussions of decision making come to us from two quite different perspectives, however. From one perspective, as illustrated above, decision making is a process that includes systematic rational steps. Such descriptions vary from lists of procedural steps intended to maximize rationality to sophisticated statistical models for testing interrelationships among elements. They tend to come out of the mathematics, scientific management, and management literature.

From another perspective, we are presented propositions, questions, and research findings concerned with "participation" in decision making: who should participate, in what decisions, how much participation is desired, effectiveness of participation, participation and structure. Other propositions consider factors that influence decisions: psychological or personal factors, power and influence, social relationships, negotiations, conflict, bargaining, values effected in decisions. These discussions tend to come from the political science, sociopolitical perspective and focus on the following three central sociopolitical activities in decision making:

(*1*) *Organizing alternatives* — gathering or collecting possible alternatives for choice. Shall there be consultation with a variety of members of a group, or shall the set of possible choices be determined by one or a few persons? What types of choices (decisions) necessitate the expertise or interest of what members? How shall the information of "experts" or interest groups be elicited?

(*2*) *Rank-ordering alternatives* by individuals or groups based on personal sets of values or priorities. What influences and wants are felt by individuals participating, and how important are those issues for the individuals or groups involved? How much conflict exists in personal priorities? What demands are placed?

(*3*) *Weighting the choices or priorities* of various individuals or groups. What individuals or influence groups shall be allowed to participate in the choice? What members are willing to participate and under what conditions? How shall the choices of various individuals or groups be "counted" — by ballot? by assent? by acclamation? by fiat? To what degree is the decision binding on all individuals?

A decision ends with a choice among competing values; there is no evidence by which priorities may be validated. The only logic appropriate to assessing values is the logic of integration, or the hierarchy of values — the logic that raises the question, "Is this value in harmony with larger values?'' The logic of decision process is the logic of preparing for choice and of carrying out the prescribed system of weighing and weighting conflicting values, in legal terms "due process."

A plan starts from chosen values, and the logic of whether proposed actions and resources are likely to achieve that value can be checked. That is, the outcome desired is specified, and the relationships among means are evident. There are internal evidences of the process of planning by which the plan itself and the process employed may be judged. The degree to which and the logic by which specific conceptual activities have been undertaken is quite evident in the plan itself.

A plan reveals the mind and the intention of the planner because it specifies both action and purpose; a decision gives no evidence of the decision maker's purposes. Concern about hidden agendas and manipulative tactics point out how frequently reasons for decisions are not what they seem to be.

A Case Example of Planning and Decision Making

A true account of an operation undertaken during World War II gives an excellent case illustration of the processes of planning and decision making. This story, *Cockleshell Heroes* by Lucas-Phillips (1957), details the establishment, development, and operation of one small unit of the British forces, the Royal Marine Boom Patrol Division (RMBPD), from its conception through planning and proposing an infiltration operation. It clearly distinguishes between plan and decision.

The RMBPD, under Lt. Hassler, was given the task of developing small boats, equipment, and techniques for deep infiltration into enemy-held waters, specifically Bordeaux Harbour, for the purpose of putting an end to enemy blockade running between Germany and Japan. When the unit was ready, Lt. Hassler prepared a plan for infiltration involving twelve men in six "cockles." He proposed to lead the exercise. The cockles would be launched from a submarine in the Channel under cover of night. The exercise would entail three nights of travel by cockle in absolute silence up the Garonne River and three days of holing up in enemy territory. The boats and equipment had been specifically designed and the men specially trained in tactics and skills.

The plan was daring and precise in detail, revealing imagination and arduous preparation on the part of Lt. Hassler. The decision was made that the operation should be undertaken as proposed. The decision itself reveals little; it would seem almost automatic, coming from the plan and from the purpose for which the RMBPD had been established. But the decision-making process was also revealing of the persons involved and of the sociopolitical process of the circumstances, and that process can only be known from observation or participation.

Lt. Hassler presented his plan for the operation to the Combined Operations Headquarters (COHQ) with Lord Mountbatten as chief of staff. By assent, it was agreed that the operation should be undertaken. After discussion, it was agreed that the operation would be deemed successful if the group successfully mined at least six blockade-running ships in Bordeaux Harbour. It was seriously questioned, however, whether Lt. Hassler should lead his men. Pros and cons were strongly pressed. All members of the COHQ staff felt strongly that the risk of losing Lt. Hassler was too great and that it outweighed his own plea that a leader must lead his men.

Finally, Lord Mountbatten polled the individual chiefs of staff. Each one voted "no." Then Lord Mountbatten said, in effect, "My own judgment tells me, too, that you should not go. However, I recognize the imperative of your plea, and you may lead the operation." The decision-making process was a personal and interpersonal process, weighing values held and weighting responsibilities, not the rational means-ends equation of the planning process.

Planning and Decision Making Distinguished

We suggest that the decision-making process is this personal-interpersonal interchange, that it is sociopolitical in nature and essentially nonrational in character. That is, it is outside of the precise means/ends logic of rationality.[3] The ends or values upon which individual choices are made are not open to inspection. The same choice of particular means

[3]It is difficult to distinguish clearly between rational, logical, and nonrational. At times in the literature, *rational* is used to mean "having clear relationships between means and ends." This sometimes also implies "employing quantitative data as a basis for choice." At other times, rational means "firmly grounded in reality." Since hopes, fears, and imaginary demons are psychological "reality," choices made on the basis of pschological "ends," it might be argued, are "firmly grounded in reality." When we bring into the discussion of "rationality" the sociopolitical forces that play in the process, we must, perforce, accept that the means/ends logic of emotional and cultural choice is rational on a different plane.

by members of a group may be based on different sets of values. The choice to base a decision on systematic analysis, to respect quantitative data such as in Decision Tree Analysis or Program Evaluation Review Technique (PERT), is a values choice, the choice to rely on system and objective data over subjective data and intuition.

Three activities, all of them sociopolitical in nature, dominate in the decision-making process, namely 1) collecting a "bank" of alternatives, 2) choosing separately by individuals and/or groups, and 3) weighting the separate choices. As in the case of Lord Mountbatten, often enough, one vote carries more "weight" than the votes of many.

The decision-making process can be made somewhat systematic. Groups and organizations establish, by law or by custom, systems for carrying out activities one and three, collecting sets of alternatives, and weighting the separate choices of individuals (from no weight in a dictatorship to equal weight by ballot). Organization charts, constitutions, labor contracts, codes of laws all attempt to systematize the decision-making process. Such documents identify who shall make what decisions, in what manner members of a group may be involved, and by what methods they may influence decisions. They attempt to make objective, even rational, a very subjective, arational process, the process of setting priorities on values held. Figure 1.3 proposes the varying emphases on conceptual and sociopolitical processes that operate in planning and decision making.

Just as it is laws, policies, and customs that attempt to regulate or make systematic the process of decision making, it is the process of decision making by which the legislative, or regulatory, function of governance is carried out, by which laws, customs, policies, and purposes are established and agreed upon. Two processes, planning which emphasizes conceptual processes, and decision making in which sociopolitical processes dominate, operate together to establish direction in an organization.

Figure 1.3. *It is proposed that conceptual processes are dominant in planning and that sociopolitical processes are dominant in decision making.*

LOGIC AND RATIONALITY IN PLANNING

All administrative action (in fact, all educational activity) is based on predictions. We predict that *IF* we do A/B/C, *THEN* X, Y, or Z will happen. Or we *assume* that X, Y, or Z will happen, without consciously thinking about cause and effect.

Planning attempts to bring those predictions into clearer focus. It consciously uses the logic of cause/effect thinking. The logic of planning should propose cause/effect relationships that can be recognized as reasonable. It should be clear that the proposed actions (IF we do ___) would, with reasonable probability, produce the desired result (THEN there will be ___).

However, logic is not sufficient, because ways and means of getting results are not always moral, ethical, or socially or culturally acceptable. So an educational plan must be feasible and ethical, as well as logical. A plan must live within the context of the situation. Logic asks the question, "Would it work?" Rationality broadens the question to, "Would it work given the real world (or school community) within which we live? Is it in harmony with values held and ends or outcomes desired? Is it firmly grounded in reality?" Logic is a mental exercise; rationality places that mental exercise into its human context. The logic of a plan can be produced in isolation; the rationality of the plan requires the multiple perspectives of those who will be affected.

A plan is logical if it is internally consistent; it is rational if it is firmly grounded in reality. Thus, the two dimensions of any plan are its rational basis in the reality of context (the values that are accepted for the community or system) and its logical consistency, the probability that the actions proposed will result in achieving the values upon which it is based.

Two kinds of process skills are, therefore, important to maintain the values-based planning perspective in education. For education plans to be rational, effective, and moral, the processes of logical thought and the processes of social relationships are critical skills. Tools have been developed over the decades of the twentieth century that can be used to enhance both domains.

The two sets of processes cannot be thought of in the same terms, however. Conceptual processes are customarily described in serial or procedural steps. Social processes are interactively incremental in nature; this is inevitable. They may be incremental in a cumulative or additive sense or in the sense of development, growth, or change. That is, people thinking together in groups accumulate pools of thought or ideas; one idea will react to, replace, or build upon the previous ones. Each stimulates development or clarification. Because they are interactive and incremental, social processes cannot be defined in procedural steps. They can be imagined more in the visual of Mandelbrot sets, forever expanding in patterns relevant to norms and customs. They are defined in terms of competing interest sectors and constituent groups, in dimensions of orientation, as person versus task, or in expanding cycles of awareness and understanding. These contexts and dimensions identify the interactive play of value bases.

This book will deal primarily with the tools of logical thought processes related to planning, and will propose methods by which the logic of planning can be kept grounded in values, and aimed at quality.

QUALITY EDUCATION

The whole purpose of planning for education and for attempting to use planning tools effectively is to bring about quality education for our students. The quality of education has never been more intensely the object of public attention than in the decades just prior to the twenty-first century.

For at least fifty years, well into the twentieth century, North America was virtually undisputed as the leader in providing universal, high-quality education to its youth. Few questions were raised about the importance of education or about the value of extended years of schooling for individuals. Young people were impressed with the fact that particular vocations were more prestigious than others, that higher income related to those prestigious occupations, and that access to them was through extended years of schooling.

By mid-century a period of increasing disillusionment with education began for students and for the public. Taxpayers questioned both costs and effectiveness of the system. Young people rebelled against what they saw as the gap between schooling and real life. Much of the student rebellion of the 1960s was directed at the depersonalization of education factories, at the lack of relevance of education as they were experiencing it, and at the discrepancy between values taught and values lived.

Timothy Leary, Bob Dylan, and other LSD gurus urged young students to "drop out and tune in," drop out of university and tune in to people or real experience. Songs like "Ticky-Tacky Houses" sneered at the values that middle-class and immigrant parents had lived and worked for. "Educated canon fodder" and "The Killing Fields" were the anguished cries of the Vietnam war years.

The great swing in North Americans' faith in the education system is represented by the contrasting visions of Counts (1932) in *Dare the Schools Build a New Social Order?* and Illich (1971) in *Deschooling Society.* The widely differing perspectives on what the purpose of schooling in North America is and should be remains in the current reform debate.

Educators such as Giroux (1983, 1992), Greene (1980, 1983), and Eisner (1992a, 1992b) argue for an orientation toward moral, ethical, and humanistic purpose. The public responds in *Phi Delta Kappan* Gallup polls (Elam and Gallup, 1989) with economic rationales for education. Reasons parents stated for wanting their children to get a good education included "job opportunities/better job; preparation for life/better life; financial security/economic stability; and better paying job." Percentages responding with this series of reasons were 77% in 1986 and 88% in 1989 (Elam and Gallup, 1989, 48).

Moreover, much public criticism of the "effectiveness" of our education systems in the *Why Johnny Can't Read* era (Flesch, 1955) focused on the proposition that North America's technological and scientific leadership had been overtaken. Current criticism is focused on the proposition that North America's economic viability is declining on the world scene (Askey, 1992; Baker, 1993).

At the same time, loudly vocal minorities cry out for educational rights. Girls must be allowed to "win" in school; older workers must be provided with new training; language minorities must be educated in their own language; special needs children must be allowed to enjoy full social experience. Few people would deny the human tragedies created by failure to respond to such cries. But the education system, designed for "mass production," is not easily redesigned, despite the fact that technology may make a totally individualized learning system reality within a few decades.

Meanwhile, "the school" exists. Educators and the public continue to struggle between visions and limitations in very human ways: social, political, emotional, and conceptual. Our visions of quality education and better life lie deep within our beliefs and values. To make those beliefs and values more consciously usable, to make them tools to create the education and life we imagine, is the continuing task of educators. We must know the implications of possible choices for our values and for the results we hope to achieve as well as a chess master knows the alternative "games" the opponent may "play."

Although ideal democratic citizenship and economic strength were considered harmonious aims in the early twentieth century, those two purposes are today often viewed as conflicting. Clarifying values, priorities, and purposes, and the means for achieving them is the realm of planning, and planning tools are available for thinking out all of the issues related to good planning.

SUMMARY

This chapter has proposed that planning is essentially a conceptual process, though that process may be undertaken by one individual or by a group. And in any group, sociopolitical processes inevitably become an important factor that must be understood and accepted.

Planning and decision making develop and establish direction for the education system and for the school. These processes are two of those needed to manage and govern the organization. They are considered critical administrative processes in an organization because they affect the organization and all of its members.

The conceptual processes of planning involve logical thinking skills: analysis, synthesis, imagining, inference, and judgment. All of these thinking skills are related to hypothesis generating and hypothesis testing. The general pattern of logical thinking in the western world follows the analysis proposed by Dewey (1933, 106–116).

It is proposed that logical thought processes and social processes are the two dimensions that all administrative activity includes and that both are "rational" in the sense that each arises out of its own domain of human reality and strives toward justifiable ends, though the basis of justification differs. Social processes stem from social reality, the psychological reality of humans in interaction. Logical thought processes stem from objective reality, the reality of the objective world (or organization) in which people live. Logical thought processes are dominant in planning, while interpersonal processes are dominant in decision making. Tools have been developed over the decades of the twentieth century that can be used to develop skills in each domain. Effective use of planning tools can increase the probability of quality education.

Chapter 2 will continue the discussion of planning and decision making and will discuss other related administrative processes and organizational functions. It will present models that propose relationships among the various processes and functions. Models such as those presented provide "visual memory hooks" that trigger review of the many factors that must be considered in creating any plan. Chapter 2 will conclude Section I.

Section II will consider the sources of our ways of thinking about planning, choice and action for education. It will move from the broad general base of understanding, our philosophy of education, toward ways of thinking about increasingly specific aspects related to educational planning.

Planning and Related Processes

RELATIONSHIPS AND INTERRELATIONSHIPS

DISCUSSIONS of administrative processes such as planning, decision making, problem solving, systems analysis, and change strategies sound much alike in the literature. This is partly because no particular process *ever* takes place in isolation. Moreover, there is no beginning or end to any of these administrative processes. All are intercyclical; each process takes place within the cycle of every other, and each contributes to and develops upon all related processes.

Analyzing takes place at several points in making a decision or developing a plan. An analysis itself must be planned, and choices of analysis base, scope, and detail take place within the analysis. Some planning almost always precedes making a decision, and choices are made at every step of the planning process. Decisions are necessarily a key factor in problem solving, and planning can be incorporated into the crisis situation of a "problem."

However, each of these processes has a cycle of events peculiar to itself, and each performs its own function and makes its own contribution to the organization. Each has its own purpose and its own place in administrative thinking. The first part of this chapter will propose some distinctions between planning and problem solving and will present some graphic models from the literature that seem particularly useful as "thinking tools" to aid planners.

The idea of planning as decision making will then be discussed and some ways in which systems analysis and system thinking relate to planning will be considered briefly. It is proposed that no one process is the "heart and soul" of administration. The question is not "Which is right?", but "Where is each process most helpful?"

Three other aspects of administrative and organizational action are also particularly important in thinking productively about planning. These are values, leadership, and participation. They will be discussed more fully in Section II. Values are the criteria upon which choices of and judgments about organizational direction are made. Values are the criteria upon which planning and decision making balance adaptability (the capacity to meet future needs) with stability (maintenance of common effort and united action). The value bases of educational planning are discussed in Chapters 3, 4, and 5, and techniques for clarifying values and making it possible to use them more consciously as tools for planning are proposed.

Leadership is a second aspect of organizational concern that is closely related to planning. The mental images that both planning and leadership project are of future action. Both are concerned with pointing the "way to go"; both give direction to the organization. Philosophies, paradigms, and metaphors of leadership enter into the discussion of values bases in Section II.

A third question that must be resolved for any planning activity is the question of participation. In the literature of educational administration, participation is discussed almost solely in relation to decision making. Of course, participation is critical to every aspect of any organization. Teaching is certainly participating in the business of education, as is hall duty, marking papers, meeting with parents, attending conferences, serving on committees, and counseling students. And participation in planning for quality education (much of which does not take place in groups, but in the privacy of the teacher's classroom) deserves more attention. Some issues relevant to the dynamics of participation in planning are discussed in Chapter 7.

Each of these three related concepts enters into the discussion of models that propose relationships among administrative processes and organizational functions and concerns. Three models from the literature are presented in the second part of this chapter. In the third part, I present my own model of the administrative and organizational relationships that are particularly relevant to planning.

THE LANGUAGE OF DISCUSSION

Classes of Phenomena

A second source of language confusion lies in the fact that we are not consistent in the use of *classifying* terminology. Careful classification of phenomena is a distinguishing characteristic of the "hard sciences" and the professions derived from those sciences: engineering, medicine, architecture. In the behavioral studies, classifying terms exist, and they are used in both theoretical and practice-based discussions. Organizational, interpersonal, and individual phenomena are commonly spoken of as processes, functions, states, conditions, principles, systems, or policies.

However, any particular phenomenon may be identified as a function, task, process, or relationship. There is no clear classification, or identification, of any of the behavioral phenomena discussed. For example, leadership has been called a process (Meath, 1971, 97), a set of tasks (Vroom and Yetton, 1973, 6), a function (Davis, 1969, 313), a control process (Parsons, 1967, 276), and it is commonly referred to as a relationship, even as a negotiated relationship.

Planning, decision making, problem solving, and systems analysis are commonly considered processes, although it will become evident as the discussion progresses that they have also been spoken of as functions or skills. In common usage, and by definition in the literature, function and process are viewed as distinct classes of phenomena. Hills defined function as a contribution to a system, thus an outcome of action (1967, 10). Kaufman gave a similar definition, "Function [is] one of a group of related outcomes (or products or subproducts) contributing to a larger outcome (or product)" (1972, 75). "Process," Griffiths proposed, "is a *cycle of events* in which a consistent quality or direction can be discerned (1959, 92, emphasis added).

If we consider the digestive system as an analogy, we might suggest that one *function* of the system, a contribution to the body, is nourishment. It accomplishes this outcome (it nourishes) through various *processes* such as "dissolving and chemically changing food in the stomach." The system itself is defined (and commonly understood) as "*an entity composed of (1) a number of parts, (2) the relationships of these parts, and (3) the attributes of both the parts and the relationships*" (Immegart and Pilecki, 1973, 30, emphasis in original). Thus, food and chemicals in the stomach are two of the "parts" (#1); the type of food, and its spicy nature, its percentage of roughage, etc., are "attributes" (#3); and the ability of chemicals present to affect the food is a relationship between parts and their attributes (#2). Physiological functions can be identified as the outcomes of processes, thus as contributions to the effectiveness of a particular system, or as outcomes of the system itself, contributions to the healthy condition of the body.

Processes (cycles of events) and systems (interrelated entities of parts and their relationships) have been designed for organizations and groups to move action systematically toward accomplishing particular desired outcomes, toward effectively fulfilling desired organizational functions. Relationships between processes, systems, and functions are common to all organizations, and each is a variable. Demographic and operational features and human values and skills create the variances in the processes and functions. Educational organizations become individual and take on their own unique identities in terms of such variances.

The process of communication in a small elementary school is more direct and personal than in a large secondary school. There is less reliance on written directives or on large assemblies for relaying information. Systems of control of student behavior (based in sets of standards, recognition, punishments) are influenced more by community pressures in a rural area than in a large city. The type and level of learning expected can differ, depending on socioeconomic characteristics of the community.

One unified high school district near Stanford University operated three secondary schools in the 1960s. The populations of the three schools were quite distinct, and the schools had very different characters. Parents of the students in all three schools worked in high technology industries in the area, but one school was populated by students whose parents were in the forefront of technological development. They were highly educated, literate, and demanding innovators and creators. That school instituted a system of course registration similar to that of a university, and competition was keen for courses with demanding teachers.

Parents of students in the second school worked in service jobs in the same industries. Parents and teachers were less demanding of high academic achievement, but more critical of actual achievement. The third school drew students whose parents worked on the less skilled jobs in the industrial park. More students in this school were programmed into shop and secretarial courses and job training programs.

Although teachers in all three schools were highly qualified and dedicated and policies and programs for the schools were technically the same, the schools visibly reflected their communities. The schools took on unique characters because the clients served differed and the community in which each school was located differed in socioeconomic characteristics, in achievement orientation, and in education level of the general population.

Policies, programs, processes, functions, and systems are designed on principles of relationship between types of action, conditions that exist, and intended outcomes. The principle might be adaptability or stability, efficiency, or effectiveness. Decision making, for example, helps to provide stability because it establishes particular modes of expected action as means to achieve desired outcomes. Planning enhances adaptability because it emphasizes ends and considers the "many roads that lead to Rome" (equifinality, in systems terminology).

Thus, the decisions made about programs and the plans made to accomplish the system's goals and objectives differed in those three schools because of the three elements of design: possible actions, conditions, and desired outcomes. Moreover, the processes of planning and decision making differed in the three schools. There was more cooperative and interactive planning in the school in the lowest socioeconomic/academic area. Teachers spent more time together thinking out adaptive means to promote academic learning in the school with the greatest need.

It becomes clear that the four phenomena we are considering in this chapter, planning, decision making, problem solving, and system analysis, are processes under the definition proposed by Griffiths. Each is always described as a cycle of events, a series of steps or stages of thinking leading in some particular direction toward some end or outcome. But every plan, every decision, every system, and every problem solution is a variable; it is affected by the situation.

It is easy to understand why planning and decision making may sometimes be called functions. They are normally considered part of the responsibility, job, or task of the administrator, so we often say, "That is his/her function." Moreover, it is easy to recognize processes as skills. If there is a series of steps to perform in a process, those steps can be learned, and we can develop greater skill in performing them. We do not speak of leadership or coordination as series of steps. It is more difficult to conceive of leadership as a skill, because it requires many skills and depends on interaction with others to exist. There are no precise steps to follow.

It is my view that some of the difficulties faced in studying administration and organizations productively lie in our lack of a common "language of discourse." As Litchfield said, "Our confusion of terminology makes it difficult to speak accurately to one another within any one field, let alone across fields and across cultures" (1956, 3).

In presenting my own model, I will use the terms *process, functions,* and *systems* as they have been defined in the literature. In presenting models and discussions from the literature, the authors' perspectives will be presented.

PROPOSITIONS MADE ABOUT CLOSELY RELATED CONCEPTS

Planning and Time

> When I dipped into the future as far as the human eye could see,
> I saw the vision of the world and all the wonder that would be.
> —A. Lord Tennyson. "Locksley Hall," 1842

Planning: Janus Peering into the Future

All discussions of planning accept its multiple time reference. As an activity it takes place in the present, derives knowledge from the past, and is oriented toward the future. All action proposed in a plan is future action, and all outcomes aimed for are future outcomes. Thus, all planning is hypothetical in nature. It attempts to predict the means to bring about desired outcomes when the conditions that will surround them are unknowable. Kaufman and Herman say, "[Planning] scans current realities and opportunities in order to yield useful strategies and tactics for arriving at a better tomorrow" (1991, xvii). Fierhaller, at the Planning Executives Institute International Conference in Montreal (1979), was asked, "What do you expect from your planners?" He answered, "I expect them to see the tip of the iceberg and tell me what it portends for us."

Friedmann (1973) depicted planning as based in the past (scientific knowledge), the near future (expectations), the historical future (hope), and the A-historical future (faith). Figure 2.1 presents his representation of the relationships among these four time frames.

From the past and scientific knowledge, planners require three kinds of knowledge: facts, trends, and proposed relationships (theories or hypotheses). Facts and trends required are both organizational and societal. Systematic recording of facts permits planners to recognize trends upon which reasonable expectations for the near future may be predicted. This "near future" is, Friedmann proposes, the domain of

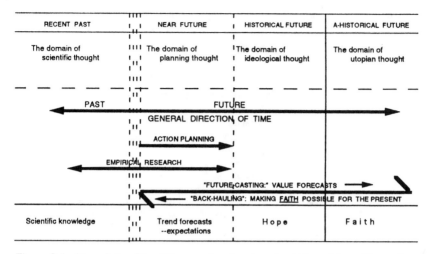

Figure 2.1. *The relationship of time to planning thought. (Adapted from Figure 6, p. 141, Friedman, J.* Retracking America: A Theory of Transactive Planning. *© 1973 by Doubleday Publishers. Reprinted by permission of Doubleday Publishers.)*

planning thought. But planning thought attempts to bring back into the near future the hopes of ideologues, the multiple interests of special needs groups. Planning attempts to make ''hopes'' possible in the near future (1973, 139–144).

Friedmann's vision extends planning still further into the ''history that has not yet been envisioned,'' that best of all possible worlds, the world of faith in full humanity. Friedmann believed such visionary planning to be the role of government. Hamilton (1991) sees it as the role of all—particularly of educators, a view that is particularly appealing to present-day educators. Educational planners, all educators, see learning as the ideal world of an ahistorical future that Friedmann (1973) models. New technologies, the growth of a better educated populace, and the growing demand for ''one world,'' are some of the indicators of efforts to ''back-haul'' that faith in learning into the ''historical future'' of hope.

Time as Cost

Time is of concern to planners in two ways: time *for* planning, as well as the time frame *of* planning. Bologna (1980) surveyed managers in private corporations to determine why managers resist planning. Several of the ten reasons most commonly given spoke directly of time from one

Table 2.1.   Ten Reasons Why People Don't, Won't, or Can't Plan, Based on First and Second Choices (in rank order).

1. Too time consuming
2. Too much work involved
3. Knowledge deficiency
4. The future being too uncertain
5. Skill deficiency
6. Attitude deficiency
7. Don't like or understand process
8. Too difficult
9. Live for today
10. Fear of failure

Source: Table 1, p. 24. Bologna, J. 1980. "Why Managers Resist Planning." *Managerial Planning.* 28(4): 23 – 25. Published by The Planning Forum, January/February 1980. Reprinted by permission of The Planning Forum.

perspective or the other. Table 2.1 reports the reasons most commonly given.

Realistically, the two time frames, the future orientation of all planning and the amount of time that effective planning requires, interact. The fact of demands on people's time and of the immediacy of demands for action often make it difficult to arrange time for thoughtful planning. Planning costs time (money, energy, effort), and returns on that expenditure of time and effort are not immediate. Yet everyone is aware of the confusion, frustration, and retrenching time involved when a school system jumps on some bandwagon to put an innovation into place without adequate planning and preparation.

Many innovations have come and gone in education, perhaps because they were implemented in a short preparation time-span frame. Many examples could be cited: MBO, PPBS, streaming, nongraded groups, and special classes. Teacher's reactions to "big" programs invariably inform us of the costs beyond dollars. Articles such as "Teachers Ask, Is There Life after Madeline Hunter?" (Garman and Hazi, 1988), "The Hunterization of America's Schools" (Slavin, 1987), and "A Complaint and a Prediction" (Breinin, 1987) should not be taken as the angry outcry of isolated individuals. They express a deep malaise in the teaching profession with the increasing demands on the schools and with the increasing burden of complaints from the public about inadequate results. Such outcries have inevitably followed implementation of some additional responsibility placed on teacher educators. Many reports emphasize the lack of proper planning and preparation for innovations.

A longer planning time frame permits opportunities for several working sessions so that implications and applications can be worked out. Figure 2.2 proposes that time spent in careful planning reduces cost in money, effort, and interest.

It is important to "count the cost" of innovations in education, not only in money, but in time, effort, interest, motivation, and frustration. Ultimately, those emotional tolls probably affect learning outcomes more dramatically than dollars.

Improvisation

Two major propositions are made in the literature about the purpose of planning: planning for control and planning for change. Our own perspective, which will be developed further in the last section of the chapter, is that planning is hypothesizing about future direction. We propose that adaptability and stability express the action principles involved in planning and decision making.

Stability (the principle upon which decisions rest) implies continuity

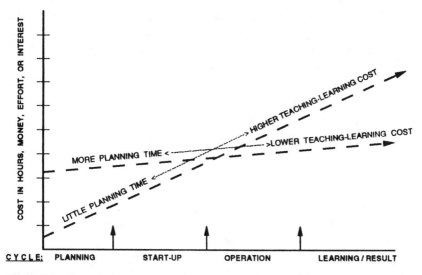

Figure 2.2. Careful planning saves in the long run. Time spent in planning saves time and cost in operation and in teaching-learning.

and the security of knowing that actions will be acceptable, perhaps *without* authoritarian control. As we have said earlier, decisions, programs, and policies are means of providing stability. Adaptability (the principle upon which planning exists) allows for the possibility of change without assuming that it is necessary. Plans, goals, and objectives offer change or continuation of desirable current practices.

Criticisms of planning in the rational comprehensive tradition propose that educators do not have the time, the resources, or the inclination for rational comprehensive planning. Critics propose that more spontaneous, serendipitous bases of choice and action should be recognized and validated. Inbar (1991) has proposed improvisation as a viable alternative approach to change.

Inbar (1991) asserted that much of the choice-making in education is necessarily done on the instant, in response to situations that arise unexpectedly in the classroom or around the school. The educator must *create* a way of approaching a learning or behavioral situation as it occurs. He proposed that much of what goes on is improvised out of the circumstances and the educator's tacit knowledge (70–81).

Inbar compared the profiles of four approaches to organizational change: the programming profile (1991, Figure 4.2, 70), the planning profile (1991, Figure 4.3, 71), the improvisation profile (1991, Figure 4.4, 72), and the randomized response profile (1991, Figure 4.5, 73). He identified five polar dimensions that affect these change approaches: 1) constraints (bounding or fluid), 2) knowledge (explicit or tacit), 3) vision (hierarchical or unconstructed), 4) vision (broad or narrow), and 5) preparation time span (short or long). He "mapped" each approach on the five dimensions.

Inbar (1991) proposed that planning and programming are oriented to a longer time frame and improvisation and randomized response to a shorter time frame. He described improvisation as opposite to planning on all dimensions except one—both deal with a broad, rather than a narrow, vision. However, he urged that improvisation is a productive approach to change as an alternative to planning or programming. Table 2.2 presents the four profiles he proposed and related profiles created for problem solving and decision making.

Inbar warns that "there is always the danger that improvisation will become increasingly vulnerable to producing faddish actions." But he adds, "[it] enables choices to be made and problems to be resolved . . . even under fluid conditions, conflicts, new constraints, changing en-

Table 2.2. Profiles of Planning, Improvisation, and Related Approaches to Change. Based on Five Polar Dimensions Presented by Inbar (1991).

Type of Emphasis	Change Orientation					
	Planning	Improvisation	Programming	Random Response	Problem Solving*	Decision Making*
Constraints (bounding/fluid)	Quite bounding**	Quite fluid	Very bounding	Minimal bounding	Quite bounding	Very bounding
Knowledge (explicit/tacit)	Very explicit**	Very tacit	Very explicit	Minimally explicit	Quite tacit	Explicit + tacit
Vision (hierarchical/unconstructed)	Quite hierarchical	Quite unconstructed	Very hierarchical	Very unconstructed	Unconstructed	Quite hierarchical
Vision (broad/narrow)	Very broad	Quite broad	Quite broad	Quite narrow	Very narrow	Quite broad
Preparation time span (long/short)	Very long	Quite short	Medium – long	Very short	Very short	Short – long

*Problem solving and decision making orientations have been added for comparison purposes.

**All range level interpretations (Minimal, Quite, Very, etc.) are interpretations of the visual graphic maps provided by Inbar. The overall pictures presented by the graphic maps offer visual comparisons that make an important contribution to understanding.

Source: Adapted from Figures 4.3, p. 71; 4.4, p. 72; 4.5, p. 73; and 4.6, p. 74 in Inbar, D. E. 1991. "Improvisation and Organizational Planning," pp. 65 – 80 in *Educational Planning. Concepts, Strategies, Practices*. Edited by R. V. Carlson and G. Awkerman. © 1991 by Longman Publishers. Reprinted by permission of Longman Publishers.

vironment and with planners and decision makers forced to act in short periods of time'' (1991, 79). However, improvisation ''does not imply the freedom to act without rules and consideration for the other participants' behavior; it is a *disciplined synthesis of one's own imagination to provide context for rules and others' behavior*'' (1991, 74, emphasis in original).

Improvisation is one possible means of responding to the fluidity of conditions in current education systems. It assumes (as in the jazz ensemble cited by Inbar) that broad, general parameters exist within which action will develop. Within those parameters, leadership can flow throughout the group as one ''player'' improvises variations on the theme and others follow and ''play off'' on that variation.

Much of the day-to-day reality for teacher or educational administrator has two of the contextual characteristics of improvisation as Inbar describes it: a necessarily short time span between thinking and acting and a reliance on tacit (experiential) knowledge. Indeed, much successful teaching and much successful leadership in a school depend on this ability to ''seize the moment.'' Inbar proposes that more credence should be given to improvisation in education in light of the fluidity of current realities and that more credence should be given to the tacit knowledge upon which improvisation draws (1991, 79).

However, there are critical differences between a jazz ensemble and a school staff. A jazz ensemble is a small, very close-knit, harmonious group melded as one unit and working always in the face-to-face group. All improvisation in a jazz group is bounded by periods of face-to-face working time. Other than inside the classroom, for educators, there are very few such intimate, face-to-face working situations that extend over periods of time devoted to development. In schools and school systems, improvisation as a planning or administrative mode of action is extremely vulnerable to that ''faddish action'' Inbar warns against.

There are schools in which close and harmonious understanding among the staff enables them to ''play together'' as an ensemble. One such school was recently described in the following conversation with a member of the staff: ''Our staff does all the planning for our school; the principal isn't involved at all. We get together as a staff in the spring and decide on what activities and projects we are going to develop for the coming year. Tasks get assigned, and when September comes, we organize and run all the programs and events we have planned.

"It all started a few years ago when we had a 'peer coaching' program. We really began to meld as a group of teachers working toward a good education program. At first, the principal resisted. He didn't want to give up the authority, but over time he found that it worked really well."

"So leadership comes from the staff as a group?"

"Yes."

"Why do you think that is?"

"Well, we have all worked at that school for twelve to fifteen years. We know each other really well — what to expect, who can be depended on, what each one is good at. We've had two principals in the last ten years, but we teachers are a really solid group. We count on each other. And we know the principal; we know his standards, and we know what he expects from us."

Like the jazz ensemble, they have had a stable group for many years, and they have a central figure or ensemble leader. Although they allow their principal to "hold the guidelines in place" — to keep the music in harmony — this school staff works within a framework they have planned and created. This kind of harmonious educational workplace is not by any means universal, but it does reflect the situation Inbar points us toward.

In a recent analysis of the 1949 Mann Gulch firefighting disaster, Weick discussed four sources of "resilience"[4] in organizations: "(1) improvisation and bricolage (creating new uses of materials at hand); (2) virtual role systems, (3) the attitude of wisdom, and (4) respectful interaction" (1993, 638). The phrase *virtual role systems* is drawn from the computer technology phrase *virtual reality.* Weick means a situation in which "each individual in the crew mentally takes all roles and . . . in the manner of a holograph, each person can reconstitute the group and assume whatever role is vacated, pick up the activities, and run a credible version of the role" (640).

It seems clear, from the description of the school presented by the staff member cited above, that just such a "virtual role system" has developed for this group of teachers. But it is important to note that the

---

[4]*Resilience* in this use of the term has much the same meaning as the term *negentropy* in systems thinking—the ability of the system to counteract entropy (the tendency of any system toward randomness, disorder, and death). *Negentropy* is the characteristic of open systems that enables renewal, order, unity, and maintenance of life (Immegart and Pilecki, 1973, 30–36).

staff does plan; it sets the broad parameters within which projects and programs will be developed. And the teacher adds, they spend many hours beyond contractual mandates in this kind of planning activity.

Weick (1993) points out that, even though the "leader" of the smoke jumper group (he questions whether it can be called a "unit") improvised a solution that saved his own life, he had not prepared the men to "image" the whole role system or the whole of the potential fire situation. He had not planned for roles to deal with unexpected danger. The men had the image of "firefighter," not of "leader and innovator," and most of them perished.

Inbar (1991) does not suggest that improvisation should replace planning. He calls for recognition of the importance of tacit, or experiential, knowledge and of the fact that, when dealing with people, much action must rely on a short preparation time frame. Judgments must be made and decisions to act taken "on the moment." Indeed, all educators have a vast store of experiential knowledge that enlightens theory, concepts, and propositions. Without the ability to relate experience to ideas, there is no judgment; there are only rules. Education is the profession of making fair and reasonable judgments about the learning and behavior of students. Improvisation, grounded in educated judgment, comprises much of the business of educators. Planning helps make experience available for use in action.

Thus, improvisation is akin to planning since it maintains the broad perspective of the whole unit and maintains a vision of goal, aim, or purpose as the guiding principle of action, even in emergency. But to be successful, it requires that the broad vision, the broad mental image, should be held by each member; it requires *common* goals, aims, and purposes.

In our view, this central core (the mental image of the whole) permits improvised action to be positive, but that particular core develops out of experience. A jazz ensemble is not "hey-nonny-noe," any more than break dancing can be done by just anyone.

"Gut feeling" is intelligent use of experience.

Problem Solving and Planning

Until well past the mid-twentieth century, planning was equated with problem solving. The problem-solving framework was derived from

Dewey's 1933 analysis of "logical thinking." Propositions of the problem-solving process incorporated all seven of the steps found to be common to descriptions of many related processes involved in administration. Table 2.3 presents four typical descriptions of planning as problem solving.

The problem-solving framework is useful for thinking about the conceptual processes of management in education, and, frequently enough in the literature, planning is still equated with problem solving. However, it is my view that problem solving is a management *style* that derives from a narrower focus than does planning and, at the same time, encompasses more of the whole set of management processes and functions than planning.

Since the context of problem solving is problems, the implied situation is crisis; the focus is inward on what is not or what has been lost and needs to be regained. Problem solving is, by implication, reactive in nature, a reaction to an undesirable situation, a problem. Planning is proactive; its focus is to anticipate and prevent problems. The situs of planning is always the future; the focus is outward, on the possible, what could be.

In addition, *solving* implies that there is a solution, a point at which the problem will no longer exist. In real life, we neither expect, nor desire, that state of endless perfection. The old fable of the priest carrying the devil on his back is the human condition of educators—if there is nothing to learn, what need for educators? Or stated as a credo, we can always learn and grow; we can always become something better than we are. Planning asserts that this is not accomplished by focusing on what is wrong, on problems, but on what could be, the end we desire.

Solution implies, too, checking the solution to determine if it is successful. It implies that the solution must be implemented and evaluated to complete the process, since action is not a solution unless it is successful. Thus, *problem solving* implies all of the stages of the administrative cycle directed at one particular issue and is properly viewed as a style of management, a style that is particularly appropriate under circumstances of stress.

Planning, on the other hand, includes planning *for* implementation and evaluation but awaits a management decision for actual implementation. That is, planning is hypothesis making; it is propositional in nature; it proposes action. A good plan should include a plan for implementation and a plan for evaluation. When the plan has been

Table 2.3. Typical Descriptions of Planning for Education as a Problem-Solving Process.

	Banghart and Trull (1973, 442)	Havelock (1974, 2)	Hostrop (1975, Figure 3.1)	Hanson (1979, 366)
1.		Initial disturbance		Problem recognition stage
2.	Defining the educational planning problem	Feeling need and decision to do "something" about need	Diagnosing the problem	Problem screening stage
3.	Analyzing planning problem area	Diagnosing of need as a problem	Formulating goals and objectives / Indentifying constraints and needed resources	Problem distribution stage
4.	Conceptualizing and designing plans; evaluating plans	Search for solutions, choosing alternatives	Evaluating alternatives; selecting solutions	Decision-making stage
5.	Specifying the plan			Decision implementation
6.	Implementing the plan	Application of a possible solution to the need	Implementating the selected solutions	Feedback stage
7.	Plan feedback, adjusting, redesign	Satisfaction that the problem is solved or dissatisfaction resulting in repeat of cycle	Feedback and evaluation	Problem resolution or renewal stage

accepted by decision, it becomes a guide to action, a guide to implementation and evaluation, but a guide only, subject to change as conditions change. Actual implementation and actual evaluation of the plan are elements of the larger set of administrative or management processes, which feed back into the cycle as data to be used in planning a modification or planning new programs.

Our Values-Based Planning System presented in Chapters 9 and 10 does not deal with implementation per se, but with planning for implementation. Moreover, we do not consider that determining performance effectiveness is a step in the planning process, as it is in the problem-solving process, although making a plan for assessing effectiveness will be proposed as a critical early stage in planning for any project.

One can always construct the vision for the future as a problem for today. Planning and problem solving are closely related because both apply processes of logical thinking; however, most discussions of problem solving emphasize describing the problem (the discrepancy); determining the cause of the problem, the fault in the system; and seeking a way to eliminate the cause. Problems are frequently only symptoms. It can be critically important to deal with a fight on the playground or to address a student's habitual absence, but putting out fires is not enough to create a healthy learning situation. A broader perspective of the system is what we ask of our educational planners, a perspective that focuses on growth, development, and effective learning. Figure 2.3 illustrates some of the differences between the planning focus and the problem-solving focus.

If teachers were to look at every initial disturbance within or by a student (question, argument, debate, refusal to comply) as a problem, we would have few competent and confident adults. Creative teachers everywhere recognize a "disturbance" as one of the primary indicators of independent thinking, lateral thinking, skill orientations, and confidence in self-determination, or simply as playful *joie de vivre*. Creative teachers build upon these "deviations" as potentials for independent growth in individuals.

> When I get up in the morning
> I look like a bear;
> I act like a bear;
> And I am a bear.
> —*Poem written by a low-level fifth-grade student*

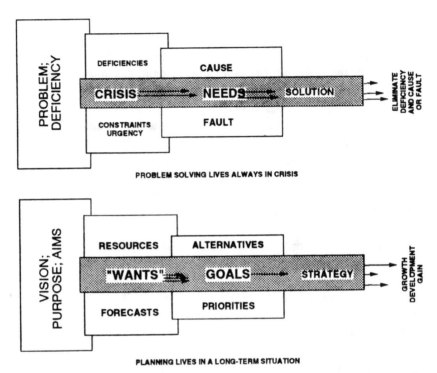

Figure 2.3. The "mind-set" for problem solving and planning are different because the time frame is different. Planning can go after results a step at a time because it is directed at the future, not at an immediate crisis.

When the student who wrote this poem was observed on video by a group of graduate students in educational administration, judgments of his behavior and attitude differed dramatically among observers. Some saw him as deliberately disruptive, a student to be "quickly put in his place," a problem. Others saw him as lively and creative, having talents that should be developed. It is easy to predict different outcomes for this boy in future classes.

In the days when teachers' "plan books" were their weekly guides to action, problems were never their source of inspiration. Skills to be learned, understandings to be developed, and knowledge to be acquired were the keystones of good teacher plans. This planning orientation is common in the classroom, and it is equally appropriate for the organization.

The major differences between problem solving and planning as effective administrative processes are mind-set (causes versus aims) and time constraints (crisis versus preparation). Problems are temporary and often hugely overwhelming; they must be dealt with by crisis interventions, but planning should help to prepare resources and skills so that crises, when they come, can be dealt with effectively.

Chance favors the prepared mind.
— *Louis Pasteur*

Decision Making and Planning

The planning process has also been considered "a dimension of the decision process" (Miklos, Bourgette, and Cowley, 1972, 5) or "the process of preparing a set of decisions for action . . ." (Dror, 1963, 50). Planning and decision making are, indeed, closely bound to each other; they are two key processes that help develop and maintain direction in the organization. Beyond the fact that both are described in the literature by the same set of activities, models that present ways of thinking about decision making also illuminate planning.

Decision making was recognized as a key process in administration in the mid-twentieth century as the social sciences began to offer perspectives on administration. Theorists such as Barnard (1938), Von Neuman and Morgenstern (1947), Griffiths (1959), Simon (1945, 1960), Thompson (1967), and Vroom and Yetton (1973) laid the groundwork for the two strands of thinking about decision making in organizations: the statistical probability analysis strand, and the participation in decision making strand.

Applications of Bayesian statistics and decision tree analysis to administrative choice were developed by theorists such as Raiffa (1970), Newman (1971), and Winkler (1972). Decision statistics still plays an important role in macro- (school board or system level) and mega- (state, province, or national level) decisions [see, for example, Estler (1988) and McNamara and Chisolm (1988)]. An example of Decision Tree Analysis (DTA) is presented in Chapter 6, Figure 6.7.

Thompson — The Decision Situation

Thompson's (1967) model of the dimensions of decision issues is one of the most useful grids for helping decision makers (and also planners) to sit back and take a look at where we are. It does not depict process or steps in the cycle of activities in decision making. Thompson asks the decision makers, ''What kind of decision situation is this one we are looking at in terms of what we know?'' He proposes two dimensions of ''knowing'': knowing where we want to go (what results we hope to achieve) and knowing how to get there (what techniques and methods are most likely to accomplish the results we hope for). Figure 2.4 presents Thompson's model.

Thompson proposed that we may be ''certain/in agreement/clear'' about where we want to go, about the outcome we desire, or we may be ''uncertain/not in agreement.'' Should the school curricula include programs on drugs, sexual behavior, religion, evolution, food and diet, competitive sports, and movies? Are the primary purposes of the school to train/prepare future workers; to develop each child's personal skills and abilities; to develop attitudes toward work, self, and others; to learn to work in groups; to become independent thinkers? Most of us, either as parents or as educators, are ''uncertain'' about where most emphasis should be placed, and there can be wide disagreement within our education communities about each of these issues and many others.

Similarly, Thompson adds, we might ''know with certainty'' how to accomplish some desired result (if we could agree on it), or we may not be sure what methods or technologies would be best suited to that end. If our community is fully convinced that the school should address the issue of drugs or AIDS, what is the best approach? Should the program

		Preferences regarding possible outcomes	
		Certainty	Uncertainty
Beliefs about cause/effect relations	Certain	**A** Computational Strategy	**B** Compromise Strategy
	Uncertain	**C** Judgmental Strategy	**D** Inspirational Strategy

Figure 2.4. Dimensions of decision issues. From pp. 134–135, Thompson, James D. Organizations in Action. New York, NY: McGraw-Hill Book Co., © 1967. Reproduced with permission of McGraw-Hill.

be based on scare tactics (bringing in people who have "been there" and focusing on the terrible effects)? Or should the program be based on group solidarity strategies (the "just say no," or postponing sexual involvement – PSI – programs)?

We are "certain" that we want special children to have a rewarding and successful educational experience. Is the best approach integration, inclusion, special classes, tutoring, or cooperative learning? Concern for the environment is important. Should that concern be addressed through an adopt a tree, park, or street program, a recycling program, or investigations of endangered species?

If we initiate such a program, where does the time come from – from academics, physical education, art, and music? The time question places the issue back into the frame of attempting to agree on relative importance of possible outcomes. Weighing the priorities of (the relative preference for) programs is often a matter of dealing with interest groups, of negotiation and compromise. School systems and individual educators are constantly faced with choices among competing aims.

Thompson proposed that different decision strategies are best suited to situations that fall in the four major quadrants. Of course, there could be degrees of certainty or uncertainty, which might lead to modifications of strategies, but Thompson's model provides a useful grid for addressing the issues systematically. Table 2.4 proposes strategy questions that might be raised when the situation falls in one of the four quadrants suggested by Thompson's model.

The fine line between decision thinking and planning thinking is apparent in the questions proposed as strategy questions. Whether the "who, what, when, where, why, and how" questions are viewed as decision data questions or as action planning questions is very much a matter of mind-set. Mind-set does have psychological impact, of course. Much frustration develops when planners assume they are making decisions. Our preference is to consider that the questions about the situation and possible strategies are planning questions, that their usefulness lies in preparing hypotheses about how to accomplish desired results; therefore, we believe that Thompson's model can be very useful to educational planners.

Many planning situations in schools might be placed in quadrant A, where computational strategy is appropriate. The school has a yearly book fair, a sports day, a music program, a fashion show, a spelling bee, a science project exhibition – or any similar schoolwide activity. The

Table 2.4. Questions to Be Raised to Determine the Appropriate Educational Planning or Decision-Making Strategy in "Certainty-Uncertainty" Situations Identified in Thompson's Model (1967).

Situation Description Questions	Answer	Strategy Questions
Agree on outcome? Are we agreed that our school should deal with this issue? On what we are trying to accomplish? On the purpose or the outcome we are hoping for?	Yes	**Quadrant A—computational approach** What all has to be done to make this program or project a success? Who will plan it? organize it? do it? (Who/When/Where/ How?)
Agree on approach? Are we agreed on the best kind of program? On the best approach for now?	Yes	
Agree on outcome?	No	**Quadrant B—compromise approach** What are the different outcomes involved? Which is more/less important? What can we give up? Which is most important?
Agree on approach?	Yes	If we agree on Proposal A, who should handle it? Proposal B?

Table 2.4. (continued).

Situation Description Questions	Answer	Strategy Questions
Agree on outcome?	Yes	**Quadrant C—best judgement approach** What are the best possible ways, the possible kinds of programs to handle this situation? to move most productively toward the kind of learning situation we hope for? In our best judgment, which is most likely to "work"? What would give us the best chance of succeeding?
Agree on approach?	No	
Agree on outcome?	No	**Quadrant D—inspiration approach** Could all of these aims be integrated in some way? Could there really be one bigger, more general aim? What kind of program could be created to deal with *all* of these aims properly?
Agree on approach?	No	If we didn't have to worry about any constraints, lack of resources or anything, what would be the *very* best approach?

choices (of outcome and of means) are already made. Planning focuses on the activities, people, and resources needed to make it a success.

Many of the decisions about learning units in the classroom might also fall in quadrant A. There is a unit on the federal election process, modern drama, square root, international trade, the Charter of Rights and Freedoms or The Bill of Rights, a Shakespeare play, fractions, or writing an essay. Perhaps there is even a guide for teaching or a textbook to follow. The specifics of how, how much time, and when, are essentially computational, or logistical, in nature. That is, they are not substantive questions of where to go or how to get there.

Many times, general units are specified as in the preceding paragraph, but the basic questions of how to approach the unit are not defined. The ''choice'' situation might be seen as requiring a judgmental strategy (quadrant C). Does this group learn best by projects, in groups, by independent study, by field approaches, by workbooks, or by discussion? The teacher makes the choice of approach, or method, on his/her best judgment and knowledge of the group.

Thompson's model is as applicable to choices made within the classroom as to choices made for the system. It can help us understand *why* certain types of decisions or planning behaviors are necessary, to know when we need to turn to a totally new approach (inspiration), or to realize when we need to compromise. But, perhaps more importantly, it may open up new possible approaches to replace some of the habits of choice that arise from following curriculum guides, textbooks, and traditional practices. One important value of every model is that it proposes alternatives. Models enhance understanding of issues because they inspire and direct questions; they remind the decision maker or planner that questions could help clarify the issue, that there are alternatives, that many roads lead to Rome.

Communication Wheels and Decision Making

Models from many different theoretical bases can be usefully applied to thinking about planning and decision making. One example could be cited from communication theory. Patterns of communication in organizations were a subject of study in the 1950s and 1960s. Communication theorists such as Haney (1960, 1973); Hovland, Janis, and Kelley (1958); and Watzlawick, Beavin, and Jackson (1967) identified primary patterns that they represented as ''wheels.'' Five of the most common patterns found are 1) all communication outward from the decision-making group; 2) all communication toward the decision group; 3) communication both toward and from the decision group; 4) communication toward and from, plus communication between all members of the participating groups; and 5) communication to representatives and from representatives to the decision group. Figure 2.5 illustrates these five communication patterns.

By relating these communication wheels to decision-making theory, the patterns could be identified with leaders' styles of participation in decision making. Wheel #1 could be considered autocratic; #2, political; #3, participative; #4, collegial; and #5, representative.

We have attached labels to each of the communication wheels because the patterns depicted closely represent patterns of participation in decision making or planning presented in the literature. For example, Vroom and Yetton (1973) describe the styles of leadership in terms of the degree of participation that leaders encourage. In the autocratic #1 style, the leader makes the decision by her/himself, based on information already known. In consultative style #2, the leader shares information with all members and gets input individually. We have labeled this style participative (wheel #3). Vroom and Yetton's group style #2 closely resembles the wheel we have labeled collegial (#4), since all members participate in generating ideas, giving information, and making the decision.

The communication wheel that we have called political (#2) is exactly replicated in Hamilton's Figure 2.7, "[an] example [that] demonstrates that a variety of different groups . . . may affect the development and outcomes of a planning process" (1991, 39). Hamilton's graphic portrayal, using human figures instead of circles, is more interesting than a simple wheel because it visualizes the types of internal and external individuals and groups that may attempt to influence the process.

Wheel #5 (representative) is the customary organizational chart with the departments or divisions ranged around the superintendent or director general in a wheel, rather than in the flat, hierarchical format in which it is customarily represented. In the 1970s, the YMCA of Montreal represented its organizational chart in just such a wheel. Their reasoning was that this visual representation would encourage more between-department communication and cooperative planning. They found, ultimately, that overlapping and repetitive discussion groups had been

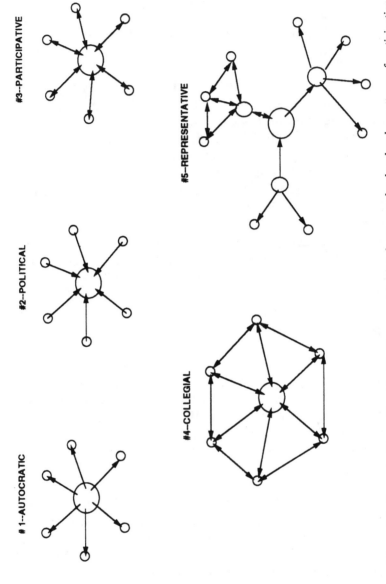

Figure 2.5. Patterns of interaction identified in communication theory are closely related to patterns of participation in decision making.

46

created, which slowed decision making down and stagnated development and growth, so they reverted to the more common flat chart and the function specification it implies.

Thus, models or illustrations from different bodies of our literature often provide insights into the processes of decision making and planning.

REM Decisions

In discussions of decision making or planning for education, three qualitative dimensions of "goodness" are always implied: rationality, effectiveness, and moral or ethical acceptability. Much of the literature addresses the question of *how* to make rational decisions. It is generally assumed that a rational decision is "good" and has a greater probability of being effective. *Effective* is, however, a dimension that escapes rationality. It is sometimes proposed as an alternative perspective that an effective decision is one that is accepted — whether some outside agency or observer considers it to have been rational or not. *Effective* is not confined to rationality.

In education, the third dimension is the basis of all choice and action — ethical acceptability or moral goodness. Thus, the decisions and the plans we aim for in education have three characteristics of goodness — they are rational (in harmony with reality), they are effective (they achieve the results we hope for), and they are morally or ethically acceptable. Figure 2.6 represents the three dimensions of goodness. REM (rational, effective, and moral) decisions and plans are to the organization what REM sleep is to the individual. They keep the creative vitality of the organization healthy.

System(s) Analysis and Planning

System analysis (or *systems* analysis) has been proposed as a framework for planning in education since the late 1960s. One of the most influential contributors to this perspective on planning has been Roger Kaufman. From his early book, *Educational System Planning* (1972), to his more recent works, *Planning Educational Systems* (1988), *Strategic Planning in Education* (with Herman, 1991), and *Mapping Educational Success* (1992), Kaufman has urged a *system* approach to planning for education.

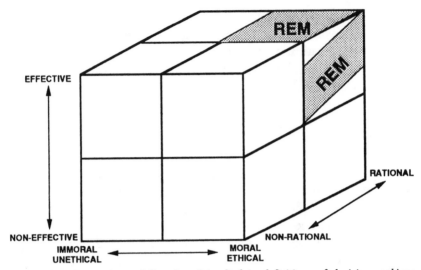

Figure 2.6. Dimensions of "goodness" implied in definitions of decision making: . *rationality, effectiveness, and moral acceptability. REM decisions are Rational, Effective, and Morally good.*

Kaufman and System Analysis

Kaufman distinguishes between *system* analysis/approach and *systems* analysis/approach. He draws this distinction based on the work of Cleland and King (1968, 1969) who defined *systems* analysis and applied it to corporate settings. *Systems* analysis, Kaufman proposes (1988, 166) deals with the how questions—how can and how should the organization's goals be accomplished? What are the alternatives, and which is the best alternative? This approach focuses on tools and techniques for determining optimal courses of action.

System analysis, Kaufman proposes, takes a more global, holistic perspective. It deals first with the ''what'' questions—what should the organization be trying to accomplish? What are the needs or goals? Thus, *system* analysis is particularly relevant to education, since the aims of education, its goals, needs, or priorities are seldom universally agreed upon.

Kaufman breaks down the process of planning with the system analysis approach into seven basic steps or stages: 1) identifying and clarifying needs, 2) mission analysis, 3) function analysis, 4) task analysis, 5) methods-means analysis, 6) selecting and implementing, and 7) determining effectiveness and efficiency and revising. These seven steps closely parallel those proposed in the problem-solving approach, but here the emphasis is on analysis—identifying the components at each stage. Figure 2.7 presents Kaufman's (1972) and Kaufman and Herman's (1992) "map" of planning using the system approach.

Kaufman proposes that, as in the problem-solving approach, the planner should start with an observed educational need, "a measurable gap between our current outcomes . . . and our desired . . . ones" (1988, 92). However, the planner should then take a step backwards to gain a more holistic perspective—should relate the "need" to "mission." A mission he defines as "an overall job—an outcome, output, or product; a completed service; or a change in the condition of something or somebody—that must be accomplished" (1988, 92).

Thus, a mission statement can be described as an objective, and the examples Kaufman gives (1988, 94 – 103) specify the mission objective in terms similar to those of behavioral objectives, with one major difference. A mission objective "should not have the methods and means for getting the results included in the statement," because including methods and means will "lock [the planners] into a solution before defining the problem" (1988, 94).

The mission profile, the second part of mission analysis is the management plan for accomplishing the objective. More detailed analysis follows, with consideration of possible strategies and tactics as the step immediately preceding the choice for implementation. Kaufman's detailed description of steps and his presentation of examples should be studied carefully. His work has been influential in focusing attention on careful, systematic planning for education.

McManama and Systems Analysis

It is not easy to maintain the distinction that Kaufman proposes in use of the terms *system* analysis and *systems* analysis. There are two domains of choice: 1) what the organization should try to accomplish (as expressed in goals, objectives, aims, purposes, mandates, expectations, desired results, outcomes) and 2) how these results, goals, or objectives can best be accomplished (see again Thompson's grid, Figure 2.4). In addition, there are tools and technologies that have been developed to

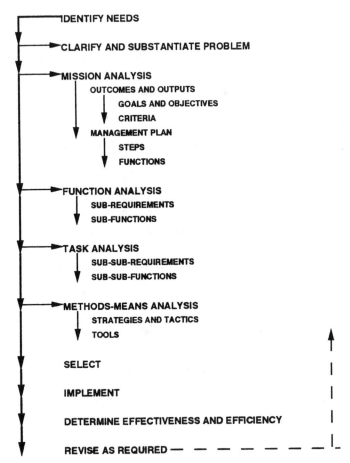

Figure 2.7. *A system analysis approach to planning.* *[Source: Kaufman, Roger A. (1972) Educational System Planning. Englewood Cliffs, NJ: Prentice Hall, Inc. and (1992) Mapping Educational Success. Newbury Park, CA: Corwin Press, Inc. Reprinted by permission of Corwin Press and Roger Kaufman.]*

help planners make better choices in both domains—the what to do domain and the how to do it domain.

Kaufman uses the term *system* analysis to incorporate all four issues, both what to do and how to do it, plus the tools and technologies that address each of these two questions. As he notes (1988, 166), Cleland and King (1968) describe tools and technologies that planners can use to develop better "how to do it" plans (question 2). They describe methodologies such as PERT and CPM networks, Gantt charts, Line of Balance, etc. They use the term *systems* analysis.

In education, what to do is seldom crystal clear. Given education's multiple constituencies, planners must always address the question of what are the end results desired in any planning cycle. This question is, as Kaufman insists, a *system* question; that is, it relates the specific planning cycle to overall system goals and objectives. By addressing the question of desired results or outcomes, Kaufman places the planning cycle in the context of the larger system, and so uses the term *system* analysis framework.

However, use of the terminology is not consistent in the literature, so some confusion may result. Although Cleland and King (1968) use the term *systems* analysis to present tools and technologies useful in developing project plans, McManama (1971) uses that term to address questions of goal clarification. Figure 2.8 presents McManama's flowchart of goal clarification through systems analysis.

McManama's systems analysis "map" focuses on preparing for choice by what is often described as "clarifying the goals and objectives." The emphasis on establishing criteria for assessing alternatives at each level of generality (1.1.2, 1.2.2, and 1.3.2 from Figure 2.8) is a critical factor in developing a clear understanding of the meaning of a goal or objective. Identifying constraints at each level (1.1.3, 1.2.3, and 1.3.3) points to the steps that keep thinking and action in harmony with reality, with the conditions that presently exist. Thus, the map provides a guide to developing immediate, or "enabling," objectives that are in harmony with the more global "terminal" objectives and goals, as well as with realistic constraints.

The Inter-Cyclical Nature of Processes

It is clear from these examples that every administrative process interacts with every other process. Analysis takes place throughout

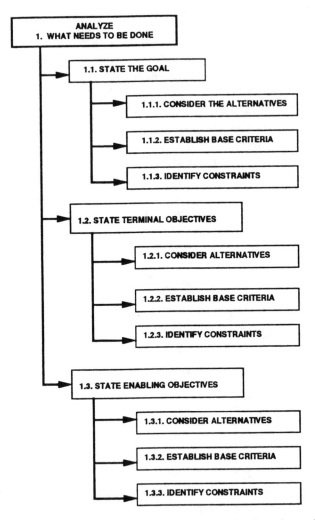

Figure 2.8. A flowchart model of major functions and subtasks to be performed in systems analysis. (Source: Figures 2 and 3, pp. 25—26 in McManama, John. Systems Analysis for Effective School Administration. *West Nyack, NY: Parker Publishing Co. © 1977. Reprinted by permission of the publisher, Parker Publishing/A division of Simon & Schuster, West Nyack, NY.)*

planning or decision making—thinking out steps, criteria, constraints, or activities and resources needed for any action plan. Equally, choices are made in any analysis—scope (system, department), limitations (time, resources), and basis (sequence, structure). Any analysis implies consideration of direction, planning, and decision making.

All administrative processes are intercyclical; they permeate all administrative action. To isolate one process for study is simply a matter of selection, a question of what activities, what thinking processes, what interrelationships we choose to focus on for the moment.

Planning has its function, an intended contribution: to provide data for making the best informed judgment about alternative ends and means available and, thus, to support leadership and contribute to direction taking for the organization. What actually comes out of any planning cycle "depends"; it depends on the nature and quality of other processes and on the variable nature of all elements involved. To describe a system for planning is to describe its "bare bones," its structural components; the essence of *system* lies, as Hills (1967) and Kuhn (1963) say, in interdependence and order among variable phenomena and on the actual states or conditions of those variable phenomena as they interact.

It is not the mission objective or the mission profile that creates a system, but the state of the mission objective—the degree to which mission objective is understood and accepted and the degree to which the mission profile is detailed and feasible, plus the coherence or harmony between objective and profile. Or, to repeat, the map is a guide to orderly, systematic planning; how well it works and the quality of planning that results depend on the effective interaction of all processes and elements involved.

THE IMPORTANCE OF CONTEXT

To this point, single administrative processes have been concentrated upon as if they exist in isolation, as separate and discrete cycles of action; however, students of organizations and administration must examine concerns both as if they were discrete phenomena and in their interaction with other concerns. We do not study only what decision making is and how to make better decisions. We also study what effects decisions may have on communication, programs, authority systems, participation, control, and a host of other aspects of the business of an organization.

Equally, those who study motivation are not concerned only with what it is and how to motivate personnel more effectively. They are also concerned with the reasons for motivating; what effects motivation will have on work, satisfaction, effectiveness, and efficiency; the quality of plans and decisions; or what lack of motivation will do to the organization as a whole and to the people involved.

Planning, too, must be examined both as a thing in and of itself, as a process that can be learned and applied, and also as interactive with all organizational and administrative action and interest. The next section of this chapter will present various ways in which authors have placed planning in context with relevant organizational functions.

Planning within Analyses of Administration

Planning has been considered a critical factor in administration from the early decades of the twentieth century. Analyses of the practice of administration became prominent during the era of scientific management as the proposition was made that *management* of work is an important factor in the *productivity* of work. Early theorists presented lists of factors in or elements of the manager's/administrator's job. Some of the best known of those early propositions were made by Fayol (1949), Gulick and Urwick (1937), Urwick (1943) and Tead (1945, 1951). All included planning.

Interestingly enough, none of the early analysts included decision making as an element of administration, although Barnard (1948) did stress policy-making, which is decision making at a broad, general level. During the period of the 1950s and 1960s, decision making was increasingly studied, and processes for decision making were developed.

To get a clearer picture of what administration is seen to involve, an analysis was made of thirty-three propositions presented between 1916 and 1992. The number of factors included on any one list varied from three (Davis, 1935) and four (Scott and Lynton, 1952; Blau and Scott, 1962) to twelve (Knezevich, 1969), thirteen (Tead, 1945, 1951), and fourteen (Southern States, 1954). Terminology varied, but thirty general tasks or factors appeared on the lists. Table 2.5 reports the thirteen most frequently cited factors. Each was included on 20% or more of the lists reviewed.

Despite the evidence presented earlier that planning has not received the same magnitude of attention in the literature as has decision making

Table 2.5. Phenomena Identified as Critical Aspects of Administration in a Count of Thirty-Three Propositions from the Literature (1916 to 1992), in Order of Frequency of Citation.

Phenomenon	Number (n = 33)	Percent
1. Planning	25	75.7
2. Organizing/systematizing	25	75.7
3. Coordination	19	57.6
4. Controlling	18	54.5
5. Leading/leadership	12	36.4
6. Assembling resources, etc.	12	36.4
7. Communication	12	36.4
8. Evaluating/appraising	10	30.3
9. Influencing/inspiring	9	27.3
10. Decision making	9	27.3
11. Directing	8	24.2
12. Implement/manage change	8	24.2
13. Budget/allocate	7	21.2

or leadership, it has consistently made the lists of critical aspects of administration. Only organizing/systematizing is cited by as many authors.

Relationships Proposed

Beyond simple lists of elements, facets, or critical factors of administration, theorists have developed propositions about how the elements interact with each other. They have proposed that all aspects of administrative action interrelate with all others and with critical factors of the organization. Models presented identify factors that can be studied (and, by implication, improved) but emphasize interrelationships.

Three models from the literature will be presented and discussed here. The first, from *Educational Governance and Administration* by Sergiovanni et al. (1980, 1992), is the most complex. The emphasis in this model is, as could be expected from the title of the book, on two broad organizational dimensions: governance, "the political function of policy-making in education" (1980, xiv), and administration, "the art and science of getting things efficiently done" (1980, 5).

The second model has been adapted for education from Kazmier's *Management. A Programmed Approach with Cases and Applications* (1980). This model relates administrative (or management) functions and organizational concerns. The third model, from Cunningham's *Systematic Planning for Educational Change* (1982), proposes planning as the foundation for all administrative functions.

Each of these models, like most of those in the literature, stresses the fact that no aspect of administrative action stands alone. The models depict graphically the proposition that all aspects (processes, functions, tasks, etc.) interact upon and affect all others. They make clear the unreality of isolating any factor for study, emphasizing that the whole set of administrative actions and organizational concerns and inter-relationships must be the perspective of the administrator.

A section of my own model, A Model for Organizational Design and Development (Burns, 1978b, 1992), will be presented in the last part of this chapter. My overall model differs from the other three presented here and from most of those in the literature, in that it makes specific hypotheses. It proposes that particular administrative processes are related to specific organizational outcomes or conditions. That is, it proposes that changes in methods of, and emphasis on, particular administrative processes are directly related to specific organizational functions and outcomes, that each process, as Getzels (1959) asserts, has a "consistent quality or direction."

The section to be presented in this chapter focuses on planning and hypothesizes interactions among planning and other organizational and administrative phenomena. It proposes that planning and decision making are parallel processes, both based in values and contributing equally to the direction the organization will take.

Sergiovanni, Burlingame, Coombs, and Thurston

The model proposed by Sergiovanni et al. (1980, 1992) is presented here because it is one of the most interesting, as well as complex, models in the literature of educational administration. It is particularly interesting because it deals with both the organization as an entity and with administrators as those members having specific responsibilities toward the organization.

These authors identified three primary sets of factors that relate to and affect each other in the conduct of the business of education systems. These are 1) critical administrative responsibility areas, 2) critical administrative processes, and 3) critical administrative skills. Each of these, they say, is comprised of a set of factors essential to proper governance and administration in the school or system.

The choice of "governance and administration" as the two focal dimensions of effective operation of a school system was a deliberate break from the more common opposition of administration versus leadership (Sergiovanni et al., 1980, 6). Sergiovanni et al. define educational administration as "concern with the process of administering, the execution of public affairs in educational organizations" (1980, xiv). They include leadership within this dimension. "Leadership and administration are operationally so interrelated that, practically speaking, both behavior modes should be considered as necessary and important *variations in administrative style*" (1980, 6–7, emphasis added). "Educational governance," they proposed, "is concerned with the political function of policy-making in education; the organization and machinery through which political units . . . exercise authority and perform functions . . ." (1980, xiv). Figure 2.9 presents their "Map of the Job of Educational Administration."

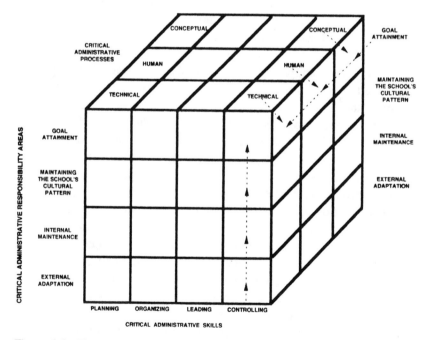

Figure 2.9. Three dimensions of the job of the educational administrator: skills, responsibility areas, and administrative processes. *(Source: Figure 1.1 in Sergiovanni, Thomas J., Martin Burlingame, Fred D. Coombs and Paul W. Thurston. Educational Governance and Administration, 3rd ed. © 1992. Englewood Cliffs, NJ: Prentice-Hall, Inc. Permission to adapt granted by Allyn & Bacon Co.)*

Critical administrative responsibilities can be seen as responsibilities of administrators *toward* the organization. Administrators are to be concerned with the organization as an entity: achieving goals that have been set, maintaining the operational viability and the community of the system, and adapting the system to external forces. The authors propose that these are achieved by "administrative functions . . . [which include, for example,] planning, organizing, controlling, coordinating, teaching, communicating, and evaluating" (Sergiovanni et al., 1980, 8). In the graphic model, such functions are identified as administrative skills, since they "comprise the administrative process."

In addition, the model proposes three "critical administrative processes" relevant to all areas of responsibility: conceptual, human, and technical. The authors refer to Katz (1955), who identified these three types of skills as the basis upon which successful administration rests. Skills in each of these three domains are seen as critical to administrative effectiveness.

The model has a great deal to offer in terms of thinking about the factors essential to understanding and developing successful governance and administration of school systems. It is particularly important in its emphasis on the fact that all three types of skills (conceptual, technical, and human) are seen to impact on every area of administrative responsibility.

Goal attainment, for example, requires *technical* skills in planning (perhaps the Delphi technique or needs assessment), in organizing (scheduling, budgeting), in leading (inspiring, clarifying values), and in controlling (feedback, records, ratings). Goal attainment also requires *human* skills in planning (participation, involvement), in organizing (task allocation, supervising), in leading (encouraging, accepting ideas), and in controlling (empathy, understanding, fairness). *Conceptual* skills are equally important in each area of operation: in planning (imaging the whole, determining the means to achieve the whole), in organizing (conceiving how the various programs can work to support each other and the goals), in leading (envisioning the potential of the future), and in controlling (exercising good judgment in choice and incentives).

Similar examples of the conceptual, human, and technical aspects of each of the critical administrative responsibility areas could be given. In Chapter 6, three somewhat similar dimensions are proposed that inhere in all organizational choice and action: conceptual, norming, and dynamics of participation. I believe that both my norming and dynamics dimensions would be included within Sergiovanni et al.'s human skills dimension. Norming processes derive from needs, expectations, customs, and norms, and dynamics of participation is the reality of involvement and contribution of members. I propose these three types of processes as dimensional, varying from highly individualized to highly generalized or organizational in orientation.

Such a dimensional character to types of processes can easily be seen to apply to Sergiovanni et al.,'s cells of interaction. For example, conceptual processes for organizing goal attainment might be highly individualized in a research organization, but highly centralized in the army, in a particular research project such as Banting's search for insulin, or in the development of a new computer as described in *The Soul of a New Machine* (Kidder, 1981).

The human skills of public relations, networking, and political influence are extremely important at education's system level as the system competes for the public dollar and for community support. Different types of human skills are important in the classroom where the issues are maintaining interest, enthusiasm, and accomplishment. The Values-Based Planning System applies the conceptual dimension to the development of a plan. Specific steps in the model bring norms, interests, attitudes, and commitment into the process, and require that the planners estimate their impact on alternative strategies.

We do not identify technical process skills as a separate dimension. There is technical knowledge related to conceptual processes, to norming processes, and to dynamic processes of participation. Any model that attempts to depict the elements of organization and the interactions of those elements is inevitably complex and, at the same time, inevitably simplistic when compared to reality. Because reality is more complex than any model one could presently design, most theorists tend to deal with only two or, at most, three dimensions. As can be seen in the presentation of Sergiovanni et al., a model can quickly develop multiple cells of interaction. Four by four by three provides us with forty-eight interactions that might be examined in considerable detail. I have touched on only a few.

I believe that the picture, the model, is more helpful than detailed discussion of each cell. No example is ever exactly like the situation the administrator is faced with. *Models are always general; real situations are always specific.* The model does not present answers to questions, but it helps the administrator to raise more thoughtful, insightful questions:

• Is this an issue of external adaptation or cultural pattern maintenance?

- Is this a matter where control is necessary or where better organizing is necessary?
- Is this an issue that requires technical knowledge or innovative imaging, conceptualization of new ideas, or new paradigms?
- Is this a situation that pressure or interest groups should be brought to or one in which more information is needed?

To have the mental "grid" clear in the mind speeds up and enlarges clear thinking about any issue. A model such as this of Sergiovanni et al., is a "thinking tool" for planning because it places planning in context with other administrative processes and with organizational responsibilities and functions. It does not incorporate specific content or specific issues that choices and action deal with in schools or school systems. It proposes that all "elements" come into play regardless of the specific focus of the planning cycle – curriculum, finance, discipline, achievement, etc.

Kazmier

The model proposed by Kazmier (1980) is less complex than that of Sergiovanni et al., and it does relate management functions to specific types of decision areas. For that reason, it may be seen as more readily applied to immediate questions. Kazmier proposed interactions between management functions and organizational concerns. Because his model was developed for business managers, the organizational concerns he identified were production, sales, finance, and personnel. Based on suggestions of graduate students in educational administration, I have adapted his model to education by identifying some of the major concerns of education systems. Figure 2.10 presents the adaptation of Kazmier's model.

The four management functions proposed, planning, organizing, directing, and controlling, are the same as the four critical administrative skills proposed by Sergiovanni et al., with one exception. Kazmier includes *directing,* rather than *leading.* Kazmier uses the term *directing* in much the same sense that others speak of implementing. This meaning, directing the operation, has connotations of the executive function in government. Directing has a different meaning when it is used in the context of goals and aims. In such a context, it implies pointing the direction and is related to leadership and, thus, to planning.

REPRESENTATIVE ORGANIZATIONAL CONCERNS

MANAGEMENT FUNCTIONS	STUDENT ACHIEVEMENT	CURRICULUM	METHODOLOGY	MOTIVATION	PERSONNEL	FINANCE
PLANNING →						
ORGANIZING →						
DIRECTING →						
CONTROLLING →						

Figure 2.10. Relationships between organizational concerns and management functions in education systems. (Based on Figure 2.1, p. 41 in Kazmier, Leonard J. Management. A Programmed Approach with Cases and Applications. New York, NY: McGraw-Hill Book Co. © 1980. Adapted for education and reprinted by permission of McGraw-Hill Book Co.)

One's own "thinking grid" could easily add other management functions or organizational concerns. Again, however, the importance of the graphic grid is that it stresses the multiple functions or aspects of administration that must all be addressed when any particular organizational concern is at issue.

If the board desires a system of supervision, it not only must *plan* how the system will operate, but it must *organize* for it, establish the responsibility for *directing* it, and *control* the system so that there is a realistic possibility that it can achieve the results desired. It must integrate the system into the schedule, provide resources, and set standards and review procedures (organize). It must make someone or some group responsible for ensuring that it operates as planned (directing and implementing). And it must control the operation; ensure that standards are met, that the same techniques are used throughout; and that appropriate incentives are applied with fairness.

It is easy to see, when we think through such a grid, where many of our education projects and programs need more development — which "functions" have not been sufficiently attended to in planning. As proposed in the planning system in Chapters 9 and 10, every plan for a proposed activity must provide a plan for allocating resources to make it feasible, in addition to a plan for determining effects, as well as a plan for organizing and directing activities involved.

Cunningham

Cunningham's model, The Five Functions of the Administrator (1982, Figure 1.1), is the most specific of the three presented here. The questions that both Sergiovanni et al. and Kazmier addressed were as follows: What is administration, and how does it relate to the concerns of the organization? How can we think more productively about administration? Cunningham's questions are more specific: What is planning? What does planning contribute to the organization? How can we think more productively about planning? Figure 2.11 presents Cunningham's model of the functions of the administrator.

Here, a general consideration of educational administration has placed the focus on planning as the key to administrative effectiveness and organizational vitality. Cunningham stressed that the concern of the educational administrator is properly with the future and that the road to the future will be less rocky if it is paved with reasonable planning.

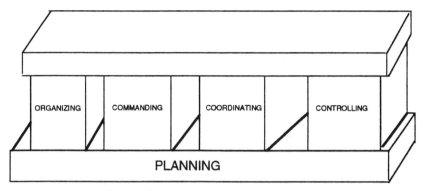

The Five Functions of the Administrator

Figure 2.11. *Planning proposed as the foundation for all administrative functions. (Source: Figure 1.1, p. 4 in Cunningham, William G.* Systematic Planning for Educational Change. *© 1982 Mayfield Publishing Co., Palo Alto, CA. Reprinted with permission of Mayfield Publishing Co.)*

This emphasis on planning is valid, and Cunningham can be applauded for counterbalancing, to some degree, the emphasis the literature has placed on decision making. Decision making is the *exercise* of power; Cunningham stresses that careful planning is one *source* of power. Planning is the process for imagining how values may become actions; decisions confirm values and provide guidelines (rules, policies, programs) to ensure that action supports those values.

The Organizational Context—Taking Direction

It has been stressed that it is important to examine interactions among processes, functions, and outcomes, as well as to study such elements as particular phenomena. The three models presented previously propose interrelationships among organizational and administrative phenomena. In this section, one set of relationships as proposed in my Model for Organizational Design and Development is presented (Burns, 1978b, 1992).

The line of interactions presented in Figure 2.12 depicts the relationships already proposed between planning, decision making, leadership, and organizational direction. The overall model makes two general propositions. They are reflected in Figure 2.12 but are not fully developed here.

GOVERNANCE DIMENSION   **MANAGEMENT DIMENSION**

REGULATION FUNCTION   POLICIES   DIRECTION   PURPOSES   LEADERSHIP FUNCTION
DECISION MAKING   PROGRAMS & RULES   GOALS & OBJECTIVES   PLANNING
PROCESS   VALUES   PROCESS
STABILITY   ADAPTABILITY

Figure 2.12. Model proposing relationships among planning, other organizational and administrative phenomena, and the direction quality education will take.

First General Proposition

Basic to this model is my definition of administration: the profession of governance and management of an organization. Thus, this agrees with Sergiovanni et al.'s (1980) premise that there are two dimensions that enter into all organizational activity. The governance dimension is a political and dynamic interaction dimension by which organizational relationships are continuously constituted, designed, and maintained. The management dimension is the dimension through which means are established and units are empowered to fulfill the purposes or mandates of the organization.

The governance dimension is concerned primarily with the people of the organization, their relationships to the organization and to each other, and maintaining reasonable and fair situations for working harmoniously and productively together. The management dimension is concerned primarily with the work of the organization, with providing people or units with resources and skills to do the work efficiently and effectively, and with ensuring that the desired quality of organizational work is upheld.

These two dimensions of administration act/function (or are intended to function) on behalf of the organization. Particular functions provide particular services to the organization; they serve to create the organization that is envisioned by participants. We readily acknowledge that the organization envisioned can differ dramatically from one participant to another. Moreover, the services that are proposed as organizational functions are not necessarily fulfilled by those individuals who hold administrative posts, nor should they be the exclusive property of administrators.

All members perform organizational functions as they go about their daily work. They make decisions that affect the group; they plan, problem solve, and analyze. Everyone contributes to the governance and management of the organization. Administrators are formally charged with such contributions, but the degree to which administrators or other participants use processes productively and fulfill organizational functions varies greatly from time to time and from group to group. We identify particular functions as management functions because they have to do with managing the work itself—not because only managers or administrators perform those functions; and other functions are identified as governance functions because they are concerned with maintaining relationships among people—not in order to assign them to governors or administrators.

Second General Proposition

I believe that there are four major concerns upon which to judge whether the organization is "good." Attention focuses ultimately on these four concerns, and we continually work to create them in the image we hold of a good organization, a good school, or a good school system. These concerns are participation (degree, kind, amount, outcomes), direction (where we are headed, whether our values are being served), operation (the kinds of results that are being achieved, whether we/our children are benefiting sufficiently), and control (whether the quality of teaching and learning, of behavior, and of programs is being maintained to our expectations).

Direction and Planning

One of the conditions basic to the health and vitality of any organization is the condition of taking and maintaining direction effectively. It goes without saying that *effective* is a relative term, that a direction that is effective for one group or organization may, in fact, be countereffective for another. The direction that is appropriate for an elementary school (the expectations held for it) may differ dramatically from that appropriate to a secondary school. The goals or aims and the programs and policies that work for an inner-city, multicultural school could be very different from those that work in a small rural community school.

The demands placed on the school by one community group will differ from those of another group. Through leadership and leadership tools such as plans, goals, and objectives and through making decisions to establish programs, policies, rules, and procedures, such differing emphases are resolved. The harmonizing criterion of all planning and decision making should be values — the values held *by* the participants and *for* the education system of the community itself.

There are two primary organizational functions directly related to ''direction taking'' in any organization: the legislative or regulatory function and the leadership function. The legislative function operates primarily by employing appropriate decision-making processes to provide stability and predictability of direction by establishing programs, policies, rules, and norms. Decisions inform members of the direction chosen and the activities expected to maintain that direction. Decisions (rules, programs, policies, purposes, and mandates) allow members to act with reasonable assurance that their actions will be considered acceptable.

The leadership function operating from values and through careful planning provides flexibility or adaptability of direction by foreseeing trends and possible developments, clarifying goals and objectives, and predicting the best means of achieving those goals. Leadership clarifies values through goals and objectives and offers direction. Legislation (or regulation) establishes or confirms direction and the values upon which action will be based by establishing programs, policies, and rules.

It is generally expected that the elected or appointed officials of an organization shall exert leadership and shall be active in decision making within the organization. Of course, members other than the administrators and factors other than administrative affect the direction the organization takes. The intensity of union activity, the nature of the clientele, the source of funding, the expertise of personnel, and the established purpose of the organization, affect the stability and adaptability of direction.

Thus, it is proposed that leadership and legislation (regulation) are administrative functions, but they do not ever, in any organization or group, reside totally within that set of persons officially designated as administrators. Leadership is the function of pointing out the direction; regulation is the function of establishing the rules, norms, and programs by which the organization acts and moves toward the chosen direction. The degree to which formal officers or other members fulfill those functions varies across organizations and within organizations across time. They always function throughout the organization.

Planning and decision making are processes through which the organizational functions of leadership and regulation are fulfilled to ensure that values become action.

SUMMARY

In this chapter, some of the ways in which problem solving, decision making, and system(s) analysis overlap with planning have been discussed. It was proposed that these four phenomena can be considered administrative processes, in that each can be described in a cycle of activities or steps. In education systems, it is expected that administrators will employ these processes to serve the welfare of the organization and its members.

The view was stressed that the welfare of the organization has multiple images and that serving its welfare might best be expressed in Weick's (1993) terminology as resilience or, in the language of open systems, as negentropy, ensuring that the organization maintains openness to revitalization and adaptation to conditions so that it does not fragment and die.

Models were presented to help clarify distinctions among the four processes discussed, which can particularly enlighten thinking about planning. Also presented were models from the literature of administration, which propose relationships among these four processes and which stress the interactive reality of all administrative processes and functions in the daily working of an education system.

Finally, I have presented my own model of the hypothesized relationships between planning and decision making as processes, leadership and regulation as functions, and direction based in values as the intended outcome of these processes and functions.

VALUES BASES OF PLANNING

VALUES, FROM GENERAL TO PARTICULAR

SECTION II proposes that thinking about and planning for education is grounded in our most fundamental beliefs about life itself and about how we live comfortably and productively together in social groups. An important assumption throughout the book is that every action, every choice, and every hope for the future derives from those beliefs, from what can be thought of as a personal philosophy of education.

Education is the means that societies have developed to try to ensure a good life for their children. The fact that there are different sets of beliefs about what that good life should be creates much of the complexity of modern life and causes continuing debate about the what and how of education. What and how are the key questions of educational planners and decision makers; therefore, understanding different sets of beliefs is essential to effective planning for quality education.

Chapter 3 looks at some of the patterns of beliefs that have developed in western thinking. Figure 3.1 suggests that views of particular aspects of education (the organization, school, leadership, planning) develop within an overall philosophy or set of beliefs. The discussion in Chapters 3 through 7 follows the pattern presented in Figure 3.1. Philosophies of education, paradigms, or world views of organizations, teaching and learning, and leadership and planning are reviewed in these chapters. Techniques for determining how they have affected practice and how they might be used productively to enhance educational planning and choice are presented.

It is assumed that such patterns of thinking underlie all planning, choice, and action in education. For the most part, these patterns or ways of thinking affect action unconsciously. A major proposition of the book is that the various patterns of thinking can become conscious bases of action. That is, they can become tools for planning.

WHAT ARE PLANNING TOOLS?

When *tool* is mentioned, the image that comes most readily to mind is of some simple physical thing used to work on a task: a saw, hammer, typewriter, computer, overhead projector, or microscope; however, the idea of *tool* includes much more than physical things. We are all familiar with such statements as, "S/he is a tool of the establishment" (a person used to carry out the designs of others, a dupe) or "tools of the trade" (in advertising, perhaps print and color, or videos and focus groups).

In legal rulings, a tool as "any instrument or apparatus necessary to the efficient prosecution of one's profession or trade" is interpreted to include intellectual products such as software programs, records of client preferences, melodies from source music, and designs. In that sense, ideas are tools of the trade and necessary for the accomplishment of many tasks. A recipe is as much a tool for a cook as a spatula; an outline is a tool for a writer; a flag or anthem is a tool for national identity, as well as a symbol; and an analysis of learning styles is a tool for a teacher, as is a seating chart, a filmstrip, or a curriculum guide. The hypothesis and research design are more important tools for a researcher than a questionnaire or a computer; rituals are tools of socialization; and goals and objectives, programs, and policies are tools by which direction is established for an organization or an individual.

The critical factor is that the "thing" (be it a physical object, an idea, or a person) is *used,* consciously and purposefully, by someone to accomplish their aims or to achieve desired outcomes. Indeed, the tool is chosen and shaped to suit the purpose. There must be a hundred different sizes, shapes, and styles of hammers, from jewelers' tappets to construction jackhammers. Each has been designed on the same principle, a known relationship between action and result, but each is shaped to suit the specific purpose for which it is used. When a screwdriver is not available, we choose the nearest approximation at hand: a nail file, a knife blade, or a dime. We choose because we know the principle of design, the relationship between action needed and intended purpose or outcome.

Thus, three bases of what a tool is are suggested: 1) It is used consciously and purposefully to achieve some desired outcome; 2) it is designed on some basic principle of relationship between action and desired outcome; and 3) it may take many different specific shapes. It is infinitely variable because it is designed on a principle of relationship.

By these criteria, it is not enough to have a leadership style to assert that it is a planning or management tool. There must be conscious choice of the appropriate leadership style to suit the situation and conscious shaping of that style to suit the group and the desired outcomes. Only then can one assert that leadership style is a tool and not a habituated personality trait.

There is a wealth of research that reveals two basic dimensions to leadership style: task orientation and personal support/needs orientation. This fact presents us with four primary styles: high task/high personal, high task/low personal, low task/high personal, and low task/low personal. This research also informs us that the effectiveness of a style is related to circumstances. Likert's (1967) work training managers in participative leadership techniques, Getzels and Guba's (1959) "nomothetic and idiographic" dimensions model, and Fiedler's (1967) well-known contingency analysis are examples.

Hersey and Blanchard (1974) also report that effectiveness differs, depending on the situation. They propose that style should be varied purposely to suit the circumstances. An important criterion for choice of the style to use, they propose, is group maturity, that is, the degree to which the group works well and productively together. Thus, Fiedler and others suggest that style ought to be varied depending on circumstances. Hersey and Blanchard suggest a way in which style can become a consciously used tool that is chosen and shaped to the conditions and the ends in view.

Similarly, it is not enough to conduct a needs assessment to be able to claim it as a tool in one's planning kit. It must be chosen as the appropriate means to accomplish specific purposes and designed or shaped carefully to fit the circumstances. Using techniques because they are the latest silver bullet is no more productive than buying the latest computer program because it presents colorful graphic displays.

It is in this broader sense that the term *tool* is used here. In this sense, the conceptual models, systems, and technologies that have been developed to assist people to think logically and plan effectively are planning tools, because planning is a conceptual process based in analysis and synthesis, logical thinking. Equally, models, processes, and technologies have been developed to enable people to work productively in groups. Social, political, and psychological norms of interaction, communication, and influence can also become tools for planning. Organizational planning is inevitably group relevant, whether it is accomplished within and by the group or by a single individual isolated from the group.

Operational Process Tools

Kaufman (1972) reviewed a number of planning tools used for education systems and placed them in what he proposed to be the overall framework of a problem-solving process, or a system approach to educational planning (see Figure II.1).

It can be seen that the tools included in Kaufman's framework are action oriented and operational in nature. Each tool deals with a specific step or stage in any systematic planning cycle. Kaufman cited only a few examples of the operational process tools that have been developed to handle each stage productively. The important contribution of such an analysis is that it relates tools to their specific purposes. It provides a practical guide to choosing which conceptual tool to apply at particular stages in the management of education. It identifies which planning tool can be most useful in thinking out different steps in the overall process.

As was pointed out in Chapter 2, planning has been closely associated with problem solving. Kaufman's five boxes (Figure II.1), plus the line "revise" that links the steps, identify six of the steps generally prescribed in the problem-solving approach. The first step Kaufman proposes (Box 1.0) is to identify the problem. Obtaining consensus of opinion about needs is an important means of clarifying a problem. Needs assessment and the Delphi technique are two techniques frequently employed to assess degree of consensus on values, goals, objectives, or needs in education. These techniques seek responses from users or other community members (for needs assessment) or knowledgeable experts (for Delphi technique).

A third common technology (tool) that seeks to clarify goals and objectives is management by objectives (MBO). This technology is addressed to internal members of the organization and develops a pyramid, or taxonomy, of objectives for the school, the system, or the organization. The intention is that each individual's personal objectives will be encapsulated in, be in harmony with, and support department,

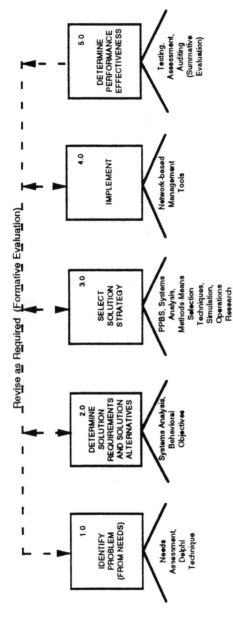

Figure II.1. Possible relation between current tools for the improvement of education and a problem-solving process model (system approach). (Source: Figure 8.1, p. 136. Kaufman, R. A. 1972. Educational System Planning. Reproduced by permission of Prentice-Hall, Inc. Englewood Cliffs, NJ and Roger Kaufman.)

school, and system objectives. Management by objectives goes beyond goal clarification, of course. It encompasses other aspects of the problem-solving cycle illustrated—review of performance and revision of objectives. These three goals/objectives tools will be discussed in more detail in Chapter 11.

In application, the perspective of any particular tool could be broad and general, concerned with the system's relationships with its environment, or it could be particular to a small unit of the whole and to problems peculiar to that unit. Kaufman's framework proposes a systematic approach to operational planning in any context.

Three Types of Planning Tools Proposed

Operational process tools are one major set of planning tools. There are many such tools available, and each is quite well defined in the literature. Also, there are useful variations of each for particular steps in the overall process. These tools are action-oriented; they help determine or clarify specific elements necessary to careful, systematic planning. Essentially, they address questions of how to do whatever step in planning the group is engaged in. They assume purpose and value, the reasons why some activity should take place.

Even a needs assessment and the Delphi technique begin with some general direction in mind. A survey question may be very broad, such as "What will be the learning needs for a young adult in the year 2000?" or "What are the most important changes young adults will face by 2000?" Even such questions direct attention and, therefore, have a values framework. They expect respondents to think about the role of the school vis-à-vis the future. They call for values and beliefs about the school, about learning, about what is important for living, and about what is or will be a good life.

Questions such as these speak to our less conscious knowledge and beliefs—to our hopes, interests, and priorities. We respond to such questions from values and beliefs learned from cultural traditions, social norms, political ideologies, psychological attitudes, personal and organizational pressures, and rumors in the wind.

The role of the social and behavioral sciences over the past several decades and of philosophies, cultures, and religions over the span of recorded history has been to identify and confirm patterns in these bases of thinking so that we can hope to live more comfortably and harmoniously as social beings. Patterns allow us to predict how others will act or react and allow us to act with reasonable confidence that our actions will be acceptable. To the degree that we can become aware of the different patterns of beliefs, values, customs, and habits that have developed, we can perhaps choose and shape patterns appropriate to the situation we are in. That is, the beliefs and values we act on can become tools, chosen and adapted to circumstances.

This is what happens to every student who undertakes and completes a Ph.D. program. S/he moves into a new world of discourse, norms, and expectations. It happens to every teacher who becomes an administrator, a matter of *they* instead of a *we*. It happens when we have the opportunity to become friends with someone of another culture, race, or language group. It happens when we move to Japan or Sweden or Italy for a year. Finding ourselves in the heart of two patterns creates uncertainty and confusion until we begin to know which pattern should be followed at the moment, that is, until we begin to use the patterns themselves as tools for choice and action.

Thus, it is suggested that there is a second (more truly, the primary) set of potential tools the administrator or educator can access. These are the subconscious patterns of thinking, feeling, acting, and choosing learned from culture, experience, study, religion, and social life. These are the ways of thinking and feeling and acting that we take for granted until we become aware of some different frame of reference.

In organizational and administrative studies different frames of reference are presented as philosophical systems; as social and behavioral science theories and propositions; as metaphors, paradigms, and definitions of concepts; and as patterns of discourse.

It is proposed, therefore, that there are three general types of conceptual tools for planners and that they may be classified according to their function. The most basic are tools that provide values sources, or values frameworks, and, thus, foundations for planning. The second set are process tools, which prioritize and operationalize values. The third group, management systems tools, integrates some particular stage in planning into an overall management system. Figure II.2 presents the three classes of tools that will be discussed.

The broadest, most pervasive tools are those that provide the values bases for thinking and acting, the perspective of the whole. We are calling these values source tools *holistic* tools. These inhere in all management action, and they underlie the choice of more specific

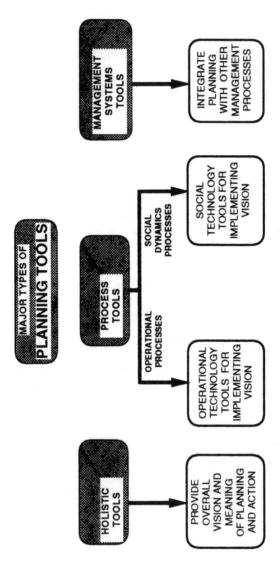

Figure II.2. Major types of planning tools classified according to purpose. Holistic tools provide the overall vision and meaning of planning and action. Process tools provide the technology for putting the vision into action. Management systems tools integrate planning with other related management processes.

planning tools. Holistic tools and values sources include belief systems; philosophies of education; paradigms or world views applied to organizations; and definitions, models, and systems of planning. Even when they are not consciously expressed, beliefs and values affect action and may be inferred from action. They are tools only insofar as they are chosen consciously and used purposefully to accomplish desired outcomes.

The most specific are *process* tools. These address planning for particular activities, events, or conditions. They are always specific whether they are used to plan for the system as a whole or for a single classroom, because each tool focuses on one element of planning: goals, allocations of time or effort, possible options, etc. The model proposed includes as process tools most of those presented by Kaufman (Figure II.1), but it also adds a set of social dynamics process tools.

The third type of planning tools, which are called management systems tools, addresses management in a general sense. These systems place the emphasis on one or another aspect of management planning [for example, program, planning, budgeting system (PPBS) focuses on resource allocation and use, management by objectives (MBO) on goals and objectives, the newer total quality management (TQM) on production]. But they arise out of some framework of thinking and may use one or more of the process tools. Process and management systems tools are both illustrated in Kaufman's system framework.

Figure II.3 details specific steps in or aspects of planning activity for which sets of tools have been developed within each of these three general categories.

A number of different tools have been developed, or invented, to address each type of question raised in planning. As we have noted above, three goal-setting tools are commonly used in education: needs assessment, Delphi technique, and MBO. Many others are also available. Some of the most common tools within each category, or type, will be described in later chapters.

Holistic tools are discussed in the next five chapters: Philosophy of Education, Paradigms and Metaphors, Planning Metaphors and Definitions, Models and Systems, and Dynamics of Participation (which focuses on social process tools).

Section III describes the Values-Based Planning System, the map to our philosophical and operational orientation to educational planning. This system maps relationships between values as goals; value as cost,

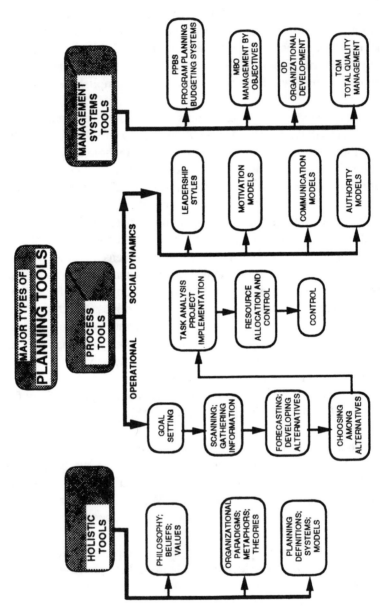

MAJOR TYPES OF PLANNING TOOLS

HOLISTIC TOOLS
- PHILOSOPHY; BELIEFS; VALUES
- ORGANIZATIONAL PARADIGMS; METAPHORS; THEORIES
- PLANNING DEFINITIONS; SYSTEMS; MODELS

PROCESS TOOLS

OPERATIONAL
- GOAL SETTING
- SCANNING; GATHERING INFORMATION
- FORECASTING; DEVELOPING ALTERNATIVES
- CHOOSING AMONG ALTERNATIVES
- TASK ANALYSIS; PROJECT IMPLEMENTATION
- RESOURCE ALLOCATION AND CONTROL
- CONTROL

SOCIAL DYNAMICS
- LEADERSHIP STYLES
- MOTIVATION MODELS
- COMMUNICATION MODELS
- AUTHORITY MODELS

MANAGEMENT SYSTEMS TOOLS
- PPBS PROGRAM PLANNING BUDGETING SYSTEMS
- MBO MANAGEMENT BY OBJECTIVES
- OD ORGANIZATIONAL DEVELOPMENT
- TQM TOTAL QUALITY MANAGEMENT

Figure II.3. Major types of planning tools classified according to perspective: holistic, process, and management systems.

choice, action; and resource use. Some of the tools appropriate to different steps in planning, for relating and integrating values and action, are described in detail for use in this system in Chapters 9 and 10.

Section IV will describe additional process tools and management systems tools that can be useful for various planning activities. Most of what can be said about planning or planning tools is relevant to almost any planning situation; however, we are concerned with education. Therefore, the focus will be on appropriate uses and applications of planning tools in education and the usefulness of various tools in educational settings. The major emphasis is on conceptual techniques for prioritizing and operationalizing values, that is, on clarifying values choices and bringing values and action (ends and means) into harmony. This, we propose, is the primary function of planning, to develop and propose programs, projects, curricula, and policies that will put values into action, to improve our ability to ensure that action (the means) reflects values (desired ends).

CHAPTER 3

Philosophy of Education as a Tool for Planning

HOLISTIC TOOLS

NO educational planning, nor any action, takes place in a vacuum. For each of us, the whole of our personal view of life and set of values is the *gestalt* that defines us as individuals, that which distinguishes us from other individuals. Holistic views of reality set the parameters within which we plan for a thing, an event, or a program; they help us define the wholeness we envision, and they help us choose directions and act in accord with that whole.

Wholeness exists at many levels: in our educational philosophy, our cultural beliefs and values; in the theories or principles through which we perceive relationships; in the paradigms or metaphors we apply to organizations and administration; and in the definitions and models of planning we assume to be valid. Every educational act is bounded by the values and beliefs incorporated in these several deep levels of wholeness that frame our thinking about education.

Views of learning and knowing and of groups or organizations are holistic and universal in nature, even while they are individual in reality. That is, they provide the whole within which we act as individuals. Indeed, one could go so far as to say that no action escapes personal gestalt. Our real gestalt not only expresses itself in, but also reveals itself in, the choices we make and in our actions.

If we orient a unit in science toward understanding the fragility of the world's ecological system, we would not be likely to emphasize expansion of national boundaries through wars in history. The two orientations conflict in basic value orientations. Someone who ''thinks'' mathematically might readily understand the structure of language or music. If we believe that teachers must be supervised, we are also likely to put emphasis on students "doing their own work" (Theory X).

Much of the stress of living comes when we are faced with words and actions that do not match. We recognize the disparity between the value expressed in words and the value expressed by action and are caught on the proverbial "horns of the dilemma." We learn ways of dealing with the dilemma, but unless we are very sure of our own values, there can be a high personal and emotional cost. Taking the time and trouble to clarify our own values can provide us with something like immunization against the stress of conflict, because our values instinctively become the heart of every action.

The deepest and most pervasive system of beliefs and values is philosophy because philosophy deals with the whole of reality and with the nature and conditions of knowledge. Definitions and models of planning deal with the nature and conditions of one kind of knowledge — knowledge about planning as a process. Thus, the models and definitions of planning that we choose and use for education lie within our overall philosophy of education. Our preference for particular models is affected by our overall view of knowledge and reality, our view of what "knowing" means, and of how we learn. Figure 3.1 presents the several levels of holistic tools that affect our educational planning and action and their relationship to each other.

Thus, I propose that the metaphor by which we characterize the school as an organization is a natural development out of our overall set of beliefs and values, our philosophy of education. Do we think of an organization as a machine, as an organism, as a text to be written? Metaphors such as these and some of the implications they may have for planning will be discussed in Chapter 5.

Paradigms or belief systems about organizations, images of leadership, definitions and metaphors of planning, and planning models and systems will be presented as following naturally from the philosophy of education one holds and the metaphors with which one characterizes an organization. In Section III, the Values-Based Planning System will be described. Thus, Figure 3.1 depicts, in a general way, the framework within which we think about planning — that all planning is grounded in our philosophy of education. It arises naturally from those broad, general values to our sets of beliefs about particular aspects of the education systems we are concerned with.

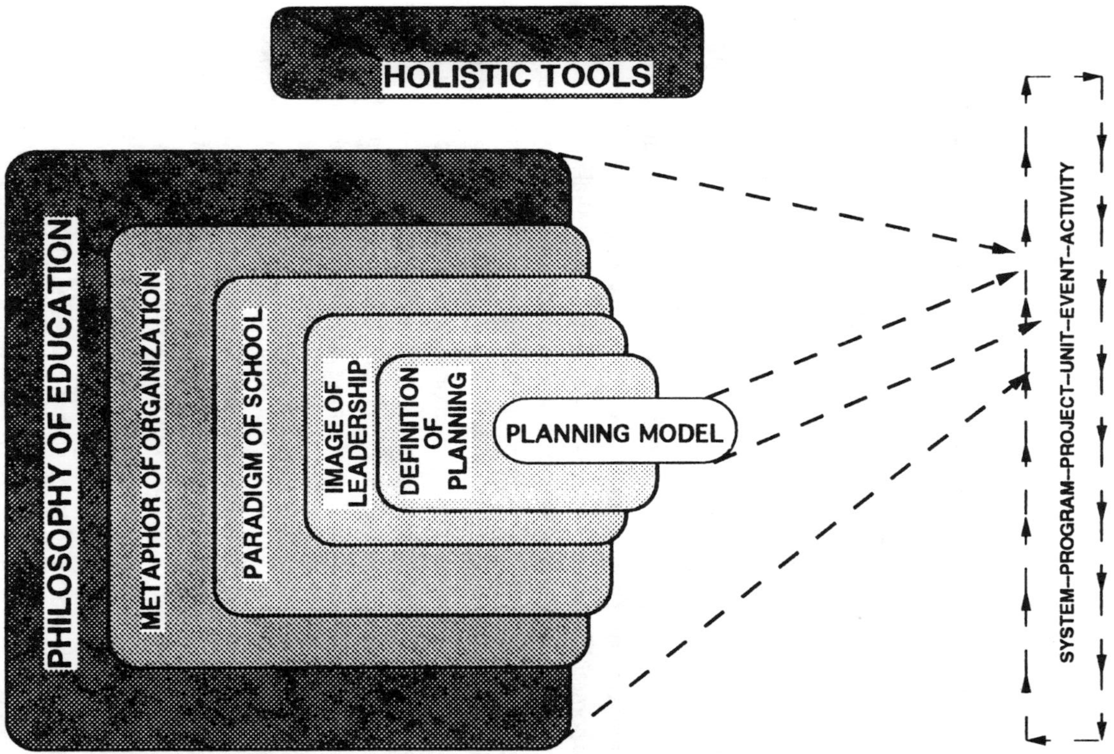

Figure 3.1. Holistic tools focus more specifically as you direct attention to some particular aspect of administration, but they nonetheless draw on one's deepest beliefs and values for the purpose they serve.

83

PHILOSOPHY AND EDUCATION

To assert that one's gestalt shapes every choice and every action is not to assume that gestalt is automatically a tool. We may be unconscious of the real values, beliefs, and images that direct and shape our choices and our actions. In large part, holistic tools act for us without conscious intent. This is particularly true of our philosophy. We might think of such unconscious values and beliefs as "body knowledge," the habits of thinking and believing.

We know that we have habits of action that allow us to ride a bicycle or to ski without thinking of each movement. Zuboff (1988) calls these "habit movements" body knowledge, knowledge that your body has and uses without conscious thought. We do also have habits of thinking, believing, and feeling that our mind uses without conscious thought. A Freudian slip is an embarrassing example. But there are many habitual responses to situations that are learned and automatic and that we never question. One of the important values of poetry and art is that they make us see something new in some everyday thing—they shake up our habits of thinking and open new windows on the world. Philosophy is the study of the ways we think, and it, too, can help us "air out the attic."

It is body knowledge that allows Jack Nicklaus or Greg Norman to play professional golf, but it is conscious awareness of that body knowledge and of alternatives available that enables them to plan their play for a tournament. Conscious use makes it possible for body knowledge to be a tool for winning or for bringing about quality education.

Our philosophical "system" can act as a tool for us in two respects. First, it can become a tool for determining our actions and choices to the degree that we use the beliefs and values we hold about education consciously for clarifying our thinking. Second, philosophy emphasizes the processes of thinking logically and recognizing the assumptions implied in normative statements. It is a tool that can help us think clearly about the truth and validity of statements. The practice of logic that is basic to philosophical thought can help determine whether the assumptions behind proposals are realistic, whether the reasons given for a project are in harmony with the values and beliefs that comprise our philosophy, our set of values.

This chapter will discuss some of the ways in which thinking about philosophy can help educators clarify the meaning of quality education and help them plan more effectively to achieve that quality. The way in which philosophies have influenced practice will be considered as well as how to use our own philosophy more consciously to aim toward a better system and toward the desired results. That is, we consider how to make our philosophy a tool for planning and creating quality education.

Why Think about Philosophy?

It is important to recognize that everyone does have a philosophy of education in the sense of a set of ideas and beliefs that frames their thinking about education, teaching, and learning. That set may be so well formulated for some as to be clearly within a school of philosophical thought. For others, it may be less consciously formulated but constitutes a personal belief system, a personal "philosophy of education," which has developed out of society and culture and out of study and experience. We vary in the degree to which our beliefs are "all of a piece," integrated and coherent, but we are more or less aware that our ideas and beliefs form a pattern.

Being aware of the patterns of ideas that have been developed in formal systems of philosophy can help establish more consciously the set of beliefs from which we ourselves will act and can help us recognize the different sets of beliefs upon which others may have based their choices and actions. Hall, speaking of cultural patterns as the root of habits, says, "The great gift that members of the human race have for each other is . . . an opportunity to achieve awareness of the structure of their own system, *which can be accomplished only by interacting with others who do not have that system . . .*" (1977, 44, emphasis in original). This could be said just as validly of one's philosophy of education. We cannot "know" our own values and beliefs until we (as Hall says) "like blind people, bump into" values and beliefs that stem from another view of life and learning. This is the potential gift of philosophy—to enable us to see our own values more clearly.

Although everyone has a fairly well established set of beliefs about education, our philosophy is hardly ever as formal and comprehensive as the systems studied by philosophers. We are concerned with some of the same questions, but we think about them in less structured and formal terms than philosophers do. Because we have a philosophy of education, whether we want one or not, and because our philosophy affects everything we say and do, we should make the effort to try to recognize and understand our own beliefs and values more fully.

We should not reject philosophy and what it offers simply because of the formality of "capital-P" Philosophy. It is important to be able to think about a philosophy of education in terms of everyday life because it is at the heart of everyday living. As educators, we are action-oriented; therefore, our system of beliefs is expressed in concrete, rather than abstract, terms; it deals with the issues of philosophy in day-to-day terms.

Most simply for the purposes of using philosophy as a tool for planning and for quality education, philosophy of education is defined as one's set of beliefs about education and the values one holds for education. It includes beliefs about the purpose of education, the content, the ways content and process should be organized and presented, the effectiveness of various methodologies, and even who should be educated. In other words, our beliefs answer for us the basic questions about education: what, how, to whom, when, why, by what means, and for whose benefit. We have beliefs about what is, about what should be, about why it should be or what is right or good, and about how to move toward those things we believe are right and good.

BELIEFS, VALUES, AND KNOWLEDGE

In ordinary language, we differentiate between know, believe, and value, though not precisely on the same bases as philosophers do. Technically, something that is "known" has been proven to be true by empirical observation. We believe many things that are not subject to empirical proof: children are born naturally good (Rousseau) or naturally bad; workers are naturally lazy (Theory X), or workers naturally enjoy work (Theory Y); children like school, or children don't like school; everything I ever needed to know I learned in kindergarten, or learning is a lifelong pursuit.

In common discourse, we frequently say *know* when *believe* would be empirically more accurate. We may "know" that students who take a laboratory science will be more objective in their thinking, that a period of physical activity will bring students back into the academic class more ready to learn, or that students respond well to challenges. Knowing, particularly in regard to human behavior, is frequently confirmed by experienced observation over time. We all have accumulated a vast body of experiential knowledge that we act on daily, and we should acknowledge it as proper bases for action. The common expression for this knowledge is "gut feeling"; Inbar (1991) calls it "tacit knowledge."

We may say *know* rather than *believe* when everyone around us also believes the same thing: students should not (or should) be permitted to use calculators for math classes; all students should (or should not) take some shop courses; we should (or should not) have a program to educate students about drugs; parents should not (or should) be encouraged to work on school curriculum committees. Moreover, we frequently say *believe* when *think it is probable* would be more accurate: "I believe (think probably) his excuse is forged," "I believe (think probably) it would be better to present it in an assembly." A term that has recently come into our education language to state a belief is *feel.* "I feel (think or believe) that the students need more experiences"; "I feel (think or believe) this history text is better than that one."

Facts and Inferences

Still another type of situation in which we often say that we know something is when we have made an inference that may or may not be justified. We have "jumped to a conclusion" because unrelated facts have been tied together in some way. This is what happens when we flip a light switch and, at the same instant, someone turns on a radio or rings the doorbell. For just an instant we think, "Did I do that?" Or you, as the principal, have been visiting a class. Just as you walk out of the door, you hear behind you a peal of laughter. What do you think? You, the teacher are at the blackboard. You hear a loud slap. (*Fact:* John just dropped his book on the floor.) You hear Mary cry, "Ouch!" (*Fact:* Mary just cut her finger on the edge of a sheet of paper.) You jerk around and see that John and Mary both look flustered. What is your first thought?

We all put two and two together and get seventy-six like this. We infer relationships between events. It is one of our greatest higher order thinking abilities and is also a source of many false assumptions. Exercise 3.1 is a chance to practice separating facts from inferences. Turn to Appendix A for the correct answers.

Despite the fact that a reasonable case can be made for "knowing" based on something less than scientifically controlled observation, it is important to acknowledge the many different bases of knowing and

Read the narrative. Then answer each statement.
T = True; F = False; ? = Not enough information to be sure
Do not make inferences.
Circle True or False only if the narrative clearly makes the statement true or false.

Narrative:
A businessman had just turned off the lights in the store when a man appeared and demanded money. The owner opened the cash register. The contents of the cash register were scooped up, and the man sped away. A member of the police force was notified promptly.

Statements about this story:	T	F	?
1. A man appeared after the owner had turned off the store lights.	T	F	?
2. The robber was a man.	T	F	?
3. The man who appeared did not demand money.	T	F	?
4. The man who opened the cash register was the owner.	T	F	?
5. The store owner scooped up the contents of the cash register and ran away.	T	F	?
6. Someone opened a cash register.	T	F	?
7. After the man who demanded money scooped up the contents of the cash register, he ran away.	T	F	?
8. While the cash register contained money, the story does not state how much.	T	F	?
9. The robber demanded money of the owner.	T	F	?
10. The robber opened the cash register.	T	F	?
11. After the store lights were turned off, a man appeared.	T	F	?
12. The robber did not take the money with him.	T	F	?
13. The robber did not demand money of the owner.	T	F	?
14. The owner opened the cash register.	T	F	?
15. The age of the store owner was not revealed in the story.	T	F	?
16. Taking the contents of the cash register with him, the man ran out of the store.	T	F	?
17. The story concerns a series of events in which only three persons are referred to: the owner of the store, the man who demanded money, and a member of the police force.	T	F	?
18. The following events were included in the story: someone demanded money, a cash register was opened, its contents were scooped up, a a man dashed out of the store.	T	F	?

Exercise 3.1. Facts and inferences.

believing. Most philosophers differentiate between knowing and believing on the basis of empirical confirmation. That is, one can 1) believe something without knowing it (because it has not been confirmed by any form of empirical observation) or 2) both know and believe something. To assert that something, some belief, is a value is to express the priority it holds in our set of beliefs, the degree to which it would be chosen over other, related beliefs. If we had to choose, would we spend more school resources on the library or on the computer lab, more time on music or on algebra, build a swimming pool or a theater, hire an extra counselor or an extra secretary? Thus, *values,* as we are using the term in this chapter, are a subset of beliefs.[5] A value expresses a belief that is "held dear," that has a high priority for choice, behavior, interest, or relationship.

North Americans value personal rights and freedoms, but some societies hold community or family needs and customs as more important. Wealthy societies value ownership of property, but many poorer societies freely share the use of survival tools. In an inner-city school, one student who took the book or pencil of another student was not stealing. They needed, so they took. If one asked the other to borrow a pencil, the other was *obliged,* by custom and belief, to give it, even though that may have left him/her without.

Our values are often labeled biases, or prejudices, by those who disagree with us. To quote a former history teacher, Miss Shurtleff, "Wars are not waged between right and wrong; they are waged between right and right." And battles between teachers and students are often waged between what the culture and values of the students say is "right" and what the teacher holds to be good. This does not imply accepting the students' standards of behavior, but it does necessitate recognizing that there are two different value bases. I found that students readily accepted the rule, "You can't take without asking in my classroom," though they would heatedly deny that they had *stolen.* They knew very well that there was one set of rules for school and another for home. They were comfortable with not being permitted, but not with being judged "bad."

Values are in the mind of the believer.

The students *knew* that taking without asking was not acceptable at school; they *believed* that sharing is good; they *valued* both sharing and acceptance at school, and these students had learned to use the value system appropriate to the place—home or school. Value systems had, for them, become a set of tools, because these students were able to choose the system appropriate to the situation. Figure 3.2 presents the relationships between believe, know, and value.

[5]In Chapters 9 and 10, one stage in the planning system is called "Value Cost Perspective." In this use, *value* is used to refer to *cost* in time, effort, and resources of some belief value (goal) for which the plan is being developed.

THINGS YOU BELIEVE ABOUT EDUCATION

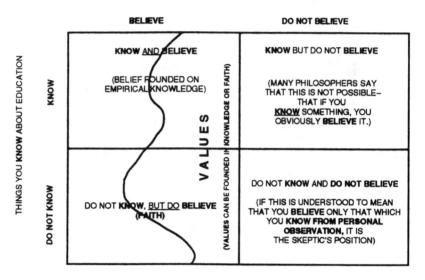

Figure 3.2. Relationships between know, believe, and value. (Values are a subset of beliefs.)

Dealing with Different Values

Our own philosophy of education cannot become an effective tool until we recognize different sets of beliefs held by different people. In order to know our own philosophy, we must distinguish between believe, know, and value. In many cases, it is simple enough to distinguish between what we believe and what we know. We (a) *know* that World War II was fought between the Allied and the Axis nations. We may (b) *believe* that the United States should have entered the war sooner. We are able to say we know "a" because evidence is a matter of public record. We can never know "b" because it cannot be confirmed; at most, it could become a belief strongly supported by reason.

We (a) *know* that many intelligent young people do not get an education beyond secondary school. We (b) *believe* that all should go to university (though other people may believe differently). We (c) *value* (place a high priority on) providing a fair opportunity and the means to go to university for all.

We (a) *know* that some students are not well developed or well coordinated physically. We (b) *believe* that students' self-esteem will be damaged if they get low marks in physical education. We (c) *value* self-esteem over physical skills achievement, so we base marks on effort, as well as achievement.

New knowledge often wreaks havoc with beliefs and values. Neil Postman, in *The Disappearance of Childhood* (1984), traced changes in the value of "the innocence of childhood" from Greek and Roman history to the 1970s. He proposed that *innocent* meant that young people were to be kept uninformed about and unaware of the "facts of life": knowledge about sex, birth, death, and violence. *Childhood* came to be defined as the period of imposed innocence. That is, he argued, *childhood* was invented when the printing press created a "secret garden" for knowledge. He argued that technology (the invention of the printing press and books) created the possibility of innocence, because the "secrets of life" could be kept from the child until s/he learned to read. Now, technology (through the invention of the telephone, radio, and television) has, Postman says, eliminated any possibility of "childhood innocence."

Meanwhile, the value of childhood innocence has remained high, so we are in a period of cultural and social strain. We have not yet invented social means of handling the dual values—the love of modern communication technology, with its inevitable open information, and the desire to maintain for our children a period of innocence and freedom from the stresses that open information generates.

These few examples illustrate some of the differences between know, believe, and value as they relate to our philosophy of education. *Know* implies that the assertion has been confirmed by some form of observation or, at least, that there is considerable objective evidence to support it. *Believe* implies that we hold the statement to be true, whether it has been confirmed or not. Every *should do* and every *should have done* statement comes under this latter group—those that could not be confirmed; they are statements of belief or opinion. Thus, *believe* would generally be accepted as including both statements that might be confirmed and those that could not be confirmed by observation.

Beliefs include those things that could be said to be known and those things we accept on faith, on the basis of cultural or social norms, or on the basis of respect for the person who told us it was true. Some people persist in believing something long after it has been refuted by much reliable evidence. There are still people who believe that the earth is flat

(the Flat Earth Society), that the Holocaust is a political myth, or that a
''witching wand'' will point to water in the right hands. All stereotypes
are of this nature, beliefs that persist despite considerable evidence that
they are not valid.

How to Know

One of the ways to think about the statements we make about education
is to consider them in terms of whether they state something that is known
or could be known. The simplest statement to confirm is one that can be
checked by direct observation: Jack is taller than Harry; everyone is
present today; three people missed problem six because they did not
''carry.''

A second type of statement common in education is one that suggests
a trend or a change over time on a fact-based criterion: vandalism has
increased; results on mathematics achievement tests are declining. Such
a belief can be supported if data are systematically collected over time
and compared on common bases. Unfortunately, such a statement is
often accepted on the basis of public opinion (''If you hear it three times,
it must be true'') or because some dramatic case hits the news. Perhaps
one school was badly vandalized, or perhaps one poor outlying area has
been amalgamated into the district, and the low achievement in that area
colors public opinion about the overall results across all schools.

A third type of statement may at first sound much like the second:
achievement in mathematics is declining. A judgment about achievement is an inference from facts, and such an inference cannot be
confirmed simply on the basis of test scores. It requires comparisons
across multiple factors—groups tested, pre- and post-test, test items
included, etc. Weakness in such bases of comparison are at the root of
many assumptions currently being tossed around about the quality of
education.

The fourth general group of beliefs about education is expressed in
two types of cause-effect statements. One type proposes a relationship
between variables (a correlation) and could be examined by data records,
surveys or opinion questionnaires, or direct observation. Academic
achievement is related to mother's work or educational status; satisfaction with teaching is related to participation in decision making. Bright
students are good athletes—or are poor athletes. Children from broken
homes are more likely than children from nuclear families to have

problems in school. We make many such statements that suggest relationships, and much of our educational research addresses questions raised by these statements.

Many of the expectations we have for particular students are based on assumptions of relationships between academic achievement and personal or demographic factors. Two specific examples illustrate how easy it is to let irrelevant factors color our expectations. One girl in our eighth grade ("Francie") was carelessly fat, dirty, and unkempt. She was from a poor, minority family, and she had had many discipline problems at school (fights, truancy, pornographic pictures). She was a poor student, and the general perception among the teachers was that she didn't much try to learn.

The assistant principal took the trouble one year to compare IQ and achievement test results on an individual basis for all 1800 of our junior high students. To the amazement of all teachers, "Francie's" scores indicated that she was the strongest overachiever in the school. Francie's achievement ranked considerably above what might be expected, given her very low IQ.

In a second case, I had an eighth-grade boy ("Richard") who was always clean and well pressed. He was polite, friendly, alert, and well liked among the students; however, he did not do his assignments well and did very poorly on tests. He was restless in class, and I assumed that he wasn't trying, that he should be able to do better.

I spoke to him several times, telling him that he had to try harder, because I was sure he should be doing better work. For several months, nothing changed, and, finally, I checked his record in the office. "Richard's" IQ was 85, close to the borderline at which he might have been considered for special classes. I realized then that I had made the assumption that his academic skills should be on a par with his social skills and his appearance. I lowered the pressure on him, and he became less tense and restless and, in fact, did do better.

The IQ's of these two students were approximately the same. In "Francie's" case, her dirty, unkempt appearance and her unacceptable behavior led us to expect poor academic achievement. In "Richard's" case, his neat, well-cared-for appearance and his polite, alert, friendly manner led me to expect more than it was possible for him to accomplish. These are two cases in which personal experience did not provide sufficient evidence upon which to make judgments; comparative data were needed to gain a proper perspective.

Table 3.1. Types of Beliefs and Statements People Make about Education. Empirical Beliefs Can Be Investigated on the Basis of Facts. Philosphical Beliefs Can Be Validated (Given Support) by Reference to Appropriate Norming Groups: Societal, Cultural, Community, Professional.

Empirical Statements		Philosophical Statements
Statements that can be investigated on the basis of facts—by observation, by collection of data, or by experiment	Possible ways to investigate empirical statements:	Statements that express personal beliefs, values, and attitudes. These statements cannot be tested on the basis of facts. They can only be validated on the bases of general philosophical beliefs of a society, a culture, a community, or a school system.
— (Girls) (boys) get better scores on (math) (language) tests.	— Examine test scores over time.	— (Girls) (boys) should all take (shop) (cooking).
— Students treat handicapped children better if they are in integrated classes.	— Pre- and postobservations in and outside the classroom	— Mainstreaming is morally right.
— Curriculum decisions made by relevant groups are more apt to be effectively implemented than those imposed from above.	— Pre- and postobservation, examination of documents, or participant reports	— Curriculum decisions made by relevant groups are *better* than those imposed from above.
— Students who have had strong academic programs in school will get high-level jobs more readily after completing.	— Examine historical records from follow-up studies.	— Students who have had strong academic programs in school will be better citizens after completing.
— Students will perform better if the teacher is informed that they are gifted, than if the teacher is given negative information.	— Experimental study with a control group	— Teachers should be given information suggesting that students are capable, even if tests indicate low ability.
— Students from different cultural groups have different beliefs about school rules and expectations.	— Surveys, attitude response questionnaires, informal interviews	— Students should be allowed to follow their own values re: behavior in school, even if they conflict with the rules and customs of the school.

List several empirical statements you have heard, and possible ways to investigate them. Also list several philosophical statements you have heard educators make as if they were facts (see again the discussion in the text).

Types of Statements You Have Heard People Make about Education.

Empirical Statements	Possible Investigation	Philosophical Statements
Statements that can be investigated on the basis of facts—by observation, by collection of data, or by experiment		Most statements of what should happen or should be make up what can be thought of as a "personal philosophy of education." They cannot be proven. They can only be validated on the bases of general philosophical beliefs of a society, a culture, a community, or a school system.
Example: Level of education is related to lifelong earning power.	**Investigation:** historical data on large groups of persons with different levels of education	**Example:** All young people should have at least two years of college.

Exercise 3.2. Types of beliefs worksheet.

The second type of cause-effect statements concerns the effects of one factor on another; it proposes differences in outcomes based on different treatments. Such a proposition should be tested by controlled experiment. Reinforcement increases positive responses; whole-language learning increases the amount of free reading that students do; school uniforms create a positive attitude. Table 3.1 presents a number of empirical belief statements and possible ways they could be investigated. It also presents a set of somewhat similar statements that express personal beliefs, values, and attitudes that could not be tested empirically. These are philosophical statements.

Why is it that we identify one statement about curriculum as an empirical statement and the other as a philosophical statement? Most of the statements that assert that we should do thus and so or that one choice is better than another arise out of personal beliefs or opinions. Since *should* cannot be tested empirically, it reveals something about the individual's philosophy of education.

If the philosophical statement were put to the test, one might say that decisions made by groups are better because they are more apt to be implemented. Often enough, such an empirical meaning lies under the surface of a philosophical statement as an assumption. Examining those assumptions for their empirical meaning is one of the basic orientations of philosophical thinking.

This is one of the important ways in which your philosophy can become a tool for clear thinking about action and choice. Exercise 3.2 asks you to list other statements you have heard people make about education and classify them as empirical or philosophical, that is, as stating ideas or points that could be tested versus those that could not.

PHILOSOPHICAL SYSTEMS

A number of formal philosophical systems have been developed across the centuries in the Western world to help us understand our essential humanness. They address the primary questions: what is being, what is knowing (how do we know), and what is truth or reality (what is real)? These questions are so intimately bound up in the business of education that we must accept the fact that whatever may be the system of education that develops in a society or culture, it finds its bases in the answers given to these questions.

The major philosophical systems differ in their answers to those questions. In North America, four philosophical systems have had considerable impact on propositions about what education means. In fact, the differing views have been at the heart of controversies over what should be the purpose, the process, and the desired products of education. Table 3.2 illustrates some of the major propositions of four philosophical systems that have influenced education.

A brief summary such as that presented in Table 3.2 may not have much meaning in relation to real situations; it may seem far removed from the daily business of a school. The purpose here is not to develop any particular philosophy nor to study in depth the systems themselves, but to recognize some of the implications and applications of different philosophies on educational thought and practice. If you do study those philosophical systems, it may become evident that you have an inclination toward one system of beliefs or another. You may lean toward one set of ideas about what ''knowing'' is and how we learn. Several additional readings that may be of interest are listed at the end of the chapter. Also, Exercises 3.5 – 3.8 at the end of the chapter present some ''choice'' situations for discussion. In such situations, choices could be based on different sets of beliefs about education.

If you have a subconscious belief that what is in a book, especially a literary or historical book, is ''true or known,'' then you may be inclined toward idealism. You may believe that to really know something, you must understand the sources of the ideas upon which it is based. You may stress the great thinkers of the past and their contributions to knowledge.

If, on the other hand, you have to see it to believe it (or feel it, or smell it, or taste it), then you may lean toward realism—visits to museums to study artifacts from other cultures, study of the structure of government, writing skills, or basic mathematics functions. You will want to learn the basic structures of language, mathematics, or music. You will learn the different periods of art and the forms used in those periods. You will want to see the thing in many different forms.

A pragmatist may believe that social action and social causes or scientific investigation are the sources of real knowing, because they are experience. The pragmatist would encourage field trips, ecological projects, work-study programs, and community service. The pragmatist would not emphasize the *facts* learned from the field trip or the community project, but the *experience* itself. Life is experience, and, therefore, experience is knowledge. The pragmatist would expect students to be able to organize experience to learn.

Table 3.2. Some of the Major Propositions of Four Philosophical Systems That Have Influenced Education.

	Idealism	Realism	Pragmatism	Existentialism
What is real?	—We can only know the idea of the thing. —The thing itself is forever beyond our knowing.	—Things are real, but in incredibly varying forms. —Reality is the thing itself in all its infinite variety.	—Change and process are the essence of reality. —Reality is experience.	—Only what you see, smell, feel, hear right now at this moment of time is real. —Only yourself and your experience.
What is knowledge?	—Understanding great ideas of the past —Conscious recognition of the "ideas" of things —Remembering	—Recognizing the common character in all possible variations of the thing —Recognizing the "thingness" within variety	—We cannot know chage/process. —Change can only be inferred from pre- and postobservation. —Knowledge is process/experience.	—Being aware of the instant and acting on the instant —Knowledge is one's relationship to the instant.
How do we learn?	—By studying the past, and ideas of great thinkers —By bringing to consciousness the ideas of things through reading and study —By listening to wise elders	—By seeing, examining, touching, sensing all the varying representations of a thing —By examining as many variations as possible	—By isolating points in the flow of process through which we can infer change	—By recognizing and acting on the instant —By recognizing the kaleidoscope of the here and now
What is the source of knowledge?	—Books, history, philosophy	—Things, people, events	—Observations under known conditions	—The chaos of existence

The existentialist might assert that, being aware of the sights, sounds, and smells that we live and breath, the "ocean of life" is knowing. Knowledge does not come to us in structured packages, the existentialist might say, but in flashes, in impulses, in feelings, and in sensings. To truly "know," the child must be able to create their own image of reality, must take the instant and see it as whole. The phenomenologist approach to research owes much to the existentialist philosophy.

Or it may be that you tend to be eclectic—to find value in all sets of beliefs and may then choose according to the circumstances. There is no right answer, although social and cultural groups develop relatively stable sets of common beliefs and values, and particular orientations become more or less "correct" in different periods or in different groups. One's philosophy is a set of personal values and beliefs. Such beliefs become the basis for action and choice, but zealous promotion of particular sets of beliefs causes many controversies in education.

Exercise 3.3 gives examples of how teachers holding different philosophical perspectives might teach the concept of "time" in a seventh-grade class.

Words and Values

In addition to acting as a tool for us by incorporating the basic set of beliefs and values we hold about education into our actions and choices, our philosophy of education can help us recognize reasons for conflict in the debates over "where to go" or "how to get there" in education. Educators act on sets of beliefs that IF we require . . . , present . . . , discuss . . . , show . . . , accept . . . , THEN our students will understand . . . , appreciate . . . , be able to . . . , know . . . , create. . . . The system itself is established on a similar proposition. Education systems are established and designed by societies on the proposition that "IF our young people understand . . . , appreciate . . . , are able to . . . , know . . . , create . . . , THEN they will contribute effectively to our society."

However, the words and phrases we all use have different meanings to different people or to the same group under different circumstances. "Effective contribution to a society" may be thought of in economic terms or in social terms; it may be oriented toward individual best interests or toward the best interests of the community or society. The meaning one holds for words is expressed in the actions that may result. The actions we expect in the name of "good citizenship" or "security"

Which of the four philosophical systems is each one leaning toward? Discuss the differences in what they believe it means for students to learn: to "know," "understand," "experience," see, or feel."

Teacher A: I would bring in some stories about how people of earlier times explained day and night; the Greek and Roman myths. Then, I would have them read about the Industrial Revolution and discuss how it affected people's reactions to time. I would have them study their geography for differences in day and night, summer and winter, north and south hemispheres, etc.

Teacher B: I would have them keep a daily record of time for two weekdays and then do the same for two weekend days. Then, I would have them compare how they felt about time during those periods and whether it was easier to keep the record for weekdays or for weekends. I would have them record any disagreements they had with their parents about what should be done at certain times and analyze these disagreements in terms of difference in the ways they and their parents think about time.

Teacher C: I would ask them how far it is from their home to other places, because many times we talk about distances in terms of time. I would give them a "sunrise-sunset" graph for different times of the year, and ask them to divide "daytime" into twelve sections. Since that would give different numbers of "minutes" in an hour for summer and winter, I would ask them to figure out how many minutes there would be in a "nighttime hour" in summer and winter. Then, we would read about what a "school day" might mean if we lived in the far north or on the equator.

Teacher D: I would bring in a big digital clock and have them "move" and "freeze" as the clock flashed. Then, I would have them get up and move around the room for as long as they wanted. But if they stopped, they would have to sit down and couldn't get up again. Then we would talk about whether they felt like they had to quit or had to keep going, how we get used to doing things by the clock, and how they feel when the clock says, "Do it now." Then, we would talk about how rock stars flash different time images in their videos and whether the flashing stirs people up or makes them confused about what they want to do.

Exercise 3.3. Four teachers describe how they would teach the understanding of "time" to a seventh-grade class.

or "a good life" have changed dramatically since the early twentieth century.

One picture is worth a thousand words, but
one word creates as many images
as there are people who hear it.

The meanings words hold for people represent their beliefs and values. With the increasing multiethnic, multiperspective nature of society, words used in planning for education may have multiple meanings. We may use the same words, and think we are saying the same thing but expect radically different actions. Therefore, it is important for educational planners to recognize the diversity of basic values represented in their community. When we meet a situation that presents a conflict of values, we choose one course or another or are not able to make a firm choice. It is particularly in such a values-conflict situation that a clear understanding of our own philosophy, a clear set of values, can become a valuable tool. It can enable us to make specific choices in harmony with our basic beliefs, our fundamental values.

Teaching in a junior high school that had a multiethnic and a mixed socioeconomic population made language an important factor of establishing reasonable rapport with students. The students' language included all of the *verboten* four-letter words. To a large degree, the students did not use that language to be purposefully disruptive; those words were everyday language in their homes and in their lives. The students used them almost unconsciously; however, I did not allow them in my classroom, and the students knew that.

Occasionally, a student broke out with a "dirty" word, and I sent them to the counselor. I learned that if I wrote on the pass that "Harry" said a "bad word," both I and the counselor got a lot of argument. But if I wrote that "Harry" said ____ (explicit), there was no argument at all. The counselor said, "Did you say it?" "Yes." "You know you can't say that in Mrs. J's class?" "Yes." End of discussion. Despite our different values on the meaning of good and bad words, the students and I both held the same value about "tell it like it is," a fact is a fact, as long as no value judgment was made about the person.

When beliefs and values are only assumed in a choice, not clearly stated, they become propositions that we ourselves might not consciously wish to make. In such a case, our philosophy is not a tool, a thing consciously used to shape our lives. If the school curricular program emphasizes sciences and math, it is based in assumptions, or beliefs, about what kind of learning is important for future adults. If it emphasizes fine arts and humanities, some very different assumptions about learning are expressed. Educate the whole child, back to basics, an educated work force, learning by doing, whole-language learning — each of these phrases is a key to some aspect of an educational philosophy, a set of beliefs and values.

As North American educators, school commitments are, to us, sacrosanct; however, to many community groups, home and family commitments take precedence over school. What absences from school are "legitimate"? Personal illness is universally accepted in North America, but is it acceptable to be absent to take part in a whale hunt or a pheasant hunt, to care for a sick younger child, to help a father at work, or to attend a religious ceremony? These are values-based questions that our multifaceted society is increasingly faced with. Do we teach all children to live by one set of values? Is it possible to create a system of universal education that can accommodate widely divergent value systems?

These are the vital, specific questions that address the meaning of the more general questions: What is the purpose of an education system, and what kinds of learning are important for our youth? Do the social learnings that the school is charged with rest in allegiance to the primary family, to the school or school friendship groups (secondary groups), or to society at large (a tertiary group)? Or do desired social learnings rest in the individuals themselves, as advocated by Timothy Leary in the 1960s, by many present-day rock stars, and by refrains such as "do your own thing," "self-actualization," and "individual rights"? How do we balance these differing values?

GOALS, VALUES, AND PLANNING FOR EDUCATION

Within our personal philosophy we have beliefs about the who, what, when, where, why, and how of education. For administrators and teachers, these are related to two general groups of beliefs about education, the proper ends or aims of education, and the best means to achieve our aims: the best areas of study and the proper content of courses and the best modes of action, techniques, and methods. Currently, questions are being raised about the overemphasis on means and ends and its demand that we specify clear relationships between them. Some authors emphasize open-ended approaches to educational planning; they propose that planning should be goal-free, exploratory, and inventive [see for example, Clark (1981), Carlson (1991), Hamilton (1991), Kaufman (1991)].

We take the position that goals are the expression of values, the desired outcomes that we aim for and work toward. Or to state it differently, values we hold dear are the real outcomes we aim toward. If we put those values up front as goals, then direction is clear, but the means chosen can vary with conditions. As systems theory tells us, all open systems are characterized by "equifinality"; they allow different approaches to the life and vitality of an organization. "Many roads lead to Rome."

We consider that goal-free and planning are mutually exclusive ideas, that goals or objectives, the values intended, are inherent in all plans, not just in "rational" plans. Goals, objectives, means, plans, and leadership are all directional in nature; they all focus on the future and are concerned with desired states. The fact that our purpose in an activity is discovery, social harmony, contribution to personal welfare, or simply new experience does not deny the reality of goals; it simply broadens the goal to incorporate larger realities and interests and to allow for growth in terms of goals themselves.

Goal-free propositions incorporate the fact that action is a mode of discovery and learning, as well as a mode of implementing. When we learn to ski or to skateboard, we do not just learn how to perform the necessary actions. By performing those actions, we learn something about balance, reaction time, alertness to the surroundings, speed, and compensation for error. We discover our own abilities and incorporate them into attitudes and interests held. We learn *from* as well as learning *to*. Since *learnings from* are not specifically stated as goals, difficulties faced in *learning to* may blot out these related learnings. Goal-free emphasizes the fact that stated goals are not necessarily the most important learnings that derive from action. The judgment abilities *learned from* are valued aims or goals at a higher level of learning, but the attitudes and behaviors that result may not all be desired. Both the desirable and undesirable outcomes must be noted and attended to.

Despite recognizing the importance of "beyond goal" or "other than goal" learning outcomes, we assume that planning is inevitably goal-oriented and inevitably value-based. We define planning as the process of preparing a conceptual model of a thing, an activity, or an event. We understand a model to be a set of *hypotheses* proposed as the means most likely to be successful for achieving that thing, activity, or event. Since hypotheses deal with the relationships between means and ends, questions of ends, means, and relationships believed to exist between ends and means have to be resolved in developing any plan for an education system. However, a plan is not a decision carved in stone. It is a set of hypotheses based on the best evidence at some point and subject to change as new evidence becomes available or as new interests develop.

We learn methods and techniques of teaching, counseling, administering—educational means—from study and from experience. Beliefs about means are generally empirical. That is, they could be tested by some form of observation, and they have been the subject of much research and thoughtful analysis and reflection. Research has provided useful guidelines for choice and action, but we do not have, and never will have, formulas for successful teaching or administering. Always, experienced judgment based on sound reasoning is the final arbiter for choice in the specific case. And every choice of means is, in reality, a hypothesis, an educated guess as to how to achieve a desired result in each particular case.

Conversely, beliefs about the proper ends or aims of education are not empirical. They cannot be tested empirically, although they can be supported (shown to be acceptable within the context of a culture or society) on the basis of common understanding and values and by evidence of desirable or undesirable effects accumulated over time.

We may choose integration, rather than special classes, as the mode of structuring learning situations for a group of students. We might explain that such a mode is better because it enhances social living skills, interdependence, and a sense of mutual respect for and responsibility among people with differing abilities. The "becauses" of our thinking express our beliefs and values. If we have clearly thought out our philosophy of education, our most fundamental beliefs, we know that we are choosing to emphasize social living skills over academic learning skills.

Historically, special classes were created to permit a space of psychological freedom from unequal academic competition for particular groups of students or to make it possible for regular students to proceed at a more rapid pace. Of course, we want to achieve both sets of valued aims, social and academic. We must then create some other modification (perhaps cooperative learning, perhaps learning games, perhaps computer-based individualization) that will provide the psychological freedom from unfair standards of competition formerly offered by special classes and allow learners to proceed at their own pace. (To say nothing, of course, about providing special training for teachers in diagnosis and remediation and support for classroom instruction.)

If the values that we aim for are made clear, it may become easier to develop effective strategies. We acquire beliefs about the purposes of education from social, cultural, and life experiences. We take such beliefs for granted, and challenges to beliefs shake up our world.

A good example of the disorienting effects of a challenge to our beliefs about the proper ends of education is the degree to which the ''Japanese way'' has shaken North American education. For decades, North Americans, educators and the public alike, have asserted that one overriding purpose of education is the development of each individual, their personal self-identity and self-esteem, and their ability to live a full and satisfying life. Academic learning has been viewed as an important means to that end. We have had faith that an educated populace will be a moral, productive, and creative populace.

We are now challenged with the apparent superiority of Japanese school children in the use of mathematics and language and in responsibility toward work and working life. We have seen the effects of emphasis on these outcomes reflected in Japanese productivity. This poses a fundamental challenge. Education is provided by the state; is, then, the proper end of education growth and strength of the self or growth and strength of the nation? Can we create a system that will accomplish both aims? Both North Americans and Japanese are wrestling with this issue.

The ''sputnik'' blow to American pride in 1957 is another example of a shattering challenge to beliefs about the ends or aims of education. So, too, are the social and technological revolutions taking place; the demands of minority ethnic groups, handicapped, and women; the increasing mobility of world peoples; the immediacy and universality of information; the changing population age curve; and the changing characteristics of work.

The fall of the Berlin Wall, and the violent disruptions of national stability throughout Europe suggest profound changes in the common person's reaction to imposed will. All of these changes in the world around us force us, as educators, to review and clarify our values and to reconsider our beliefs and practices. A belief that is not thoughtfully examined in light of new circumstances becomes an assumption, and assumptions are the icebergs that endanger education. Philosophy insists on thoughtful appraisal of beliefs, assumptions, and assertions.

Thus, the first way that a philosophy of education can serve as a tool is by continually helping us know ourselves better, helping us develop a clear set of beliefs about education. When we are clear about our basic beliefs and values, they become tools for planning and action, consciously used and consciously held as bases for choice. Exercise 3.4 suggests a set of questions to develop a values profile about educational issues.

The first big question each educator has to resolve individually is which perspective they will lean toward: the system perspective (common subject matter, best teaching methods, etc.) or the student's perspective (personal learning styles, individual interests and abilities, etc.). From which perspective does the educator think about most issues that arise daily? To date, most education literature (supervision, leadership, curriculum) has focused on the system perspective.

With the technological tools that are rapidly becoming available, the focus could shift to the student's perspective. There is no valid reason that all math students should spend the same amount of time on a particular skill. Nor is there any reason that all students should be expected to read at the same rate, a chapter a day, for example. Some may already be reading far beyond grade level, and some may not have the ability to concentrate attention for extended periods of time. The technology of the future could free us from the system orientation – the fifty-minute class period syndrome.

The second way in which philosophy can help us is to develop the ability to think logically, to recognize the assumptions implied in normative statements, and to think clearly about the truth and logic of proposals. Chapter 8 deals with the logic of IF ↔ THEN and how that logic relates to planning. That chapter lays the groundwork for building a plan based in values, as described in Chapters 9 and 10.

For the most part, our sets of beliefs have developed in terms of practice, action, and expectations, and each of us has sets of beliefs focused on specific aspects of our lives. Different patterns focus on organizations or on people in organizations and have developed out of different philosophical bases. Chapter 4 discusses the broad general approaches to thinking about organizations that have emerged in the past

Develop possible alternative values profiles. Choose one subject field and give examples.

The answers to questions such as these express one's educational philosophy—one's beliefs and priorities for education.

Values issues that underlie all educational planning must be faced, individually by educators and collectively for education systems.

Which set of questions is easier to answer?

From the Perspective of the System: How Best to Educate All Students	From the Perspective of the Student: How, What, and When to Learn
SUBJECT MATTER What should be taught?	SUBJECT MATTER What should the student be expected to learn in school?
TEACHING METHODS What are the best methods of teaching each?	LEARNING STYLES How do learners learn best?
GRADE LEVEL CURRICULA To whom should each subject/skill be taught?	LEARNING READINESS What is each student capable of learning?
SPECIALIST FIELDS When should it be taught to particular students?	LEARNING INTERESTS When can students best learn particular things?
WHOSE BENEFIT: THE PUBLIC Why should a thing be taught?	WHOSE BENEFIT: THE STUDENT What is the purpose for learning a thing?
WHO SHOULD DECIDE The educators—the experts?	WHO SHOULD DECIDE The students/parents/community?

Exercise 3.4. Developing alternative values profiles.

century. These patterns are called paradigms, or world views. They are views of the world that have provided, and limited, the focus of research. They have influenced practice in organizations, generally, and in education.

APPLICATION QUESTIONS

Exercises 3.5−3.8 are sample questions to apply your knowledge. Examples of responses given to several of the exercises in the book are presented in Appendix A. (One analysis presented in response to Exercise 3.6 is included, for example.) It is important to remember that, in most cases, there are no right answers. These exercises are intended to stimulate thinking and debate.

Make a list of teaching techniques you frequently use, and state your reasons why these have been good choices. Which philosophical system do the techniques and reasons seem to come from?

Exercise 3.5. Teaching techniques.

Choose some major current education proposal and discuss it in terms of the philosophical systems it seems to originate from. Give specific examples from the proposal (examples of proposals: America 2000, Total Quality Management, régime pédagogique, authentic testing, any Royal Commission report on education, etc.).

Exercise 3.6. Education proposals.

Assume you are the principal of an inner-city secondary school. A former graduate has bequeathed the school $50,000 to spend on something for the school's programs. The decision of what to spend it on must be made by a staff vote after open consultation. You have all four philosopher-types in your staff. You have asked for suggestions and have received many. What might have been suggested and by which "philosophers?"

Exercise 3.7. Spending suggestions.

Discuss the question: Should education systems be based on the proposition that students must know, or on the proposition that students must be able to _____?

Exercise 3.8. Basis of education systems.

SUGGESTED READINGS ON PHILOSOPHY AND VALUES FOR EDUCATION

Adams, H. 1988. "The Fate of Knowledge," in *Cultural Literacy and the Idea of General Education. Eighty-Seventh Yearbook of the National Society for the Study of Education, Part II*, I. Westbury and A. C. Purves, eds., Chicago, IL: The University of Chicago Press, pp. 52–68.

Adler, J. J. 1982. *The Paideia Proposal.* New York, NY: Macmillan Publishing Co.

Campbell-Evans, G. H. 1991. "Nature and Influence of Values in Principal Decision Making," *The Alberta Journal of Educational Research,* 37(2):167–178.

Fitzgibbons, R. E. 1981. *Making Educational Decisions. An Introduction to Philosophy of Education.* New York, NY: Harcourt Brace Jovanovich, Inc.

Giroux, H. and D. Purpel, eds. 1983. *The Hidden Curriculum and Moral Education. Deception or Discovery?* Berkeley, CA: McCutchan Publishing Corp. Articles by P. W. Jackson, M. Apple, M. Greene, P. Friere, and others address issues related to moral bases of education practices and choices.

Hague, W. J. 1987. "Teaching Values in Canadian Schools," in *Contemporary Educational Issues: The Canadian Mosaic,* L. L. Stewin. S. McCann, and J. H. Stewart, eds., Toronto, Ont.: Copp Clark Pitman, pp. 241–251.

Hodgkinson, C. 1970. "Organization Influence on Value Systems," *Educational Administration Quarterly,* 6(3):46–55.

Hodgkinson, C. 1978. *Towards a Philosophy of Administration.* Oxford, Eng.: Basil Blackwell.

Hodgkinson, C. 1983. *The Philosophy of Leadership.* Oxford, Eng.: Basil Blackwell.

Love, J. M. 1985. "Knowledge Transfer and Utilization in Education," in *Review of Research in Education,* No. 12, E. W. Gordon, ed., Washington, DC: National Educational Research Association, pp. 337–386. The question of whether "utilization" is the most desirable value base for education.

Maddock, T. 1990. "The Relevance of Philosophy to Educational Administration," *Educational Administration Quarterly,* 26(3):280–292.

NSSE. 1972. *Philosophical Redirection of Educational Research. The Seventy-First Yearbook of the National Society for the Study of Education, Part I,* L. G. Thomas, ed., Chicago, IL: The University of Chicago Press. Of particular interest: Section II, Criticizing Current Concepts (which points to some of the current issues of research), and Section III, Developing New Models.

NSSE. 1981. *Philosophy and Education. Eightieth Yearbook of the National Society for the Study of Education, Part I,* J. F. Soltis, ed., Chicago, IL: The University of Chicago Press. Chapters on philosophical issues related to curriculum, teaching, aesthetics, society, and science. Also chapters on the basic questions of philosophy: epistemology, logic, ethics, and metaphysics.

NSSE. 1985. *Learning and Teaching: The Ways of Knowing. Eighty-Fourth Yearbook of the National Society for the Study of Education, Part II,* E. Eisner, ed., Chicago, IL: The University of Chicago Press. Curriculum reforms; modes of knowing (scientific, interpersonal, intuition, narrative, practical, and spiritual); implications for practice.

Nucci, L. P., ed. 1989. *Moral Development and Character Education, a Dialogue.* Berkeley, CA: McCutchan Publishing Corp.

Ozmon, H. A. and S. M. Craver. 1990. *Philosophical Foundations of Education*, Fourth ed. New York, NY: Macmillan Publishing Co. Chapters on the many philosophical systems that have had an impact on education: idealism, realism, pragmatism, reconstructionism, and existentialism. Also chapters on other systems of thought.

Pajares, M. F. 1992. "Teachers' Beliefs and Educational Research: Cleaning Up a Messy Construct," *Review of Educational Research*, 62(3):307–332.

Robertson, E. 1992. "Is Dewey's Educational Vision Still Viable?" in *Review of Research in Education*, #18, G. Grant, ed., Washington, DC: American Educational Research Association, pp. 335–381.

Starratt, R. J. 1991. "Building an Ethical School: A Theory for Practice in Educational Leadership," *Educational Administration Quarterly*, 27(2):185–202.

Straughan, R. J. Wrigley, eds. 1980. *Values and Evaluation in Education*. London: Harper and Row Publishers. Perhaps of particular interest: Ch. 1, "What are the Main Issues?" by the editors, and Ch. 6, "Values in Education" by C. Ormell. Also chapters on particular subject areas.

Tom, A. R. 1984. *Teaching as a Moral Craft*. New York, NY: Longman Inc. Contrasts teaching as an applied science versus teaching as a moral craft.

Venn, G. 1970. *Man, Education, and Manpower*. Washington, DC: The American Association of School Administrators. "Today" and "Tomorrow" from the perspective of 1970: Ch. 3, "Schools Yesterday"; Ch. 4, "Schools Today"; and Ch. 5, "Schools Tomorrow."

CHAPTER 4

Paradigms and Metaphors

The axis of the earth sticks out visibly through the centre of each and every town or city.
—*Oliver Wendell Holmes,* The Autocrat of the Breakfast Table [vi]

PARADIGMS AS SUBSETS OF A PHILOSOPHY OF EDUCATION

SETS of beliefs that comprise one's philosophy arise from the most basic questions about being human: What is existence? What is real? How do we know? What is learning? In some profound and almost subliminal sense, everyone has beliefs about the "right" answers to those questions. Although those beliefs affect every choice and every action in every aspect of our lives, we express them in practical terms about the practical situations we live in. They are very "real" to each of us; they are the truth as we see it and know it. Thus, customs, traditions, norms, and habits of thinking, feeling, acting, and believing develop.

Since each of us lives in many different worlds, our philosophy expresses itself in many different world views, or in sets of assumptions that frame our way of thinking about each of those worlds. We form a holistic view of, or set of beliefs about, the school, the family, religion, teaching or learning, a community, leadership, authority, marriage, work, or play. All of those worlds overlap and integrate for each of us, and the world views of individuals in the same setting have much in common. But it is increasingly being acknowledged that every individual develops his/her own particular view of each of the worlds we live in.

When a particularly informative world view, or set of propositions, is expressed in the research and scholarly study of some aspect of our lives, it has an impact on the work of others in the field. Other researchers formulate questions to test aspects of the set of propositions; names are given to relationships proposed and to the type of research being done. Naming the research creates a frame within which thinking then proceeds. Naming also creates a communication link between researchers and their partners, practicing educators. A name gives character to a set of ideas.

But a funny thing happens on the way to understanding. Once the frame is named, it will be abstracted and generalized. The set of propositions will be analyzed into elements and the proposed relationships between elements, and the whole will be represented graphically with boxes, circles, connecting lines, and arrows. The graphic representation, the picture, raises a thousand questions to be studied, and a community of researchers grows. The underlying propositions may have become assumptions, and particular views of a world begin to dominate scholarly work.

Such world views, called paradigms, are holistic views of specific subworlds within which researchers raise questions and within which we live and act. As educators, we have integrated holistic frames of reference that govern, or affect, the way we think about teaching, about the school, about curriculum, about methodologies, about parent involvement, about the proper relationships between teachers and pupils, about how a classroom should be organized, and about every aspect of education.

We recognize that others may not hold the same sets of beliefs and attitudes and may not believe in the same ways of doing things. Seeing the different paradigms compared makes them available as tools to choose from in particular situations. Much of the recent work of researchers is directed toward clarifying those differing sets of assumptions and propositions, those different paradigms, so that they may become more readily available as tools to be used consciously for planning and action.

Paradigms in Behavioral Studies

The term *paradigm* has been used in the sciences for many decades to identify a pattern of assumptions, propositions, questions, and methodologies within which a convention of research has developed. Paradigms have been defined by Gage as ''models, patterns, or schemata . . . [as] ways of thinking or patterns for research that, when carried out, can lead to the development of theory'' (1963, 95; 1972, 73). Kuhn (1962) described paradigms as ''ways of seeing the world . . . which determine the problems available for scientific scrutiny and provide . . . an intertwined body of theoretical and methodological belief'' (p. 17). Shulman used paradigm as generally interchangeable with ''research program.'' He said, ''Each of the extant research programs grows out of a particular perspective, a bias of either convention or discipline, necessarily illuminating some part of the field of teaching while ignoring the rest'' (1990, 2−3).

Thus, the idea of paradigms has generally been applied to research communities−groups of researchers testing propositions within the same overall framework (Shulman, 1990, 2). That framework, which Simon might call "a simplified model of the real situation" (1957, 199), frames one view of the immediate world and sets boundaries on what will be attended to. Kuhn (1962, 1970) noted that physical scientists proceed from a commonly accepted base of assumptions about the nature of their discipline and the appropriate methods of study within the field. He argued that the social sciences were less mature than the natural sciences because they have a confusing multitude of paradigms−that a mature science accepts one paradigm until a revolutionary new world view emerges. He cited Copernicus, Darwin, Newton, and Einstein as examples of natural scientists who introduced a new world view that changed not only the course of research, but also the direction of progress. Such a dramatic change is called, in currently popular change literature, a paradigm shift (Barker 1992; Guba, 1990; Tapscott and Caston, 1993).

In the social and behavioral sciences schools of thought may have been called research communities or traditions, as in Collins' *Three Sociological Traditions* (1985). Collins described three scholarly communities in sociological thought, the Conflict, Durkhemian, and Microinteractionist Traditions, which have the characteristics of paradigms. Each has a common base of assumptions, common world view, and common methodology or approach. These traditions did not replace each other, however, as Kuhn says is the nature of a mature science (1962, 23). According to Collins (1985), they developed in roughly parallel time frames: Conflict Tradition 1800−1960 and beyond (p. 48), Durkhemian Tradition 1740−1960 (p. 120), and Microinteractionist Tradition 1870−1960 (p. 181).

Ways of Viewing the World of Education

Chapter 3 discussed philosophies of education, the broadest, most inclusive holistic ways of viewing our education worlds. This chapter presents world views of or ways of viewing organizations, education, and leadership. Chapters 5 and 6 will present ways of viewing planning in education. Each of these world views, or views of specific worlds within which we live and work, is holistic in perspective, although each is specific in its focus. Particular ways of viewing our worlds develop out of research and scholarly study and become the basis of practice.

Research, theory, and practice in education face broad, general issues such as the nature of the organization, the nature of leadership and administrative processes, decision making, planning, and motivation. They also face issues that are particular to education: the nature of the school, teaching effectiveness, and the process and meaning of learning. Separate bodies of research and literature have developed, and, within each, paradigms or propositional world views have framed research and practice. In the following sections, paradigms of organizations, the school, and leadership are presented. First, however, the question of multiple paradigms is discussed.

Supplant—Supplement—Complement

Supplant or Supplement

If it can be suggested that the existence of different paradigms directing different bodies of inquiry and practice is good, how do they enlighten each other? How can multiple paradigms do other than confuse, as Kuhn acknowledged being confused during his year in the behavioral science "think tank"? How do educators and researchers avoid myopic, kaleidoscopic, or situational fragments of "facts" that do nothing to advance knowledge, understanding, or practice? Gage (1978) and Erickson (1986) proposed that different research programs should supplement or add to findings and suggested cycles of research on teaching. Gage proposed a cycle of case study → process-product studies → field testing (1978, 90). Erickson proposed that, at every stage generalization should be supplemented by ethnographic studies for thick detail (1986, 2).

Other researchers appear to mix research methodologies without really changing the world view or underlying assumptions. Shulman says, "One of the strategies . . . is a form of eclecticism run wild, with little or no discipline to regulate the decisions. In these studies, many *forms* of research are incorporated and thrown together with little thought for the differences in their purposes, assumptions, or perspectives" (1990, 83, emphasis added).

Within any paradigm, the research methodology is a function of the assumptions being made about the world in view, not the reverse. Methodology is chosen because it is the best (or only) way by which specific questions can be answered. A sequence of methodological approaches to a question may contribute insights, but sequencing and intermingling are essentially supplementary in nature.

Complement

An approach that appears to hold more promise for bringing conceptual clarity to sets of paradigms in a field can be found in organization studies literature. A growing group of scholars has begun to identify and generalize the assumptions underlying different sets of paradigms or models. These scholars identify polar dimensions upon which a set of models can be "mapped." Generally, two dimensions are proposed as basic to the set, creating four quadrants.[6]

The quadrants are then characterized on the underlying assumptions inhering in models mapped into the set. Three examples are presented in the following pages. Figure 4.1 [from Burrell and Morgan (1979)] maps paradigms or world views of the organization. Figure 4.2 [from Scott (1978)] maps theories of behavior in organizations. Figure 4.3 [from Astley and Van de Ven (1983)] maps paradigms of organizational action. These three examples are chosen because they approach the question of sets of beliefs, or world views about organizations from different perspectives. Each contributes to understanding some of the issues involved in thinking about organizations.

WAYS OF VIEWING ORGANIZATIONS

Paradigms of the Organization (Burrell and Morgan, 1979)[7]

Burrell and Morgan (1979) and Morgan (1980) proposed that four major communities of scholars exist who study and research organiza-

---

[6]Inbar (1991), however, posited five dimensions and mapped orientations to organizational change on the five dimensions: The Programming Profile, Figure 4.2, p. 70; The Planning Profile, Figure 4.3, p. 71; The Improvisation Profile, Figure 4.4, p. 72; and The Randomized Response Profile, Figure 4.5, p. 73. See the discussion in Chapter 2.

[7]The discussion in this section is based on Burrell, G. and G. Morgan. 1979. *Sociological Paradigms and Organizational Analysis*. London: Heinemann; and on Morgan, G. 1980. "Paradigms, Metaphors, and Puzzle Solving in Organization Theory," *Administrative Science Quarterly*, 25(4):605–621.

tions. They proposed that research (and practice) can be oriented toward regulation (maintenance and control) or toward change (the necessity for change or the impossibility of change). The largest group of researchers and theorists in organizational and administrative studies addresses objective bases of regulation such as contracts, job descriptions, organigrams, functions, and budgetary rules. For other researchers, the focus can be on subjective bases of regulation, as cultural beliefs, interests, or psychological dispositions. Thus one defining characteristic of the paradigms is the polar dimension subjective ↔ objective.

Other theorists, they argued, are oriented toward the need for change, either because the organization itself has become a "prison" within which some members or classes of members are subjugated by tradition or custom (subjective forces) or by groups that dominate by controlling or manipulating rules, power, and resources (objective forces). These two polar dimensions reveal four paradigms, or world views, of research and theory. The defining characteristics of these paradigms are the two polar dimensions subjective ↔ objective, and regulation ↔ change.

Thus, they proposed that the four broadly general views of the "world of the organization" can be identified by their primary orientations and by metaphors that shape and "image" their perspectives. They mapped the propositions and theories of scholars in the field of organization studies into the quadrants formed by the horizontal and vertical axes, identifying each quadrant as a general world view, or paradigm. Figure 4.1 presents Burrell and Morgan's map of paradigms of organizations.

The Objective-Regulation Paradigm

Those scholars whose work employs an objective approach and is oriented toward regulation (structure and function) employ two metaphors: machine and organism. One, machine, images the organization as inert, a thing to be worked, to be operated. The other, organism, images the organization as a living thing, with the capacity to grow or die. Both are external to the participants and to the scholar, so they can be examined objectively, in terms of structure and function. Functionalism has been the dominant paradigm in organization studies, and it dominates organization practice.

Many of the well-known propositions about organizations are in-

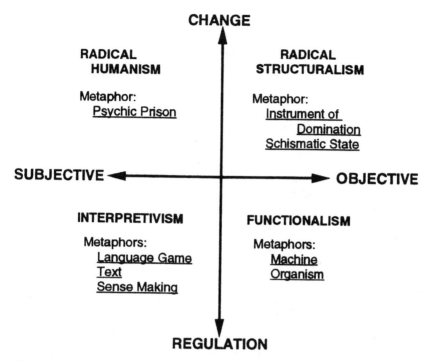

Figure 4.1. Paradigms of the organization proposed, based on change – regulation and subjective – objective dimensions. (Source: W. G. Burrell and G. Morgan. 1979. Sociological Paradigms and Organizational Analysis. London: Heinemann. Reprinted by permission of W. G. Burrell and G. Morgan.)

cluded in this paradigm. Table 4.1 gives examples of scholars who employ the machine metaphor and some who employ the organism metaphor. All of the propositions classified in this paradigm assume that the organization is a real thing, that real relationships exist whether they are formally structured or they develop out of organizational or human needs. It seems reasonable to propose that the functionalist paradigm, or way of thinking, is most comfortable for a practicing administrator. It is practical for administrators to assume that they are dealing with something that actually exists.

The fact that several metaphors are employed within this objective-regulatory view—the functionalist paradigm—means that the administrator must be aware of the different forces that shape the organization. This view includes propositions about formal and informal structures, the intended and actual, and hidden agendas since such views

Table 4.1. Examples of Scholars and Researchers Whose Propositions Are Classified by Morgan (1980) as Belonging in the Functionalist Paradigm.

Organism Metaphor	Machine Metaphor
Roethlisberger and Dickson (1939): Hawthorne Studies	Taylor (1911): Scientific Management; efficiency of worker
Selznick (1948): Structural functionalist	Fayol (1949): Scientific Management; efficiency of manager
Parsons (1956): Process analysis of functions	Weber (1946): Bureaucracy; the structure of authority systems
Argyris (1957): Satisfy needs of organizational members	Gouldner (1959): Organizational rationality
McGregor (1960): Managerial styles	Etzioni (1960): Goal models
Katz and Kahn (1966): General systems approach	Georgiou (1973): Goal models
Lawrence and Lorch (1967): Modern contingency theory	
Likert (1967): Managerial styles and effectiveness	

Other Metaphors in the Functionalist Paradigm	
Cybernetic systems:	Feedback and control
Loosely coupled systems:	Real structure not neat and "tidy"
Political systems:	Conflict of interest and power structures
Theatre:	Human actors in various roles

Source: pp. 613–616. "Paradigms, Metaphors, and Puzzle Solving in Organization Theory," G. Morgan. 1980. *Administrative Science Quarterly*, 25(4):605–621. © 1980 by Cornell University. Reprinted by permission of *Administrative Science Quarterly*.

assume a "real" set of relationships, whether created and displayed on an organizational chart or growing out of custom and example.

It also includes human relations and human resources views, which are directed toward shaping relationships among mutually connected and interdependent parts of the organization. It is this assumption, that the organization is an objective thing existing in reality outside of the participants' personal interpretations, that distinguishes the *objective-*regulatory from the *subjective*-regulatory paradigm.

The metaphors themselves direct our interpretation of events and infiltrate our language. "It's the squeaky wheel that gets the grease"; "Throw a monkey wrench into the works"; "big wheel"; "The early bird gets the worm"; "the brains of the operation"; "Light a fire under ____"; "Get to the heart of the question." All of the criterion of effectiveness group of scholars who study teaching effectiveness, effective schools, and leadership effectiveness would be placed in this quadrant, although Burrell and Morgan do not deal with this body of literature. Exercise 4.1 asks whether some of the current proposals for educational reform could be characterized by either of these two metaphors, machine or organism.

The Subjective-Regulation Paradigm

The second group of scholars identified by Burrell and Morgan have shifted the approach from objective to subjective. This group would include the group of educational researchers that Shulman (1990) discussed in relation to classroom ecology and interpretivist studies and the phenomenological and ethnographic approaches. This group of scholars does not deny the existence of order (regulation) in the organization, but they assert that it is subjectively formed and reformed by each participant within each situation. The approach to study is participant observation and "thick" description.[8] Wolcott's *The Man in the Principal's Chair* (1973) and Rutter et al.'s *Fifteen Thousand Hours* (1979) are well known examples from the literature of education. Scholars such as Apple, Giroux, van Maanen, Georgiou, and Leithwood also are oriented toward "thick" observation and description.

Two research studies by Ahola-Sidaway (1978, 1986) are an interesting application of this approach to the study of behavior in secondary schools. Ahola-Sidaway (1978) studied student life in a small and a large suburban high school. She expanded that study (1986) by following students from a highly academic elementary school into the large high school. She lived in the high school for an extended period of time, followed students to classes, had a student locker, joined clubs, and generally participated quite fully in student life. Since she was young looking, she "passed" quite well and was accepted by the students as almost one of themselves.

Ahola-Sidaway found that the impact of the sixth-year elementary

---

[8]"Thick" observation and "thick" description are not exactly the same. Thick observation implies hours of participant observation, note taking, interviews, and recordings. These data are sometimes analyzed and reported as general ideas, conclusions, or types of information. Sometimes, they are described as incidents or reported as interpretations, commentary, or quotations and, thus, become thick description. In the first case, qualitative data are, to some degree, quantified. In the second case, they are reported as received, as individual perceptions, ideas, and opinions.

Many proposals for reform of education and restructuring of schools are presently being studied, implemented, and tested in North America. Some are listed below. Consider their basic assumptions, and decide if they would be placed under one of the metaphors in the functionalist paradigm proposed by Burrell and Morgan.

	In Functionalist Paradigm?*		If Yes, which
Proposal	**Yes**	**No**	**Metaphor?** **

Goal-Free Planning _____

Madeline Hunter Model _____

Site-Based Management _____

Garbage Can Model of Decision Making _____

Program Budgeting _____

Authentic Assessment _____

Merit Pay _____

Criterion-Referenced Tests _____

Competency-Based Certification _____

Recertification of Teachers _____

Peer Supervision _____

Clinical Supervision _____

Empowerment of Teachers _____

De-Schooling Society _____

Union Control of Teacher Placement _____

Whole Language _____

Home Teaching _____

Add others: _____

_____

_____

*Does the action proposed in this reform movement rely on, arise from, or promote *objective* functions, structures, rules, and regulations? Yes, objective = functionalist. Or does it rely on *subjective* beliefs, feelings, customs? Yes, subjective = not functionalist.

** If the proposal relies on *objective* patterns (F), do these patterns suggest a *machine* (a mechanical organization) or an *organism* (a dynamic, growing organization)?

Exercise 4.1. Metaphors in the functionalist paradigm.

teacher appeared to have important implications for the ease with which students adapted to high school life. Students whose elementary school teacher cared about them as individuals were more apt to report that they liked high school than were students whose elementary teacher had been described as not caring. She found, also, that the character of the high school differed from that of the elementary school. She used the terms *Gemeinschaft* and *Gesellschaft* to distinguish between the close "family feeling" of the elementary school and the impersonal, fragmented life reported by students in the high school (1986).

The subjective-regulation quadrant is named the interpretivist paradigm by Burrell and Morgan (1979). Until recently, scholars and researchers whose work is identified in this domain have not been as significant a force in administrative and management literature as those in the functionalist paradigm. Few textbooks on educational administration deal with proposals such as Wittgenstein's that organizational activity is little more than a game of words (1968). Yet could we not propose that much of the feminist literature and the antifeminist literature, as well, is just that—a game of the words with which we discuss organizational activity. Should we say "each to (his)(his/her)(their) own taste?" Should we speak of chair<u>man</u> and chair<u>woman</u>, or chair, or chair(er)(ess)? For that matter, say the antifeminists somewhat tongue-in-cheek, should we not be concerned with words like wo<u>man</u> and fe<u>male</u>?

The game of words is not an insignificant matter in education. Should we speak of a multi<u>racial</u>, a multi<u>cultural</u>, or a multi<u>ethnic</u> society? Should we say blacks, coloreds, or African-American, Mexican-American, British-Caribbean? The use of hyphenated identification is less prevalent in Canada than in the United States, but the language game is strong nevertheless; it takes a different form. The first question asked of a black person in Canada is "Where are you from?" They may be third or fourth generation Canadian, but they are thought of first as being *from* some other part of the world. This is also true of other nonwhite Canadian citizens. It may be explained in part by the fact that there is a large multiethnic population in Canada whose members have come by choice from both French-speaking and English-speaking islands and countries.

Language establishes identity, role, and status. One does not say "I *work* at Peter Jenkins School"; one says "I am a *teacher* at ____, I am the *nurse* at ____, I am the *head custodian* at ____, I am the *principal* at

_____.'' Certainly, one hopes that no one still says ''I am *just* a teacher.''

Language also stereotypes in subtle ways, ''His sister was _____,'' ''She is one of the _____.'' One of my most unforgettable experiences as a junior high school teacher is an example of that subtle typing of a student. I had heard many reports of ''Janet Bernstein'' (not her real name) in the teachers' lounge, but had paid little attention, except to know that ''Janet'' spelled trouble in a big way. One day, the principal told me that ''Janet'' was going to be moved into my seventh-grade low-stream English class. When I came into class, she had not arrived, but the rest of the students were already in their seats. I was met with a chorus of, ''Is 'Janet Bernstein' *really* going to be in our class?'' So we all got ready to work with one ear cocked to the door. When it opened, I nearly gasped. I hadn't expected one of the most beautiful children I had ever seen, and I hadn't expected *black*. (I'd done a bit of stereotyping myself.)

I said, ''Come on in, Janet, this is your seat here.'' (I had moved someone from front-row center.) Janet came in and stood by the desk with her head thrown proudly and defiantly back, looking at the students more than at me. I said, ''Come on Janet, sit down, we're getting to work.'' ''I don't got no book.'' ''OK, bring your book tomorrow. Right now, we're going to do some writing.'' ''I don't got no pencil.'' ''Well, OK, I'll loan you one today, but bring yours tomorrow.''

Still ''Janet'' stood, but her air was not quite so defiant. I touched her lightly on the arm and said, ''Come on Janet, sit down so we can get to work.'' She melted into her seat and went to work with the rest of the class.

That had, indeed, been a language game—not just between myself and Janet, but within the whole group. They had all watched her intently, giving not one sign of favor or disfavor. Silence is one of the most important ''languages'' there is in a group. Janet knew that she would lose face with the kids if she treated me badly; I had a reputation in the school, too. But I could have lost the whole group if I had dealt with her in the language I had been taught about her in the teachers' lounge. Exercise 4.2 asks for phrases that may be heard around the school which reveal some underlying assumptions.

Scholars in the interpretivist paradigm search for the meaning of events to participants in order to understand organizational life. Metaphors used are language text (each participant is ''writing the story'' of events in their minds as they happen) and sense making (each

Scholars in the interpretivist paradigm often speak of an organization as a language game. We hear some people play that game with others all of the time with phrases that identify high and low status and phrases that reveal high or low expectations for particular students or groups of students. This results in individuals or groups being treated more favorably or more unfavorably than one would really expect from the facts of their situation.

High Status for Teachers

Example: S/he's one of the in-crowd
          Got the principal in his/her pocket

Low Status for Teachers

S/he just teaches _____
S/he just does enough to get by

Give some other examples of phrases that identify:
     high status among teachers   vs.   low status among teachers

High Expectations for a Student

Example: His/her father's a lawyer, you know
          S/he's always so well-dressed

Low Expectations for a Student

They're from that _____ area
Why bother—what will they ever do?

Give some other examples of phrases that reveal:
     high expectations for a student   vs.   low expectations for a student

Exercise 4.2. The metaphor "language game" applied.

tries to ''make sense'' out of events in the context of their own life and culture). A metaphor that might characterize the researcher's approach in this quadrant could be taken from Edmund Burke's ''Intimations of Immortality'':

> To see a world in a grain of sand.
> *—Edmund Burke*

Subjective-Change and Objective-Change Paradigms

The two remaining paradigms have had less direct impact on administration studies, although scholars in those domains have had tremendous impact on our views of the world. The dominant metaphor proposed for the radical humanist paradigm (subjective-change quadrant) is that organization is a psychic prison. The metaphors of the radical structuralist paradigm (objective-change quadrant) are organization as an instrument of domination, or a schismatic state.

These two paradigms, both oriented toward change, and the metaphors through which they are expressed lie close to each other. A major difference is that individuals create their own psychic prison but that others employ the organization as an instrument of domination, or the nature of organization itself creates schisms. That is, the difference lies between a dominating force *subjectively* interpreted and subjectively reacted to, but not necessarily objectively observable, versus one considered *objectively* created (real in the external world) with external forces dominating. Table 4.2 presents some of the scholars identified in each of these two quadrants and a brief phrase representing propositions they have made.

The scholars in the radical humanist paradigm are not focused on the structures and functions of the organization as it *is,* a "thing" that could be changed. Their concerns are with the impact the organization has had on particular groups or individuals and the sense those members have of being caged in, of having no recourse against the fate of organizational life. People are captives because they have been taught to believe that their fate is inevitable. Change must take place, they assert, but people are powerless to create that change because they believe they are powerless. These authors may rail against the apathy and defeatism of the people.

Scholars in the radical structuralist paradigm, in contrast, believe that it is the rules, regulations, practices, and established power positions that dominate the worker. Workers do not believe that they are born to be in subjugation but that they have few resources at their disposal to fight the system, to change the power relationships. Scholars may study how groups begin to "go their own way," to develop power groups and schisms and fragment the organization.

In each paradigm, Burrell and Morgan have traced the underlying assumptions to their philosophical origins. They proposed that a paradigm expressed in sets of research and scholarly work develops directly from the system of philosophical thought that forms the world view of particular scholars. The answers to the question "What is an organization?" grow out of the larger questions "What is existence; what is reality?"

Table 4.2. Scholars Identified in the Change-Oriented Domain: The Radical Humanist and the Radical Structuralist Paradigms (Morgan, 1980).

Scholar	Proposition
RADICAL HUMANIST PARADIGM (pp. 617–618)	
METAPHOR: PSYCHIC PRISON	
Marx (1844)	Individuals think of their institutions as "real," something that exists independent of their own will and action.
Freud (1922)	Organizations and organizational behavior can be seen as individuals acting out their own repressed tendencies.
Freud (1922)	Individuals are captives of their own unconscious processes.
Marcuse (1964)	Individuals believe that those in power use ideologies to manipulate people to their own ends.
Jung (1965)	(As Freud): Individuals are captives of their own unconscious processes.
Habermas (1972)	(As Marcuse): Individuals believe that those in power use ideologies to manipulate people to their own ends.
RADICAL STRUCTURALIST (pp. 618–619)	
METAPHOR: INSTRUMENT OF DOMINATION	
Taylor (1911)	Scientific management—analysis of worker's tasks
Weber (1947)	Bureaucracy is a mode of domination, an "iron cage."
Michels (1949)	"Iron law of oligarchy"
Fayol (1949)	Scientific management—analysis of management tasks
Friedman (1977)	Those in power use all means to dominate their members.
METAPHOR: SCHISMATIC STATE	
Bateson (1936)	Processes through which organizations develop factions.
Gouldner (1959)	Members drive toward functional autonomy, leading to fragmentation.
Morgan (1980)	Organizations tend to fragment because of internal tensions.

Source: pp. 617–619. "Paradigms, Metaphors, and Puzzle Solving in Organization Theory," G. Morgan. 1980. *Adminstrative Science Quarterly*, 25(4):605–621. © 1980 by Cornell University. Reprinted by permission of *Administrative Science Quarterly*.

The language used to name the paradigms—to name the polar extremes of the dimensions—and the metaphors associated with each paradigm suggest much of the character of the research and propositions that are to be found. But the language used does much more than reveal—it directs us to think in those terms. Thus one of the major contributions of a map, such as that developed by Burrell and Morgan (1979), is that the languages of each can be seen in context with the others. The map becomes a tool for thinking.

Metaphors have been named because organization members talk about organizational life in patterns that reveal their underlying assumptions. Although we seldom use the terms psychic prison, instrument of domination, or schismatic state, we do use phrases that suggest these ways of thinking. Give some other examples from your own experience or similar phrases you have heard:

Psychic Prison Metaphor

Examples:

1. You'll never change anything; everyone's so traditional.
2. You have to be "politically correct" or you'll be on the black list.
3. You don't dare say what you really think around here.

Instrument of Domination

Examples:

1. The rules box us in.
2. The in-crowd keeps the power in their own group.
3. We're like robots to them; we're not allowed to think for ourselves.

Schismatic Metaphor

Examples:

1. Learning is too fragmented, nothing seems to hang together.
2. Each department is a law unto itself.
3. Let's get our act together; we're going in a thousand directions at once.
4. There's no such thing as "professionalism" anymore; it's dog eat dog.

Exercise 4.3. Metaphors of the "psychic prison" or "schismatic state" applied.

Exercise 4.3 seeks examples of phrases we often hear in education that reveal the underlying assumptions of "psychic prison," "instrument of domination," or "schismatic state."

Burns proposed that an important source of this contribution is that "such models . . . use a visual format to present the different conceptual bases of the separate paradigms. This allows us to call to conscious consideration quite readily, the clearly contrasting views and their relationships to each other. Thus we can use the model for understanding our own choices, and for understanding the choices and actions of others'' (1993, 250). We can compare and contrast ideas and their implications; we do not have to be caught up in one frame of thinking. We can ''carry on a conversation with ourselves'' (Zuboff, 1988, 196).

Paradigms for Choice-Making in Organizations (Scott, 1978)

Scott (1978) reviewed models of choice-making in organizations and proposed that four paradigms dominate the literature. He proposed two polar dimensions that define the paradigms within which those models can be characterized: closed system ↔ open system, and natural ↔ rational models. Figure 4.2 presents Scott's map of models for organizational choice.

Scott presented human relations and cooperative systems models as closed system models, which are parallel to scientific management and bureaucratic models. Both of these groups might be seen as residing within the functionalist paradigm proposed by Burrell and Morgan. Type II models (natural, closed system) might be viewed through the

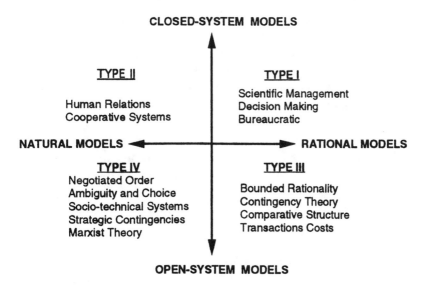

Figure 4.2. *Theoretical map of choice-making models, based on closed system ↔ open system and natural ↔ rational dimensions. (Source: Table 1, p. 22. "Theoretical Perspectives," W. R. Scott in* Environments and Organizations: Theoretical and Empirical Perspectives, *M. W. Meyer and Associates, eds., © 1978 by Jossey-Bass Inc. Reprinted by permission of Jossey-Bass Inc.)*

organism metaphor and Type I (rational, closed system) through the metaphor of the machine. Types III (rational, open system) and IV (natural, open system) are not as clearly equated with Burrell and Morgan's change orientation dimension. They are not focused on the imprisoning and dominating character of organizations but are focused on factors in the environment that affect, and perhaps limit, the probability of effective change.

It is interesting to observe that Scott proposed that rational choice could be found oriented toward both closed and open systems. There is often an implication in current literature that closed systems are not rational, that they do not face the realities of the environment. To the degree that the orientation (world view) is toward maintaining the system in its present state, rational choice is characterized by the propositions of scientific management, traditional decision processes, and a bureaucratic design. If the world view is that the organization is an open system, a subsystem of its environment and fully interactive with its environment, rational choice has the character of contingency theory, bounded rationality (satisficing), and transactions costs.

The map thus becomes a tool for planning and choice because it makes possible a "conversation" about the way to approach an issue. If economic conditions make budget cuts necessary, the map of choice models makes it easier to debate, or converse about, different approaches. The model, a visual device that is easy to call to mind, raises the questions of contingencies, ambiguity of goals, human relations, and the existing structure, whether bureaucratic or loosely coupled. The map becomes a mental checklist against which to consider choice-making issues, a picture of different ways one could look at an issue. It can be used as a tool by mapping any choice issue according to the aspects that require consideration and by reminding the decision makers of alternative perspectives. Exercise 4.4 poses several discussion questions directed at the four choice-making perspectives presented by Scott.

Paradigms of the Manager's Role (Astley and Van de Ven, 1983)

The paradigms mapped by Astley and Van de Ven (1983) present views of the role of the manager within differing orientations toward direction-taking in organizations. They oppose the dimensions of macro level ↔ micro level and deterministic orientation ↔ voluntaristic orientation as

Discuss the following questions related to the paradigms proposed by Scott (1978).

1. Is "the school" a natural model or a rational model (Type I, II, III, or IV)?

2. What are some of the "contingencies" (the factors that must be taken into consideration) that affect planning or choice in education?

3. What is the difference between a "contingency plan" and "contingencies that may affect a plan"?

4. What are some of the ways in which "scientific management" has contributed positively in education (technology, structure, growth of knowledge, services, furniture, subject fields, etc.)? Give specific examples of things we take for granted.

Exercise 4.4. Discussion questions.

defining characteristics of the paradigms existing in the field. Figure 4.3 presents the model proposed.

Astley and Van de Ven (1983) propose that one of the major determinants of the manager's role is the scope of responsibility: macro (national or state/province level) or micro (board or system level); the other determinant is the action orientation: deterministic or voluntaristic. ''Seen from the voluntaristic orientation, individuals and their

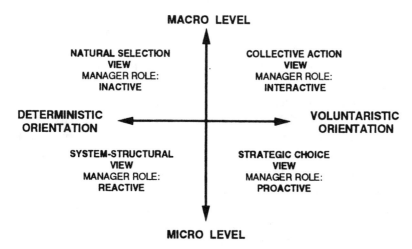

Figure 4.3. Paradigms of the manager's role proposed based on macro↔micro level and deterministic↔voluntaristic orientation dimensions. (Adapted from Figure 4, p. 247, "Central Perspectives and Debates in Organization Theory," W. G. Astley and A. H. Van de Ven, published in Administrative Science Quarterly, 28:247. © 1983 by Cornell University. Reprinted by permission of Administrative Science Quarterly.)

created institutions are autonomous, proactive, self-directing agents. . . . The deterministic orientation focuses not on individuals, but on the structural properties of the context within which action unfolds . . .'' (1983, 247). The authors place collective action view and interactive managerial role at the macro level (national or state/province). Strategic choice view and proactive managerial role are placed at the micro (board or system) level.

In some respects, a school system might be considered an ''organization of organizations'' (the macro level), with the individual school being at the micro level. This is not the level of analysis Astley and Van de Ven are dealing with, however. They might examine the set of school boards at the province or state level as macro. Recognizing that distinction, it is interesting to consider current school restructuring proposals in terms of Astley and Van de Venn's map.

School Restructuring Considered within Paradigms of Manager's Role

Murphy (1991) identified four major strategies that have been proposed for restructuring schools: school-based management, choice-voice, teacher empowerment, and teaching for understanding. Each of these strategies, he suggested, affects organization and governance, work design (redesign), and core technology (1991, 19). Specific proposals within each strategy address issues at the macro level – the role of the central administration to be changed from control to support (p. 24) – and at the micro level – the student, not the teacher to be considered the prime worker [p. 51, citing Seeley (1980), 7]. Each strategy also addresses issues of voluntaristic orientation versus deterministic orientation: parental choice versus teacher empowerment or partnerships; teacher empowerment versus self-contained classrooms versus contracting out for teaching services (p. 68); and partnerships versus labor negotiations (p. 87). The issues of level (macro/micro) and orientation (deterministic/voluntaristic) raise questions for all restructuring proposals. What sector are they aimed at, and do the specifics of the plan support the general propositions?

Reavis and Griffith (1992) distinguished between site-based management and decentralization on the one hand and restructuring on the other. They said, ''In contrast to these two [site-based management and decentralization which delegate some powers but retain the basic bureaucratic structure], restructuring requires a change in the basic operational assumptions of the organization; it requires a change in the

Consider your own role as a manager in an organization in terms of the manager's roles proposed by Astley and Van de Ven (1983). (Refer back to Figure 4.3 and the discussion following.)

If you are a teacher, assume that you are a "manager of learning experiences" and describe your role in terms of inactive, interactive, reactive, and proactive.

1. What portion of your work would you characterize as:

    Manager Role: Inactive   _____

    Manager Role: Interactive   _____

    Manager Role: Reactive   _____

    Manager Role: Proactive   _____

2. What portion of the work of central administrators would you characterize as:

    Manager Role: Inactive   _____

    Manager Role: Interactive   _____

    Manager Role: Reactive   _____

    Manager Role: Proactive   _____

3. In what aspects of your work are you most able to act in each of the four manager's roles in the model (for example, in curriculum development, in instructional leadership, pupil control, goal setting, financial management, personnel development, personnel selection, or other)?

    Inactive: Natural Selection:

    Interactive: Collective Action:

    Reactive: System Structural:

    Proactive: Strategic Choice:

Exercise 4.5. Manager's roles.

culture of the organization; it requires *shared* decision making and collaboration'' (p. 16, emphasis added). Such a vision clearly seems to shift the school from a deterministic orientation to a voluntaristic orientation.

Do the specific propositions made about restructuring support that collaborative, or voluntaristic, vision? The authors, Reavis and Griffith (1992) provided an implementation checklist at the end of six of their eight chapters. In total, eighty-eight statements are included in the checklists. Seventeen, or 27.3%, of the statements either make specific reference to parents and community members being actively involved in some decisional or operational process or are worded broadly enough that involvement can be inferred; however, all eighty-eight state or imply action by staff members. The emphasis is still heavily system-structural in orientation. The collaborative focus that is stressed throughout the discussion of restructuring is primarily between school-site administrators and staff. (*Subordinates* is the term frequently used to identify staff other than administrators.)

In these two discussions of restructuring, the proposals being presented currently seem to be based in the micro level-deterministic orientation paradigm, although collective action is strongly supported. It could be proposed that collective action is more readily implemented at the school (micro) level, while strategic choice may be more appropriately examined at the macro (or system) level. In school systems, then, the characteristics of ''collective action view and manager role: interactive'' might be placed in the micro level dimension, and ''strategic choice view and manager role: proactive'' in the macro level dimension. In Exercise 4.5, review your own situation in light of the sets of orientations proposed in the four quadrants.

WAYS OF VIEWING THE SCHOOL

Within the broad world view of organizations in general, educators develop frameworks for thinking about the school as an organization and as a living and working system. Concerns about the school as an organization have focused on a number of issues arising out of basic social and cultural purposes of education. Four of them—the teacher and teaching, the student and learning, the principal and leadership, and the classroom as a learning environment—have always been at the heart of debates. Each has produced a significant body of research and literature and a number of schools of thought. All are presently the focus of restructuring and reform strategies and proposals.

The Teacher and Teaching

In the first *Handbook of Research on Teaching* (1963) Gage identified three influential paradigms in research on teaching: criteria of effectiveness (or process-product), process (interaction), and machine. He discussed each in considerable detail in Chapter 3 of the *Handbook* (pp. 94–141), and in Chapter 6 of a later book, *Teacher Effectiveness and Teacher Education: The Search for a Scientific Basis* (1972, 84–113). The criteria of effectiveness paradigm has been, until recently, the most powerful in the field. Criterion variables have been used in research and in design of teacher education programs, supervision programs, and evaluation systems. By a natural process, the paradigm has colored all teaching practice. Figure 4.4 shows the elements that may be found in criterion of effectiveness research on teaching.

The current focus on school effectiveness might be seen as an extension of the criterion of effectiveness paradigm in teaching research. Many of the variables identified in the school effectiveness literature parallel those in the teaching effectiveness paradigm. Leader personality and characteristics replace similar teacher variables; contingency factors are identified, as are school behaviors (replacing classroom behaviors); pupil growth and attitudes remain as Type IV variables.

Leadership effectiveness research has also been framed by the criterion of effectiveness paradigm. Halpin's Leadership Behavior Description Questionnaire (1966), Getzels and Guba's nomothetic-idiographic dimension paradigm (1959), Reddin's 3D model of leader effectiveness (1971), Likert's management styles research (1967), Fiedler's Contingency Theory (1967), and Thomas's conflict management research (1976) could each be considered a paradigm in that they have generated their own bodies of research and literature; however, each could also be located on the broadly inclusive criterion of effectiveness paradigm.

The Source of Criterion of Effectiveness Thought

All criterion of effectiveness research and theory incorporate the basic input ↔ output model of a scientific approach to the study of change. The

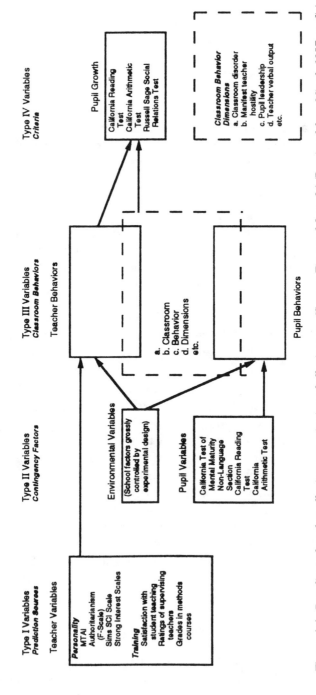

Figure 4.4. *Paradigm of teacher effectiveness: criterion of effectiveness. [Source: Figures 6-8, p. 94 (Reprinted from Mitzel, 1957, p. 6) in N. L. Gage, Teacher Effectiveness and Teacher Education: A Search for a Scientific Basis. © 1972 by N. L. Gage and Pacific Books, Publishers. Palo Alto, CA. Reprinted by permission of Pacific Books, Publishers.]*

134

first assumption of the whole body of effectiveness research, literature, and theory is that if the right combination of inputs exists, the desired output will result. The concept of input dominates all of the studies and all of the practice derived from the paradigm, and the source of input is the system: teacher, structure, curriculum, methodologies, teacher behavior, classroom interaction moderated by the teacher. Figure 4.5 presents an input↔output model of the school.

Although the input↔output model suggests that output is the ultimate concern, research on teaching effectiveness, on school effectiveness, and on leadership effectiveness has, until recently, been focused on input. Shulman says, "In the research programs we have been discussing thus far [the process-product research]. . . . The teacher has been very much the center of classroom life, the source or starting point for teaching. . . . In the research programs that collectively define the study of classroom ecology, however, this matter of causal direction is itself problematic" (1990, 44).

A Paradigm Shift

Greenfield's (1975) challenging comment, "There is no such thing as *an* organization" (Greenfield, 1975) blew the top off the mountain of the criterion of effectiveness paradigm. Anthropologists, ethnographers, case studies enthusiasts, and sociolinguists had for a long time asserted that each individual lives in a world of their own making. When this proposition was placed in the context of the classroom, a dramatic shift in the orientation of research resulted.

Shulman says,

> While process-product researchers view classrooms as reducible to discrete events and behaviors which can be noted, counted and aggregated for purposes of generalization across settings and individuals, interpretive scholars view classrooms as socially and culturally organized environments. . . . [Individual participants] discern meanings intended by other actors and they engage in the continuing *invention and reformulation of new meanings.* (1990, 47, emphasis added)

Thus, students each create their own meaning out of the environment. If they learn to strive or learn to quit trying, this paradigm proposes, it is because the whole environment and the whole situation present that message by word, gesture, seating, pace, opportunity, and recognition.

Classroom ecology research, the interpretivist perspective, and the

INPUT <---> OUTPUT MODEL OF AN EDUCATION SYSTEM

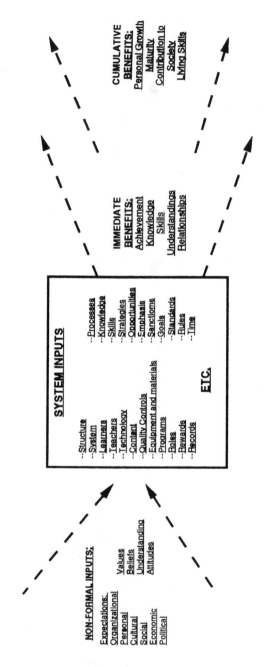

NON-FORMAL INPUTS:

Expectations:
Organizational
Personal
Cultural
Social
Economic
Political

Values
Beliefs
Understanding
Attitudes

SYSTEM INPUTS

--Structure
--System
--Learners
--Teachers
--Technology
--Content
--Quality Controls
--Equipment and materials
--Programs
--Roles
--Rewards
--Records

--Processes
--Knowledge
--Skills
--Strategies
--Opportunities
--Emphasis
--Sanctions
--Goals
--Standards
--Rules
--Time

ETC.

IMMEDIATE BENEFITS:
Achievement
Knowledge
Skills
Understandings
Relationships

CUMULATIVE BENEFITS:
Personal Growth
Maturity
Contribution to Society
Living Skills

Process Effectiveness = relationship of **Immediate Benefits** to **Inputs** (In-school assessment)
Social and Human Effectiveness = relationship of **Cumulative Benefits** to **Inputs** (Judgment of a healthy society)

Figure 4.5. Input→output effectiveness model of an education system, based on expectations and the system as inputs and immediate and cumulative benefits as outputs.

136

phenomenological approach form a new paradigm or world view of the place called school. Scholars took the assertion, "Learning emanates from teaching from the school" and asked it as a question, "What is the controlling source of learning?" The new question produced a new answer, "The child's interpretation of the total environment." A new community of scholarly researchers and a new body of scholarly study of the school developed.

If this paradigm still employs the input ↔ output model of thinking, the emphasis and the specific elements differ radically from those in Figure 4.5. Figure 4.6 suggests the model if the child's interpretation of the total environment is the controlling source of learning.

Using this model, researchers attempt to discover how the child "sees" the world of the classroom. Much of the child's interpretation of what takes place arises from background, so researchers place emphasis on cultural patterns and beliefs as screens through which the child sees the classroom. The aim of research in this domain is to inform educators about the child's view of the world, their *interpretation* of gestures, words, activities, and their *understanding* of directions, explanations, purposes, and goals. Is the goal to "get ten problems done" or to "know how to do long division?" Research in this domain is of the "thick description" variety, such as that of Wolcott (1973), Rutter et al. (1979), and Aloha-Sidaway (1986).

The Meaning of Learning

A second thread that has run throughout the literature on education parallel to the criterion of effectiveness paradigm has addressed the issue of the meaning of learning. While a large portion of the criterion of effectiveness literature has come from teacher training educators and social psychologists, studies of learning have largely come from learning and cognitive psychologists. The body of that research has had two streams, the *process* of learning and the *meaning* of learning. A paradigm of the meaning of learning is proposed in the following discussion. It is based on the article, "A Paradigm by Any Other Name" (Burns, 1993).

The author has proposed (1993, 249−255) a paradigm of basic orientations toward the meaning of learning that exist in educational theory and practice. It is suggested that two dimensions characterize sets of ideas about "learning." One dimension is the polar axis action ↔

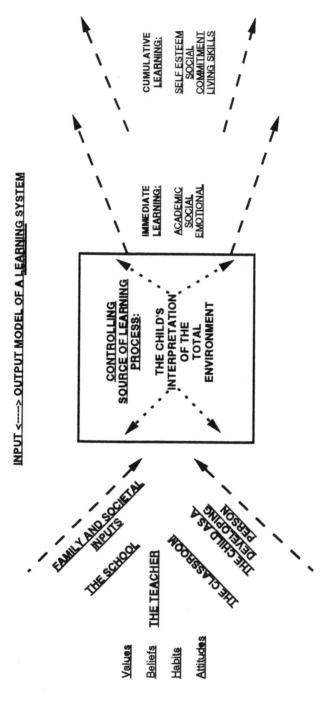

INPUT <—> OUTPUT MODEL OF A LEARNING SYSTEM

CUMULATIVE LEARNING:

SELF ESTEEM
SOCIAL COMMITMENT
LIVING SKILLS

IMMEDIATE LEARNING:

ACADEMIC
SOCIAL
EMOTIONAL

CONTROLLING SOURCE OF LEARNING PROCESS:

THE CHILD'S INTERPRETATION OF THE TOTAL ENVIRONMENT

FAMILY AND SOCIETAL INPUTS

THE SCHOOL

THE TEACHER

THE CLASSROOM

THE CHILD AS A DEVELOPING PERSON

Values

Beliefs

Habits

Attitudes

Process Effectiveness = relationship of Immediate Benefits to Inputs (Judgment of the child in school)
Social and Human Effectiveness = relationship of Cumulative Benefits to Inputs (Judgment of the adult in society)

Figure 4.6. Input→output effectiveness model of an education system, based on personal, social, and system inputs, the child's interpretation of the total environment as process, and immediate and cumulative learning as outputs.

138

ideas; the other polar axis proposed is holistic ↔ particularistic. That is, one group of educators, including pragmatists and experimentalists (particularists) on one hand and existentialists and impressionists (holists) on the other, is oriented toward *action* as the mode and meaning of learning. A second group, including realists and functionalists on the one hand and idealists and humanists on the other, is oriented toward *ideas* as the mode and meaning of learning.

Particularist Orientation

The model proposes that four paradigms, or basic orientations, have resulted, which characterize different concepts of learning and different models of teaching. Figure 4.7 presents the paradigm proposed.

The model suggests that certain subject fields generally express the meaning of learning within the four paradigms created. When educators, or the general public, speak of ''getting back to the basics,'' they are

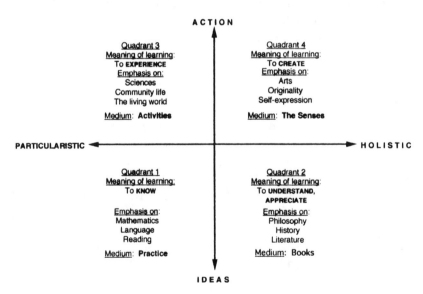

Figure 4.7. Paradigms proposed as orientations that exist in our thinking about the school, based on two dimensions of the meaning of learning: action ↔ ideas and particularistic ↔ holistic. [Source: Figure 2, p. 253, in M. L. Burns, "A Paradigm by Any Other Name," International Journal of Educational Reform, 2(3):249–255. © 1993 by Technomic Publishing Co., Inc. Reprinted by permission of Technomic Publishing Co., Inc.]

commonly thinking of the subject fields that comprise the building blocks of communication and further learning: reading, language, and mathematics. A vast body of complaints about the education system has been levied against schools, crying out that students' abilities to function well in these subject areas do not satisfy expectations. Learning in these subjects entails knowing the elements with which ideas are expressed through these basic conceptual tools and knowing the rules of combining elements to communicate ideas. In this domain, the body of knowledge is developed by analysis and is oriented toward structure. In the particularistic-ideas domain, learning "means" knowing and being able to use correctly; such learning is acquired by practice.

The sciences, government, social life, politics, and the natural world are also oriented toward particular settings, and particular issues, relationships under particular circumstances. In these fields, learning is acquired by investigation and involvement, by activities designed to find out how things work, how they relate to each other under specific conditions. Learning can only happen by observing change or differences under different conditions. Learning in this domain (particularistic-action) is the experience of finding out. It is personal because each individual "experiences" an event from their own perspective. Activities are the medium of learning.

Holistic Orientation

History, philosophy, and literature are holistic, not particularistic, in their nature. They are the sum and substance of ideas. They are a reason for learning the basics because they present the "big ideas" of humanity in some form: dramatic, reporting, or analytical. It is the ideas of literature, history, and philosophy that one strives to understand and appreciate with the basic tools. It is through these subject fields that the fragmented nature of learning so often lamented can be counteracted and that visions of the wholeness of humanity can be renewed. These ideas of the whole meaning of humanity are expressed in the literature of ideas, in books. Books and the ideas of great thinkers over history are the medium of learning.

The arts, drama, dance, and shops where things are created use the sentient powers, the senses, as the medium of creating, of learning. Sacks (1985) tells the poignant story of Rebecca, who is seriously mentally handicapped. In the world of competence testing, IQ's, and

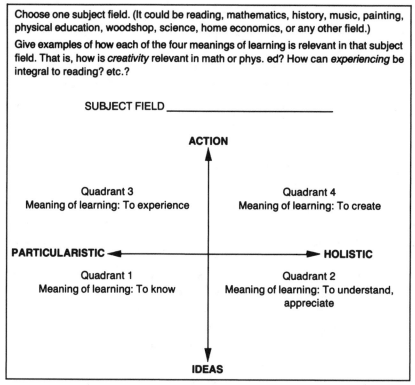

Choose one subject field. (It could be reading, mathematics, history, music, painting, physical education, woodshop, science, home economics, or any other field.)

Give examples of how each of the four meanings of learning is relevant in that subject field. That is, how is *creativity* relevant in math or phys. ed? How can *experiencing* be integral to reading? etc.?

SUBJECT FIELD _____

ACTION

Quadrant 3
Meaning of learning: To experience

Quadrant 4
Meaning of learning: To create

PARTICULARISTIC ◄——————————► HOLISTIC

Quadrant 1
Meaning of learning: To know

Quadrant 2
Meaning of learning: To understand, appreciate

IDEAS

Exercise 4.6. The four meanings of learning applied to a subject field.

achievement, the world of knowing, Rebecca reveals herself to be a hopeless intellectual cripple. But the tests, Sacks said, "had given me no hint of her positive powers, her ability to perceive the real world . . . as a coherent, intelligible, poetic whole. . . . Is it possible, I wondered, that [she] can *use* a narrative [or dramatic] mode to compose and integrate a coherent world, in place of the schematic mode, which, in her, is so defective that it simply doesn't work?" (1985, 181, emphasis in original).

Sacks goes on to say that Rebecca, "placed in a series of workshops and classes as a part of our Developmental and Cognitive Drive" failed miserably (p. 183). However, when she was enrolled in a theater group, "she became a complete person, poised, fluent, with style in each role" (p. 185). The recent Public Broadcasting Services series on dancing emphasizes the natural spirituality and the holistic sense of humanity expressed through rhythm, music, and dancing. These are important media of learning. Burns (1993) proposes that it is important to incorporate all four meanings of learning into *each* subject field. Some examples are cited in the article. Further examples exploring applications of the four orientations in various subject areas (developed by workshop participants) are presented in Appendix B. For Exercise 4.6, choose one subject area and give examples of how each meaning of learning is or could be incorporated.

WAYS OF VIEWING LEADERSHIP

In addition to the issues of teaching and learning, a third concern is closely tied to the idea of quality education. Leadership within the school is a focus of study and research fundamental to educational planning. One framework has provided the basis for much of the research and study on leadership in organizations and has formed a strong core of beliefs about good leadership in education.

That paradigm has proposed a bidimensional character to leadership behavior. It is evident in the literature of organizational life at least from the publication of *The Federalist Papers* in 1788. In those papers, Alexander Hamilton distinguished between "all of the operations of the body politic" and "executive details" (March 18, 1788). Woodrow Wilson (1877) also distinguished "the broad plans of governmental action. . . . [and] The field of administration (as) a field of business" (p. 97). Again, in 1905, Goodnow stressed the distinction. "The two functions of government . . . may, for purposes of convenience, be designated respectively as Politics and Administration. Politics has to do with policies and expressions of State Will. Administration has to do with the execution of these policies" (pp. 6, 15). A similar duality is developed by Sergiovanni et al. in *Educational Governance and Administration* (1980).

The Two Dimensions of Leadership

The distinction made in those early works was between the state and its policies and the business of the state or execution of policies. With the government of the new nation designed on the principle of separation of powers, the focus of scholars was on clarifying the nature and implications of that principle. "Of the people and by the people" meant through political action and legislative representation. "For the people" meant through implementation of the mandates granted by the people. "The people" were granted an active role in determining the nature and conduct of the nation.

In contrast to this political statement about "a nation," management literature of the day was concerned with corporations, with production, survival, and growth. It was assumed that the worker should be dedicated to the goals of the organization. In the scientific management literature prior to the 1920s, the concepts "of the people and by the people" held little sway. However, research such as the Hawthorne Studies (Roethlisberger and Dickson, 1939); the work of such scholars as Elton Mayo, Mary Parker Follett, Chester Barnard, and Herbert A. Simon; and union drives forced corporations to acknowledge the needs of "the people."

Thus, it is easy to recognize from these beginnings the historical basis of the two dimensions of social behavior in organizations proposed by Getzels and Guba in 1959. As early as 1939, Lewin, Lippet, and White had studied the effects of leadership styles on the social climate of groups. In their studies, *style* was a manipulated variable, determined and imposed by the leader: autocratic, democratic, and laissez-faire. Getzels and Guba proposed, however, that the social behavior of the group might be mutually agreed on between leader and followers. Figure 4.8 presents the social behavior model of the administrative process proposed by Getzels and Guba.

Nomothetic-Idiographic Dimensions Proposed by Getzels and Guba

The model proposed that there are two sets of demands placed on participants: organizational needs and human needs. Some leader-follower groups, Getzels and Guba proposed, perceive that "the most expeditious route to [achieving an agreed upon] goal is seen as residing in the institutional structure rather than in any particular persons" (1959, 436). This style of leadership-followership social behavior they called "nomothetic" deriving from "normative," or structured roles and norms. "The *idiographic style* of leadership-followership . . . places emphasis on the requirements of the individual, the personality, and the need disposition . . . [as] the most expeditious route to the goal" (1959, 437; emphasis in original).

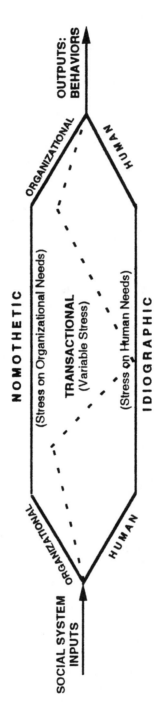

Figure 4.8. Social behavior model of the administrative process. [Source: Figure 1, p. 429, from "Social Behavior and the Administrative Process," J. W. Getzels and E. B. Guba, The School Review, 65(4):423–441. © 1959. The University of Chicago Press. Reprinted by permission of the University of Chicago Press.

Getzels and Guba assumed, for the purpose of theoretical analysis, a situation in which the goal was agreed upon by both leader and follower. In such a situation, they assumed, the social behavior was also agreed upon; the style was a leader-follower style, a relationship mutually agreed upon. It was not a leader or administrative style imposed on followers. It is important to note this, because most of the research and theory that developed within this two-dimensional framework has assumed a different situation.

The nomothetic relationship did not imply "Theory X" management style, although it is hard to divorce nomothetic from such descriptive phrases as task oriented, autocratic, or bureaucratic today. The idiographic relationship, the belief that the goal can best be achieved "by making it possible for each person to contribute what is relevant and meaningful to him" (Getzels and Guba, 1959, 437) is clearly the direct parent of the personal support or human relations dimension of administrative style advanced in today's literature and practice.

We might, then, assume a situation in which both leaders and followers want to achieve organizational goals, want to work, want to contribute. In this situation, Getzels and Guba imply, the leader and followers could strike a sort of social compact and agree 1) that the best way is to "follow the book" or conversely, 2) that the best way is to allow personal initiative.

Further Proposals of a Bidimensional Character to Leadership

Most of the literature and research that has developed within this school of thought, world view, or paradigm of leadership has assumed that "style" is "leadership style" and that it arises from the leader/administrator/manager's personal value orientations. Some well-known examples of the research related to this framework are discussed briefly here.

Style and Productivity

Likert (1967) studied the relationship between manager's style and two types of organizational results: employee satisfaction and output/efficiency. Figure 4.9 shows the relationships found in his research.

Likert found four styles of management: authoritative/exploitative, benevolent authoritative, consultative, and participative. Where the

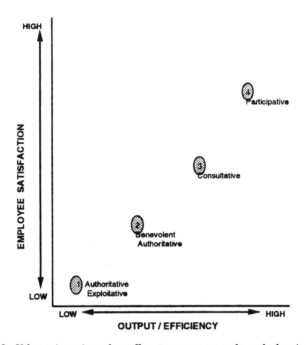

Figure 4.9. *Value orientations that affect management style and planning in an organization.* (*Based on R. Likert, 1967.* The Human Organization: Its Management and Value. © *1967 McGraw-Hill, Inc. Reproduced by permission of McGraw-Hill, Inc.*)

manager's style was authoritative/exploitative, both satisfaction and output/efficiency were low; where the style was participative, both output dimensions were high. Moreover, when managers were given training in participative style management, output rose.[9] In common discourse, nomothetic (oriented toward the demands of the organization) and authoritative are often considered synonymous, as are participative and idiographic (oriented toward the needs of individuals). However, that inference cannot be made directly from Getzels and Guba's model. The various names for dimensions of leadership style have accumulated connotative meanings from each other. One set, those naming an orientation toward task, the organization, or production, are considered related, as having similar meanings or implications. Those naming an

---

[9]It has often been concluded, based on Likert's work and on such research as the Hawthorne Studies (Roethlisberger and Dickson, 1939), that the two output dimensions are directly related, that satisfaction and production correlate positively. In Likert's research, at least, the emphasis was on manager's style as a mediator of both satisfaction and output/efficiency.

orientation toward personal or interpersonal consideration and support and participative decision making have also acquired a common base of meanings.

The Leadership Behavior Description Questionnaire (LBDQ)

In his studies using the LBDQ, Halpin (1966) described two basic dimensions of administrative behavior, initiating structure and consideration. Brown's studies using an updated version of the questionnaire (1967) supported the two-dimensional character proposed, naming the dimensions system orientation and person orientation. These studies had considerable influence on the developing paradigm of leadership research.

Using similar dimensions (concern for production and concern for people), Blake and Mouton (1964) developed a "managerial grid," proposing five potential combinations of the two dimensions. In their studies, more than thirty between 1960 and 1980, they consistently found that the manager, combining high concern for production with high concern for people (the team builder), offered the greatest benefits to the group and to the organization (Blake and Mouton, 1978).

Contingency Theory

Fiedler (1967) studied the relationship of proposed administrative styles and various output factors. He concluded that a single administrative style was not equally successful in all circumstances. He proposed that certain contingencies affect the success of a particular chosen style. His work anchored the effective leadership paradigm in the criterion of effectiveness paradigm proposed for the study of teaching effectiveness by bringing in Type II variables — environmental and participant variables — as well as Type I variables — leader's personal characteristics and background.

Hersey and Blanchard (1974) proposed that one of the factors, or contingencies, that should be considered in choosing leadership style is the maturity of the working group. By maturity, they meant the degree to which the group works well together and is productive, not just how mature group members are as individuals. They found that if a group is not cohesive and task-oriented, not a mature working group, the leader should use a high task/low relationship style. If the group is a mature working group, the preferred style is low task/low relationship—that is, stay out of the picture and let the group get on with its work (p. 29).

Returning to the Group Process Perspective

Thomas (1976) proposed two additional factors that affect the ability of groups to deal effectively with their problems, particularly in conflict situations. However, he considered conflict resolution to be the concern of the group as a whole, not just the problem of the leader. He proposed that "the degree to which parties involved have common interests and values" and "the degree to which they have a personal stake in the outcome" interact to affect the ability of the group to resolve or manage conflict (p. 922). With Thomas's analysis, attention returns to the proposition in Getzels and Guba's model of social process. Thomas found that style is a matter of relationships between parties; it is not simply the choice or the personal style of the leader. Figure 4.10 presents the styles of conflict resolution behavior proposed by Thomas.

The words chosen to name the points in the two-dimensional field of conflict situation resolution are not leader-based words. They are group behavior terminology. The message is quite clear that style or manner of resolution of conflict develops in the group; it is *not* chosen by the leader to fit the circumstances. In Thomas's model, style is group style, totally interactive in nature, and it grows out of interaction. Competition is not a solitary state; neither are collaboration, avoidance, compromise, and accommodation.

This language is quite different from Likert's (1967) authoritative-exploitative, benevolent authoritative, consultative, and participative. All of the named points on Likert's range imply top-down action. All of the named points on Thomas' imply action within the group and among group members. Thus, a different world view is proposed, more in harmony with the emerging view of organizations as freely associating groups that have as much influence on the leader as the leader has on the group.

Getzels and Guba (1959) assumed a situation in which the goals were held in common by leader and followers. Thomas adds that, when group members *do* have values and interests in common, they may take one of two routes. They may accommodate themselves to, or adapt to, some

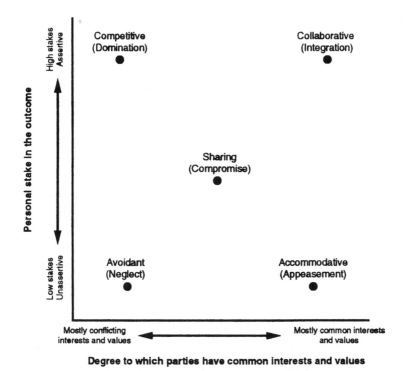

Figure 4.10. *Modes of reconciling divergent interests and values, and personal stakes in the outcome in group planning. (Source: Figure 8, p. 922, "Conflict and Conflict Management," K. Thomas. © 1976. In M. D. Dunnette, ed.* Handbook of Industrial and Organizational Psychology. *Chicago, IL: Rand McNally. Reprinted by permission of Marvin D. Dunnette.)*

outcome if they will not be seriously affected by it (have low stakes), or they may collaborate with others to integrate ideas and strategies if they have high stakes in the outcome.

On the other hand, Thomas suggests, it may be that group members have conflicting interests and values. Then, they may choose one of two quite different group-oriented behaviors. Some may avoid the issue, not attend meetings, do paperwork, tune out, if they assume the outcome will not affect them anyway. Others may become very competitive and domineering, trying to force their own values on the group. Thomas does not propose these as group leader behaviors only. They are some of the dynamics of the group as a whole.

Through these few examples, we can see how the leadership styles propositions and the social process model have developed as a comprehensive leadership effectiveness paradigm. We can see, too, how the propositions themselves and the language with which they are discussed, the names applied, lead us to think, in many ways, from the leader as the strength of the pack to the pack as the strength of the leader.

PARADIGMS AS TOOLS

It is clear, therefore, that a paradigm can both enlighten and limit understanding. It enlightens by virtue of the fact that it produces propositional rules. Shulman says, "Such general rules [about teaching] include propositions about assigning praise or blame, allocating turns, sequencing instruction, checking for understanding, and the like" (1990, 79). It limits for precisely the same reason. General rules should be "properly construed as grounds, not prescriptions," and should be complemented with "knowledge of richly described and critically analyzed cases" (Shulman, 1990, 80–81).

Any paradigm excludes some factors, some types of data. Since the human child lives in many worlds at once (personal, peer, student, family, culture, etc.), many world views are relevant. The same general point is true for all studies of people in groups or in organizations. One paradigm or world view, or framework for study, in the social and behavioral sciences complements, rather than supplements, another.

The Contribution of Paradigms and Maps of Paradigms

We have spoken of paradigms, paradigm models, and maps of paradigms. We are calling the graphic model of a paradigm, which appears as a set of lines, boxes, relationship arrows, and dimensional sectors, a paradigm model. Neither a paradigm model nor a paradigm is the same as a theoretical model, although a theoretical model may initiate the school of research that develops the scope of a paradigm. A paradigm model (like the criterion of effectiveness paradigm of teacher effectiveness) is not a predictive model. It is descriptive of a set of research issues, propositions, and questions that are related in a body of research and that are thought to be evident in practice. The model represents graphically, in generalized abstraction, the primary characteristics of the world view or framework, which directs, limits, and provides the body to life events in some particular scholarly or practical world (as the world of classroom teaching and learning; the world of the organization; the world of school effectiveness, of decision making, or of planning).

The theoretical model or proposition from which a paradigm (the way of looking at particular relationships) develops may incorporate relatively few elements, as Pavlov's model of operant conditioning or as the Getzels-Guba nomothetic-idiographic model of the administrative process. Such a model makes a basic proposition about human behavior or relationships, and models, or represents the proposition graphically. However, the proposition made is broadly general in applicability. It is recognized immediately that the model explains behavior in many specific situations; therefore, it initiates research in many domains and may be said to have initiated a school of research, hence a research paradigm.

The paradigm itself is not the graphic representation; the paradigm includes both idea and action or, in Collingwood's terms, both "the inside and the outside" of events [1946, 213, cited in Shulman (1990), 75]. The paradigm is the whole; it is not abstract; it is a particular world as we see it. In terms of research, the paradigm is the whole set of research studies that have emanated from the original proposition, all of the specific questions raised by the model. In its impact on practice, it includes all of the ways we study, talk about, and act out the abstract ideas represented graphically in the paradigm model.

A map of paradigms opposes two or more paradigms on dimensional characteristics so their particular contributions to our thinking can be more readily examined, so we can carry on a more productive dialogue with ourselves or with others about specific proposals. Such a map enables us to compare and contrast the basic characteristics, assumptions, and propositions of paradigms that express different world views. It enables us to test statements, ideas, and proposed programs against the assumptions they may be making.

The paradigm map of criterion of effectiveness research on teaching proposed four sets of variables related to effectiveness. Each set has generated a body of research as Gage has described (1963, 1972, 1978). Thus, the map proposes relationships among the sets of variables within four schools or traditions of research on teaching. Following the pattern of meta-research, the kind of model we are calling a map of paradigms might be thought of as a meta-paradigm, a paradigm of paradigms.

Impact of Paradigms on Thought and Practice in Education

Although paradigms develop in research and scholarly communities, their influence goes far beyond research. They frame the view of a world for practitioners as well. A paradigm focuses attention on particular factors, relationships, and methodologies, and "it also specifies what is necessarily excluded from the list of permissible topics" (Shulman, 1990, 5). A paradigm prescribes the kind of language that will be used to discuss ideas and, thus, may make it less probable that new questions will be asked.

For example, all the world had always said that a thing falls to the ground. Newton suddenly said something like this, "An apple, at some point in time *leaves the tree.* Why does it not move upwards toward the clouds, or across the orchard to another tree?" By simply replacing the idea *fall* with the idea *moves from,* he was able to ask a new question. Whether we understand the physics or not, all the world now knows that the earth *pulls* the apple toward it, even though we still say the apple *falls.* We know why we do not fly off into space as the world turns.

In planning literature, the most common first question in process has been, "What has happened here; what is the problem?" A "problem" always exists in the present and is related to the past; the use of the word *problem* directs attention away from the future, the situs of planning. It also directs attention to "recovery" rather than "growth," to "regain" rather than "invent." Since planning is, by definition, for the future, the first question should be, "Where are we heading; what do we want to achieve; what would be the best of all possible worlds, the ideal?"

The problem-solving paradigm, based on Dewey's process of logical thought, limits creative imaging. It has generated a basic orientation, not only to planning, but also to teaching, particularly to teaching mathematics and science. It has directed teacher training programs, encouraging teachers always to seek out the child's problem. It has resulted in the common practice of marking those things on a paper that are wrong, instead of marking those things that are right—an equally viable approach. It has directed every phase of educational practice toward eliminating problems, rather than toward reinforcing accomplishment.

Paradigms and the words with which they are discussed direct our attention and our practice.

Language, Metaphors, and Paradigm Shifts

The language we get in the habit of using as we talk about organizations and about schools reinforces our tendency to think in certain ways. Metaphors are particularly powerful pieces of language. A metaphor calls up a holistic image of a specific "thing" that has specific parts that relate to each other in known ways. Therefore, the metaphor leads us to expect similar relationships in the organization and to act as if those expected relationships really exist.

If reality does not conform, the inclination may be to shape reality to fit the image. A student who has never seen a tree is expected to talk about trees instead of polar bears. A student who has never seen snow reads about sleds and sings about sleigh bells jingling. The metaphor images the poor reader as a defective piece, or as an unhealthy organism, and directs us to think of "repair," "restoration," or "healing." We might, with equal reason, direct ourselves to the child's strengths and allow those strengths to direct further learning. Such a world view may be increasingly possible with new technologies and new focuses on the child as the center of learning.

Metaphors are powerful tools of understanding because they are partially true. The image brought to mind is well known, and the image makes available to our minds some of the aspects of the organization or the school. But we should be wary of metaphors and paradigms. They can blind us to other realities. The road to a paradigm shift is through a question. One takes an assertion, turns it into a question, and "tries out" a different answer. "An organization is a thing that exists as an entity. → Is an organization a thing that exists as an entity? → No, I see the organization differently from the way you see it, therefore I live and act differently. → There are as many entities of an organization as there are people associated with it."

"The key to learning in the school is the teacher. → Is the key to learning the teacher? → No, students make what sense they can out of all that is going on in the classroom. They absorb what they can understand, appreciate, relate to from the whole environment. → The key to learning is the learner."

"The principal should be the instructional leader. → Should the principal be the instructional leader? → No, teachers know the students, their abilities, their needs, and teachers know the body of their particular curriculum. → The teachers should be the instructional leaders in the school."

"Students should be kept with their age and learning level peers. → Should there be this pattern of grade levels by age? Are age levels and learning levels the same? → No, students learn at very different rates, in spurts and plateaus. → Perhaps, they should be grouped by competencies regardless of age, like in the old one-room country school."

All of these are paradigm shifts that have led us to think in new ways about the place called school and about the meaning of learning.

SUMMARY

This chapter has presented some of the world views that have shaped our thinking about schools and education. We have proposed, following the structure presented in Chapter 3, Figure 3.1, that paradigms are a subset of philosophies of education. Paradigms, world views, or holistic views of some particular world map, shape, and limit our thinking about that particular world (be it the classroom, group dynamics, teaching effectiveness, or leadership). At the same time, paradigms open windows on that world, raise new questions, offer new insights, and sharpen our understandings. They are powerful tools for planning. The degree to which we can comprehend and consciously use many paradigms is the degree to which planning for education can respond to the worlds of all of our students and all of our communities.

CHAPTER 5

Planning Metaphors and Definitions

ERAS OF STUDY AND RESEARCH ON ADMINISTRATION

EVERY general textbook on educational administration and many summary articles, as well, trace the history of management or administrative
thought through eras, periods in which particular patterns of thinking
developed and dominated the literature. Sergiovanni et al. (1980) identified three "strands of thought": "One is characterized by a concern
for *efficiency*; the second, a concern for the *person*; and the third, a
concern for *politics and decision making*" (p. 41, emphasis in text).
They dated these periods as, roughly, 1900s – 1930s, 1930s – 1960s, and
1940s – 1980s, respectively.

Toward the end of that second period, Bertram Gross had identified
major contributors to the first two of these streams of thought: the
"gospel of efficiency," and "the Pioneers, the New Beginnings." Representative of the efficiency stream were, he proposed, Taylor, a major
contributor to analysis of production tasks and scientific management;
Fayol, who applied task analysis to administration to create a general
approach to administration; and Gulick and Urwick, who continued
Fayol's approach and proposed principles of administration (Gross,
1964, 34 – 44).

The second period, Gross proposed, contributed two major streams
of thought, the human relations approach and the process approach. He
included five scholars in the group of pioneers in these new directions.
Follett, with a political science and economics background and a
humanistic approach, added "power" to the lexicon of administrative
considerations. Mayo, an industrial psychologist, and Roethlisberger, a
sociologist, are best remembered for the Hawthorne Studies. This series
of studies probably had the greatest influence on the movement of

155

administrative research and theory toward the human relations and social psychology orientations (Gross, 1964, 44 – 56).

Gross identified Barnard and Simon with the emerging process approach (56 – 72). This strand of thought has more recently been termed, by Hoy and Miskel (1987), for example, as the behavioral science approach. Hoy and Miskel termed the first two eras ''Classical Organizational Thought'' and the ''Human Relations Approach.''

Reactions against the behavioral sciences approach have stressed the individual and personal interpretation of life in organizations, as well as the place of the organization in, and its dependence on, larger contexts in the environment. Open systems propositions, phenomenological theories, ethnographic approaches to research, and cultural and philosophical belief systems as sources of perspective and action characterize research and theory from the 1980s to the present. Thus, a new stream of thought may well be identified as emerging in the late 1970s. Figure 5.1 presents a summary of the relative emphasis on the several streams of thought from the early 1900s.

It is important for educational administrators and educational planners to recognize the heritage of the several approaches to the study of administration. No approach is ''sufficient unto itself.'' Each has provided knowledge, understanding, and technologies that may become, more or less urgently, the focus of attention at various times but do not cease to exist.[10]

A fascinating review of thought about administration has been provided by George (1968) in *The History of Management Thought*. His time line reviews the history of various administrative practices often thought to be modern inventions. He reports that, in 5000 B.C., the Sumarians practiced scripting and record keeping; in 2700 B.C., an Egyptian manager reminded his subordinates that an interview to ''get it off your chest'' is therapeutic; in 1480 A.D., the Arsenal of Venice built ships along the canals using the assembly line concept (pp. xiii – xvii).

In a recent review of ideas that have provided foundations for administrative thought and practice, English (1994) reminds us that the

---

[10]The changing emphasis in approach might be related to Maslow's "hierarchy of needs" concept. As task analysis provided stable bases for mass production and education for all children, the need in organizations moved up the hierarchy to social or personal relations. Today's emphasis on humanism, values, and individual belief systems could be considered as responding to higher order needs. But technical production needs still exist and come to the fore at various times in the life of a school system.

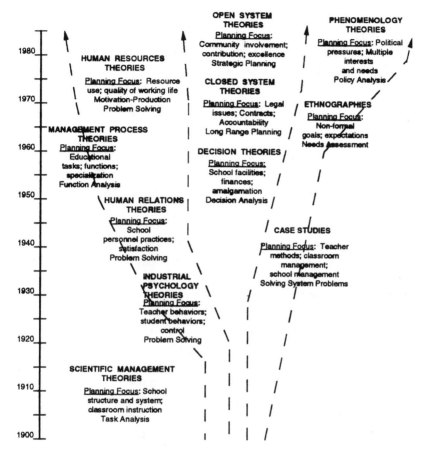

Figure 5.1. *Varying focuses on the study of management over time and suggested planning emphases in school systems.*

legacy of scientific management is evident today in many practices. "The so-called *effective schools* movement has ushered forth new indicators of Taylorism that emphasize routine inspection, tests, and standard criteria, as well as continued centralization of control within systems of education. . . . While 'scientific management' as a term is outdated, it has been replaced by 'quality management,' or *total quality management* (TQM) . . ." (p. 20, emphasis in original).

Plus que ça change, plus c'est la même chose.

Even as one moves from the more holistic propositions about planning, such as definitions, to the more particular propositions about how to do it (planning models and systems), the world view embraced remains the framework for thinking and acting. Two questions will be discussed in the following sections: 1) the image of the planner that may be implied in metaphors and world views of the organization and how the image affects plans and action in education and 2) focuses on planning implied in definitions and propositions about planning.

Images of the Planner Implied in Metaphors of the Organization

Within the major schools of thought that have had particular impact on organizational and administrative theory and research, metaphors of organization developed. Two common metaphors of the organization from earlier eras are machine and organism. Other metaphors that have developed more recently include system, team, language text, and garbage can. Such metaphors encapsulate an "image" of the organization; these images help the researcher and practitioner address complex aspects of organizations, by suggesting similarities with known things.

Chapters 3 and 4 stressed that one's broad, general views and beliefs become the bases for orientations toward choice and action in particular situations. This view assumes that the image or metaphor subconsciously held affects one's approach to all aspects of administration. Table 5.1 summarizes some of the major schools of thought and the metaphors associated with them. It then suggests possible analogies of those metaphors in terms of the roles of the administrator or manager and the planner.

Planner as Technician

The metaphor most commonly associated with the early scientific management school of thought is the organization as a machine. Within this metaphor, administrators or managers may be subconsciously thought of as machine operators. They oversee the operation and production of the machine, noting how it (the total organization or unit) works and what it produces. English (1994, 104) quotes George Howland's (1896) description of the school principal's duties: "His is the life, the impulse of the school, its controlling and directing power, . . . *adjusting and harmonizing its various parts,* encouraging here and checking there, . . . alive to the *working of the mental and material machinery* entrusted to his care" (p. 152, emphasis added).

Table 5.1. Metaphors of Organizations Presented in the Literature and the Image of the Planner That Might Be Inferred from the Metaphor. Ways of Thinking about Planning in Organizations.

School of Thought	Organizational Metaphor	Focus	Concern	Administrative Analogy	Planner
Scientific management	Machine	Functions	Production	Operator	Technician
Human relations	Organism	Interactions	Motivation	Head/chief	Problem solver
Behavioral sciences	Closed system	Behaviors	Maintenance	Executive	Decision maker
System theory	Open system	Environments	Development	Diplomat/politician	Analyst
Games theory	Team	Strategies	Success	Coach	Strategist
Phenomenology	Sense making	Unique situations	Quality of life	Reflective practitioner	Interpreter
Radical structuralist	Garbage can	Unique situations	Opportunities	Pragmatist	Forecaster

Planners, then, could be seen as technicians determining what the machine/organization needs, how many parts are needed, how long each part could be expected to work properly, and how to make the part more efficient. Workers and tools were considered equally replaceable and should be selected or designed to fit the task at hand (Taylor, 1913). Thus, the metaphor of machine leads to task simplification and specialization, replacement (no job security), the quota system of production, work week, work life expectancy (mandatory retirement at some specified age), and merit pay (variable pay for levels of efficiency).

It is very easy to accept the pejorative connotations that have encrusted certain words in our literature. *Scientific management* and *technician* are two vulnerable terms, but it is important to respect and learn from all perspectives. Is there a "technician dimension" to all planning? The technician continually seeks information to make predictions and choices. In the 1950s, Sacramento, California's district planners sought information from housing and land developers and bought land for schools ten years before a new growth period was predicted for an area.

In Quebec, the province funds school districts on the basis of actual students present in the school on September 30 of each year. The Ministry of Education does periodic audits to ensure accuracy of counts. "Moving day" in Quebec is July (practically all leases end on June 30), which leaves a short time span for school planners to predict changing enrollments and staff needs, but because telephone, hydro (electricity), and cable TV orders are generally in hand nearly two months ahead of moving day, school planners can get reasonably accurate indicators of enrollments by late May.

Friedmann (1973) said that when rational planning is most needed, as in times of crisis and social upheaval, it is least possible. Pressures of events leave no time for investigation and thorough examination of options. Therefore, he added, planning must become a way of thinking, a total way of looking at the environment and its indicators to have information absorbed so it can be automatically available. Collecting data systematically and examining it thoughtfully is like taking out an insurance policy; the information is already integrated into your thinking if you need it. The motto of the technician/planner might be

Gather ye data while ye may
A crisis might strike almost any day.

Exercise 5.1 asks you to identify data presently collected in your

List some types of school data and the kinds of choices or decisions these data might affect.	
Part I	
Data presently collected:	Choices/decisions they may affect:
Example: dropouts, test scores	special programs, alternative schools
Data that might be useful:	Choices/decisions they could affect:
Example: life expectancy of books, equipment	budget planning, programs
Part II	
Changes that have been made in the past decades	What brought about these changes (factual evidence) (political pressures)?
Example: variable sizes of desks, salary schedules	different heights of students (data) union activity (pressures)

Exercise 5.1. Data collection.

school or system and the choices that may have been affected by those data. What additional data might be useful to provide information for choices that may have to be made in the future? What changes have taken place over the years and on what types of information (objective data, stakeholder pressures, etc.)?

Planner as Problem Solver

The human relations school of thought was influenced by psychologists, humanists, philosophers, and activists. Industrial psychologists such as Roethlisberger and Dickson, and Mayo, and political scientists such as Follett put the emphasis on interpersonal relationships and human motivation. The organization chart took on the appearance of the human skeleton, and concepts such as line and staff acquired organic connotations. It was natural to speak of the head of the organization, the brains of the operation, feeding resources into the system, or sowing seeds of discontent.

During that same period, Dewey defined the process of rational thought in terms of an approach to solving problems, and planning became identified with problem solving. Issues that arose were addressed as problems to be solved, the first step being to identify, or clarify, the problem. Case studies in organizational problems were presented to students for analysis of salient factors. Administrators and managers learned to seek out the faults or causes of breakdown in the system and to propose solutions.

Examples such as the well-known "Parable of the Spindle" [Porter (1962), cited in Carzo and Yanouzas (1967)] led students to believe that the language of the various sciences might differ, but the problem, properly clarified, would present its own solution. In the parable, three social scientists, a sociologist, a psychologist, and an anthropologist were asked to observe practice in a restaurant and identify the cause of breakdown between an order being given to the kitchen and being mounted ready to serve. All three identified the cause in terms of power conflict but couched the problem in the language of their particular discipline. In essence, the conflict arose from the waitress (lower status, subordinate, child) giving orders to the cook (higher status, boss, father). All three recommended the same solution, a rotating spindle upon which orders could be placed, thus saving face for the higher status person.

Exercise 5.2 presents a situation in which the problem might be clarified or expressed quite differently by different groups of people involved, and solutions proposed would also differ.

Changing Metaphors and Changing Images

Metaphors changed across the decades of the twentieth century as awareness and understanding of different aspects of organizations and human behavior in organizations were enhanced. Metaphors that take the world view of phenomenology and of individualism are still being clarified, but several have received credibility in the literature. Two of these newer metaphors may be identified with the phenomenologist school: sense making and language game. (These were included in the discussion of paradigms proposed by Burrell and Morgan in Chapter 4. Exercises related to these metaphors were also presented in that discussion.)

Newer schools of thought addressed life in organizations from the perspective of multiple realities, rather than from one structural-functional perspective. "The" organization could be understood only in the multiple interpretations of all members, ever changing and read through subjective, personal sets of beliefs and customs. Thus, "the" organization was envisioned as texts being "read" through personal lenses or as

A committee of English consultants has chosen the following list of books to be required reading for tenth and eleventh grades.

The Merchant of Venice	Shakespeare	Not Wanted on the Voyage	Findley
Lord of the Flies*	Golding	Who Has Seen the Wind?	Mitchell
The Apprenticeship of Duddy Kravitz*	Richler	Huckleberry Finn	Twain
		To Kill a Mocking Bird	Lee
Lives of Girls and Women	Munro	The Handmaid's Tale	Atwood
Pride and Prejudice*	Austin	Brave New World	Huxley
Wuthering Heights	Brontë	The Scarlet Letter	Hawthorne
Great Expectations*	Dickens		

*(Those starred are already in the school class sets)

Complaints have been made from many concerned groups, including

English teachers	Ethnic parents	School principals
Community fundamentalists	Community liberals	Student leaders
School counselors	School board members	Religious leaders
Women activists	Male activists	

A meeting has been called. The chair says, "The first thing we have to do is clarify the problem with this list."

— How might some of the groups express the problem?
— Propose three possible solutions that might be worth considering.
— Or name three possible ways that the group might go about reaching a decision.

Exercise 5.2. Clarify the problem.

language games being played, each player using rules learned from their own experience and culture.

The analogy for administrator, as well as for teacher, quite common in this domain is "reflective practitioner" (Schon, 1983). Emphasis is placed on moral or ethical values, on service to the human family, on the reality and complexity of the specific situation. The role of the planner in sense making or in the language game might be seen as interpreter. The planner must attempt to read from many texts and must look for meanings elsewhere than within the formal structures of the organization.

Two other current metaphors that have reacted against the propositions of functionalism are organization as a garbage can (March and Olsen, 1976) and organizations as organized anarchies (Weick, 1982; Firestone and Herriott, 1982; Kennedy, 1984). Both metaphors recognize the fact that real organizations are never "neat and tidy" as functionalists design them. Both present life in organizations as a series of unique experiences and events, real in an objective sense, but not structured to achieve aims, purposes, or goals in the classic organizational perspective. These propositions argue that change happens by chance or by the use of power. In this respect, garbage can and anarchies as metaphors differ from the perspective of interpretivists who do not deny order and regulation. Interpretivists accept that there are sets of organizing beliefs and values based in culture or society, that there are regulating forces, even though those forces are not necessarily organizational. For a useful discussion of the intended meanings of these two metaphors and some misunderstandings that have resulted from the labels themselves, see Estler (1988).

Both metaphors, the garbage can and organized anarchies, imply an objective orientation and change by juxtaposition of circumstances, chance, or manipulation. It is proposed from this perspective the analogy of administrator as pragmatist whose motto might be *carpe diem*. In the fluid organization, pragmatism might take one of several directions: laissez-faire, entrepreneur, or opportunist. Thus, the pragmatist might act to serve the organization productively or to serve personal ends. The planner must then be able to forecast probable circumstances and developments. The role might become forecaster or "bricoleur," Weick's term for using what is at hand in new ways to serve the ends in view (1993, 640).

In any case, it seems that "planner," distinct from entrepreneur or opportunist, has little place in the organized anarchy or the garbage can organization. To speak of organizational planning, that is, for planning to have any organizational perspective, some unity is necessarily assumed, some common sense of purpose, values, and direction. If there are no common values or purposes, if all is fluidity, change, or personal choice, planning is also personal, not organizational. Entrepreneur is leader or administrator because of being planner, because of seeing and seizing the opportunity. Planning may become either a negative or a positive force: "turning into the wind," "building an empire," or, as many native philosophies propose, "moving in harmony with nature."

The role of planning in an organization inheres in the image held of the organization itself, and that image is often expressed in the language used. An exercise that has been used many times in a masters level planning course at McGill University presents four brief scenarios that differ in specific ways. The language with which the situation is described inevitably steers responses into particular frames of reference. The scenarios are presented in Exercise 5.3.

For this exercise, students are divided into four groups, and each is given only one scenario. They are asked to list eight things the principal (as planner) would do in the order they would be done. Typical patterns of responses accumulated over the years are presented in Table 5.2.

From the results of this exercise, it is clear that the language used affects the pattern of thinking of the various groups. The juxtaposition of two factors in Scenario 1 (amount spent and vandalism) has inevitably created the assumption that the two were related, inevitably elicited the problem-solving frame of reference. We propose that the use of problem-solving language directs attention to the present and the past and to human "faults" or error. Planning looks for windows and doors; prob-

---

Scenario 1:

You, the Principal of _____ High School, have observed from requisitions that the amount spent on textbooks and library books has been increasing rapidly for the past several years. You have the feeling that carelessness, vandalism, and theft are also increasing.

You resolve to plan a program to do something about it and propose it to the board at an early meeting. List eight things you would do in the order you would do them.

Scenario 2:

You, the Principal of _____ High School, have observed from requisitions that the amount spent on textbooks and library books has been increasing rapidly for the past several years.

You resolve to plan a program to do something about it and propose it to the board at an early meeting. List eight things you would do in the order you would do them.

Scenario 3:

You, the Principal of _____ High School, have observed from requisitions that the amount spent on textbooks and library books has been increasing rapidly for the past several years.

You resolve to prepare a five-year budget plan for textbooks and library books and a rationale for that plan to present to the board at an early meeting. List eight things you would do in the order you would do them.

Scenario 4:

You, the Principal of _____ High School, have observed from requisitions that the amount spent on textbooks and library books has been increasing rapidly for the past several years.

You resolve to prepare a five-year plan for a project of the use of community resources in the educational program of your school and present it to the board at an early meeting. List eight things you would do in the order you would do them.

Exercise 5.3. Textbooks and library books.

Table 5.2. Typical Patterns of First Order Responses to Four Library/Textbook Exercises, in Order of Actions Proposed.

Exercise 1 (suggests carelessness, vandalism, and theft):

1. Educate students that the library and the school are for their benefit and should be cared for.
2. Keep better check on book checkouts from the library and who has overdue books.
3. Establish and enforce clear rules regarding punishments or charges for vandalism and theft.
4. Encourage teachers to keep closer watch over textbooks assigned.

Exercise 2 (suggests increasing amounts spent and proposes program):

1. Make inventory of books.
2. Survey future program needs.
3. Plot requisitions over time and project costs.
4. Assign coordinator to purchase and distribution of books.

Exercise 3 (suggests increasing amounts spent and proposes five-year plan):

1. Project student enrollments for five years.
2. Survey possible program needs.
3. Determine relative library/textbook purchases and set priorities.
4. Comparison shop re: costs, quality, durability (including hardcover vs. paperback).

Exercise 4 (proposes plan for use of community resources):

1. Set up task force (staff and parents).
2. Survey staff for potential uses of community resources.
3. Survey and tour community resource facilities.
4. Establish preliminary budget.

---

lem solving stays within the walls. Many situations characterized as problems are really signals of future trends or potential directions. One administrator's problem is another administrator's opportunity.

Varying Emphases in the Literature

Indeed, all images of the organization exist in our thinking and action today. There has been, historically, a general shift in the literature from technician, very much bound by immediate specifics, to visionary thinker, expected to foresee opportunities and dangers to the organization and/or to its participants. As Shulman (1990) suggested, in human thinking and in human behavior new images do not replace the old but take precedence at various times and supplement each other. If it could be proposed that each new image adds dimensions to our thinking, then it is possible to see metaphors and analogies as tools that planners can use as the circumstances demand a particular focus.

As metaphors of organization have changed, the images of the administrator and planner have changed, and the locus and issues of planning in education have changed. Worth proposed that, in Canada between 1957 and 1987, educational planning moved from the provincial to the provincial + local level and began to focus on a shorter time frame and more precise, basic issues, and it involved more qualitative investigation (1988, 2). In the United States, the movement was seen by Johnston and Liggett as moving from the level of the classroom, with the focus on instruction, to central office and federal program planning, with the issues being efficiency and equity, to a present focus on excellence, with planning at the state level (1991, 110).

Hamilton (1991) traced the change as a shift from individual-based planning action to moral-based planning action. Figure 5.2 presents Hamilton's hierarchy of developing focuses.

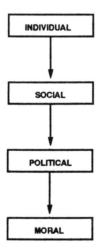

Figure 5.2. Differing focuses of planning action over time as proposed by Hamilton. [Source: Hamilton, D. N. (1991). Figure 2.6, p. 43, "An Alternative to Rational Planning Models," pp. 21–47, from Educational Planning: Concepts, Strategies, and Practices, *Edited by R. V. Carlson and G. Awkerman. Copyright © 1991 by Longman Publishing Group. Reprinted by permission of Longman.]*

The setting is a large (1800 population) junior high school in a southern area. The school is built in wings with outdoor passing areas. It has a large outdoor lunch patio space with snack bar service. At lunch time, the students rush to the snack bar, forming a large, pushing, yelling crowd. No student has been seriously injured, but some have been hurt. There have been many complaints by students that they have been crowded out and threatened.

Which "planners" might have made some of the proposals listed? Which proposal(s) do you think most likely to be successful? Why?

Planners: **Proposals Made:**

A) Technician asks: Where is the   1. Close down the snack bar
   breakdown in the system? How can   2. Teacher monitors and detention
   we "repair" it?   3. Student monitors
B) Problem solver asks: What is the   4. Stagger lunch hour dismissals
   problem here? Who is at fault? What 5. Paint line-up lines on the patio
   did they do wrong?   floor
C) Decision maker asks: What are   6. Hold an assembly on the topic
   possible actions to take? What are   7. Give courtesy badges
   our choices?   8. Have student council set up a
D) Analyst asks: Are there particular   behavior code
   groups of students causing this?   9. Serve only sodas in the snack bar
   What sets them off?   10. Have counselors talk with worst
E) Strategist asks: Who are the   offenders
   leaders? How can we get them on   11. Have counselors talk with student
   board?   leaders
F) Interpreter asks: How do students   12. Have a "courtesy poster" contest
   feel about the snack bar? about   13. Hand the problem over to the
   other students? about the lunch   student council
   period? What can we do about
   different attitudes?
G) Forecaster asks: Do the students
   line up other places? How could we
   "trigger" an automatic habit of
   lining up?

Exercise 5.4. Snack bar case: case scenario for "the planner."

Hamilton's discussion and his model are propositional, or normative, as well as descriptive. He proposed that the more effective direction for planning in a human sense will be toward incorporating moral values as bases of all planning. Table 4.1 proposed that this is one of two current trends, both of which arise from recognition of multiplicity of values, meanings, interests, and beliefs. One move (phenomenology) reflects the interpretivist metaphor of planning. It is oriented toward subjective (tacit) knowledge and regulation, order, and structure. The other is oriented toward an objective view of the world and radical change.

Hamilton's view would move organizations and social groups, in general, toward a search for unity, harmony, and mutuality, toward moral and ethical bases of action. Educational planners, all educators, see learning as the ideal world of ahistorical future. New technologies, the growth of a better educated populace, and the growing demand for One World are some of the indicators of efforts to "back-haul" that faith in learning into the "historical future" of hope.

The radical change direction, the direction of amorality, is implicit in Hamilton's model as well. There are tensions in modern social life, tensions that become political, that press toward regulation (self-imposed in the interpretivist world view, or group imposed in the functionalist view) or toward anti-regulation and fractionalization. There are tensions also between the drive for "excellence," a characteristic of open systems theories, efforts to address multiple human needs, characteristic of phenomenologist theories, and the quality of working life, the human relations orientation.

Such tensions are values issues that planners and all participants in educational enterprises must address. The first imperative is to recognize and understand the differing perspectives and to "stand in the other's shoes" on occasion. Exercise 5.4 presents a brief case and asks how various ones of the planners proposed in Table 5.1 might approach the situation.[11]

WHAT IS PLANNING?

Metaphors of planning are given shape and substance by definitions, descriptions, and propositions. But when we examine the definition statements made about planning in the literature, we find much diversity. First, we can say that there are three primary types of definition statements made: metaphorical, descriptive, and conceptual. Second, within the descriptive group, there are five different bases of description: steps, elements, purposes, relationships, and characteristics. Third, in their specifics, there is even greater variety. In an analysis of twenty-eight statements about planning, twenty-seven different action verbs were used to make forty-one different action statements.

---

[11]See Appendix A, Exercise 5.4 results, for the proposal that was actually implemented successfully.

Perhaps even more confusing, a separate analysis of thirty-three statements about five different administrative processes found seven steps commonly included in each. It seems that "planning" has more feet than a centipede, more arms than an octopus, and more eyes than a fly. In short, planning, like a giraffe, is an animal that cannot exist. Yet it does. It forms every human activity. We might not go as far as Hart to say that "the ability to make plans and carry them out is the key aspect of human intelligence . . ." (1983, 49), but we would not linger far behind that proposition. What can be made of all of this? In the next paragraphs, each of the general statements made about the meaning of planning will be dealt with.

Types of Statements

The three general types of statements we have identified are metaphorical, descriptive, and conceptual. Each type serves a particular purpose in helping us understand the nature and the reality of planning. Table 5.3 gives a set of representative examples of each.

Metaphorical Statements

Metaphorical statements actually serve two purposes. They inspire because they image a future result, and they inform because they give shape to a rather amorphous process. Thus, a "blueprint for action" (McManama, 1971) shapes our thinking because we know that blueprints place separate "things" into a harmonious, workable whole. It inspires because it tells us that actions are such things and makes us believe that actions, too, can be placed into a harmonious, workable whole. A similar example is Carlson's statement, "Planning is the bridge between present and future" (1960). The image is different, but it serves much the same purpose. We want to get there—from the present to the future—and we believe it is possible to build a bridge.

Metaphors are powerful instruments. Their importance is not just that they inspire; they also instruct. We know something about building bridges and making blueprints, so they help us know something about building a plan.

Table 5.3. Examples of Types of Statements That Have Been Made about What Planning Is.

Metaphorical

McManama, 1971: A plan is a blueprint for action.
Steiner, 1969: Planning has been described as projective thought, or "looking ahead." Planning in this sense is an attitude, a state of mind, a way of thinking. (p. 133)
Bologna, 1980: Planning is the design of a desired future. (p. 24)

Descriptive

Of Steps:
    Miklos, Bourgette, and Cowley, 1972: Planning involves (1) the identification and refinement of alternative goals; (2) the development of alternative means for achieving selected goals; (3) the identification of the most promising (most efficient and effective) means. Implementation processes are excluded; however, planning could also include: (4) monitoring the extent to which goals have been achieved, and (5) on the basis of the information gained, revising means and possible goals or targets. (pp. 5 – 7)
Of Elements:
    Anthony, 1965: Strategic planning is the process of deciding on objectives of the organization, on changes in these objectives, on the resources used to attain these objectives, and on the policies that are to govern the acquisition, use, and disposition of these resources. (pp. 16 – 18)
Of Purpose:
    Coombs, 1970: Educational planning: the application of rational, systematic analysis to the process of educational development with the aim of making education more effective and efficient in responding to the needs and goals of its students and society. (p. 14)
    Kaufman and Herman, 1991: Educational planning intends to create a better future for individuals, groups, organizations, and society. Planning identifies where to go, why to go there, and provides the basic criteria for determining if and when you have arrived. (p. 4)
Of Relationships:
    Sergiovanni and Carver, 1980: Planning is a process that precedes decision making. The planning process is differentiated from other predecision activity in that it is systematic, deliberate, and continuous. (p. 284)
Of Characteristics:
    Hamilton, 1991: Planning is first and foremost a social and political activity. (p. 32)
    Sergiovanni and Carver (ibid.)
    Coombs (ibid.)

(continued)

Table 5.3. (continued).

Conceptual
Anderson and Bowman, 1964: Planning: a process of preparing sets of decisions for future action. (p. 9) Hartley, 1968: Planning is used in a broad sense to encompass a rational means-ends assessment of resources and objectives by all interested parties. This process relates inputs and outputs and directs attention to the preparation of time-phased future activities. (p. 2) Burns, 1980: Planning is the process of preparing a conceptual model, a visual representation in some scaled form, of a thing, an operation, or an event. A model is a set of hypotheses, a prediction. (p. 5)

Conceptual Statements

The third type of statements in the literature is conceptual statements. (Descriptive statements will be discussed again in the next section.) Conceptual statements define; they identify the type of thing we are talking about. In administrative studies, three common generic types of phenomena we read and think about are processes, functions, and principles. We cannot distinguish among them as easily as we can distinguish between saws and planes as physical tools or between cutting and shaping as physical actions.

But we have some general understanding of the differences. If we are told that leadership is a process, we want to know how to do it. Then we are told that it depends on the people and the circumstances, so we mentally make the adjustment to "function." Leadership is a function of "$(A + B) \times C$," for example, or "*l'homme, l'heure, et le milieu*," to quote Voltaire.

Planning does not really depend. The outcomes and effects a plan will have do depend on many things, but planning can be done alone in your ivory tower. Leadership cannot. Griffiths defines process as "a cycle of events in which a consistent quality or direction can be discerned" (1959, 92). Planning is commonly accepted as a process, and a conceptual definition places it in that class.

We define planning as "the process of preparing a conceptual model, a visual representation in some scaled form, of a thing, an operation, or an event. . . . A model is a set of hypotheses, a prediction" (Burns, 1980, 5). We will discuss the reasons for relating a plan to hypotheses rather than decisions (Anderson and Bowman, 1964, 9) in Chapter 6. Both are conceptual, or classifying definitions, however.

Descriptive Statements

Most statements about planning are descriptive. Table 5.3 presented examples of the five following types of descriptive statements:

(1) Descriptions of the steps to be taken or the cycle of events that comprise the process

(2) Descriptions of the elements that must be included in the plan, the parts that must be related to each other to ensure that the event will be successful

(3) Descriptions of the purposes for which planning is undertaken, the direction the process is leading toward

(4) Descriptions of how planning relates to other administrative processes or functions

(5) Descriptions of the characteristics of planning [systematic, deliberate, and continuous in Sergiovanni et al. (1980, 284); social and political in Hamilton (1991, 32)].

Analysis of Descriptive Statements

The statements included in Table 5.3 are only a sample of those in the literature. To understand and appreciate planning as an administrative process, all of these viewpoints are necessary; however, it can also be useful to organize the statements and the language of the statements to reveal their unity and diversity. An analysis was made of twenty-eight statements, all of which would be classified as descriptive of steps. Table 5.4 reports the results of that analysis.

Four primary categories of analysis were developed: generic behavior, broad general statements (process and product), statements about three stages of creating plans (early, middle, and final), and statements about related general management behaviors. Two points can be noted.

The first is that only ten of the twenty-eight statements identified a class of behaviors or phenomena to which planning belongs. That is, only ten said *what it is*. No one would consider trying to explain a dog without saying first that it is an animal. The sun is a star; hunger is a

Table 5.4. Analysis of Propositions about Planning. Summary of Behaviors Identified as Relevant to the Planning Process in Twenty-Eight Propositions.

Generic Behavior Category	
Process = 8*	Dimensions of decision process = 1
Function = 1	None given = 18

Broad General Process Statements		Broad General Product Statements	
Apply	rational analysis to process of educational development	Prepare	set of decisions for action
Apply	research (systematically) to problems of policy	Prepare	decision as basis for action
		Prepare	time-phased future activities
		Prepare	blueprint for action
		Make	set of decisions to increase likelihood of achieving desired outcomes
		Devise/design	something
		Form	scheme or method for doing, achieving
		Formulate	rationally feasible courses of action
		Arrange	some action to be carried out
		Plot	use of time, resources and effort toward aims

Early Stages of Planning Process		Middle Stages of Planning Process	
Obtain	pertinent information	Analyze	pertinent information
Identify	elements of project as activities	Develop	alternative means for achieving goals
Identify	alternative goals and means to achieve goals	Develop	solutions to problems
Identify	requirements for meeting needs	Develop (refine)	(see formulate and determine on p. 175)
Identify	how to get (where want to go)	Refine	alternative goals

174

Table 5.4. (continued).

Early Stages of Planning Process (continued)		Middle Stages of Planning Process (continued)	
Foresee	desired objectives	Arrange	means or steps for achievement of purposes/objectives
Generate	series of objectives to meet responsibilities	Arrange	elements of project (activities) in order
Determine	appropriate goals and objectives	Assess	rational means-ends relationship of resources and objectives
Determine	where to go	Relate	inputs and outputs
Formulate and determine	objectives, plans, budgets, standards, procedures, policies, programs, schedules, methods, organizational criteria	Relate	means to ends
Decide on	objectives, changes in objectives, resources, policies		
Anticipate	problems		
Anticipate	changes		

Final Stages of Planning Process		Related General Management Behaviors	
Evaluate	set of decisions to increase likelihood of achieving desired outcomes	Obtain agreement	on steps and procedures to meet needs
		Direct	changes
		Coordinate	operations
		Monitor	extent to which goals are achieved
		Revise	means and possible goals

*Number of times the generic category was given.

feeling; life, liberty, and the pursuit of happiness are rights; defense of those rights is an obligation. One difficulty that arises in establishing classes of organizational behaviors is that behaviors clearly involving cycles of actions (processes) are often assigned to people in various positions. Although *function* is defined formally as an outcome or a contribution to a system (Hills, 1967, 10; Kaufman, 1972, 75), it is often used to mean task or responsibility. A process may be called *the* function of particular people. It is in this sense, as of a task or responsibility, that Jucius and Schlender (1965, 46) classified planning as a function.

There is no need to belabor the point since it is generally recognized that planning comprises a cycle of activities leading toward some outcome, a process; however, it is important to take the position that classification of administrative and organizational phenomena is important for the profession. Classification is a critical first step toward communicating ideas effectively.

The second point that might be noted is that, within twenty-eight statements, twenty-seven different action verbs were employed and forty-one different statements were presented. It is true that many of the statements have similar meanings, so there is general similarity. The hope is that the profession can move toward more precise definition and description.

Will the Real Planning Please Stand Up?

In addition to the confusion that may arise from different definitions of *planning* itself, since all three types of statements are presented as definitions, there is another factor that contributes to lack of clarity. As we read, we discover that descriptions of planning, decision making, systems analysis, change strategies, problem solving, and even Dewey's description of thinking all sound very much alike. In an attempt to develop a coherent idea of planning, statements about planning were compared to statements about other administrative processes. An analysis of thirty-two such descriptions revealed that seven steps or actions were commonly included, regardless of which process was being presented (Burns, 1978a, 5). Table 5.5 presents the results of this comparison.

The set of activities listed in Table 5.5 covers a more global phenomenon than planning, decision making, or problem solving, the

Table 5.5. Summary of Activities Proposed as Steps in Five Administrative Processes Demonstating the Similarity across All Aspects of Administration Considered "Processes" (Burns, 1978a, 5).

	Planning ($n = 6^*$)	Problem Solving ($n = 6$)	Decision Making ($n = 8$)	Systems Analysis ($n = 4$)	Change Models ($n = 9$)
(Identification) (clarification) of (needs) (goals) (problems) (objectives)	6**	8	12†	6	12
(Documentation) (getting information)	5	5	7	5	7
Identification of alternative (strategies) (tools) (methods)	5	5	7	4	6
Listing advantages and disadvantages of each set of alternatives (analyzing alternatives)	7	2	4	4	11
Deciding on action	4	4	8	1	6
Arranging for (implementation) (test) (execution)	4	5	4	1	7
Determining performance effectiveness	2	3	4		3

*Number of statements reviewed.
**Number of statements citing this step.
†Some statements cited the same step more than once, at different stages in the process.

phenomenon of undertaking systematically to maximize the effectiveness of any operation. The set of activities proposes, in effect, an orderly or systematic approach to undertaking and completing activities or operations having complex interrelationships. It seems reasonable to believe that system or order will maximize the logical, means-ends dimension of the whole. It is my view that, within an organization, that set of activities approximates the broader, more general phenomenon of administration and that processes such as planning or decision making are subsumed within the set.

In fact, Simon, Griffiths, and others have argued quite convincingly that administration *is* decision making (or decision making is the heart of administration) on the basis that such a set of activities describes decision making and comprises the activities inhering in administration. The terms *systems analysis, planning, decision making,* and *problem solving* are confused in organizational literature; common usage tells us, however, that the processes they name are definitely not the same. We propose that they are not separable or discrete processes, that they cannot take place in isolation from each other, but that identifiably different phenomena exist. It is important in the study of administration to differentiate among them.

Planning, decision making, and analyzing are processes fundamental to every organization. Formalized and systematized or not, depending on specific purposes and aims, they are keys to the vitality and development of all organizations. Attempts to describe any one process must take all relevant processes into account. Some of the relationships among the processes included in Table 5.5 were discussed in Chapter 2 through the models developed by Sergiovanni, by Kazmier, and by Cunningham.

A Definition of Planning

Each of the statements presented in Table 5.3 and many others in the literature offer insights into the planning process; each is informative in many respects. Most appealing is the definition proposed by Anderson and Bowman, derived from Dror's earlier definition, ''Planning is the process of preparing a set of decisions for action'' [Anderson and Bowman (1964), in Adams (1964), p. 4]. Anderson and Bowman, and Dror (1963), emphasize *set* as a key word in their definitions—*set* implying integrally related.

Although that definition is more precise and conceptually clear than many proposed, it is still somewhat lacking. A group of decisions can be a set, integrally related, without having been planned. They can, and often do, arise naturally out of circumstances, one decision leading naturally and relatedly to the next. The whole is not clearly visioned before the stream of decisions commences, although the integrative character of the stream is recognizable after the fact. Because beliefs and values are the basis of all choice and action, the holistic nature of personal gestalt always comes into play at the moment of choice. So coherence is evident, but the set of decisions cannot be called a plan. This reality is expressed in Braybrooke and Lindblom's disjointed incrementalist model, which suggests that decisions often move indirectly but in an incremental pattern toward a more desirable situation.

Intuitively, however, we know that a plan is something more than a set of decisions. Certainly, a plan cannot be developed without making decisions, but decisions are often made without planning; moreover, a plan has an emotional pull because it is a proposal for some future, desirable state. It is set before us to pull us *toward* something in a way that a set of decisions for action does not. A set of decisions is like digital time: each event is discrete.

A plan has more of the character of a clock face with hands showing the relationship of the particular minute to the framework, the hour of sixty minutes. Thus, a decision, like a digital minute, exists within the framework but does not speak to the framework, does not place the minute into any context.

A decision is an organizational fragment. The plan that the decision implements places the fragment into the context of values, goals, aims, and purposes, into the context of wholes. A set of decisions can be a plan if they are integrally related not only to each other, but, more importantly, to a specified determined end result or outcome. The whole — the end result aimed for — is an integral element of a plan.

To develop our definition of planning, therefore, we started by examining different types of plans, the outline, blueprint, and design, to discover what is missing in previous definitions. What do all of these plans have in common?

First, they are all presented in some visual format, which identifies elements of a whole and visually proposes relationships between the parts. Those things that we call plans are physical things. Blueprints, designs, and models show visually how the parts fit together to compose the imagined whole. Even an outline has a visual representation of relationships, the relationships of main and supporting ideas to each other and to the topic at hand. From the plan, we immediately begin to see the vision of the planners; we get a sense of the whole.

Second, plans present the ''whole'' in brief. Each plan is a scaled down version of some whole. That is, the relationships of separate parts to each other are presented on a scale of sorts — time (a schedule), size (a blueprint), quantity (a budget), inclusion (an outline), and distance (a map). The scaled relationships instruct how to proceed, yet every plan is an abstraction, infinitely variable in detail. Implementers can become engaged actively because they see the parts and the end product but can adapt the whole to particular interests.

There are, of course, different scales relevant to any representation. An architect's blueprint of a house and the prospective owner's drawings are not on the same scale. One is on the logic of measurement and proportion, the other on the logic of value.

Third, the "whole" that a plan represents may be a thing, an operation, or an event. Fourth, plans are conceived, designed, and developed in the mind, in the minds of many perhaps, but they are conceptual, ideational. The idea is often a sudden inspiration, but plans do not just grow; they are ideas of a whole thing, conceived as a desired result. By back-tracking, the whole is designed in its necessary parts. It is carefully represented in a scaled down form, so relationships can be reviewed and tested in the abstract *before* being produced in fact.

To repeat the definition, then, a plan is a conceptual model, a representation in some scaled form, of a thing, an operation, or an event. By common practice, most plans are presented as visual models. Planning is the process of preparing that conceptual model as a set of hypotheses, a prediction. A model has a logic of its own; it hypothesizes (predicts) that certain elements (things or actions) arranged in a particular set of relationships will produce a specified outcome.

A plan, a miniature whole, invites implementers to try it out in reality, to see how well it works, to find out. A set of decisions assumes that prescribed action should be followed. A plan leads the viewer to think about the whole, the end product, and try to achieve an envisioned result. If a plan is accepted as a set of decisions, implementation may tend to move inflexibly through prescribed steps. If a plan is accepted as a set of hypotheses, it can be modified as circumstances change without losing the focus on the end intended.

> de Forge's first principle: if the facts don't fit your plan, make your plan fit the facts
>
> *— Frizell, 1972, in* The Grand Defiance

It is our view that the distinction between plans as sets of decisions and plans as sets of hypotheses can have an impact on the mental set for pursuing goals and objectives. No predictions are perfect; all plans must be modified as they are implemented. A plan viewed as a set of hypotheses gives two safeguards. It requires that every real operation and every event be checked (or tested) against its desired whole, the ideal outcome hoped for, before risking resources and results in reality. It also encourages reality to be tested against the ideal as action proceeds and permits adjustment to new reality as it develops without losing the concept of the whole. Plans lead into action because they keep the spotlight on the end result intended.

In summary, everyone carries in their mind a metaphor, or mental image, of a planner, and, because of the historical baggage we carry around, that mental image may be favorable or unfavorable. Yet everyone plans, and everyone has a pretty good general idea of how to go about it. No one would start out on any enterprise, small or large, without some image of how it should take shape.

Moreover, everyone accepts the fact that the planning part of preparing for some activity endures much investigation, debate, and mental testing. And everyone knows that plans are only a probable means to an end; the person who has a second best alternative route in mind is not defeated by a roadblock. Knowing what the second best alternatives are is part of effective planning.

CHAPTER 6

Models and Systems of Planning

> We talk about learning from experience, but we cannot do that unless we
> . . . organize our experience, that is relate the parts. Unrelated experience
> is of little use to us. . . .
>
> —*Follett* (1924, 305)

THE broad, general frameworks within which we plan—philosophies, paradigms, metaphors—are useful to practicing administrators mostly for helping us recognize our own patterns of thinking and the patterns of those around us. Seldom do we start planning by creating a philosophy of education or even by identifying our own philosophy. For the most part, we deal with specifics, the here and now. However, just as Schon (1983) describes the architect professor reflecting on the "lay of the land" and on the principles of design before sketching in a school, so it is important for us to reflect on the bases of our administrative thinking.

It will have become clear to the reader that the discussion is moving from broad perspectives on organizations and administration in general to more specific, focused perspectives on planning in education in particular, as was depicted in Figure 3.1. Chapters 4 and 5 also moved from a broad perspective, from paradigms or world views to metaphors (images) of the organization and of the planner, to the more specific definitions (conceptual identification) of planning.

Models and systems of planning are the day-to-day tools of planners. They instruct more specifically in what orientations to take, what to be concerned with, and how to proceed. This chapter will discuss different models and systems of planning and how they contribute to effective planning.

But there are so many models and systems in the literature, how can their practical usefulness be assessed? Can they be organized in some useful way? Can the different models and systems be related to each other so that we can, as Follett proposes, understand planning better by thinking about the different models and systems as a set? Does the set provide greater understanding of planning because we can see relationships among the different aspects? The following points will be addressed in this chapter.

First, three questions will be addressed: 1) Can we distinguish productively between ''models of planning'' and ''planning systems?'' 2) Do various models or systems differ in terms of what they are useful for? 3) On what bases can the countless models/systems presented in the literature be assessed? What are the issues about organizational life that models and systems of planning address, and how do the answers they propose differ?

Second, three process dimensions will be proposed as useful bases of comparing and contrasting planning models/systems, and a number of common models will be identified at poles on these dimensions. Specific models and systems will be compared and contrasted.

Third, common models and practices of planning will be mapped on two of the three process dimensions identified.

ARE MODELS AND SYSTEMS OF PLANNING DIFFERENT?

Both models and systems can be found in the literature in three different modes: presented graphically, using visual symbols to represent ideas and relationships; presented mathematically, using statistical symbols; and presented descriptively. Mathematical models are most useful for aggregated data and, therefore, at the mega (province, state, national) and macro (board, system) levels of planning. This section will be concerned, for the most part, with graphic and descriptive presentations, since the book is addressed to issues at the level of the individual school and to the work of the practicing administrator or educational leader in the school.

The terms *models of planning* and *planning systems* are often used interchangeably. Although there is, implicit in all discussions, a more theoretical, abstract meaning to planning models than to planning systems, there is no clear distinction between them in specific instances. Particular planning models and planning systems may be described similarly; however, it seems that they might profitably be distinguished in several ways. First, they might be distinguished by their proximity to action, using *models of planning* to identify the more abstract, or theoretical, presentations and *planning systems* to name those that specify, in some detail, the steps or series of actions necessary to develop effective plans.

A second distinguishing characteristic is that those we might call *models* put emphasis on approach, style, or perspective. They propose, or describe, relationships among elements of a plan or the planning process. Thus the rational comprehensive model instructs the planner to approach the issue rationally and comprehensively. The disjointed incrementalist model proposes that, in the real world, a plan is not an integrally related set of anything (decisions or hypotheses); it is built day by day from the circumstances that exist. "You take what they give you and make the most of it," as the bag lady tells the socialite in the movie *Face of a Stranger*. Those we would prefer to classify as planning systems advise one on the steps to take to ensure rational comprehensiveness or incremental progress.

To compound any attempt to discuss types of planning systematically, they are often characterized by focus. That is, financial planning, budget planning, curriculum planning, and program planning appear as quite separate bodies of educational literature. Thus, in moving into a specific planning situation, there are three primary questions planners respond to: 1) What are we planning about? (focus or content); 2) What approach is practical and appropriate? (model); and 3) What are the steps we should follow? (system). There is a wide range of possible combinations of answers to those three questions, and discussions show that thinking has changed over the past several decades. For example, budget planning theoretically and traditionally is considered rational but realistically is acknowledged to be political; curriculum planning has moved from rational to learning-adaptive, formative, or political and moral.

There are large bodies of literature that address planning in particular contexts, the context of budgets, financing education, curriculum, special programs, human resources or personnel, community relations, buildings and facilities, etc. For the most part, these bodies of literature address the issue of ends or aims to be attained and adopt some relevant model or propose specific programs or projects. This chapter is concerned with models that have been presented regardless of the context for which they may be considered most relevant. We are concerned with how the many models differ from each other and what they add to our overall knowledge about planning, that is, how seeing them as a set can assist administrators to choose a useful approach to planning and useful techniques of planning.

Any assignment made of individual presentations to the classification of models or systems would be hopelessly arbitrary and would add little to clarification. Certainly, one is just as apt to find reference to rational systems as to rational models, to the learning-adaptive model or system, to strategic planning models or systems, or to political models and systems.

The term *system* is not used in such references in the context of "systems approach" or with the theoretical precision expressed by Hills (1967), Bertalanffy (1968), Immegart and Pilecki (1973), and others. The systems approach and some implications for educational planning were discussed briefly in Chapter 2. The phrase *planning system* is used in the literature in the more common or colloquial meaning of *system*, as is expressed in comments such as "My system works well for me," or "We have a good system for registration." In this sense, *system* implies a series of activities performed in an orderly fashion to accomplish a task. It takes on much of the technical meaning of *process*, as defined by Griffiths (1959, 92), "A cycle of events in which a consistent quality or direction can be discerned."

Process, however, presupposes some nonobservable transformation that takes place within the subject, such as is implied in the input-output model of a learning system, as presented in Figures 4.5 and 4.6. That is, the subjects observed for process (as students in learning, or plants in photosynthesis) participate themselves in the input-output relationship. Therefore, models and systems will be discussed as one general category, while identifying the characteristics that might place specific examples in one class or the other. For the most part, we will use the term *models* to mean the general group, including *systems*.

PRACTICAL USEFULNESS OF PLANNING MODELS/SYSTEMS

The most important distinction for practicing administrators seems to be their proximity to action. In this respect, three types of planning models or systems are found in the literature. Although they overlap in many particular instances, they differ primarily in terms of generality and specifics. They may usefully be classified as conceptual, operational, and procedural mapping (or more simply, mapping) models or systems. Within each of these three types may be found models that differ in terms of orientation and focus. Figure 6.1 presents the three primary types of planning models and systems proposed and some ways in which the models are useful for practicing administrators.

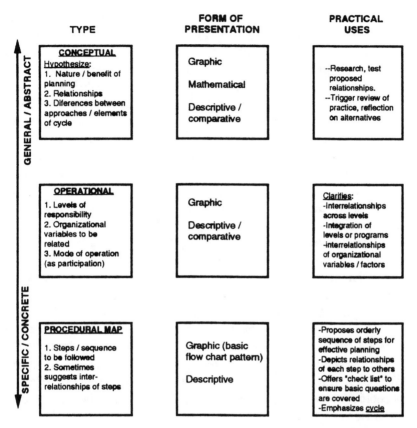

TYPE	FORM OF PRESENTATION	PRACTICAL USES
CONCEPTUAL Hypothesize: 1. Nature / benefit of planning 2. Relationships 3. Diferences between approaches / elements of cycle	Graphic Mathematical Descriptive / comparative	--Research, test proposed relationships. --Trigger review of practice, reflection on alternatives
OPERATIONAL 1. Levels of responsibility 2. Organizational variables to be related 3. Mode of operation (as participation)	Graphic Descriptive / comparative	Clarifies: -Interrelationships across levels -Integration of levels or programs -interrelationships of organizational variables / factors
PROCEDURAL MAP 1. Steps / sequence to be followed 2. Sometimes suggests inter-relationships of steps	Graphic (basic flow chart pattern) Descriptive	-Proposes orderly sequence of steps for effective planning -Depicts relationships of each step to others -Offers "check list" to ensure basic questions are covered -Emphasizes cycle

GENERAL / ABSTRACT ← → SPECIFIC / CONCRETE

Figure 6.1. Three types of planning models or systems found in the literature and some of their practical uses.

Conceptual Models

Planning models and systems that should be classified as conceptual models are general and abstract in nature. They may propose a general hypothesis about effects or intended effects of planning, or they may make a general statement about the importance of planning for the organization. Examples are the cost/benefit model presented in Figure 2.2 and Friedmann's (1973) model of the relationship of time to planning thought presented in Figure 2.1.

A second type of conceptual model is analytical and descriptive. Such models may identify changes over time, as Hamilton's (1991) model of changes in the focus of planning thought presented in Figure 5.2, Worth's (1988) model of changes in the locus and focus of planning for education in Canada, and Johnston and Liggett's (1991) similar analysis of changes in planning for education in the United States.

Some analytical or descriptive models propose relationships between planning and other organizational and administrative phenomena. Examples include the models of Sergiovanni et al. (1992), Kazmier (1980), and Cunningham (1982), which were presented in Figures 2.9, 2.10, and 2.11, respectively. My own model proposing relationships between planning, decision making, and direction was also presented in Chapter 2, Figure 2.12. These models place planning in perspective of some general set of processes and functions that must be considered in any educational plan. They remind the planner of the larger setting of action.

A third type of conceptual model may make a proposition about one particular element in the whole planning cycle. "Behavioral objectives" is an example of such a model. That body of literature presents the rationale for, and the nature of, behavioral objectives. There is little emphasis in that literature on other steps in the planning cycle. Authentic testing and total quality management are newer bodies of literature that focus on some particular step in the planning cycle. Pyke's (1970) distinction between exploratory forecasting (effect oriented) and extrapolative, or normative, forecasting (goal oriented) is an example of a conceptual model that compares two different approaches to one particular step in the cycle.

Conceptual models present a general proposition about planning or propose a general orientation or approach, and they hypothesize relationships between elements or variables, the effects of certain variables or activities on others. Such models may be presented graphically (as those already cited), mathematically (Simon, 1945, 1960; Johnstone, 1974; Game Theory models), or through description and comparison. Inbar's (1991) comparison of planning and improvisation presented in Table 2.2 is an example. Bologna's (1980) analysis of long-range versus strategic planning and Friedmann's (1973) distinction between allocative and innovative planning are presented in a later section of this chapter (Tables 6.1 and 6.2).

Conceptual models imply that relationships proposed should be tested—perhaps for the goodness of fit with the reality of organizational behavior, as in the extensive case studies of Mintzberg (1973, 1976, 1980; Mintzberg, Raisinghani, and Thoret, 1976), perhaps for the differential effects of one approach, one set of proposed relationships, against the other. Or perhaps the models themselves should be tested for their usefulness under differing organizational conditions. Thus, a major value for practicing administrators is that, by proposing possible relationships between organizational approaches or phenomena, conceptual models may trigger review of or reflection on current practices and thereby suggest alternative means of achieving desired effects.

Operational Models

A second primary type of planning model found in the literature is frequently called operational. Many strategic planning models can be classified among this group, since many such models present the organizational levels at which particular planning issues are addressed. They depict *who* should do *what type* of planning. In general, strategic planning is presented as the responsibility of senior administration; operational, or administrative planning of middle management; and tactical, or implementation planning of front line management [see, for example, Ansoff (1968), Steiner (1979), Naylor and Neva (1980), Cunningham (1982), de Vasconcellos (1982), Sawyer (1983), Sufrin and Odiorne (1985), Newberry (1990), and Kaufman (1991)].

Some models of strategic planning combine conceptual and operational, or conceptual and mapping (procedural map) model elements. Newberry's model, "Filters of Analysis Applied to Strategic Planning," is one such example. His full model (1990, 14) identifies sources of planning issues (external and environmental, plus internal SWOT analyses: strengths, weaknesses, opportunities, and threats). It then distinguishes between strategic and operational planning and proposes levels of responsibility varying between board and administration. It also proposes that planning questions and issues are filtered or flow somewhat sequentially through such stakeholder variables as purpose, values, mission, and vision. Thus, the model combines some characteristics of conceptual, operational, and mapping models.

Kaufman and Herman's framework for strategic planning (1991, 42) also combines characteristics of operational and mapping models. Figure 6.2 presents Kaufman and Herman's model of strategic planning for education.

Kaufman and Herman propose a detailed flow of activities necessary for strategic planning, which is "applicable at all educational operations

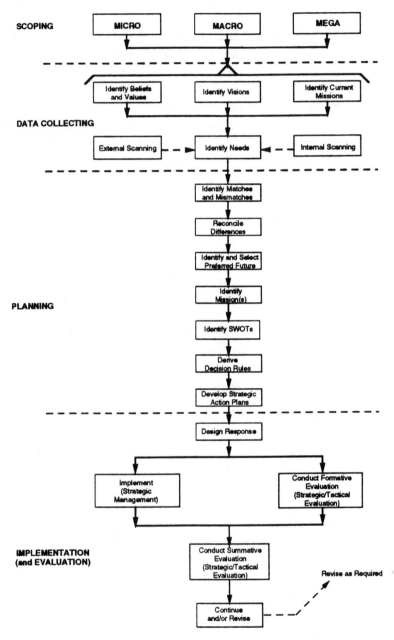

Figure 6.2. Framework for strategic planning. (Source: Figure 3.1, p. 42, in Kaufman, R. and J. Herman. Strategic Planning in Education: Rethinking, Restructuring, Revitalizing. *© 1991 by Technomic Publishing Co., Inc., Lancaster, PA. Reprinted by permission of Technomic Publishing Co., Inc.)*

and levels'' (1991, 4). This detailed flow of activities is characteristic of those we have classified as mapping models. However, rather than the common assumption that strategic planning takes place *at* and *for* the macro level, they propose that micro, macro, and mega planning issues are relevant for all operations and at all levels. Thus, society (mega), the school system (macro), and individual school or small group (micro) issues must be addressed in all planning[12] (1991, 6).

This is a more holistic organizational framework or world view for strategic planning than is found in many strategic planning models. At the same time, the model has characteristics of procedural mapping models, in that it presents a sequence, or flow, of activities.

Mapping Models

The third primary type of planning model is called a mapping model. Mapping models are the most common, including all problem-solving models, most systems analysis models, and many models of planning for change (change strategies.) Such models present a sequence of activities essential to good planning. They propose a systematic procedure for good planning. Their most important characteristic is that they present a step-by-step map to follow for good planning.

Procedural "maps," or mapping models may vary in such respects as the degree to which they incorporate analyses of the external environment or in the detail of steps included. They frequently include characteristics of operational models as Kaufman and Herman's strategic planning model (Figure 6.2). Planning maps often include, for example, post-planning management steps of implementation, monitoring, review, and modification or preplanning steps such as continuous environmental scanning. They also make the conceptual proposition, visually by arrows and, frequently, by placing the steps in a circle or a spiral, that the sequence of tasks is a continuous cycle. Procedural maps are the most immediately practical type of planning models; they instruct the practitioner in how to do it well.

Mapping models in the literature almost universally include steps associated with problems or with needs, defined as the gap between actual and desired. A problem is generally clarified in terms of needs.

[12]The step called "Identify SWOTs" refers to a management concept: Strengths, Weaknesses, Opportunities, and Threats.

It was suggested in Chapter 4 that the heavy emphasis on problem solving might be traced to Dewey's philosophy of pragmatism and his definition of logical thinking. At any rate, maps of a rational problem-solving approach to planning have been prevalent in the literature since the mid-twentieth century. Typical examples include Miller, "A model of a systems approach to problem solving" (1969, 37); Banghart and Trull, "A problem solving approach to educational planning" (1973, 442); Havelock, "The planning of alternatives" (1974, 2); and Hostrop, "Planning for change: a seven step process" (1975, Figure 3-1). Figure 6.3 presents a problem-solving model based on the steps identified as typical in Table 5.5.

Each of these maps to successful planning is presented as a cycle of the seven basic steps included in most descriptions of administrative processes, whether the specific process is planning, decision making, problem solving, systems analysis, or change strategies, as presented in

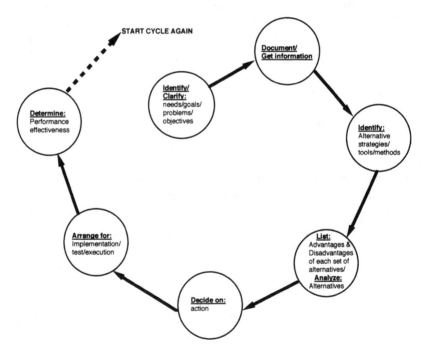

Figure 6.3. A problem-solving model of planning, based on steps identified as typical in problem-solving models presented in the literature (as presented in Table 5.5).

Table 5.5. It seems clear that problem solving as a mode of operation dominated rational propositions about administration in general and planning in particular into the 1970s. More recently, strategic planning and strategic management have dominated that body of literature. Other models that place emphasis on rationality or objectivity will be discussed in the next section.

Maps based in either the problem-solving or the strategic planning ''mental set'' represent a logical approach to planning; however, it has frequently been stressed by authors presenting such maps that there is no one exclusive starting point in the cycle, that the cycle is continuous and that planning is a way of life in organizations. Every plan creates new ideas, new opportunities (or new problems).

My own map of the planning process and how to use it effectively is presented in Chapters 9 and 10, with the same proposition—that procedural maps (planning maps) do not represent the order of thinking in planning; they represent the logic of relationships among issues that must be addressed for effective planning. A plan may start at any point in the logic of issues, but all must be considered in terms of their relationships to each other and to the whole.

DIFFERENT APPROACHES TO PLANNING

The dimension of ''proximity to action,'' upon which are distinguished three types of planning models or systems, responds to three basic questions about planning. The first, what approach or orientation to planning would be most productive for the immediate situation, is answered in various ways by the conceptual models proposed. The second, who should make what type of plans, has produced particular operational models. The third, how you go about developing a good plan, leads the planner to choose a map to follow.

The three types of models or systems cannot be ''chosen'' independently, of course. The approach or orientation preferred leads to a mode of operation (who will be involved, to what extent, at what level) and to the map to be used (the steps that will be included, in what order, and with what emphasis).

This section will discuss different conceptual models and how the approaches they present influence the planning process. It is important to note here that many of the planning models to be discussed were first presented as decision-making models or as problem-solving models. As stated in Chapter 2, planning, decision making, and problem solving are closely linked, both in reality and in administrative literature. The models proposed for all three processes are so similar that they "pass for" each other; they are seldom treated as distinct.[13] Chapters 2 and 5 address questions about how the three processes relate to each other and what each is particularly suited for. In this section, decision-making models, problem-solving models, and planning models will be considered variations of each other.

The Origin of Models of Planning

The reality of planning and of "effective" planning has, of course, been around for centuries. The face of the earth bears its marks and its scars—the pyramids and irrigation systems of Egypt, the Taj Mahal, the Great Wall of China, Roman viaducts, sky scrapers, railroads that cross continents, major league sports, and worldwide communication systems. Chernobyl, Treblinka, Hiroshima, and devastated forests and animal populations testify that plans produce destruction, as well as beauty and service. But the idea of trying to learn (or teach) how to plan better is of relatively recent origin.

The idea of systematic planning as a process that could be studied may have begun with the Cameralists during the sixteenth century. At least, Sargent and Belisle (1955) credit them with inventing the term *organization* and with developing the ideas related to systematic organizing and managing as a field of study. Certainly, planning has been accepted as an element of good administration or management in the literature since the late nineteenth century.

The more immediate ancestor of planning models is, no doubt, Dewey's (1933, 105–116) description of the process of logical thought. He proposed the following basic steps in thinking:

[13]An illustration of the interchangeable use of planning and decision making can be found in Cunningham's (1982) Chapters 3 and 10. In Chapter 10, "Decision Making," a count of words referring to decision making versus planning reveals a 13:1 ratio in favor of decision making. In Chapter 3, "Planning Theory," one might expect a similar ratio in favor of planning. However, the actual ratio is only 2:1 in favor of planning. This fact is dealt with here by considering decision making, problem solving, and planning models in terms of their implications for planning.

(*1*) Clarify the problems.

(*2*) Identify the needs and constraints.

(*3*) Identify the possible alternative solutions.

(*4*) Test the alternative solutions against the problem definition and constraints.

(*5*) Predict outcomes.

(*6*) Assess the results in terms of the problem definition.

The steps Dewey proposed presage the five steps in planning proposed by Simon (1944, 26)

(*1*) Clarify (define) the problem.

(*2*) Identify alternate strategies and tools.

(*3*) List advantages and disadvantages of alternatives.

(*4*) Analyze and evaluate (problems) (alternatives).

(*5*) Decide on action.

Thus, it has only been since the mid-twentieth century that models of planning have been presented in the literature. Even then, the model that Cunningham (1982, 28) calls "the benchmark against which all others are measured," Simon's (1947) rational comprehensive model, was presented as a decision-making model.

However, by 1949, the University of Chicago had established a program of education and research in planning. Friedmann (1973) describes Rexford G. Tugwal, Edward C. Banfield, and Harvey Perloff as instrumental figures in that program. Tugwall, he says, "conceived of society as a complex organism and of planning as a central function – similar to the brain and central nervous system in the human body – specifically concerned with coordinating its (society's) diverse elements for the benefit of the whole" [Friedmann (1969), cited in Friedman (1973), 2]. He adds that Banfield promoted Simon's rational decision-making model (p. 3), and Perloff "evolved the outlines of what eventually came to be known as the Planning-Programming-Budgeting System. His emphasis on 'strategic' or policies planning had a profound effect on the thinking of his students" (Friedmann, 1973, 4).

Nearly all models of planning, problem solving, decision making, systems analysis, and change strategies proposed in the 1950s, 1960s, and 1970s were adaptations of the seven basic steps first proposed by Dewey. For a summary of such models, see Table 5.5.[14]

Major Issues Raised

Beginning in the 1950s and 1960s, however, questions were raised about the viability of the rational comprehensive model, which had been taken as gospel. The early case studies of planning for public housing in Chicago by Meyerson and Banfield (1955) found that the model did not describe reality as planning was practiced. Friedmann, from his 1960s studies of the Tennessee Valley Authority (TVA), was similarly struck by the gap between "the narrow and sterile context of decision making" as a planning model and the reality of action (1973, 46). He proposed that "if the focus of planning is shifted from decision making to actions, it is possible to assert that any action that is deliberate is also to a certain degree planned. The problem is no longer how to make decisions more 'rational,' but how to improve the *quality of action*" (1969, quoted in 1973, 311–318, emphasis in original).

Newer models of planning (or decision making) began to raise basic issues and to propose radically different approaches to questions that had been raised. There appear to be three particularly divisive issues from which different models have been developed.

The first is the degree of rationality that is possible and desirable in planning: maximum rationality based on specific goals and objective sources of knowledge versus maximum individualization based on intuition, insight, and serendipitous goal discovery.

The second is the orientation of planning: toward organizational control and the support of organizational goals, norms, needs, and interests versus orientation toward maximizing needs, abilities, satisfaction, and morale of all members.

The third issue, which actually divides practice more than current

---

[14]For examples, see the following: *Planning:* Newman, 1950, 88–89; Carlson, 1960, 34; Smalter, 1969, 155; Kaufman, 1972, 6. *Problem Solving:* Umstattd, 1953, quoted in Dill, 1964; Lynn, 1968, quoted in Cleland and King, 1969, 230; Kaufman, 1972, 143; Havelock, 1974, 2. *Decision Making:* Tannenbaum and Massarik, 1950, 410; Griffiths, 1959, 94; Simon, 1960, 2; Dill, 1964, 201; Blankenship and Miles, 1968, 107; Marshall, 1970, 11–12; Mintzberg et al., 1976, 252–263. *Systems Analysis:* Lynn, 1968, quoted in Cleland and King, 1969, 216–231; Quade, 1969, 195–196; McManama, 1971, 25–26; Kaufman, 1972, 13–18. *Change Strategies:* Clark and Guba, 1967, 35–36; Stufflebeam, 1967, 1971; Smalter, 1969, 154; Bushnell and Rappaport, 1971, 10.

literature, is the degree and type of participation different individuals may or should have in planning activities.

These three issues arise from three types of processes that inhere in all organizational activity and have particular relevance for educational planning. The first may be considered conceptual processes, concerned with rationality and the source of knowledge. The second might be called norming processes, which are concerned with the orientation of activity—whose goals and interests are to be maximized, those of the organization or those of individuals in the organization. The third type, reflected particularly in current planning literature, is dynamics of participation, concerned with the degree to which and the means through which diverse groups and individuals participate in the planning process.

These three processes are not mutually exclusive, of course, but models make different propositions about which direction processes should take, which is right, good, or effective. The processes, therefore, become dimensions, with the characteristic of continua or dichotomies. Models and practice can be identified at various points along each dimension. In summary, it is proposed that three process dimensions are apparent in discussions of planning models and systems and in the reality of planning for education. Figure 6.4 illustrates the three processes and the polar dimensions implied.

Although all three processes inhere in planning practice, we find that operational and mapping models and systems of planning are designed on the basis of conceptual and norming processes. We propose that the basis of knowledge employed and the norming orientation assumed are expressed in the plan itself as it develops. The direction proposed by a plan and the means chosen to achieve the aims themselves reveal the orientation toward maintaining organizational norms or supporting personal needs and interests. They also reveal the degree to which the plan is able to incorporate subjective, intuitive knowledge as one of the bases of preparing for action.

The third dimension, the dynamics of participation, appears to be of a different nature. No plan reveals who developed it, although personalities can often be read from a plan by people in the know. The plan itself does not reveal the degree of participation in planning. A researcher must "shadow" the planners as the plan develops in order to describe the dynamics of participation in planning. The degree of participation incorporated into organizational activities, decision making, planning, supervising, and communicating is generally

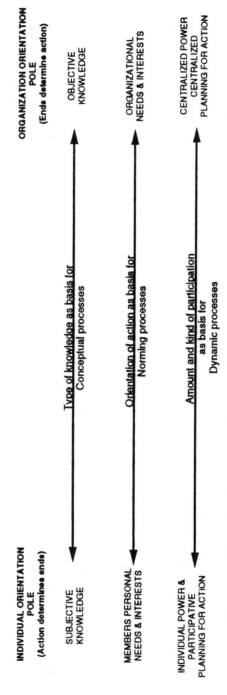

Figure 6.4. *Three process dimensions that represent different orientations to organizational action and the poles toward which planning may be directed.*

proposed as, primarily, a matter of leadership or administrative style. It is reflected more readily in certain modes of practice than in planning models [see, for example, Vroom and Yetton (1973), Tannenbaum and Schmidt (1973), and Hamilton (1991)].

The conceptual and norming dimensions will be discussed in more detail in the following sections. A number of planning models, systems, and practices will be mapped on two dimensions (conceptual and norming) and discussed in terms of those dimensions. The dynamics of participation will be discussed in Chapter 7.

THE CONCEPTUAL AND NORMING PROCESS DIMENSIONS

There are several critical elements involved in the conceptual processes of planning. Among them are rationality, the basis of knowledge, and comprehensiveness of exploration and analysis. Rationality, by definition, means "having good reasons" for choice, propositions, or action. Unfortunately, in Western usage, reasoning accepted as good is often confounded with the basis of knowledge – objective or subjective, quantitative or qualitative. Throughout the early twentieth century, the tendency was to assume that the only reasons good enough were those that could be verified by observation based on quantitative data.

The debate in the 1950s and 1960s about the validity of perception data as a basis for choice is an example of the debate about the meaning of rationality. At one extreme was the argument that perceptions do not reflect reality and therefore are not valid bases for choice or action. The objective researcher must provide data that describe reality. At the other extreme, it was argued that the true reality is that people act on perceptions and that perceptions must be taken into account in choice [see Tagiuri and Petrullo (1958) for a discussion of this debate].

The current trend has been to place more credence in subjective bases of knowledge: attitudes, feelings, perceptions, cultural and social beliefs, and customs. Acceptance of universal education as a social, political, economic, and personal good has led inevitably in North America to recognition of multiple perspectives on education and on administration of education systems; however, the debate continues. It is currently expressed as the demand for triangulation of data, for supportive evidence from several sources as necessary bases for conclusions, and in the pros and cons of authentic testing and the whole-language approach.

Thus, the current demand is for thick description of choice situations, for detailed observations and personal reports, and for multiple interpretations and their implications for educational planning. The pendulum has swung from objective to subjective knowledge as an appropriate basis of choice and from quantitative reasons to qualitative reasons as valid bases of rationality. Comprehensiveness is thought of in terms of universal interests and needs, rather than in terms of alternative strategies and probabilities, as it meant in the rational comprehensive model. The very assumption that comprehensive analysis of probabilities is necessary for effective planning can, it has been proposed, freeze the organization into inaction and resistance to change. The plan, the document itself rather than action, can become the end or goal. The danger, then, is that administration will see only itself reflected in its own mirror.

A second common thread found in planning literature and in organization literature, generally, is the identification of opposing role orientations in administrative and organizational behavior. One orientation proposed is toward maintenance of organizational norms, interests, and needs. The opposite polar orientation is toward support of personal purposes, interests, and needs. Getzels and Guba (1959) identified that dichotomy as the norming dimension of administrative role behavior. Thus, the norms that define appropriate role behavior for some planning groups come from the organization and for others, from the needs and interests of individuals in the organization.

That dichotomy is characterized as the nomothetic-idiographic dimension in Getzels and Guba's (1959) model of administration as a social process. It appears also in Likert's (1967) model of the relationship of output efficiency and employee satisfaction and in Thomas's (1976) model of modes of reconciling common and conflicting interests and values. (These three models were presented as Figures 4.8, 4.9, and 4.10 in Chapter 4.)

Similar propositions of the tension between administrative orientation toward organizational ends and aims versus responsiveness to personal needs can be found in the work of Hersey and Blanchard (1973, 1974) and Reddin (1970, 1971) and in Fiedler's Contingency Model (Fiedler, 1967; Fiedler and Chemers, 1974), the LBDQ (Leadership Behavior Description Questionnaire) studies, and in much other research. The dimension is implied also in work that prescribes a position at one end of the continuum or the other [see, for example, Peters and Waterman's emphasis on organizational excellence (1982) and Hamilton (1991) on a moral orientation to planning. Inbar (1991), Murphy (1991), Reavis and Griffith (1992), and McDonald (1993) all emphasize the individual pole].

In fact, awareness of that basic tension in organizational life is the source of Greenfield's (1975) dramatic assertion that "there is no such thing as *an* organization." Every proposition about planning responds in some way to that tension. The norming processes continuum forms the second dimension, upon which a sample of planning models, systems, and practices will be mapped.

Rational Organization Goal Models

Models and systems that emphasize objective bases of knowledge are generally considered rational and are seen as arising from a positivistic epistemology. The key characteristics of models identified as rational are analytical and systematic process, scientific approach, and empirical bases of choice. Since these models may rely on highly technical expertise, they are also often characterized as residing in the hands of specialists and soliciting little input or participation from interest groups or front line implementers.

Models or systems that propose subjective knowledge as an essential basis of choice and action are said to arise from an open system perspective, or phenomenological orientation, and to be political or participative in process. Intuitive or subjective knowledge is the expertise of persons closest to the action, those most affected. It is gathered from action and is subjectively accumulated, generalized, and applied. Thus, rational processes (which are assumed to rely on technical expertise and empirical knowledge) and participative processes (which actively seek input from all groups involved) are viewed as incompatible. The implication is that rational and participative are polar opposites [see, for example, Beach and McInerney (1986), Leithwood and Montgomery (1986), and Adams (1991) for analyses of planning behavior, which make that assumption].

In practice, that distinction is no doubt generally valid. A planning activity, far too often, takes place at the state, provincial, or national level or at the system or board level and from the generalist perspective suggested by data banks such as average achievement, national or international comparisons, and normal circumstances. However, rational planning and participative involvement in planning are not necessarily incompatible. Groups, participating interactively in planning, can employ rational conceptual processes, as Doyle and Straus (1976) assert in *How to Make Meetings Work,* and Grove (1985) asserts in *High Output Management.* Many consulting services have developed group planning processes that incorporate both dimensions, participation and rational conceptual processes. Examples include Kami and Martz (1979), Tregoe and Zimmerman (1980), and Canadian Pacific Consulting Services (CPCS) SPEC® processes.

Conceptual processes, such as analysis and synthesis, may rely on subjective, intuitive knowledge as usefully as on objective, empirical knowledge. Interpersonal processes may be centralized in character (with participation taking the form of compliance as under a charismatic leader) or participative (commonly implying that members have reasonable influence on choice and action). We will return to the question of participation in Chapter 7.

The rational comprehensive model of planning maximizes the organization orientation pole of the conceptual process continuum proposed. It is characterized by clearly specified goals and ends prescribed by the organization; by action chosen on the basis of objective, quantitative data to support those ends; and by comprehensive exploration and analysis of alternative means available.

The goal-free and learning adaptive models maximize the individual orientation pole of the conceptual processes. They are characterized by an exploratory approach to goal development and by the assumptions that action determines goals or ends; that action produces understanding; and that attitudes, values, beliefs, and customs are primary determinants of action. Many other models proposed in the literature and many practices that have developed in particular organizations or groups lean toward one pole or another. Figure 6.5 identifies a number of well-known models and practices that are oriented toward one end of the conceptual and norming continua or the other.

Rational Comprehensive and Bounded Rationality

In Figure 6.5, there has been no attempt to range or rank the different models and practices on the process dimensions; however, specific models do differ in emphasis. Even though they may direct planning to the same set of orientations, they can be compared and contrasted in

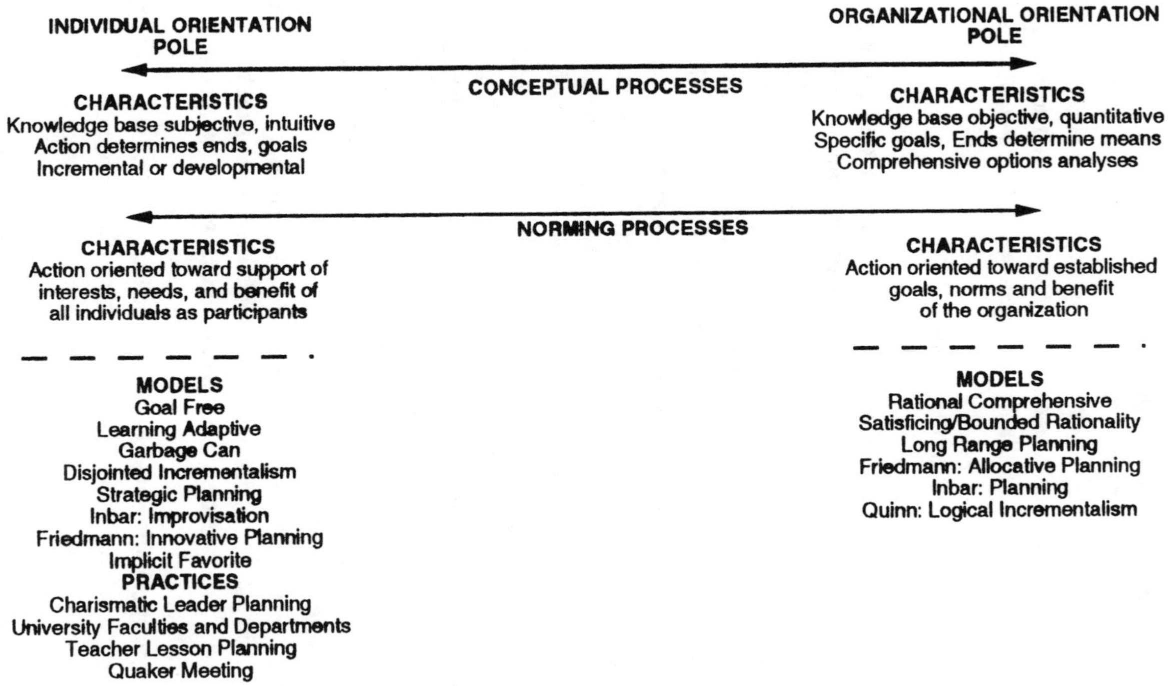

INDIVIDUAL ORIENTATION
POLE

CONCEPTUAL PROCESSES

ORGANIZATIONAL ORIENTATION
POLE

CHARACTERISTICS
Knowledge base subjective, intuitive
Action determines ends, goals
Incremental or developmental

CHARACTERISTICS
Knowledge base objective, quantitative
Specific goals, Ends determine means
Comprehensive options analyses

NORMING PROCESSES

CHARACTERISTICS
Action oriented toward support of
interests, needs, and benefit of
all individuals as participants

CHARACTERISTICS
Action oriented toward established
goals, norms and benefit
of the organization

MODELS
Goal Free
Learning Adaptive
Garbage Can
Disjointed Incrementalism
Strategic Planning
Inbar: Improvisation
Friedmann: Innovative Planning
Implicit Favorite
PRACTICES
Charismatic Leader Planning
University Faculties and Departments
Teacher Lesson Planning
Quaker Meeting

MODELS
Rational Comprehensive
Satisficing/Bounded Rationality
Long Range Planning
Friedmann: Allocative Planning
Inbar: Planning
Quinn: Logical Incrementalism

Figure 6.5. Planning models and practices that might be placed at one pole or the other of the processes dimensions.

particular respects. Certainly, the model Simon first proposed in 1947, the rational comprehensive model, and the modified "satisficing" or "bounded rationality" model proposed by March and Simon (1958) differ. Although both emphasize rationality of means↔ends relationships for analysis and objectivity as the source of knowledge, the later model recognizes that comprehensiveness, as it had been defined, is not a practical reality for most planning or decision-making situations.

Rationality Data — Rating and Ranking

Sets of planning and decision-making tools that are closely identified with rationality models have been developed for each of the steps in planning: goals-objectives rationalization, means↔ends analysis, task or activities analysis, and resource allocation and budgeting. Management by Objectives (MBO), Decision Tree Analysis (DTA), Program Evaluation and Review Technique and Critical Path Method (PERT and CPM), and Program Planning Budgeting System and Zero-Based Budgeting (PPBS and ZBB) are examples of tools developed to maximize rationality at particular steps. All have had some impact on education and could be said to "have had their day." As tools for planning they have not been lost, but educational administrators must be aware of the situations in which and the means by which such tools can be useful.

DTA is one of the best known of the rationality tools. For in-depth discussion of the statistical bases for the technique, see, for example, Newman (1971) and Winkler (1972). Decision tree analysis requires educators to set numerical values to subjectively valued outcomes. Educators often resist the demand to rank or rate values numerically; however, it would be easy to make the case that Westerners (North Americans in particular) have a well-established habit of ranking every observation, every experience (from one to ten as a recent movie impressed upon us).

An electronic polling system called Consensor® used in management consulting consists of a set of individual, autonomous response units and a video display. Figure 6.6 shows the Consensor system and its components.

Three important propositions were made in the design of the Consensor® system. First, each participant registered a personal opinion, judgment, or assessment on a small, hand-held unit. Second, response units were designed so that opinions could be kept anonymous; in addition,

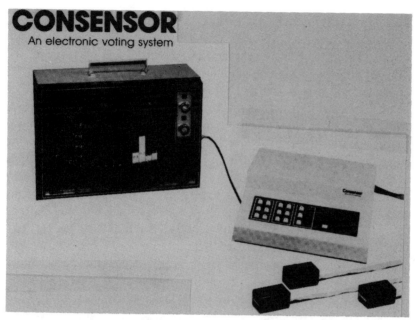

CONSENSOR
An electronic voting system

Figure 6.6. The Consensor® system. The system integrates a set (up to 100) of individual hand-held terminals, a microprocessor that continuously scans the terminals for responses, and a video display unit that displays the bar graph of the group's responses. Consensor is a registered trademark, now held by Reactive Systems, Inc. This model of the Consensor system is no longer produced, but other, more sophisticated systems provide similar capabilities for group planning and choice.

the analysis program in the microprocessor did not track individual responses. Third, the visual bar graph summary of responses was presented instantly, so discussion was not interrupted by counting or tallying up responses. There were many important advantages to a group using the system. Newer, more flexible and practical systems are now available.

In a study in Ontario schools, parents, teachers, and students were asked to rate issues that faced their schools and a number of factors related to those issues. They had no hesitation in rating their school's reputation, program, morale, effectiveness, etc. Moreover, they enlightened *themselves* on their own true perceptions of the school. Parents who were well known in their communities as severe critics of their school shocked themselves by acknowledging a rating of seven or eight on a scale of zero to ten (Burns, 1988a).

The Western world has a firmly developed habit of thinking in dichotomies: right and wrong—the law books provide a mountain of detailed distinctions; good and evil—religions, philosophies, and cultures specify the behaviors that qualify; beautiful and ugly; useful and useless; genuine and phony; innovative and conventional; motivated and apathetic; and responsible and irresponsible.

Western education systems take much of their structure from this tendency to rank. First, tasks are ranked. Reading tasks are rated third-, fourth-, or fifth-grade level. Particular cognitive manipulation tasks are pegged at grade levels. Student groups are then organized by grade levels, and students are rated above or below grade level on their ability to perform tasks prescribed for their grade. The tendency to ascribe ranks to all behavior, indeed to all attitudes, to judge on the basis of dichotomous dimensions, is firmly fixed by the time we have earned a few "gold stars" in kindergarten.

We believe that it is important to acknowledge the fact that we subconsciously rate, or rank, most things we observe, that, indeed, as educators it is our professional mandate (at present at least) to rank and rate students on work, attitudes, behaviors, abilities, and knowledge. One alternative, it seems evident, would be to rely on standardized tests of some sort—whether standardized achievement and IQ tests or authentic tests "standardized" through some method of expert validation. We may have taught the public too well that numbers and ratings are important, and we no doubt have to deal with numbers and rankings until expectations and desired outcomes change.

Rationality Tools—DTA

Of the rationality tools, DTA is often proposed as an important technology for rational decision making and rational planning. The format of DTA will be discussed here as an example of rationality tools available. The process of computing DTA and other tools for rational choice will be presented in Chapters 11 and 12. The "tree" discussed here was developed by Cunningham and presented in his book *Systematic Planning for Education* (1982, 186–189). In this example, decision tree analysis was applied to screening and program choices for exceptional children. Figure 6.7 presents the decision tree; the discussion that follows is based on that example.

DTA is particularly appropriate for mega and macro analyses, and educators should not reject DTA simply because of its quantitative and

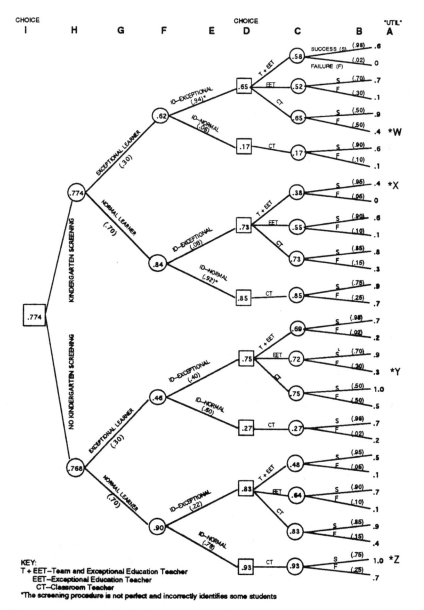

Figure 6.7. An example of a decision tree analysis considering the possible outcomes of two alternative choices for dealing with exceptional children: kindergarten screening and no prescreening as the basis for placement in four possible programs. (Source: Figure 10.6, p. 188, in Cunningham, W. G. Systematic Planning for Educational Change. © 1982, Palo Alto, CA: Mayfield Publishing Co. Reprinted with permission of *Mayfield Publishing Co.)*

207

statistical emphasis. There are reservations about the technique for general use because of its complexity, and the relatively simple choice situation described by Cunningham reveals that complexity. The following factors are involved in the situation presented:

- two screening situations: kindergarten screening
                               no kindergarten screening
- two real populations: normal students
                               exceptional students
- four outcomes of screening: normal identified as normal
                               normal identified as exceptional
                               exceptional identified as exceptional
                               exceptional identified as normal
- three programs: teacher + excep ed teacher
                               exceptional education teacher
                               classroom teacher

Given this set of factors, thirty-two outcomes related to success and failure are specified.

This is by no means the most complex educational situation we could imagine. For example, all of the factors identified are operational, choice, or demographic factors. That is, they can be known or can be controlled by the organization. The problem would be more complex in reality because parents' willingness to have their children in special classes, or in regular classes with special learners, would become issues, as they certainly have in Quebec since many school boards have adopted mainstreaming.

In a simple, preliminary example, Cunningham (1982, 178–186) incorporates an environmental factor, the probability of rain. This example makes very clear that the decision factor is not the probability of an event (rain) occurring; that is a data factor. The decision factor is the probable effect of rain on the happy outcome of the graduation ceremony. Objectivity of data (the probability of rain) is not the issue; subjective data are the deciding concern—the estimated relationship of event and choice to outcome.

Plus on est objectif, plus on est subjectif.

Decision tree analysis is a technology for assessing the compounding effects of one decision/choice, or factor, on subsequent choices and, ultimately, on outcome. It requires the decision maker to add the outcome effects of all possible choices at any one point to determine the "effect value" of the choice to be made. A change in any one value or estimate requires all values to be recomputed. Although it is becoming easier to do this with new technology, it is no easier to maintain understanding of the numbers generated.

Numbers in themselves have no value; they must be understood to make meaningful choices. It is not easy, when DTA paths have many branches, to follow the line of thinking and understand the meaning of interaction of thirty-two effects on each other and on results obtained. Thinking requires mental debate, playing the "what if" game. "What if" the kindergarten screening were not as successful as is predicted (94% and 98%), or "What if" classroom teachers were given training in recognizing clues to exceptional learning problems. Using DTA, it is not easy to think through possible different combinations of probabilities and effects; one is forced to rely on the numbers without necessarily understanding the meaning and the implications of the possible choices.

For the most part, decisions in education are not made using complex mathematical analyses. At the national, state, or provincial level and at the system or board level, statistical data are collected on such factors as demographics, costs, and outcomes. They are less commonly used analytically to make specific decisions, such as in the example cited. More frequently, they are used in reviewing programs. Perhaps such analyses should be and perhaps they will be used more frequently as electronic tools make complex mathematical paths easier to follow. It is important, however, to recognize the complexity of the judgments we do make and to make those judgments as systematically and as openly as possible.

Bounded Rationality Tools—Matrix Analysis

Recognition that comprehensive rationality, as it was developed in early decision literature, was not practical in many real choice situations soon led to other tools for decision making. Matrix analysis is one of the most common of these alternate tools. It is based on simple additive, rather than compounding, effects for analysis, and it is a multiple use tool.

In my experience as a planning consultant with Canadian Pacific Systems Services, matrix analysis was used for such planning and choice situations as the following:

- establishing goal priorities for federal government departments
- assessing possible suppliers for purchase of a multi-million dollar paper mill

- evaluating possible locations in the Caribbean for a resort hotel complex
- assessing the impact of merger of major internal departments on each other
- evaluating personnel for promotion potential
- assessing possible security procedures for the Pope's trip by rail across Canada

Matrix analysis has also been used successfully in our work with schools and school boards in Quebec and Ontario. Some examples are the following:

- assessing possible strategies for dealing with the public in regard to closing schools
- determining marketing strategies (Quebec has a strong private sector, and public schools are beginning to use marketing strategies.)
- estimating possible impact on various school concerns for a single-gender school considering change to open enrollments
- establishing goal and issue priorities for schools
- analyzing programs for professional development
- assessing alternative options for creating adequate phys. ed. facilities for a private school

Whether matrix analysis is used to assess possible strategies for a single educational outcome in one class (how best to teach understanding and appreciation of the Parliamentary system of governance) or for a multi-million dollar choice of design and construction for a community college, the process is very much the same. Factors to be considered are placed on the two axes, X and Y, and are estimated for some relationship to each other. A simple matrix format is presented in Figure 6.8.

Such a matrix can be used for many different analyses, but the question asked will differ. For establishing goal priorities, in strategic planning, for example, the question to be asked is, ''How much more, or less, important is Goal A (understanding government) than B (ability to apply the scientific method), than C (appreciate good literature), than D (physical fitness), etc.?''

For predicting possible impact (impact analysis), trends are listed as rows (A, B, C, D). Educational programs, costs, achievement, etc. (the concerns potentially affected), are listed as columns (1, 2, 3, 4). To assess impact of trend on educational concern, always read from row to

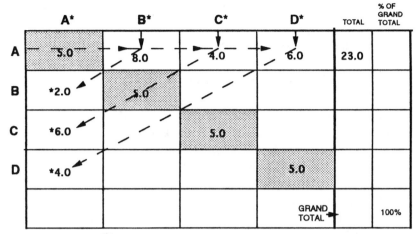

DECISION QUESTION: (reading from row to column, range = 0-10):
Is 'A' more important than B*--Yes. Score = 8
than C*--No Score = 4
than D*--Yes Score = 6
* INVERSE SCORES: Is B more important than A*--compute inverse: 10-8=2, etc.
WEIGHT = PERCENT OF GRAND TOTAL

Figure 6.8. Example of a simple matrix used to determine "weights" or goal priorities.

column. ''Equal'' could be set at 5, with scores ranging from 0 to 10. Other scoring ranges (−5 to +5 with 0 as midpoint) are often used also. In a sense, this is what we have done when we have set time allocations for teaching subjects, although such allocations are probably more a matter of custom than of any conscious analysis. An example of a matrix used to plan time allocations for an elementary school program based on themes is presented in Chapter 10, Figure 10.5.

When a matrix is used for impact analysis, the question asked is different. ''How will the trend that is developing in 'A' (growing sophistication of children in the use of computers, teaching population nearing retirement age, public concern about immoral and unethical behavior among people holding positions of trust) affect B, C, D, etc.?'' To be most useful, the factors included should be both quantitative and qualitative. Time, money, facilities, and equipment, as well as attitudes, interests, expectations, customs, and abilities, may be equally important. The use of the matrix for strategic options analysis is presented in Chapter 10, Figures 10.9 and 10.10, and in the discussion following these figures. Examples of strategic options analyses incorporated into project plans by planning students are presented in Appendix C.

For most situations in education, matrix analysis is sufficient to give reasonable bases for planning and decision making. It serves within the bounded rationality frame of March and Simon and is more precise and directed than disjointed incrementalism.

Other Models Compared and Contrasted

There are a number of other planning models that are largely based on the precepts of rational planning. Among them are long-range planning, problem solving, what Friedmann calls allocative planning, and management systems such as PPBS, TQM, and MBO, which incorporate rational planning models. Each of these models takes as its primary focus the organization and its needs and goals. The aim is to maximize organizational vitality; the purposes of planning are maintenance, stability, and economic benefit. The data for rational planning models are primarily economic and demographic trends, which are based on historical data and organizational factors.

Long-range planning, which was well established in the corporate world by 1960, is easily placed on the rational/objective pole of the conceptual continuum. Projections upon which plans were based were essentially extrapolative from historical data; however, limitations of the long-range model began to be apparent in the 1960s and 1970s as the pace of change in globalization, technology, and social conventions accelerated. The strategic planning model was developed in recognition of the fact that the past was no longer a sufficient base for prediction of the future. Doing more of the same or even building a better mousetrap was no longer the issue. Different questions must be asked, and different data must be looked at.

The strategic planning model called for a wider focus, a multidimensional perspective. It called for greater attention to be paid to the unusual, to the unexpected, and it required consideration of unique events as possible clues to the future or indicators of future trends. Consensus was no longer the sole criterion for choice of direction. Divergent thinking was encouraged as a potentially useful basis for conceptualization of vision.

Bologna (1980) compared long-range planning and strategic planning models on a number of factors. Table 6.1 presents his comparison on factors that are particularly relevant to education systems.

We have placed the strategic planning model at the nonrational/subjective pole and the long-range model at the rational/objective pole of

Table 6.1. *Comparison of Some Characteristics of Long-Range and Strategic Planning Relevant to Education.*

Distinguishing Characteristics	Central Tendencies in Long-Range Planning	Central Tendencies in Strategic Planning
Conceptual Process Dimension		
Analytical method:	Rational, scientific	Nonrational, speculative
Analytical tools:	Systems analysis, convergent thinking	Trend analysis, divergent thinking
Measurements:	Quantitative, economic	Qualitative, social
Information sources:	Historical economic and demographic data	Social data and ecological implications
Norming Process Dimension		
Value added:	Efficiency	Effectiveness
Global assumptions:	Static world, predictable	Changing world, dynamic
Output focus:	Economic benefits	Social need satisfaction
World view	Mechanistic	Organismic
Other Relevant Characteristics		
Outlook:	Optimistic, realistic	Pessimistic, idealistic
Mind-set:	Offensive	Defensive
Spatial view:	Narrow focus, linear	Wide angle focus
Planning cycle time span:	Shorter	Longer
Psychological bent:	Behavioristic	Humanistic
Advocates:	Accountants, statisticians, educators	Social scientists, artists
Teaching mode:	Content	Process
Objective:	Control	Release

Source: Based on Table 4, p. 25, in Bologna, J. 1980. "Why Managers Resist Planning," *Managerial Planning.* 28(4):23–25. Published by The Planning Forum, January/February, 1980. Reprinted by permission of The Planning Forum.

the conceptual process dimension in Figure 6.5. Bologna's analysis also suggests that placement. Several of the factors he identified distinguish the two models as lying at opposite poles conceptually: analytical method (SP: nonrational, speculative versus LR: rational, scientific); analytical tools (SP: trend analysis, divergent thinking versus LR: systems analysis, convergent thinking); measurements (SP: qualitative, social versus LR: quantitative, economic); and information sources (SP: social data and ecological implications versus LR: historical economic and demographic data).

These distinctions are similar to those proposed by other authors in the field. Friedmann's (1973) differentiation between allocative and

Table 6.2. Comparison of Allocative versus Innovative Planning, from Friedmann (1973).

Allocative Planning	Innovative Planning
ORIENTATION	
Toward functional rationality	Toward substantial rationality
Competing interest/operating groups	Institutional change
Short term (competing views of needs)	Long term (permanent change)
Financial choice (resource availability)	Political choice (not morally neutral)
Toward means (assumes ends)	Toward ends (alternative means evolve as action proceeds)
Quantitative analysis—the art of probability analysis	Inventive—the art of the possible hierarchy of values
BENEFITS/RISKS	
Minimize risk of innovativeness	Maximize innovativeness—take risks
Benefits status quo/those in power	Produces new power groups
Maintains norms	May be seen as predatory
Established procedures in place	Initially uncoordinated and competitive
COMPREHENSIVENESS	
All objectives stated explicitly	Objectives are evolved during the course of the action itself
Incremental budget alternatives —uses of resources available	Considers "new money" (nonincremental budget allocation)
Analyzes all competing "problems"	Addresses single set of problems —improve overall guidance system

Source: abstracted from pp. 51 – 66, in Friedmann, J. *Retracking America. A Theory of Transactive Planning.* Garden City, NY. © 1973 by Doubleday Publishers, by permission of Doubleday Publishers.

innovative planning proposes many of the same oppositions as those ascribed to long-range and strategic planning. Table 6.2 presents Friedmann's comparison.

Friedmann's and Bologna's comparisons also address the second dimension of planning processes proposed in Figure 6.4, the norming processes. Friedmann considers allocative planning to be oriented toward maintaining norms, the status quo, and established procedures. These characteristics would place allocative planning at the organizational pole of the norming processes dimension in Figure 6.4. Similarly, Bologna's analysis of orientations of strategic and long-range planning on such characteristics as value added, global assumptions, output focus, and world view relate to the two poles proposed for the norming processes dimension. Pyke's (1970) discussion of extrapolative projection from historical data and exploratory projection based on emerging signals highlights the important change of world view or framework for thinking about planning. Strategic planning calls for attention to "the tip of the iceberg," as well as to a body of evidence critical for planning.

However, long-range planning was often believed to be strategic planning, and historical evidence was, into the 1980s, still considered the best data for projections. This was particularly true, perhaps, in education since education had been in a long, continuous, steadily rising state. When school populations began to decline, the "steady state," now of decline, was frequently expected to hold true.

For example, between 1966 and 1981, the primary school population of one Canadian province dropped from 990,000 to about 560,000, a drop of 37% (called "the revenge of the cradle"). Predictions made by many educational planners were that, by 1991, the primary school population would drop nearly 200,000 more to about 350,000. In reality, the population in 1991 was just a little under 600,000. Figure 6.9 shows the percentage change, plus or minus, for periods between 1966 and 1991.

Extrapolative projection resulted in costly studies of the probable impact of closing schools. These studies, to some degree, created a domino effect, with families moving out of the province because of the expectation that neighborhood schools would close and the resulting uncertainty about whether a stable environment would exist for children's education.

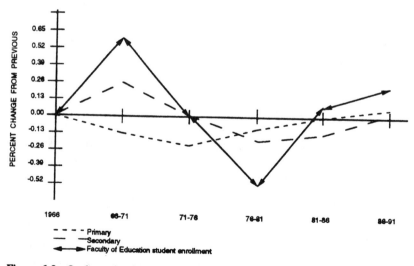

Figure 6.9. *Quebec school trend data, showing percent change from previous period (assuming 1966 as base for all sectors).*

At the same time, the planning department of a major university was using a ten-year extrapolative long-range planning model. Projected school closings were reflected in declining enrollments in teacher training programs between 1971 and 1980. The slope of the decline was projected to a ten-year continuing pattern, and budget allocations were based on those projections. The faculty of education entered an extended period of austerity and pessimism.

Since the decline in faculty of education student enrollment had, in reality, ended by 1981 (see Figure 6.9), continuing budget cuts were felt as particularly harsh. Ultimately, a change in perspective at the university level resulted in replacing the long-range model with a strategic planning model based on the concept of exploratory projections described by Pyke (1970).

This Canadian university was not an exception. An ERIC search for the period 1975–1985 found that 93% of universities and state or provincial departments of education reported demographic and historical data as the basis of their planning, a characteristic of the long-range planning model.

Educators are not the only group that can be afflicted with the "disease" of extrapolative projection of course. One could cite hundreds of examples of doomsayer predictions based on limited sets of factors. Recall that, in the 1950s, we were bombarded with predictions that, by the year 2000, human beings would have to live in space in tiny capsules, with "sensations" projected to them. Of course the best-known example is the *1984* prediction. I personally benefited from that prediction because one of the most beautiful hotels in Canada offered a $19.84 one-night rate in January of that year (much to the embarrassment of registration personnel).

In actual fact, most strategic planning incorporates both quantitative and qualitative data and relies heavily on internal historical data, as well as on Fierhaller's tip of the iceberg data from the environment. A survey of the strategic planning practices of a sample of Fortune's 300 "most admired corporations" (Baig, 1987) was conducted in 1988 (Burns, 1988b). Corporate planners were asked to consider eighty-one factors gleaned from strategic planning literature and to identify key factors that affect thirteen different strategic marketing choices. Forty-four of the factors (54.3%) were considered internal, related to the corporation itself, its suppliers, and distributors. Thirty-seven (45.7%) pertaining to the industry, competitors, a potential target, and the general economic environment were considered external. Results from the survey found an almost exactly parallel distribution, with 53.5% of responses indicating internal factors as critical to strategic choices and 46.5% indicating external factors.

However, the degree of emphasis on internal and external factors varied considerably, depending on the particular strategy being considered. If the strategy involved increasing market share for a current product (doing more of the same, doing the same a little bit differently, or doing the same for a different client group), the focus was on internal factors (66.7%). If the strategy involved purchase of another business, creating a joint venture with some government or corporate group, taking on a new business, or cutting back, external factors took precedence in about the same proportion, 67.9% (Burns, 1988b).

Some Implications for Education

When we talk about corporate marketing strategies, it may seem far removed from education. But translated, those strategies simply refer to planned changes in operation that would affect in major ways the organization's success with its client group. Education is no stranger to that concern. Table 6.3 lists the thirteen market strategies identified in corporate literature (Abell and Hammond, 1979; Tregoe and Zimmerman, 1980; David, 1985) and gives examples of educational decisions that may be viewed in a similar light. Although such educational decisions do not have growth as their purpose, they do have, as a primary aim, increasing the system's success in meeting the needs and demands of its client groups. (In business settings, meeting client needs is considered a means, not an end, the end being survival and growth).

Each of these educational strategies is directed toward client groups, toward serving new groups, or toward serving current groups better. In the corporate world, such strategies are referred to in marketing language because the client groups are both the product users and the direct source of financing. In education, our clients (students) are only indirectly the source of funding, so we tend not to think of better programs, better services, etc., as marketing strategies.

Current economic trends, tight budgets, and changing school popula-

Table 6.3. Corporate Market Strategies and Examples of Education Decisions That May Be Viewed as Marketing Strategies.

Marketing Strategy	Educational Decision Reflecting "Marketing Strategy"
1. Buy or start own distribution system (Forward Integration)	Own a school bus transportation system Provide a library Site based management
2. Buy or start a supply division (Backward Integration)	Contract for state series textbooks Run a system print shop Run an A/V materials production shop
3. Take over a competitor in a present line of business (Horizontal Integration)	Amalgamate with private school Run a summer camp program for a church
4. Increase clients by advertising and promotion (Market Penetration)	Parent nights School fairs/shows Sports/competitions
5. Go after new area, new target group (Market Development)	Continuing education Nursery/preschool Literacy program Distance education
6. Substantially improve present products or start new products of similar types (Product Development)	Mainstreaming Professional development/ supervision Cooperative learning Ecological studies
7. Join other groups whose line of work and clients are similar (Concentric Diversification)	Unify districts French/English or Spanish/English school combined
8. Join other groups whose products and clients are not the same (Conglomerate Diversification)	Work/study program with industry Literacy program in prison School/museum program
9. Join other groups whose line of work is not the same, but whose clients are (Horizontal Diversification)	Program for disturbed children in psychiatric ward/hospital Dropout school in juvenile hall
10. Form temporary partnership (Joint Venture)	Rent YMCA facilities Get Federal grant for project School/business project
11. Cut back, sell assets (Retrenchment)	Increase T:P ratio Cut services/supplies Cut program
12. Sell or close major unit (Divestiture)	Close school Sell transportation system
13. Close entire system (Liquidation)	Close small school district

tions are creating a greater demand for more of the "satisfy the customer" emphasis that is basic to marketing, however. Many schools, school systems, and, indeed, the education profession in general are increasingly concerned with service to the clients. This focus is very forcefully represented currently in such highly regarded practitioners' journals as *The Kappan, Educational Leadership, The Principal, Administrators' Notebook,* and *Education Canada,* as well as in count-less current books.

In business, planning takes the market as its major strategic focus for several reasons, one of which is that its customers are both directly and indirectly the source of funding. In education, the clients are only indirectly the source of funding. Government and the general public, which includes nonusers, are the major financing bodies, either through tax elections or through negotiations at government level. Education competes politically with all other public services for funds.

In education, therefore, not only marketing strategies are necessary for survival – political strategies are also critical. The administrator must be successful at public relations, and at political relations, as well as at organizing and operating the system and as well as being an educational leader. Moreover, in education, an employee group – the teachers – is a large and powerfully united professional group. Although they take confrontational action less frequently than unions do in industry, they have a unity of purpose and values that transcends state and national boundaries and acts as a major norming force for planning. Such a national and international community of values does not exist for most corporate employee groups.

In the survey of Fortune 300 companies cited, personnel concerns (talent pool, competence, morale) were cited as critical in only 8.3% of the responses (Burns, 1988b). However, school systems and govern-ments, when they consider changes in education systems, must take into account the professional group. School systems must include personnel (human resource) strategies in their strategic planning.

Thus, a major difference exists between strategic planning for busi-ness and for education. For corporations, strategic planning is and can be essentially unidimensional: toward the market and clients. In educa-tion, it must be tridimensional: toward clients/students (market strategies), toward personnel (human resource strategies), and toward funding agencies (political strategies). The tridimensional strategic plan-ning model was developed and presented for discussion in graduate

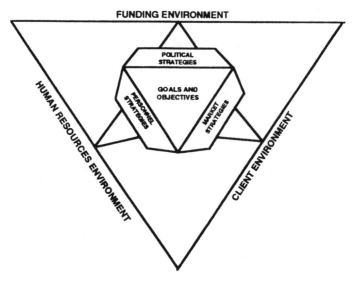

FUNDING ENVIRONMENT

POLITICAL STRATEGIES

GOALS AND OBJECTIVES

PERSONNEL STRATEGIES

MARKET STRATEGIES

HUMAN RESOURCES ENVIRONMENT

CLIENT ENVIRONMENT

Figure 6.10. Three-dimensional model for strategic planning in education.

classes at McGill University. Figure 6.10 presents the model (Burns, 1986).

The model was tested by Bailey (1992) in her doctoral study of strategic planning in Quebec cégeps.[15] Bailey surveyed all forty-four public Quebec cégeps, forty French (of which thirty-six responded) and four English (all responded). The major questions of Bailey's study were concerned with how the Directors General approached strategic planning, what groups they addressed on which issues, and what policies or practices were developed as strategies. Table 6.4 reports a summary of her main findings as they relate to the three strategic planning sectors proposed by Burns.

Bailey concluded that

> Burns' (1986) strategic planning model is a useful one for colleges to use, both in developing a strategic plan for the college and reviewing and revising an existing one. . . . Because the cégep is dependent on the State for funding, the cégep must negotiate for scarce funds for local initiatives.

---

[15]Cégep is an acronym for Collèges d'enseignement génerales et professionelles, which has taken on the status of a word. These are Quebec's postsecondary colleges that are somewhat equivalent to junior colleges or community colleges. A major difference is that all Quebec students are *required* to complete two years in a cégep before being admitted to a Quebec university.

Table 6.4. Summary of the Major Findings from Bailey's (1992) Study of Strategic Planning in Quebec Cégeps as They Relate to the Three Planning Sectors Proposed by Burns (1986).

Sector	% Responding Yes
1. Market/client strategies	
a) Consultation: in regard to academic programs	
— with all internal groups: unions, senate, administrative groups, cadres (professional, nonteaching) and service departments, in addition to academic departments	50.8
— with academic departments considered separately	100.0
— with business and industry advisory committees (such committees are mandated by law)	56.7
— with feeder schools, universities, students, and other external groups	43.3
b) Response: changing programs or adding new ones in response to needs and interests	
— revise program or introduce new program	74.3
— increase range of programs offered in an area	51.3
— provide special services/expertise to local industry	71.6
2. Staff/human resource strategies	
— staff deveopment and evaluation	54.3
— staff re-deployment for special programs	38.9
3. Political/funding strategies	
— government has high degree of influence on programs and operation	76.9
— have sufficient resources for mission	32.5
— have flexibility to use resources as needed	35.0
— generate additional funding (by contracts, etc.)	52.5

Source: Summarized from the following tables: #12, p. 112; #13, p. 113; #15, p. 118; #16, p. 120; #17, p. 121; #19, p. 125; #21, p. 131; #24, p. 135; #27, p. 143; #32, p. 155; and #33, p. 158, in Bailey, M. 1992. "The Status of Strategic Planning in Quebec's Cégeps." Ph.D. diss. Montreal, QC, McGill University.

Burns' strategic model captures the political dimension. [1992, 176–177]

Nonrational/Individual Orientation Models

At the other extreme of what we have identified as the conceptual and norming process dimensions lie models that assume either that rationality is not possible or that it is not desirable. They stem from paradigms or world views that are radically different from those represented by such models as rational comprehensive, bounded rationality, long-range, or allocative planning.

Rationality models have their bases in the functionalist paradigm and philosophies of realism and pragmatism. They assume a real world, a real organization. They assume that this real organization can and does establish goals and reasonable means for achieving its goals and that organizational goals and means are thereby ''real'' for members also. Rationality models assume that leaders can go beyond mere decisions and make plans for some purposive future, with reasonable expectations that members will work toward achieving those goals. These models imply that organizational variables can be controlled if the planners are systematic and scientific in their approach.

Models that describe planning and decision making as oriented toward individual needs and the interests of participants differ among themselves. Most of these models are descriptive, rather than prescriptive. They describe planning and decision making in various realistic modes. Reality is not always the best of all possible worlds; certainly, it is not the predictable, controllable world of rational models.

Some of these individualist models describe reality as desirable; others see reality in a less desirable light. March and Olsen (1976) described a reality at the opposite extreme from the rational comprehensive model of the 1950s. Their phrase, the garbage can model of decision making was not presented as a model to be emulated and applied, but as a description of the reality that decision makers must live with. In this view, the organization is a swirling stew of problems, resources, talents, and ideas. Concerted action seems to be the result of chance, of coincidental alignment of problem, solution, and resource. Figure 6.11 presents a schematic illustration of the garbage can model as interpreted by a student, Philip Clavel, in the masters program at McGill University (1985).

Clavel described his schema as a set of streams within streams, each of which flows continuously in changing directions. Thus, it would be, as he explained his diagram, chance or some external force applied to streams that would bring particular combinations into alignment. When educators try to develop programs, improve the system, or create more effective learning situations, it often seems that reality is a garbage can. Certainly, it is critical for educational leaders to be aware of the fluid nature of factors that affect planning and decision making.

But the garbage can model is not a true model for planning or decision

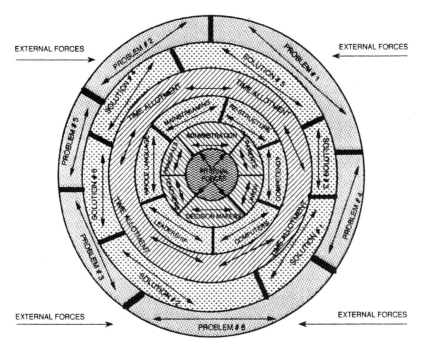

Figure 6.11. *Cylindrical diagram of the garbage can model of decision making in school systems. Based on course submission by P. Clavel. (1985) Montreal, PQ, McGill University.*

making. It is an image that is more (or less) true of reality at different times. It is a metaphor for the life of an organization within which planning and decision making may have to take place. True models of planning attempt to show how best to bring the right set of factors into alignment so that concerted action (the essential nature of organization as Barnard has said) can take place.

Another image of the ideas expressed in the garbage can model is presented by Inbar (1991) in his representation of "the fluid organization." He described the organization as a continuous flow of four streams—choices, problems, solutions, and energy from participants (pp. 74–75). Metaphors such as the garbage can, which image the reality of organizational life, help keep planners from an arrogant assumption of omniscience. They are reminders that reality and rationality are not necessarily the same thing. They also help vent natural frustrations by giving a name to them. Unfortunately, they also sometimes produce a "what's the use, why plan, it's a waste of time" reaction.

Even more unfortunately, the garbage can model and Soelberg's "implicit favorite" model open the door to manipulation. They give credence to the use of power, and the use of power can be oriented to personal advancement. If there is no system that is real, that members and participants adhere to, then individuals may seize opportunities to promote their own interests at the expense of others. A metaphor is an image, a mental picture, and as the saying goes, "One picture . . ." The garbage can metaphor should not become a "star to steer by," but a lens through which the picture can be seen more clearly.

It seems evident that the garbage can model of decision making represents assumptions common to the radical structuralist paradigm, and the metaphor of the schismatic state proposed by Burrell and Morgan (1979). It is in accord with the ideas of fragmentation, factions, and tensions by which that metaphor is characterized by Bateson (1936), Gouldner (1959), and Morgan (1980) as presented in Table 4.2.

Other planning models that respect or promote the individualist character of logical thinking and organizational action are less radical. Most of the models placed at the individual orientation pole have the characteristics of the interpretivist paradigm proposed by Burrell and Morgan (1979) and the phenomenologist perspective. These planning models assume some structure to the process and some structure in the nature of the organization.

Models such as goal-free planning, learning adaptive, and even disjointed incrementalism assume purposive direction and sets of values that may structure action. They differ in the degree to which they propose a structured approach to planning and in the effective source of structure in valuing. The degree of structure incorporated in these models decreases from strategic planning to logical incrementalism, disjointed incrementalism, learning adaptive, and goal-free. Strategic planning, which in many respects could be considered organizational in orientation, has been presented as representing the nonrational, individualist pole because it emphasizes active search for potential influences, active search for the flutter of the butterfly's wing. However, as is illustrated in Kaufman and Herman's model (Figure 6.2), it presents a structured set of issues to confront and a directed flow of activities.

The disjointed incrementalist model assumes very little structure in the planning process. Braybrooke and Lindblom (1963) suggest that, realistically, planners are "muddling through" the events of organizational life, that they are much more subject to the vagaries of events than even strategic planners would admit. However, *incrementalism* implies purposive action, direction. The image that comes to mind for this model is of Liza jumping from ice floe to ice floe, but trying desperately to reach safety on the other side of the river;[16] there is a direction and a goal.

In education, there is passionate will to keep learning alive, even though the particular system may require massive change. Of course, it does seem at times that the "will" is directed more toward keeping the system alive, because it is not easy to agree on what a good education really means. We do muddle through much of the time. One might go so far as to propose that every child is the subject in a continuing experiment in learning.

There are many occasions when the model describes very accurately the frustration of trying to decide what progress in education really means and of trying to move an unwieldy system toward that progress. We swing from streaming to integrated grade levels, from whole language to Hooked on Phonics, from management by objectives to goal-free planning, and from the whole child to back to basics, or national standards.

Is progress intensive emphasis on math and sciences in the Japanese model or developing each child's own interests and talents? Is progress an internationally competitive work force or creative humanists? This debate about what a good education means is not new. Carnochan (1993) says it has been in progress at least since the early 1800s. "Liberal education remains a belief system that survives not so much through institutional self-understanding as through continued acts of faith. . . . In other words, I don't think we know very well what we're doing" (quoted in *The Stanford Observer,* September 1993).

Education is the great human experiment, and there are many dimensions to humanity. It is not surprising that we may move in "disjointed" steps; what is awesome is that we may also move in increments. Certainly, if we compare dropout rates from the 1950s with those rates today, we find a dramatic change: in Canada from about 56% to the present average rate of 16%. And historic events in 1992 and 1993 provide some evidence of progress in world relationships. If education must accept the blame for riots, violence, family breakup, and disturbed children, may it not also accept the credit for "a giant step for mankind,"

[16]Stowe, H. B. *Uncle Tom's Cabin.*

for a handshake between historic enemies, for wonder drugs, for Stephen Hawking's contribution to knowledge, and, through his example, for our greater awareness of human potential?

Nonrational, individualist models recognize that individual members and participants do not have one world view. Goal-free and learning adaptive models are similar in many respects to disjointed incrementalism. They propose that organizational development is a learning process, that learning and development are particular to the individual, and that each member "writes their own text" of the organization.

If we apply the logic of these models to curriculum and schooling, we are struck with awareness that each child "writes his own curriculum," learns within his own frame of reference. Such awareness is at the heart of many of the recent proposals for change in education. Goal-free planning, disjointed incrementalism, and learning adaptive models assume that change takes place slowly and only within the individual's own bounded reality.

This world view asserts that adapting to the complexities of organizational life is both more realistic and more humanistic than controlling all variables. As Burrell and Morgan demonstrate, people who hold this world view do not deny structure, but they see structure as multiple, fluid, and individual. Therefore, planning must be conscious that there are many "butterflies in Mexico," in Chicago, in Whitehorse, in Bakersfield, Toronto, Paris, Halifax, Atlanta, or Johannesburg. Planning is not a process for controlling results, but for controlling parameters and preparing for variation in order to increase the probability of accomplishing what has been defined as success.

Thus, planning as a real activity may often be disjointed, muddling, or unclear in goals or in means, or it may be arbitrary, rigidly myopic, or self-serving. But any activity that is labeled *planning* is intentional; it has direction and purpose. It is no longer reasonable, or even possible, to have one meaning for good education, for success. But it is possible and necessary for educational planners to plan for something, for the best system and the best results that we can imagine at this moment, in this place. If there is one lesson that is brought home again and again in teaching graduate students and in working with educators in the community, it is that there is a passionate desire for our children to have a better education and a better chance than we had. That is a powerful force, a force that is channeled and made effective by plans.

Quinn's (1980) logical imcrementalism model is an adapted strategic planning model. It has the characteristics of a procedural map that does not differ radically from other strategic planning models; however, the mental image, the mind-set of logic plus increments is somewhat different. It "says" that the power of logic is a useful tool, that planning is for getting somewhere, but that increments are acceptable.

For most situations in education, logic plus increments is a modest model for development. At the present moment as we move toward a new century, social, economic, political, technological, and psychological pressures are such that incremental change is not keeping pace. Explosions are occurring in every education system around the world. There is a tendency to conclude that planning for the long term is wasted effort, that, at best, we should focus on immediate issues. In fact, we believe that just at such a time as this is when the "long view" is most important and useful.

Cybernetic theory tells us that we need not strain ourselves to keep constantly on course. We may swing back and forth, but the image of the target will keep us on a generally true path. That is the underlying message of incrementalist models. *Disjointed* is a descriptive term, and disjointed incrementalism is more descriptive than prescriptive. It tells us what did happen, how it looks in retrospect, not how to take the next step. For this reason, we prefer the image of logical incrementalism, which proposes that we take the next logical step, which gives a map to follow, and assumes that planning for education is worthwhile. We propose that logic based in values is the most effective basis of planning. A plan that is logically derived from values is adaptable to changing conditions. It can accept progress through increments, while keeping the focus on the holistic end desired.

The third issue raised in all current discussions of organizational planning is who shall be involved in developing the plan and how and when shall they be involved. It has been said that this is more an issue of managerial style than of a planning model. But it is an important issue for planning, since plans are intended to point out the desired direction for future action by all participants. Chapter 7 addresses issues related to the dynamics of participation in educational planning and choice.

Dynamics of Participation

THE DYNAMIC PROCESSES DIMENSION

THE processes proposed as the third dimension involved in planning and decision making are what we have called in Figure 6.4 the dynamics of participation. This dimension is of a different nature from that of the conceptual and norming process dimensions. One basic difference arises from the fact that *participation* has meaning only in terms of a formed group. We do not speak of participating in a group of people waiting on a street corner for a bus, although we could speak of norms of behavior for such a group. We do not speak of participating in a conversation with one other person, although we might say we thought it out or developed the idea with her/him.

Participation in organizations has developed an even more specific meaning or connotation. It is used almost universally in reference to bringing subordinates or interest groups into decision making and planning. That is, it is thought of from the perspective of the administrator; however, the issue of participation has expanded greatly in recent decades as teachers, parents, and community groups have become increasingly insistent upon involving themselves in choices made for education.

Demand for participation in planning for education is a growing social phenomenon. Interest groups call for review and revision of systems of education to make them more relevant to new visions of the future. Participation is at the heart of proposals being debated in well-known, practice-based journals such as *The Kappan, Educational Leadership, Education Canada, Administrators' Notebook, NASSP Bulletin,* and *The Principal* and in newspapers and TV documentaries. School choice, teacher empowerment and teacher recertification, restructuring schools,

229

national standards, authentic testing, moral curriculum, mainstreaming, and the place of the Arts have all brought new voices into discussions about the nature and purposes of North American education systems. In all of these debates, questions raised are whose voice shall be heard, who shall decide, and whose interests shall be attended to.

School choice would grant a stronger voice to parents; national standards give more power to federal education specialists. Restructured schools would result in more participation in school operation by community members; teacher empowerment would have a greater professional impact. The call for moral curriculum and strengthened values comes from one set of voices, for emphasis on needs of special groups from another. These are the practical, operational questions that arise from a general, growing demand by the people for more ''say'' in the education of our children.

How to deal with these multiple voices raises all of the issues of participation in planning and choice in education. The questions to be asked about participation are not new. They are the same questions to be asked about all organizational activity: who, what, when, where, why, how, and how much? But participation is a complex phenomenon not easily pinned down. It is like mercury; if you try to put your finger on it, it slips off in some unexpected direction, or it fragments and scoots in all directions at once. An action can be seen as effort to increase participation by one member or to strengthen control by another.

Participation is no longer concerned only with who shall be involved in planning and determining organizational direction, how and when they shall be involved, or how much influence (weight) the different members or groups shall have. These questions come from the position of authority, the organization. The same questions from the perspective of individuals are: who will get involved, when will they become active, how much influence can they develop?

In Figure 6.4, the dimension of dynamics of participation proposes that two forces operate to determine the structures of participation in planning. The poles identify the organization and the individual as being agents of influence, as determining who will participate and in what manner. The two perspectives, organizational and individual, define the meaning of participation in operational terms. If these two forces are, indeed, the agents that determine participation, then we must recognize that participation does not have the simple straightforward meaning one would infer from the literature.

Questions of the dynamics of organizational life are not unilateral. Who will and who shall participate in any planning activity both help determine whose voice will be heard—the voice of The Prince, as Beneviste (1989) calls the organization (or as common parlance would have it, *they,* as in "*they* won't let us; *they* decided"), or the voice of The People. *How* participation will take place is the question of the structures of organizational life, and there are structures that govern life in all organizations. Charters, contracts, policies, job descriptions, schedules, and norms all define formal structures of participation.

But that only raises the more fundamental question of who will determine the structures. Few are content now with formal, hierarchical structures, so who determines how many voices will be heard, in what forums? Who determines whether particular voices will make a difference? Who determines whether a voice will speak or how it will speak? The answers to these questions are critical, because whose voice will be heard determines, in large part, how a plan will be developed, whose interests will be served, and what sources of knowledge will be accepted.

The reality of organizational dynamics is much more fluid and subtle than the relationships spelled out in formal documents and agreements. The reality of participation ranges from enforced or willing compliance to determining direction. If, at one pole, centralized authority establishes directives, policies, regulations, functions, and responsibilities, then participation implies acceptance and compliance. At the opposite pole, a group of members, acting in concert, may force or persuade the central authority to accept a policy or program. Such a group could be a union, an association, a group of parents, or community activists. Or the mass of individuals, acting independently as individuals for their own personal interests and benefit, could cause policy to form, as principles of market economy or Jeffersonian democracy propose will happen.

Changing planning and decision making from an administrative action to a group process creates a whole new dynamic of interaction. Every member of an organization and, in particular, every member who becomes involved in a planning group for an organization has habits and preferences that orient them in one direction or another. They have habits of thinking, perhaps of thinking analytically and logically, with a preference for objective knowledge. Or their habits of thinking may be intuitive and projective, and their preferences may incline them toward subjective perceptions, attitudes, and values.

Similarly, they have habits of acting. For some, norms and customs may lead them to accept the organization and its goals, interests, and needs as the proper regulator of action. For others, expectations, customs, and personal ideas of "right" lead them to consider that the organization will prosper most by supporting and developing needs, interests, and goals of all members.

The third set of habits and preferences that each individual brings to planning sessions is habits of will. Individuals differ in strength of will, in commitment, and in confidence in their own powers to act. Will, commitment, confidence, and one's powers to act determine whose voice will be heard in a group and in an organization. It is through the will of individuals (groups of interested parties) or the organization or the "powers that be" (the central authority, which Beneviste calls The Prince) that choices of orientation are made in planning.

Is it the organization, the powers, that establishes the structure for making decisions, by contract, constitution, or job descriptions. Or has the will of the stakeholders, the people, acting through democratic vote through silent persistence, or through violent resistance, shifted the balance of power to the individualist pole? The balance of power shifts constantly in organizations as in national life.

Until quite recently in education, efforts to maintain the system or to gain better working conditions, to change and develop programs, were not thought of as political activity. Politics was considered unethical or unprofessional; efforts to shift power were discussed in terms of leadership style, group dynamics, or negotiation. Accepting as reality the fact that power and influence are factors inherent in participation may make it possible for members to focus on issues, rather than on personalities. At the same time, it reminds members that their greatest power may lie in concerted action.

Certainly, the balance of power in education systems has shifted greatly since the early 1900s. In many systems, it has been as recent as mid-century that a uniform salary scale existed, that individual teachers were not subject to the whims and fancies of board members or their children for security. In 1943, a woman teacher was reprimanded severely for wearing slacks downtown on a weekend in a bitterly cold Nebraska winter. Today, women teachers often wear slacks to work. As recently as the 1940s in many systems, a woman who married was immediately dismissed; today, women continue to work in the last trimester of pregnancy.

In mid-century, male professors and university students were expected to wear jacket and tie in classes. Today, both men and women students frequently wear shorts in university classes. Acceptable appearance for male teachers at all levels today often permits long hair, jeans, bare feet in thongs, earrings—all manner of dress that could have resulted in immediate dismissal only a few decades ago. In mid-century, elementary teachers were paid less than their secondary colleagues; today, almost uniformly, salary is based on education and experience, not on level of teaching. Today, contracts frequently spell out teacher-pupil ratios, number of periods of teaching required, number of work days, kinds of teaching, and work assignments that may be made. Dismissal of a teacher is a long and arduous process that requires involvement of associations or unions. All of these changes are evidence that teachers have participated successfully (through representative unions or associations) in decisions that affect their security and working conditions.

Unionization and anti-monopoly legislation are two of the great social movements that shifted the balance of power in regard to organizations. Although teachers' unions never gained a strong foothold in the United States (in contrast to Quebec where the syndical units wield great power in education), unionization changed the balance of power internally for all organizations in regard to working conditions, safety, and security. Even though it is professional associations that have been the voice of educators in most of North America, unionization in the private sector demonstrated the powers of unified voice and action. Unionization in the private sector aided teachers in gaining a measure of power over their personal life in the organization.

In education, decisions that importantly affect teachers' personal organizational life have to do with salaries, work, and working conditions. Few would deny the fact of participation in such decisions, regardless of their opinion of the results. Therefore and increasingly, the focus has shifted from what Maslow might have characterized as safety and security decisions (or McGregor as "satisficing" decisions) to motivating or self-actualizing decision questions. What constitutes a good education? What is the role of the school in society—to create a competitive work force and economy or to enhance the humanity of a people? How shall teaching and learning be balanced; what are the priorities for education; how can both standards and individual differences be maximized?

Questions such as these are the issue of participation debates in the late twentieth century. They are planning issues more than decision issues, because they require a long view, and they recognize the fact that although control of the future is not possible, preparation for the future is essential. These questions inevitably bring in the public, the clients of the system, and inevitably raise questions about fair access and proper service in education. Anti-monopoly regulation changed the balance of power externally regarding public access to fair prices and services in the marketplace. Proposals for vouchers, school choice, and local school management are direct attacks on the monopoly of public school systems.

These issues, the issues of planning for the future, require a broad view of participation, a view of participation as more than delegation of decisions or voting on key issues. Chaos theory tells us that every action is an act of participation; every act is an independent decision that nudges the organization in one direction or another. Participation, therefore, can be seen as very close to leadership, very close to involvement in the direction education should go and in the road it should take to get there. Participation in planning and decision making should be thought of as involvement in leadership for education. Hamilton (1991) sees the change as a shift toward political and moral perspectives on planning.

Until the late 1970s, educational literature focused more attention on decision making than on planning. That is still true, although to a lesser degree. An ERIC search for the period from 1982–1993 gives the following picture of relative emphasis:

Planning Citations		Decision-Making Citations	
Planning	1472	Decision making	8862
Models of planning	87	Models of decision making	35
Planning and participation	12	Decision making and participation	0
Planning and leadership	28	Decision making and leadership	189

Participation – 722 citations

The primary consideration of this book is planning and tools useful for planning quality education. The aim in this chapter is to consider what has been learned, both through research and practice, about participation as a leadership tool in planning activities. Since, in the literature of educational administration, participation has, until recently, been associated with educational decisions, much of the discussion that follows will necessarily be concerned with participation in decision making. A later section will discuss some of the work in aspects of education other than administration that provide insight into participation in planning. The last section will present philosophies and processes used in specific groups as tools for effective participative planning.

Participation and the Dynamics of Participation

The phrase *dynamics of participation* in this discussion has been used, rather than simply *participation,* because it implies that we will attend to the continuous cycle of action as decision theory and planning theory both describe it, rather than to the tip that is visible at the moment of choice. The dynamic processes of organizational life are interpersonal, social, and political. They may be initiated by the administrator (the organization) or by an individual or a group of individuals, and they affect structuring for action, action itself, and the effects of action. Thus, the dynamics of participation include preparing for participation by structuring situations where planning takes place, the actual participation that does take place, the effects on members and the organization, and activities that take place as a result of those effects.

Definitions of participation found in the literature and, indeed, most analyses and studies that address issues of participation are more specific, although the perspective may be that of the organization or of the individual. Mohrman, Cooke, and Mohrman characterized most research in the domain as "limited to the vertical distribution of decision-making involvement and influence" (1978, 13). However, Bacharach et al. say, "While some researchers characterize participation as the delegation of decisions from superiors to subordinates, others characterize it as the 'bottom-up' influence subordinates have on superiors' decisions" (1990, 127). Duke, Showers, and Imber (1980) used the phrases *participation, involvement in decision making,* and *shared decision making* as synonymous. All of these definitions focus attention on actual participation at the point of making decisions and on immediate effects.

Firestone (1977) gave an even more specific definition, one which is more limiting to the researcher, but which could open the door to a much wider interpretation. He defined participation as "formal opportunities for teachers *to be present* during the process of making decisions about school improvement'' [quoted in Firestone and Corbett (1988), 332, emphasis added].

Firestone is making a distinction between participation and involvement. Of course, the term *participation* implies involvement for most people, not just presence. Although many educators would agree that ''being present'' is a necessary condition for participation, few would accept it as a sufficient condition. In fact, teachers are often heard to remark, ''Well I was at that meeting, but I didn't have anything to do with that decision. (I didn't vote) or (I voted against it).'' Strangely enough, both behaviors are viewed as not participating in a decision. The point Firestone is making is that, by not voting or by voting ''no,'' they *did* participate in the decision. His point is very similar to the well-accepted position that a decision not to decide *is* a decision.

A fascinating incident that took place during the Consensor® study cited earlier (Burns, 1988a) illustrates very well the strangely limited perception of the meaning of participation often held and underlines the distinction Firestone is making. In one student group, the faculty advisor had a very good relationship with the thirty or so students on council. There was easy give and take in discussions, and the group was very clearly one that both listened well and developed ideas well. One student proposed a ''slave day,'' and the teacher immediately reacted, ''Oh, no! We're not going to have that kind of thing.'' The students persisted, giving ideas about how it could be worked. Still the teacher responded, ''Oh, no, never.''

Finally, one of the students said, ''Let's vote with the Consensor.'' The Consensor video showed the bar graph of responses, with votes ranging from two to ten, giving a mean of 7.4. The teacher then said, ''Well, you voted . . . no, I mean *we* voted to have it, so we will.'' The student said, ''That's right, sir, you were in there too. You were on the low side, but you added to the 'yes' '' (Burns, 1988a). This was a most important insight into the reality of participation. It is perhaps unfortunate that we are not able to express, and see, the *strength* of a ''yes or no'' more often, to see that every response is a contribution to choice. Abstaining, or absenting, oneself adds to the powers of the winning side. It is a form of participation not generally acknowledged in research, although it is often purposeful, being intended to make a statement of position.

Conway defined participation in decision making as ''the sharing by two or more actors . . . in *the process* of reaching a choice'' (1984, 19, emphasis in original). He identified two loci of PDM (participative decision making), internal and external, and identified three variable formats of participation found in education systems: *mandated versus voluntary, formal versus informal,* and *direct versus indirect* (by representation). Conway considered his definition of variable types of participation comparable to those of Dachler and Wilpert (1978) and Locke and Schweiger (1979). The inclusion of voluntary, informal, and indirect forms of participation recognizes that participation is as much the prerogative of the individual, as of the administrator. That duality of forces structuring participation in decision making is not universally acknowledged in the literature, however.

Traditional Views of Participation

Participation in decisions has been organized in many formats. A decision is a relatively concrete, or specific, point in action. It is easy to identify, and a number of well-accepted practices have been developed by which participation takes place. There may be formal voting or informal agreement by consensus. There may be surveys or polls. There may be a directive and ready acceptance. There may be negotiations and arbitration. There may be quietly passive resistance or violently active conflict, either of which might lead ultimately to negation of the decision. All of these modes of participating in decisions exist in every organization.

However, studies of participation in decision making have generally assumed that the process consists of open discussion and debate, have assumed with Firestone that a necessary condition is presence, and that the process ends at the point of decision (confirmation and establishment of one alternative). The view held by the general public is much the same as this research perspective. So when the researcher asks, ''How frequently do you participate in the decision (on one issue or another)?'' (Mohrman, Cooke, and Mohrman, 1978, 18), the response will no doubt be couched in terms of this quite limited definition.

Moreover, traditional studies of decision making have viewed postdecision issues only in terms of such outcomes as satisfaction, morale, and productivity. They have not included as part of the study the follow-up steps generally incorporated into definitions of decision making, the steps of evaluation and modification of the decision. Thus, in traditional studies, coming from management and administrative theory, there is a hiatus between definitions of the decision-making process and assumptions about the nature of participation in decision making.

Rationales for Participation

Rationales expressed in the literature also reinforce the organizational perspective on issues of participation. Propositions about the reasons for incorporating participation in decision making into organizational action arise from several different value systems. Greenberg (1975), in a review of the literature, found four basic rationales proposed. He found that, within the management school of organizational theory, which includes both the scientific management and the human relations schools, the primary focus is *productivity,* the proposition being that participation increases productivity.

In the humanistic psychology school, which includes personnel management and human resources, the rationale he found is the healthy development of the individual (self-actualization, quality of life). Two other schools of thought based the rationale for participation on education of the worker — the democratic theory school proposing to develop and encourage democratic action and the participatory left aiming to educate workers to an anti-capitalist, revolutionary perspective. Dachler and Wilpert (1978) found four similar sets of reasons proposed: democratic, socialistic, human growth, and efficiency and productivity.

Conley (1991) and Bacharach and Conley (1986) proposed that the orientation toward productivity is bureaucratic and that most research combines the bureaucratic model with a human relations perspective. They offered an additional rationale for participation, a professional model that

> emphasizes the professional discretion and expertise of teachers in diag-nosing and addressing student learning needs. . . . The bureaucratic model suggests that participation serves to gain teacher compliance with administrative decisions. The professional model suggests that an aim of participation is to accord teachers the rights they expect, as professionals, in the school workplace. (Conley, 1991, 228)

Shedd (1988), like Beneviste (1989), proposed that the distribution of participation in an organization should be considered in terms of power. Teachers negotiate for power and for control over policies and direction on the basis of expertise. Their expertise is knowledge of needs of the students, the clients, and the processes of learning. Although couched in terms of politics and negotiation, Shedd's rationale for participation of teachers in decision making is also the professional model. The rationale is power to determine what constitutes contribution (good service) to the clients, rather than to the organization as an employer. The professional rationale proposed by Conley and Bacharach and Conley and the powers of expertise rationale proposed by Shedd emphasize the role of individuals, the members, in determining the meaning and structure of education. These rationales place the people in balance with the powers, to act as full partners.

Participation as a Factor of Administrative Style

Because of the limited definition and the focus on the moment of decision, most organizational literature on participation considers it a factor of administrative or management style—how much involvement in decisions does the administrator (the powers) permit or encourage. Vroom and Yetton's well-known proposition (1973) identified five levels of participation (AI, AII, CI, CII, and GII). Their "tree" analysis of how to decide which style to use further reinforces participation as an administrative or leadership style. Is it a decision that everyone will accept without question—use AI (Autocratic #1); is it a decision that will require widespread understanding and commitment—use GII (Group #2). Similarly, Tannenbaum and Schmidt's (1973) seven-level model of choosing a managerial style relates the possibility of involvement in decision making by subordinates (the area of freedom) to managerial style. Models of leadership style proposed by Reddin (1971), the 3D model of administrative style; by Hersey and Blanchard (1977), group maturity analysis; and by Blake and Mouton (1978), the managerial grid, all involve degree of participation permitted/incorporated as a major criterion of style of management.

The levels of administrative style proposed by Vroom and Yetton and by Tannenbaum and Schmidt are hierarchies of the degree to which an administrator brings subordinates into the process of making a decision. A parallel taxonomy could be identified describing the degree to which an individual chooses to involve him/herself in a particular decision. Table 7.1 presents the two parallel taxonomies.

The taxonomy of individual participative styles proposes that mem-

Table 7.1. Taxonomies of Participative Style. Administrative Style Based on Vroom and Yetton (1973). Individual Style Proposed as Parallel.

Administrative Styles	Individual Styles
Taxonomy of Participative Styles of Leadership	Taxonomy of Participative Styles of Involvement
AI (Autocratic method #1) Administrator solves problem or makes decision alone, using information available to self at the time.	SI (Self solitary #1) Individual does not involve self in decision. Does not discuss it with others.
AII (Autocratic method #2) Administrator obtains necessary information from subordinates. May or may not tell them what the problem is; they provide information requested only. Makes decision alone.	SII (Self solitary #2) Individual decides not to involve self but does discuss it with a few friends. Wants to find out what others think about the question.
CI (Consultative method #1) Administrator shares problem with relevant subordinates individually. Gets their ideas and suggestions. Makes decision alone, but it may reflect ideas and suggestions of subordinates.	SVI (Self voting #1) Involves self by talking with colleagues. Listens to ideas and suggestions. Attends faculty meeting. Does not speak out but does vote.
CII (Consultative method #2) Administrator shares problem with subordinates as a group. Obtains ideas and suggestions from group. Makes decision alone, but it may reflect ideas and suggestions of group members.	SVII (Self voting #2) Attends meetings on the topic. Expresses ideas and opinions to the groups. Tries to persuade others. Attends faculty meeting, speaks out, votes.
GII (Group method #2) Administrator shares the problem with subordinates as a group. Together group generates ideas, alternatives. Group evaluates ideas and tries to reach consensus. Administrator acts as chair, and accepts group decision.	SLI (Self leadership #1) Takes active role in meetings, perhaps chair. Expresses ideas and opinions. Listens to ideas of others. Speaks to other members and leaders individually and tries to persuade them. Attends faculty meeting. Speaks out and votes.

240

bers differ in their willingness to commit time and energy to matters outside their immediate area of responsibility. Moreover, individual interests vary from project to project and from issue to issue. As the zone of indifference proposes, there is, no doubt, a large number of activities that are important to the school, but that lie outside the zone of commitment of particular individuals. Teachers, in order to fulfill their own responsibilities to their own satisfaction, must leave some planning and choice to others.

The extreme position of noninvolvement is to ignore the decision, not to discuss it with others, to "stay out of it." That position may reflect many different underlying attitudes and perceptions. It may come about after a conscious acknowledgment that the issue should be decided or planned by others. Or it may result from a general unwillingness to do more than is absolutely required. At the other extreme, reasons for taking a very active, leadership role in a planning activity may be equally varied. Of course, it may be that the issue will affect the daily work of the individual; but it may equally be that the issue is one about which the individual has very strong feelings and so is willing to dedicate time and effort to resolving it.

The point being stressed in Table 7.1 is that both the administrator and the individual member (potential participant) have a range of approaches from which they choose to act in the specific instance.

Costs and Benefits of Participation

In most propositions of variable administrative style, it is assumed that there is, or will be, a positive relationship between a participative style and desirable organizational outcomes such as satisfaction, morale, and productivity. McGregor (1960), Odiorne (1976), and Argyris (1978) proposed such relationships. Studies in management by Drucker (1976), Driscoll (1978), Miller (1980), and Miller and Monge (1986) investigated the general pattern of relationships between participation, satisfaction or morale, and/or productivity.

One of the most frequently cited studies in this domain, Likert's 1967 study in the General Motors Corporation, found that "System Four Leadership" (participative) affected production positively. He introduced a training program in participative leadership techniques in various divisions of GM with positive results. More recently, reviews of Likert's data have raised the question of whether it was the attention given to managers through the training programs or goal setting, rather than the style employed, that produced the positive results (Melcher, 1976; Mitchell, 1979). These questions remind one of the serendipitous findings that came from questions raised after the fact in the Hawthorne Studies.

However, all of these studies pay scant heed to the role the individual plays in the reality of participation, to the fact that, in the final analysis, it is the individual who decides simply to comply or to become actively and productively a participant in determining choice and direction. Although the propositions in the literature assert desirable results for the individual worker—human growth, healthy development, and learning—studies of participation itself, as well as studies that investigate the outcomes of participation, have, until recently, accepted the organizational or administrative frame of reference. They have raised questions about the costs and benefits to the organization of greater participation. But individuals also weigh costs and benefits for themselves as each opportunity to participate arises. As folk wisdom has it, some people don't count the costs and others never "stick their necks out."

Duke, Showers, and Imber investigated costs and benefits of participation for teachers. They proposed five potential costs, and three potential areas of benefit. The greatest cost was found to be in terms of time. Benefits in the areas specified were uniformly seen as high. In individual interviews with the fifty participating teachers, other costs and benefits were proposed. Table 7.2 lists the areas hypothesized for the study and other costs and benefits revealed by the interviews (1980, 95−105).

While reported benefits outweighed costs, Duke, Showers, and Imber found that, "most teachers felt less than anxious to participate in school decision making and found little satisfaction when they did participate. . . . The majority felt that they had benefited little from participation . . . [and] voiced skepticism over whether their involvement had actually made any difference" (1980, 103−104). Only 20% of the teachers reported that they believed "shared decision making led to greater effectiveness or improved student outcomes." However, 38% believed that better decisions and better relationships among faculty members resulted, and 34% believed that teachers complied more readily with shared decisions (1980, 102). Figure 7.1 suggests cost/benefit questions that may be raised from the perspective of the organizational and individualist poles.

Table 7.2. Costs and Benefits of Teacher Participation in Decision Making, as Found by Duke, Showers, and Imber (1980, 95 – 105).

Costs	Benefits
Proposed for the study	*Proposed for the study*
Time	Self-efficacy
Loss of autonomy	Ownership
Risk of collegial disfavor	Workplace democracy
Subversion of collective bargaining	
Threats to career advancement	
Suggested by teachers	*Suggested by teachers*
Greater responsibility	Higher quality decisions
Blame for bad decisions	Greater effectiveness
Perceived as "rubber stamping"	Improved student outcomes
Feelings of frustration	Teachers more likely to comply with
Energy loss	decisions
Disillusionment	Closer relationships among faculty
Powerless	Enhanced chances for advancement
Possible poorer decisions	Greater appreciation of complexities of
No real influence	running a school
Probability of benefits low	

Source: Duke, D. L., B. K. Showers, and M. Imber. "Teachers and Shared Decision Making: The Costs and Benefits of Involvement." *Educational Administration Quarterly,* 16(1):93 – 106. Copyright © 1980 by Sage Publications, Inc. Reprinted by permission of Corwin Press, Inc.

Both administrators and teachers have to face realistically both sets of cost and benefit issues: organizational, and personal and professional. Recent reviews of the literature on participation in educational decision making have attempted to organize the sets of propositions made in the literature and clarify a generally fuzzy picture about the duality of costs and benefits.

Conley, for example, identified seven factors that have been considered in propositions and research, all of which need further careful analysis and study. The factors she identified are related to the general questions cited above as being inherent in all organizational activity: rationale for participation and possibility of influence (why), effects and outcomes of participation (what), form of participation (how), expectations and zone of acceptance (how much), inhibiting factors such as time and isolation (when), teachers' role (who), and domains in which participation may be desired or effective (where) (1991, 237 -256).

Similar questions have been identified in earlier reviews by Bridges (1967, 1970), Lowin (1968), Schmuck and Blumberg (1969), Green-

COSTS AND BENEFITS OF PARTICIPATION

THE INDIVIDUALIST POLE

SHALL I PARTICIPATE?
<u>Questions "The Individual" asks:</u>
Is this something I care about?
How will it affect me?
Will it make my work easier?
Do I have the time to do this?
Are there others who feel the way I do?
Will the others stand up too?
Can we make a difference?
Would my opinions be respected?
Is it worth the risk?
Do I have something to learn from this?

THE ORGANIZATIONAL POLE

**SHALL WE ENCOURAGE
PARTICIPATION?**
<u>Questions "The Organization" asks:</u>
Do we need special information?
Will this group be helpful?
Can we keep the trouble makers out?
Do we need everyone on board for this?
Do we have time for "participation?"
Can we keep control?
Can we risk getting them into the act?
Will it create a better working climate?
Is it worth the risk?
Do we have the skills to handle it?

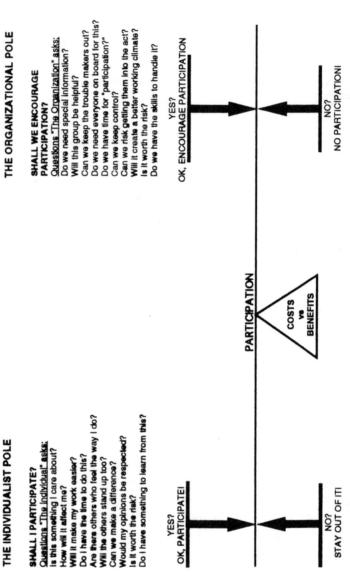

YES?
OK, PARTICIPATE!

NO?
STAY OUT OF IT!

PARTICIPATION

COSTS
vs
BENEFITS

YES?
OK, ENCOURAGE PARTICIPATION

NO?
NO PARTICIPATION!

Figure 7.1. Both the organization and the individual weigh the costs and benefits of participation.

244

berg (1975), Dachler and Wilpert (1978), Wood (1984), and Conway (1984). Many historic contributors to administrative studies such as Barnard, Simon, Griffiths, Argyris, McGregor, and Katz and Kahn have addressed these questions as well. Indeed it would be difficult to find any serious student of administration or organizational behavior who has not been concerned, from one rationale or another, with issues of participation.

But all of these factors imply questions that are asked by members, as well as by administrators. Research and practice are increasingly faced with balance between the powers and people. The fact that we do not have definitive answers, that we do not have formulae for participation, should be seen as evidence both of the reality of social change over those years and of the growing recognition of education as a profession. As such, it demands judgment and not rules, not formulae.

We should certainly work towards greater clarity and precision in analyses of and research into participation. But research will never provide the practicing administrator with rules that fit specific cases; research supplies only general guidelines, possible approaches. Every administrator and every participant has to deal with those same seven questions (who, what, when, where, why, how, and how much) in every specific instance. The greatest likelihood of effective participation results when benefits are maximized and costs are minimized for both teacher and administrator, but benefits and costs are both particular to the situation and to the individual. Figure 7.2 suggests the most effective combination of costs and benefits for administrators and teachers.

The perception of costs and benefits in any activity is very personal. To some degree, most individuals can vary their approach to working in and with a group for planning and decision making. However, most people have a comfort zone and a tendency to approach situations in a general pattern. The combination of approaches that will follow the minimum-maximum line differs with the time, the issue, and the people involved.

Studies of Participation in Education Systems

In education, most studies of participation in decision making or planning have investigated relationships of participation with measures of satisfaction and relationships of satisfaction with various organiza-

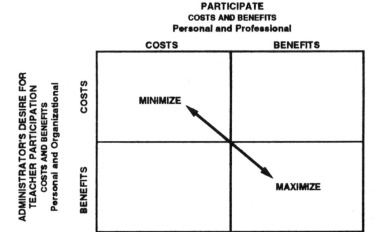

Figure 7.2. *The greatest likelihood of effective participation results when benefits are maximized and costs are minimized for both teacher and administrator.*

tional outcomes. In general, a three-stage hypothesis of relationships is proposed:

Participation → Satisfaction → Motivation and/or Productivity

There is a huge body of such studies, much of it found in the human resources field. Within this body of literature, factors such as stress, autonomy, and job design may be examined as causes of satisfaction/dissatisfaction or as outcomes of those conditions. Many of the studies propose a relationship between satisfaction and productivity; however, in the studies that have attempted to measure educational productivity, results are ambiguous and dependent on other factors such as goal clarity, decision domain, and personality characteristics.

Participation is generally measured by self-report. Responses are recognized as perception data, and some studies have compared actual and desired participation to determine areas in which teachers wish more involvement. Belasco and Alutto (1972) studied satisfaction with participation as a global score across twelve areas of possible involvement in decisions (also Alutto and Belasco, 1972, 1973). They found that teachers who were most satisfied with their level of participation (participation saturated) were also most likely to remain in a position despite inducements to leave (considered a definition of satisfaction).

This group was comprised of older women teaching in elementary schools. Feminists interpreting these findings in the 1990s might not be willing to accept the definition of satisfaction posited. Being likely to remain in a position has as much to do with realistic options available and family constraints as with satisfaction. In the 1960s and early 1970s, women were still glad just to have an interesting, well-paying job, particularly one that gave them holidays and work hours that corresponded to those of their children. They are less satisfied with such rewards in the 1990s. In the current job market, "realistic options" is an important factor of choice for men, as well as for women, of course.

Mohrman, Cooke, and Mohrman (1978) used Alutto and Belasco's domains but measured the difference between desired and actual participation in each of the twelve areas to compute a deprivation score in each area. They hypothesized that decision opportunities are related to two general domains in education: technical and managerial. They found more participation and less deprivation in the domain related to instruction (the technical domain). They found less participation and a greater sense of deprivation in the managerial domain (hiring, budgets, assignments, PR, etc.). They concluded, "In general, participation in the Technical Domain decisions was related to various affective responses of teachers to their job situation. Participation in Managerial Domain decisions . . . did not have a significant direct relationship with satisfaction or role stress scores" (1978, 25). Isherwood and Taylor (1978) also used Alutto and Belasco's instrument in a study of teacher participation in mandated school councils in Quebec secondary schools. They found no significant relationship with job satisfaction.

Bacharach et al. (1990) examined nineteen areas that are similar to the twelve presented by Alutto and Belasco within which teachers might participate in decisions. They distinguished between approaches that investigate actual participation as a global phenomenon [as, for example, the study by Alutto and Belasco (1972)] and approaches that investigate differences between desired, or expected, participation and actual. They characterized the first type as nonevaluative and the second as evaluative. They took the position that the evaluative approach (determining differences between desired and actual) would yield more insights than the nonevaluative, because it would identify more clearly areas in which increased participation could be productive.

Rather than the two domains, managerial and technical, they hypothesized four:

(*1*) Organizational-Operational (O-O) focuses on development and evaluation issues.

(*2*) Personal-Operational (P-O) focuses on technique and use of materials.

(*3*) Organizational-Strategic (O-S) examines issues related to resource allocation.

(*4*) Personal-Strategic (P-S) examines issues related to career.

The highest levels of deprivation were reported in the Organizational-Operational (O-O) and the Organizational-Strategic (O-S) domains. Both elementary and secondary teachers wanted more participation on issues of development and evaluation and on resource allocation issues. This finding fits well with one's personal sense of what might be closest to teachers' concerns. Resource allocation has to do with teacher-pupil ratios, supplies and support, and work assignments. Development and evaluation affect the teacher's personal sense of security and fulfillment in work.

Correlations with measures of affective outcomes (job satisfaction, role ambiguity, role conflict, and goal commitment) differed, but deprivation in three domains – development and evaluation (O-O), technique and use of materials (P-O), and resource allocation (O-S) – correlated at the .05 level or better with all outcome measures. Deprivation in the career issues domain – Personal-Strategic (P-S), accounted for a very small proportion of variance.

Bacharach et al. underlined the fact that global participation may be a "politically correct" idea but that teachers are not as concerned about participation in some areas as in others. They suggested that administrators look at participation more thoughtfully and analytically. They said, "For example, administrators concerned with increasing teacher commitment to organizational career goals may wish to restructure teacher opportunities to participate in particularly those decisions concerned with . . . [development and evaluation and/or resource allocation] . . . matters" (1990, 165). Exercise 7.1 asks you to review recent decisions made in your school or planning activities that are currently in progress and identify which domain they belong in and the level of participation that was (or is being) employed in reaching a decision.

A summary of responses given to this exercise in workshops is presented in Appendix A. Participants have frequently suggested that

1. List decisions that have recently been made in your school or planning that is currently in progress.
2. Identify which "domain" of participation each belongs to: O-O; P-O; O-S; P-S (see Key*).
3. Estimate the degree of participation that took place or is taking place. Use Vroom's Taxonomy: AI, AII, CI, CII, or GII (see Key**).
4. Estimate the degree to which you participated. Use the self-participation scale provided: SI, SII, SVI, SVII, or SLI (see Key†).

Issue	Domain	Organizational Participation	Self-Participation

*Domain

O-O: Development and evaluation (Organizational/Operational)
P-O: Techniques and use of materials (Personal/Operational)
O-S: Resource allocation (Organizational/Strategic)
P-S: Career development (Personal/Strategic)

**Level of Organizational Participation:

AI—Admin. Solves problem and makes decision alone
AII—Admin. Gets needed information from others; analyzes and makes decision alone
CI—Admin. Shares problem with individuals; gets information and ideas; makes own decision
CII—Admin. Shares problem with group; gets ideas and suggestions; makes own decision
GII—Admin. Shares problem with group; group gets ideas and alternatives; group makes decision

†Level of Self-Participation (your own actions):

SI—(Self, Level One) You do not get involved; do not discuss it.
SII—(Self, Level Two) You decide not to get involved but do discuss it with a few friends.
SVI—(Vote, Level One) Talk with colleagues, listen; attend faculty meeting, don't speak, do vote.
SVII—(Vote, Level Two) Attend meetings; give ideas to group; try to persuade others and vote.
SLI—(Leadership One) Take active role in meetings; express opinions; speak to leaders; give ideas and vote.

Exercise 7.1. Decision participation exercise.

this exercise could also be used with groups in a school to compare teachers' perceptions with those of the administrator.

Studies of the relationship between productivity and participation in educational decisions are, as can well be appreciated, less common and also more ambiguous in results. Measures of productivity used in various studies reviewed by Conway (1984) included student tests, student ratings of teacher effectiveness, and critical incidents analysis. Conway concluded from his review of reviews and studies that there are many myths prevalent in the profession and in the literature. The strongest support can be found for a positive relationship between participation and satisfaction (Myth No. 5), but even that relationship depends on the type of decision and the degree of involvement (Conway, 1984, 32). He proposed that there are many more mysteries than absolutes, a situation that is particularly true in regard to productivity.

However, the recent profusion of studies of effective schools and proposals for school reform[17] leads to the conclusion that participation of teachers in determining goals and policies and in program design and development is a characteristic of effective schools. These domains for participation would be consistent with the Organizational-Operational (O-O) and Organizational-Strategic (O-S) domains in which Bacharach et al. (1990) found the highest deprivation scores. These researchers pointed to the demands for school-based management and teacher leadership proposals and concluded, "This study suggests the need to move beyond policies aimed at achieving across-the-board increases in participation in decision making . . . which may be well intentioned and politically popular [but will not] have the desired effect" (Bacharach et al., 1990, 164). The demands for reform and the issues that teachers seem willing to spend time participating in seem to be moving in the same direction. However, as Duke, Showers, and Imber caution, "Since the benefits of shared decision making accrue, not from mere involvement, but rather from a combination of involvement and influence, it would seem unwise to offer opportunities for shared decision making which do not include provisions for actual influence over decisions" (1980, 104).

---

[17]For examples of reports on effective schools, see Filtgaard and Hall (1973), Rhine (1981), Reid, Hopkins, and Holly (1987), and Stellar (1988). For examples of educational reform studies and reports that emphasize teacher and/or parent participation in planning and decision making, see Boyd (1990), Zager and Rosow (1982), Doyle (1990), Lane and Walberg, (1987), and Murphy (1990). See also many recent issues of the practice-based journals cited.

Participation Viewed from Other Perspectives

There are studies in some areas of education that fit into the gaps left by administrative studies between participation, as it is generally defined, and the dynamics of participation. Recent studies in the field of curriculum planning and development, for example, have proceeded from a perspective termed *formative evaluation* [see Perry-Sheldon and Anselmini-Allain (1987), Clifford (1988), Saroyan-Farivar (1989), Patton (1990), Elliott (1991), Carson and Sumara (1992), Delamont (1992), Pinar and Reynolds (1992), Cunningham (1993), Rossi and Freeman (1993)]. These studies consider a decision as the beginning of a process or as merely a point in a continuing process. The cycle continues with investigation and analysis of post-decision activities and learning, modification of the curriculum plan in light of findings (new planning), further investigation, and, again, modification.

In the language of decision theory, this model might be called formative incrementalism, a model that has a definite goal, good learning or understanding, a goal that is relevant both for educators (the planners) and for students. This model assumes that a plan, a curriculum, is tentative: a hypothesis, rather than a decision. It assumes users as participants in the planning process and assumes that both groups of participants learn from what takes place *after* the decision is made, the formal commitment to implement a curriculum. The model assumes that both decision makers and students move toward better understanding through the process.

This orientation to curriculum development seems to provide one of the missing links between decision theory and participation research. It considers action before and after a decision point; in fact, the decision itself is seen as of less importance than what develops after the decision. This orientation arises from the phenomenologist base and makes the assumption that life in an education organization is a continuous flowing stream, moving from one state (decision point) to another, affected by every leaf and grain of sand. The stream is flowing inexorably forward, and the leaf and the grain of sand participate in the changing of states, the decisions.

An experience in a junior high school in California in the 1960s illustrates this broad view of participation. Back then, in the "way it used to be" world, boys wore dress shirts to school, with long sleeves, collars, and shirttails. We had a rule (had made a decision) that shirttails must be tucked in.

Suddenly, one year, it became a fad for the boys to pull their shirttails out and let them hang. Well, rules will be rules, so we spent a great deal of time stopping boys in the halls. ''Put your shirttail in'' became a constant refrain. We didn't get any argument, they tucked the tail in, walked on down the hall and pulled it out again until they met the next teacher. That dance of the shirttails continued until school let out.

That summer, the market was deluged with sport shirts with short sleeves and no tails. When school started in September, no shirts were tucked in. We shrugged our shoulders and accepted the inevitable ''change of state.'' A thousand little decisions had made the big one irrelevant, but if asked, would anyone say they had participated in a decision?

The direction an education system goes is more the result of a thousand grains of sand than of decisions. Plans point the way we hope to go, and decisions point the way we expect to go, but actions determine the way we *do* go. This is what Friedmann (1973) argued when he proposed that we should worry less about the quality of decisions and more about the quality of action. Every action is a grain of sand in the life of the school. Every act is an act of participation that leads toward the future.

PARTICIPATION AND RATIONALITY

The fact that every action is a decision, or choice, and that every intentional action can be seen as, to some degree, planned, does not suggest, however, that there should not be formal planning for concerted action and concerted direction in school systems. It suggests, on the contrary, that comprehensive planning should take into account the realities of social life and social values, as well as the history that precedes the present. Planning takes the emphasis off present states and habits and places it on possible futures, on where we would like to be.

Questions about the importance of and the outcomes from participation in planning by subordinates and interest groups are currently a major focus of attention, both in the literature and in practice. Several recent books are good examples: Carlson and Awkerman's 1991 collection of essays and research reports, *Educational Planning, Concepts, Strategies, Practices,* addresses issues related to participation in planning for education. Beneviste's 1989 book, *Mastering the Politics of Planning,* focuses directly on issues of the dynamics of planning in, for, and by groups. Kaufman and Herman's book, *Strategic Planning in Education: Rethinking, Restructuring, Revitalizing* (1991) emphasizes the continuous search for future directions in the light of changing technologies and social forces. All recent discussions of planning are concerned with questions of how to engage members in organizational planning and how to ensure that engagement, involvement, and participation move the system toward better programs and quality education for all.

Although effective participation is a critical factor in planning, it does not lend itself to being incorporated into planning models or systems. As stated in Chapter 6, the conceptual processes of planning are spelled out in procedural maps, in the step-by-step logic of relationships of individual elements of a plan to each other and to the whole. The logic is expressed in the relationships proposed between goals and standards, between goals and action alternatives, and between priorities expressed (value-cost perspective) and resources committed. Norming processes are expressed in the specifics of goals set and activities included. These two aspects of a plan arise from two logics: a serial logic and a logic of wholes. Both of these logics are potentially the impetus for change and are technologies of change, but, as a technique, each is essentially static; they exist as describable states.

Participation processes, group dynamics processes, are not serial, nor are they holistic. They are interactional and developmental. If life generally exists as chaos, that state between order and randomness (as chaos theory proposes), then participation is the effort of individuals to "nudge" life toward some order, some vision that leads away from the brink of randomness, entropy, and stagnation. One participation event produces countless subtle waves of action and reaction. Like waves in a pond disturbed by a stone, the waves of participation spread and rebound, cross each other, and create new waves. An act of participation can come from subjective beliefs, intuitive insights, objective data, or logical inference. There is no way to predict the effect of one idea, one suggestion, one question, or even one frown or smile on the whole. There is no map to, or model for, participation in planning. And yet there are patterns and tendencies that shape the whole.

All individuals come into a planning situation with their own conceptual orientation—toward a rational comprehensive or a learning adaptive mode of thinking—and with their own norming orientation—toward an organizational or an individualistic mode of action choice. We might say that individuals "own" their own positions on conceptual and norming dimensions. When they plan by themselves, their positions are clearly reflected in their final plan.

Individuals own their position on the dimension of dynamics of participation as well – toward power residing in members, toward power residing in the organization, or toward a sense of being in control of their own destiny (and thus "writing their own texts") or of control belonging in the organization (with the organization as an instrument of domination). When planning takes place in an organization, the question becomes whose position will dominate at any particular time and what will trigger *group* orientation.

That question is basic to the dynamics of participation. It is the question reflected in the poles of the third dimension in Figure 6.4 – whose will shall dominate: the will of members or the will of the powers. In this sense, *members* includes, of course, all stakeholder groups, clients, employees, professional groups, community activists, and parents. Members may be individuals or groups; they are the interested parties, the people.

To determine who shall participate and whose participation will be validated has a great deal to say about the nature of the plan that will be developed; therefore, structuring participation is a fundamental process in an organization. The dynamics of structuring participation is one of the primary forms that organizational activity takes. It may take place through use of force, by negotiation, by silent compliance or noncompliance, or by public protests and mass action; in any form, it is *political* activity.

Political activity involves the use of many techniques intended to shape and direct the voice of the people, but political activity also includes the voice of the people speaking. Participation, in the sense that dominates organizational literature, implies that there are provisions made to let the voice of the people be heard. Participation opportunities are intended to provide the forums for bringing into debate the different knowledge bases, beliefs, attitudes, interests, values, and needs of all interested, concerned parties.

Participation in planning or decision making means the way that action of members, the interested parties, is structured and structures itself for the purpose of developing a plan, making a decision, implementing an activity, or promoting a project. Therefore, the two poles of the continuum, organizational and individual, take their meaning not from the orientation that the plan itself takes, but from the group through which the structures of participation are realized. The formal answers may be spelled out in constitutions, charters, contracts, job descriptions, and the authority of the organization, the powers; however, the reality of participation is also dependent on personal interest, willingness to be involved, interpersonal relationships, and the shifts in power and influence among organizational members.

Differing Sources of Meaning of the Three Processes

The reality of participation is not solely activity that can be observed. It does not take place only within the group sitting as a group. Much of what should be seen as participation in planning or decision making takes place in the hallways, in the lounge, in the car pool, over the phone, or one-on-one in the union or association meeting. It takes place through research, surveys, interviews, workshops, advocacy approaches, letters, and casual conversations. It takes place through parent interviews, open house, and volunteer parents. It is this reality that has given the phenomenological approach its power as a tool for studying groups. All of these forms should be thought of as part of the dynamics of participation in education, just as customer purchases are part of the dynamics of participation in determining the direction any business takes.

Moreover, it cannot be assumed, as much of the organizational literature on participation assumes, that broad, general participation of members and interested parties in an organization is based on subjective, nonrational, intuitive knowledge. There is no reason to believe that knowledge from experience is less valid, less rational, less objective, less empirical than knowledge from statistical analysis.

A very interesting essay by Richard Nelson (1993), in a recent issue of *Audubon,* is titled ''Understanding Eskimo Science.'' He says,

> I believe their greatest genius, and the basis of their success lies in . . . the nexus of mind and nature. For what repeatedly struck me above all else was their profound knowledge of the environment.
>
> Several times, when my Inupiaq hunting companion did something especially clever, he'd point to his head and declare: ''You see – Eskimo scientist!'' At first I took it as hyperbole, but as time went by I realized he was speaking the truth. Scientists had often come to his village, and he saw in them a familiar commitment to the empirical method. (p. 102)

Teachers also have an accumulated fund of knowledge – about student and class group behavior and about abilities, interests, and values. As Maeroff says, ''Knowledge is the currency in which a teacher deals; yet the teacher's own knowledge is allowed to become stale and devalued, as though ideas were not the lifeblood of the occupation'' (1988, 474). Perhaps the biggest mistake the organization (the powers) makes in education systems is that it does not encourage and validate sufficiently the exchange of and accumulation of that knowledge. It is too often relegated to the teachers' lounge and is treated as gossip. Living discourse is a proper means of transmission of knowledge if it is accorded that status.

The traditional assumption that underlies almost all discussions of planning models is that participative planning is not based in objective knowledge—is not rational. This position is clearly presented by Adams (1991) in his Figure 1.1. In this figure, Adams places subjective, interactive and consensual models of planning at one pole of a continuum and objective, rational, and technicist models at the opposite pole. He concludes, "Attempts to remain 'as rational as possible' are not necessarily helpful and are sometimes harmful; they suggest, in effect, even though planners have acknowledged that the assumptions and techniques of rational planning are inappropriate, the only hope of achieving even partial success, nevertheless, rests on proceeding as if they were appropriate'' (1991, 18).

Friedmann, too, equates objective knowledge with expert knowledge and rational planning (1973). All discussions of planning or decision-making models in organizational literature begin with an explication of the rational comprehensive model and move through incrementalism toward what may variously be termed consensual (Adams, 1991), moral (Hamilton, 1991), innovative (Friedmann, 1973), improvisation (Inbar, 1991), strategic (Kaufman, 1992), political (Beneviste, 1989), or collaborative (Sheathelm, 1991). In essence, all are proposing a general movement from rational and organizational to participative or individualist, leading to the conclusion that rational is at the opposite end of a continuum from participative, individualist, and subjective, that rational and participative or rational and subjective cannot coexist peaceably.

My experience leads to a different conclusion. My position is that objective knowledge and rational planning and decision making can come from individuals, that, indeed, rationality can be based in subjective interests, wants, and needs. Would not everyone recognize the rational plan in the illustration by Joel (aged ten) of the life cycle of the walnut (Figure 7.3).

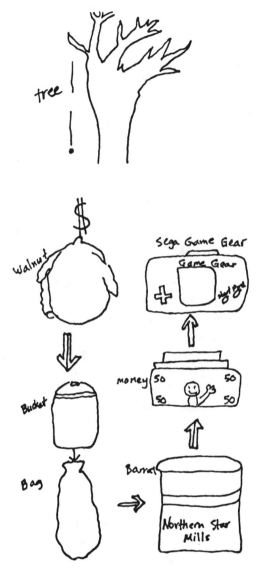

Life Cycle of a Walnut

Figure 7.3. *Rational planning is a part of the everyday thinking of everyone. Joel (aged ten) creates a plan for getting new electronic gear: the life cycle of a walnut.*

Joel had an objective, the purchase of Sega game gear, and he collected walnuts and sold them to accomplish his aim. But the fact that a ten year old could conceptualize the process as a process demonstrates very clearly that rationality is not the property of statisticians, technicians, and experts. It is a part of the everyday thinking of everyone. Thinking that is based in cultural beliefs, social norms, or human needs has its own good reasons, the empirical facts of common ways of viewing life.

Interacting Dimensions

In Figure 6.4, it is proposed that three sets of processes are involved in all organizational planning and decision making and that each of those processes is variable. We proposed that each set of processes (conceptual, norming, and dynamics of participation) varies in orientation from the organizational and generalizable to the individualist or personal pole. We presented those dimensions as parallel. The point we have been developing in the last section is that these dimensions are not actually parallel: they intersect, and their intersection may be at different points on the three continua. That is, a planning activity could take place in a group (be participative) and yet rely heavily on objective, quantifiable data. Or the Autocrat I (Vroom and Yetton, 1973) could conceivably attempt to support the needs and interests of particular interest groups, becoming the benevolent monarch or the charismatic leader. Figure 7.4 reorders the three dimensions to represent two of the opposing perspectives commonly found in the literature.

The organizational perspective, which dominated theoretical propositions in early twentieth century literature, proposes (or assumes) that functional factors, internal to the organization, dominate at the point of intersection where the three processes meet for action. Organizational aims, needs, and interests are the focus of norms; objective, quantifiable knowledge (considered rational) is the basis of conceptualization; and centralized, technicist members are those involved in planning activities and projects. Such a perspective tends to look inward, toward maintenance and control. It easily falls into an elitist and hierarchical mode, which may explain the ''ivory tower'' image that planners earned in that early period.

Certainly, North American businesses developed almost magically in the early twentieth century by turning people, as well as products, into masses. Education systems followed suit, and planning for education

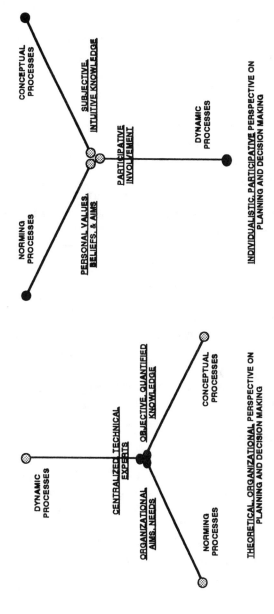

Figure 7.4. *The configuration of processes in planning and decision making is a function of knowledge base, norm orientation, and involvement preferences:* ⊛ *individualistic pole,* ● *organizational pole.*

259

turned its attention to how to accommodate masses of students and batches of knowledge. The formula that developed was (number of students) × (age level – as a surrogate for ability) × (specific skill to be learned) = (efficiency and low cost) + (effectiveness and good learning). Certainly, it seemed reasonable to expect that programming (forty students) of (similar ability) to learn (fractions at the same time) should be low in cost and should produce a high level of knowledge because attention could be focused.

Such a formula worked well, too, when *knowing* was the desired aim. Today, when such aims as thinking skills, creativity, and adaptability to change have gained priority, the rational comprehensive, generalist, batch approach to planning for education is less appropriate. The demand is for more awareness of and sensitivity to individual development, and those aims are in addition to general national educational achievement. Thinking about planning in education has refocused from organizational to individualist and societal or national.

The individualistic, participative perspective on planning as it is developing in the literature tends toward the intersect of broad participative involvement; subjective and intuitive (and experience-based) knowledge as a source of rational thinking; and personal values, beliefs, and aims as appropriate bases for educational programs. The locus of planning at the individualist pole on the three dimensions takes planning out of the system boundaries into the many environments from which members come. In Figure 7.4, inverted arrow-blocks are used to suggest the internal versus external orientation of these two planning perspectives.

Other Configurations

The two configurations presented in Figure 7.4 represent intersections at opposing extremes of the three poles. Realistically, action varies much more dynamically than at the extremes; the three processes of planning could and do intersect at many different points on the three continua. There are very few occasions in real planning on which data bases are totally objective or totally subjective. Equally, there are few occasions, today at least, when planning or decision making is the exclusive property of a technical expert or central administrator without reference to interested groups. Truman's sign, ''The buck stops here,'' did not mean that he had not heard and heeded the advice of many concerned parties. It is a rare administrator in education today whose

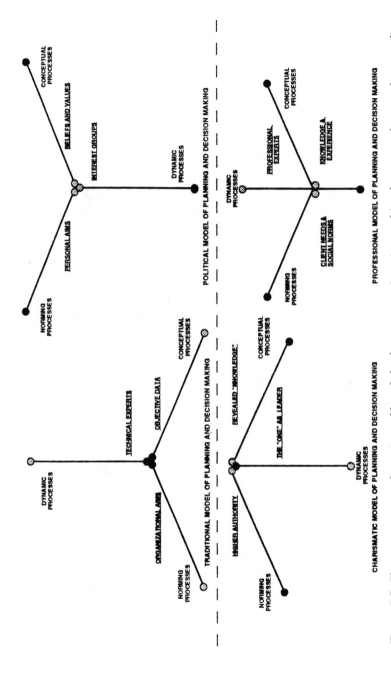

Figure 7.5. *There are many configurations of knowledge base, norm orientation, and involvement preferences that may direct planning and decision making:* ○ *individualistic pole,* ⊗ *individualistic pole,* ● *organizational pole.*

261

life is not filled with meetings where school issues are debated. Figure 7.5 suggests four other possible configurations of the ways the three types of processes might intersect under differing models of planning for education.

It is proposed that, in the *traditional* model of planning, all three types of processes are oriented primarily toward the organizational pole of the continuum. There is a senior management office or division, and technical planning experts prepare plans essentially by themselves. Theoretically, at least, they base choices on objective, quantifiable data and on organizational norms and aims. In education systems, this model might be used for some system planning such as for buildings, budgets, and transportation systems. Even in such planning, however, the traditional model would almost invariably be modified.

The *charismatic* model is proposed because charismatic leadership is often looked upon very favorably by practicing educators. The charismatic leader often pulls people together, creating a powerful force for concerted effort. Ideal goals are stressed, and the right way is made clear. Charisma is, however, highly centralized, with direction coming from the "one." The leader leads, and the followers follow. The basis of knowledge is subjective-intuitive or revealed to the "one," and the definition of good is from a higher authority, the intuition of the leader.

The terrible effects of charismatic leadership gone beyond the bounds of reason have been brought home to the North American public in such recent events as the Waco confrontation and the mass suicide led by Jones. Such things could not happen in education systems? Not too many years ago, a school principal who was beloved by his community thought nothing of demanding a complete reworking of a 2000-student high school schedule into a modular schedule two weeks before school opened for the fall term. The subordinate charged with the task worked without sleep for ten days, completed the task, and had a total physical and emotional breakdown. The principal graciously received the plaudits of the community and board for his innovative approach and farsightedness. That is an extreme example, but perhaps most educators can recall one administrator who made choices on the basis of personal preferences, brooked no alternative suggestions and no questioning of decisions, and did not seem to count the cost in heavy time and effort burdens placed on teachers.

The third model suggests the points on each dimension that are generally characteristic of the *political* model of planning. In the political model, interest groups participate, contribute, and attempt to influence decisions. Groups whose need has a high social profile develop powerful political pressures for change in education. Physical education in the 1960s, parents' access to cumulative records, sex education, condoms in dispensers, politically correct reading lists, and fair treatment of boys (the 1960s) or girls (the 1990s) have all been the focus of debate and pressures for change.

Such issues are not "provable" in the scientific sense; positions are taken on the basis of personal, social, and cultural norms, beliefs, and values. Thus, while the dimensions intersect at the personal, individualist pole, the political model is oriented to the larger society, the environments within which the school exists.

In the fourth model presented, the *professional* model, the dimensions are also depicted as intersecting close to the individualist poles. However, the dynamics of participation is seen as less broadly participative than in the political mode. Participation may involve professionals with different kinds of expertise, so a multidimensional perspective is probable. Professionals may also consult and involve nonprofessionals (parents, interested groups), but the professional model tends to assume that choice should ultimately be in the hands of professionals. Conceptual processes rely on knowledge, experience, insight, judgment, and hypothesis — both objective and subjective processes. The needs and best interests of the individual client are considered paramount and are examined both in terms of personal development and social and cultural norms.

These four models are only examples of the possible ways in which the three processes — conceptual, norming, and dynamic — might interact with each other in any specific planning cycle. It would be nice if a perfectly balanced model could be said to be ideal. Would an absolute balance of organizational and personal needs, of objective and subjective knowledge, and of participation by organizational experts and interest groups be most productive or most useful in all situations? Obviously not.

What the best, most useful, most productive combination might be for developing a particular plan can never be proven. The "proper" mix depends on many factors related to each dimension — knowledge and conceptualizing skills available, social climate related to various needs and interests, and interest and determination to be involved. Participation is a human activity, and it requires a great deal of humanity on the part of every member to make it work well.

The movement toward decentralization in North American school systems has demonstrated that the three processes interact and affect each other. *Time,* in its Education Section, December 1989, said, "Parent-led councils (in Chicago) have also been handicapped by their lack of training, particularly in budgetary matters." With broader participation comes the necessity for factual knowledge (quantitative), as well as values and belief positions (qualitative knowledge). About New York City, *Time* said, "New York City decentralized in 1969; since then, many of the 32 district school boards have become nests of political patronage and criminality. A third are currently under investigation for charges ranging from embezzlement to drug dealing." Decentralization brings to the fore the importance of balance between personal interests and group needs and between subjective and objective knowledge.

The bimodal model of educational leadership or administrative style based on degree of participation involved (Vroom and Yetton, 1973; Tannenbaum and Schmidt, 1973) presents a limited perspective on factors that comprise choice of planning approaches. However, the literature taken as a whole reveals that there are three essential processes that affect planning — conceptual, normative, and dynamic. Educational planners, whether acting on behalf of the powers or the people can contribute more productively when they recognize the many possible orientations that arise within the three process domains.

PARTICIPATIVE PLANNING GROUPS THAT WORK

Planning and decision making are the two processes that determine direction in an organization — where action is to be headed and what action is considered most likely to take the organization where it wants to go. Whether the organization is understood to be the powers or the people is the issue of participation. Are the people to be just implementers of choices made and projects developed by the powers, or are they also to be choosers and planners? Is participation of the people to be a battle from outside the Walls of Jericho? Is the "underground economy" principle (seen as subversive by the establishment) the only effective means at hand for influencing choice? Or is it possible to structure participation both broadly and effectively?

Common School Planning Groups

Many of the situations in which planning in schools is routinely a group activity are not described in administrative literature. Perhaps this is because they are particular to the situation in which they take place and cannot be readily generalized. They exist essentially within the context of the group involved and are a product of that group. Perhaps, also, it is because such groups are action-oriented (have not been research-oriented), so results from such group planning and decision making have not been codified and made available for debate and development.[18]

Every school could provide examples of such groups that have been important in the life of the school. They are usually small and may have as few as two participants. They are not part of the formal structure of the school (as are departments, councils, and core groups, although such groups may also work effectively together), but they generally have the blessing of the principal and are not seen as subversive or disruptive. They usually are planning something that they, themselves, will implement, a project that is accepted as within their ''zone of performance'' by both administration and colleagues. Processes in such groups would probably take the form of the professional model presented in Figure 7.5.

Other participative groups may be more formal, being established by the administration, though temporary. Curriculum study groups that meet to plan instructional units, choose new textbooks, and develop evaluation procedures exist in every school system. Project groups plan and implement successful music or drama presentations, art fairs, sports field days, fashion shows, and academic contests or demonstrations. Such groups cut across many specialist and hierarchical lines and also tend toward the professional model of process proposed.

Participative groups that incorporate members from the general public may be called a task force. They may be established state/provincewide or as national task groups. In general, their mandate is to study the system of education for some general purpose. The recent task force in the United States that examined proposals for innovative schools and funded eleven is one example. The annual Phi Delta Kappan Gallup Poll of public assessment of the schools is another type of broad, general participation in the business of education.

---

[18]Recent work called "action research" has begun to transmit the living discourse of daily life in education systems to a broader public. That work is context specific and anecdotal, and therefore it is difficult to learn from it, to apply understandings gleaned to new contexts. The body of that reflection on action should, however, ultimately provide important insights into interests, needs, and ways of enhancing learning [see, for example, Elliot (1991), Carson and Sumara (1992), Pinar and Reynolds (1992), Cunningham (1993)].

In Canada, Royal Commissions are established to study the status of education in one province or another and to make recommendations. Such a Royal Commission is funded for a period of three to five years. It calls for and studies thousands of "briefs" (statements of position) from hundreds of interested groups and individuals. It may make recommendations regarding the structure of the system, curriculum, standards, testing, finance, teacher preparation, and a host of other issues. Quebec's Parent Commission and Alberta's Worth Commission are two of the best known examples.

The Parent Commission (so named for its chair, Monseigneur Parent) presented its conclusions and recommendations in five volumes from 1963 to 1966. Some of its main proposals were

- Establish a ministry of education (somewhat comparable to a state department of education).
- Provide free public education for all Quebec youth through grade thirteen (this includes two years of cégeps).
- Establish comprehensive high schools to accommodate these students through grade eleven.
- Put curriculum emphasis on math, sciences, and technology to develop a modern competitive work force.
- Establish a system of low-cost universities located in seven regions of the province, accessible to young people after completing cégep.

All of these recommendations were implemented in the decade that followed submission of the report.

Thus, it cannot be said that participation in the business of education does not exist; nor can it be said that participation has no impact. On the contrary, it would be hard to find any new practice, program, or technology in schools today that did not have much of its origin and impetus from the people, teachers within the system, university research and development groups, community interest groups, and general social, cultural, and technological changes in the environment.

What, then, does the continuing call for more participation mean, and what are the implications? We have discussed the willingness of members to participate in planning and decision making in terms of cost and benefit. Both the organization and the members must weigh costs and benefits. We have proposed (Figure 7.2) that the greatest likelihood of effective participation results when benefits are maximized and costs minimized for both members and organization. Costs and benefits are not measurable only in dollars or in time, of course. The emotional drain of failure and the emotional "value added" of success are also factors that weigh in when participation is at issue. Thus, an important element of effective participation is creation of a "win-win" setting.

Mary Parker Follett proposed long ago (1924) that there are three types of resolution of conflict: domination (win-lose), compromise (lose-lose), and integration (win-win). Domination, or win-lose, can result in an autocratic situation but also in a democratic vote. One party wins, and the other loses. A vote is always a test of dominance, and it does not reveal the strength of commitment or willingness to implement a decision. Dominance should be a last resort technique for schools, the order from above. It should be reserved for situations in which neither compromise or integration has been possible.

Compromise, lose-lose (or win some-lose some), resolution results when both or all groups give up something to gain some part of their aims. It is probably the most common form of resolution in education and in regard to work situations generally. Labor or contract negotiations are a very public illustration of the technologies of compromise, but negotiations occur at every level in education and on every aspect. Daily, students test the limits of each teacher's "zone of acceptance" of behavior permitted in the classroom, due dates on assignments, or acceptance levels for marks. Who has not scaled up or down the marks/grades on a particular assignment? Are not some teachers well known for high or low marks?

To achieve integration, the win-win outcome from a decision-making situation is, Follett proposed, the most satisfying and most positive form of resolution. Follett proposed that, when there are conflicting proposals on an issue, each is focused on a subordinate part of the issue—on some secondary aspect. By stepping back and looking at the issue from a larger perspective, it can be seen that the parties involved have already accepted the main issue at hand, the goal or outcome, and are only disagreeing on the means. The recent NAFTA debates are an example. Both sides wanted a strong North American economy, a strong work force, and a strong world trade position, but there were passionate disagreements as to whether NAFTA would be the best means to achieve these valued ends.

Values are the "big view," the focal areas of common ground. When such focal areas, the underlying values, are recognized, it is often possible to invent a new alternative approach that will accommodate both of the seemingly conflicting proposals. It is by recognizing that planning requires inventing new means to a desired end that integration of conflicting proposals is possible.

Integration requires depersonalization of issues, the most difficult task to achieve in a participative group. Depersonalization of issues results when members give up personal emotional attachment to ideas ("that was my idea, and attacks on the idea are attacks on me") and personal attitudes toward the people who presented them ("s/he's always trying to run things; s/he never listens to anyone else's ideas"). Without the subliminal issues of who presented an idea and how it makes one look to win or lose, discussion can face the question, "Which, or what combination, of these proposals would benefit us all most?" It was to create the win-win climate that the SPEC® planning philosophy and process were created at Canadian Pacific, Ltd.[19]

SPEC Planning Philosophy and System

The SPEC (Structured Planning, Evaluation, and Control) System was designed as both a philosophy of planning and as an integrated set of technologies that supported the philosophy. Bob Irwin had taken to heart Marshall McLuhan's "the medium is the message." He proposed that the physical setting, the processes used, and the way information was developed and structured should all send the same message: the task of a planning group is to *build a plan together* using the best information available.

With this message in mind, he designed a physical space and a set of equipment and furnishings that would enhance the message of working together and of building a plan. The three main components of Irwin's design were 1) the physical space, which included room design, furnishings, and materials; 2) a common SPEC process, including composition

---

[19]The SPEC planning philosophy and process were developed in the 1960s as a technology for servicing departments and divisions of Canadian Pacific, Ltd. in project planning. The service group responsible, Canadian Pacific Systems Services (CPSS) later expanded to sell its services to corporations and governmental bodies. Ultimately, it was integrated into Canadian Pacific Consulting Services (CPCS), which had originally contracted only for overseas development projects. SPEC is a registered trademark of CPCS, Ltd., and SPEC process is copyrighted. This discussion is based on my experience as a senior planning consultant with CPSS for a period of five years. A key person in the development and successful use of SPEC process was Bob Irwin, Director of CPSS. I am greatly indebted to him for the opportunity to work with the group and to contribute to the technologies used.

of the group, roles of participants, and the way information was to be handled; and 3) common information space, the way information was structured to build a plan. Each of these three components will be discussed in turn.

The SPEC Theater

The first important element of Irwin's concept was that the room where group planning takes place should be a theater-in-the-round. He believed that sitting around a conference table creates a confrontational or power negotiating "mental set" that immobilizes people and stagnates ideas. He designed a room in which participants would be able to move around easily. The room was large, well carpeted, and furnished with comfortable, roll-around arm chairs and low tables. There was no boardroom table around which participants could negotiate for influence positions. Figure 7.6 shows the SPEC theater in use.

The second major proposition was that participants should not be taking notes, nor should there be a secretary. All notes should be visible to all participants at all times; therefore, all walls of the room were white enameled sheets of steel. Each note or comment was written on an individual card (3 " × 7 ") and clipped to the wall with a small magnet. These cards were disposable, so if someone questioned a statement or the use of a word, the card could easily be thrown away and a new one written. Often enough, one comment put up on the wall triggered a whole new set of factors that should not be overlooked and that might not have been brought into the picture without the building process that was taking place on the walls. The floor was often littered with discarded cards, but the version being worked on at any one point in time had been developed by the group.

The product of that use of space was that everyone had the same "picture memory," the same knowledge of how the plan was developing. But even more important in terms of group planning, the psychology of taking an idea from one member and placing it on the wall in context with what was already there turned it into group property to be worked on and developed by the group. Thus, the process allowed the group to avoid repetition, the endless summarizing of "where we are" or "what we have said," and the endless recycling of debate. If it was on the wall, it was on the wall; it could be reviewed silently or publicly, and the context of new ideas could be the issue. Does it go with personnel

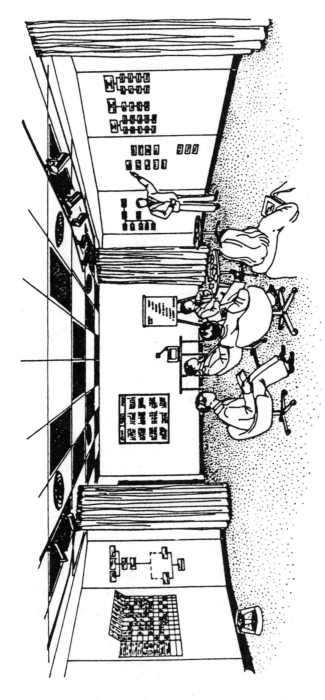

SPEC THEATRE IN USE

Figure 7.6. SPEC theater in use showing, from left wall to right, RAC (responsibility, authority, communication) matrix; hierarchy of goals analysis; planning calendar with days numbered from one to 365; participants board; SPECNET®; session plan; and (far right) work breakdown structure. [Source: Canadian Pacific Consulting Services (1985). SPEC is a registered trademark of CPCS Ltd. and SPEC process is copyrighted. CPCS Ltd. Montreal, Canada. Reproduced by permission of Canadian Pacific Consulting Services.]

development or with program content? Does it remind us of other issues that must be considered?

After a planning cycle was completed, all participants received a hard copy printout of everything recorded on the walls, in the same format as it had been created – network chart, work breakdown structure, matrix, etc.

Schools cannot generally afford the munificence of a planning theater. Even school districts would be unlikely to dedicate a room and furnishings full-time to planning – the more so because, once people became accustomed to working in such a flexible space, one theater would not be able to accommodate all demands on it. CPSS had four theaters operating, and demand was heavy. A simple alternative is to hang temporary sheets of plastic against the walls. Walls in schools are often light beige, so the plastic sheet serves well. It readily takes the 3M Magic Plus (on and off) Scotch Tape, and plastic can also be written on with erasable ink. We used this modification whenever we went out of Montreal for a consulting session, and I used the same technology in planning sessions at McGill.

Figure 7.7 presents the SPEC Planning Philosophy, identifying the elements of the three major components, physical space, SPEC process, and information space.

Common SPEC Process

The second major component of Irwin's planning philosophy was the common process, which included how the group should be composed, who should be participants, the roles they played in the group, and the way information was to be handled. Each element of the SPEC process was developed to contribute to the potential of a win-win planning climate.

There were always two moderators, one to animate discussion and one to record ideas and information and structure them on the theater walls. The moderators were senior planning consultants, neutral to the project being planned. (Neutral and objective are not the same. Objectivity is a value position; neutrality requires acceptance of both objective and subjective positions. The role of a neutral moderator is not to demand objective proof of a statement, but to put it before the group for discussion and judgment.) Each moderator had experience in developing the structuring tools commonly used for planning – networks, matrices,

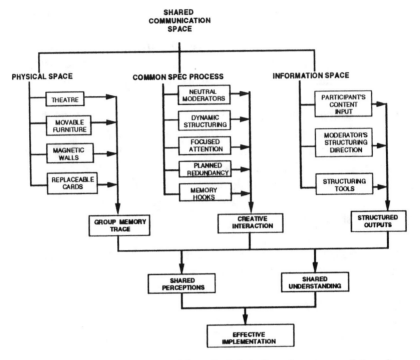

Figure 7.7. *The SPEC planning philosophy is based on the concept of shared communication space: the physical theater, the SPEC process, and shared information structured on the theater walls. [Source: Canadian Pacific Consulting Services (1985). SPEC is a registered trademark of CPCS Ltd. and SPEC process is copyrighted. CPCS Ltd. Montreal, Canada. Reprinted by permission of Canadian Pacific Consulting Services.]*

etc. Thus, drawing out information from participants and organizing the information to make it most understandable and useful was the role of the moderators. Providing information and ideas was the role of the participants.

In planning for schools, the use of consultant-moderators is not generally possible. It is more difficult for educator-leaders to remain neutral in a group planning session, but there should be an effort to be as neutral as possible while ideas are being generated. It is also important for such leaders to know different structuring tools and how and when they can be used productively.

A third important element of the SPEC process is that all points made are written on 3 × 7 cards and clipped to the theater walls. Personal note taking has a tendency to focus a participant's attention on their own "thinking out" process—how to say it, how to get the idea down. As this goes on, the participant "tunes out" of discussion temporarily. Since in a SPEC session, all notes are taken by one of the moderators and clipped to the theater walls, attention is focused on the plan, and the thinking of *all* participants is directed at the best way to say what has been said, the best way to make a particular idea clear. Attention is also focused on the structure of the whole picture—where does this point fit into the whole and what other issues does it raise. In "SPEC speak," this was called dynamic structuring.

Planned redundancy, another SPEC term, referred to three facts: that note cards were disposable, that a card clipped in one place could easily be moved to another as the whole plan developed, and that it was important to have a "fall back" or "fail safe" position. Nothing was "fixed" until the whole plan was built; moreover, this flexibility reinforced the idea of continual review of the whole, given the "new" that had been added.

This technique is, I believe, from all of my experience with it, one of the most useful techniques for planning or for developing ideas in a group situation. This use of a single, disposable card for each idea, with each card clipped temporarily to its place in the structure of thinking, is far superior to flip charts with lists of points inscribed. It does away with scratching out and writing over. There is always a clean copy in front of the group, and, in that copy, every point is in its rightful place. Cards assist and encourage the group to be flexible and developmental in approach.

The fifth element of the SPEC process was called memory hooks. This concept encouraged participants and moderators to work always toward "the heart of the matter." The consultants believed that the heart of any idea, expressed in telegraph style would be easier to remember than long explanatory sentences. The aim was to use few words to focus on the key aspects of the point being made. The guiding rule was one verb, one object noun, and one identifying adjective if needed. The 3 × 7 cards used contributed to this focused brevity. Examples might be

Verb	Adjective	Object	Verb	Adjective	Object
Prepare	survey	instrument	Clarify	contract	terms
Report		progress	Consult	—"X"—	group
Assign		tasks	Get	central	approval

All five of these elements enhanced participation and interaction among the members of the group. Many graduate students, after receiving training in modifications of these techniques, reported using them successfully in their school planning groups.

Information Space

The third major component of the SPEC planning philosophy was the information space created. As has been said, the role of the moderators was to stimulate thinking, questioning, and development of ideas. They were responsible for making sure that ideas were recorded correctly, that the recorded note expressed precisely the meaning intended. They were responsible, also, for the structuring pattern, for the planning tool being used, and for ensuring that the structure built reflected and clarified thinking.

An important principle that guided moderators was "structure absorbs complexity." By this principle, Irwin meant that organizing ideas, facts, or issues into sets (integrally related groups) creates a framework for reflection and development of related elements. Structures aid memory, reveal relationships, and trigger expansion and clarification while, at the same time, reinforcing holistic perception.

Participants always included senior officials, support staff whose information was critical, and operating staff—those who would be responsible for implementing a project. Participants were responsible for contributing data, ideas, and implications for their own group and for the organization as a whole; questions, challenges, and clarifications; and opinions and judgments.

Although it may not be feasible to adopt the whole of the SPEC process in school planning groups, the three major components, somewhat modified perhaps, can be incorporated into any group planning situation. Group space that is arranged to enhance openness, interaction, and unity; processes that encourage flexibility, neutrality, and development of ideas; and stimulation of ideas and information, plus structuring those ideas—these three components of a philosophy of participation can help create a productive environment for planning.

BUILDING A PLAN BASED IN VALUES

The ability to make plans and carry them out is the key aspect of human intelligence.
—*Hart (1983, 49; emphasis in original)*

A METAPHOR FOR PLANNING

THIS section will present the overall model of the Values-Based Planning System proposed. It will discuss the logic of relationships between elements in a constructed plan and how those elements are sequenced in the planning process, and it will describe how to create each of the elements of the plan.

As suggested earlier, the reality of how we customarily go about planning in education differs from steps that planning models propose. General planning systems described in the literature propose that effective planning starts with a clear statement of goals, objectives, wants, or needs and moves through a series of procedural steps to choice, implementation, monitoring, and modification [see, for example, Carlson (1960), Cunningham (1982), De Angelis (1985), Kaufman (1972), Sergiovanni et al. (1980)].

When planning is equated with problem solving, the first steps specified are to define the problem and then clarify the needs or goals (Ackoff, 1978; Cooke and Rousseau, 1981; Havelock, 1974). Both planning and problem-solving systems resemble a research model and can be characterized as hypothetico-deductive in orientation. Operational planning systems propose repeated analytical cycles expanding in detail as they move from mission or strategic planning to implementation or operation planning (Kaufman, 1972; McManama, 1971). These systems are based in analytical deduction, the serial logic described by Hart.

Other authors assert that there is no real possibility of a goal-based view for planning. Braybrooke and Lindblom (1963) suggest that we move in myopic, disjointed increments toward change. March and Olsen (1976) imply that decisions and change are the result of chance events,

275

fortuitous circumstances rather than planning, and that goals produce problems. Much of the curriculum theory and program evaluation literature today advises that the great potential for serendipitous learning is lost if evaluation is construed to mean determining success in meeting predetermined goals. Educators proposing this view think of evaluation as a goal-seeking experience, rather than as goal testing. They imply, or assert, that rational planning with clear goals and standards inhibits creativity and productive change.

It is my view that, if we accept the definition of evaluation as formative, we have not eliminated the reality of ''goal''; we have construed process as goal. Of course, educators continually attempt to refine programs and techniques, to make them work better. But what do we mean by *work better*? The ideas of work better and goal-free cannot be reconciled with each other; they are inherently contradictory. ''Will work'' always has some meaning to us. If it refers to process, it focuses on efficiency. If it assumes some end, aim, purpose, or goal outside of the process itself, it focuses on effectiveness. ''Better'' implies a valued level of outcome. Educators institute programs because . . .; we use technologies in order to. . . .

Thus, it can be assumed that all planning and all choice have goals, purposes, aims, or intended outcomes. Moreover, it is assumed that it is not possible to judge *better* unless we have defined that purpose or goal. However, it is also assumed that educational planning almost never starts with defining the goal. It almost universally starts with a proposal for action. I believe that ''goal check'' should be the first step after action proposal. Choosing action without a goal check could become ''weathervane'' choice, turning whichever way the wind is blowing.

The metaphor that I use to express the concept of planning is a camera. In this image, the focusing lens is a goal that expresses a value. The camera can focus broadly on a whole or narrowly on a particular. There are two camera techniques for focusing on an event as explained to me by M. Jacques Béique, former director of camera technology for Radio Canada in Montreal. ''Dollying in'' moves the camera toward the particular but maintains the focus on the whole, the setting. This technique is used when the setting itself affects the action—when the story or event could *only* take place in Paris or Calcutta or San Francisco. This is the planning focus. Goal check requires the camera to dolly in and out to see the overall perspective of the whole and to maintain that perspective in the particular.

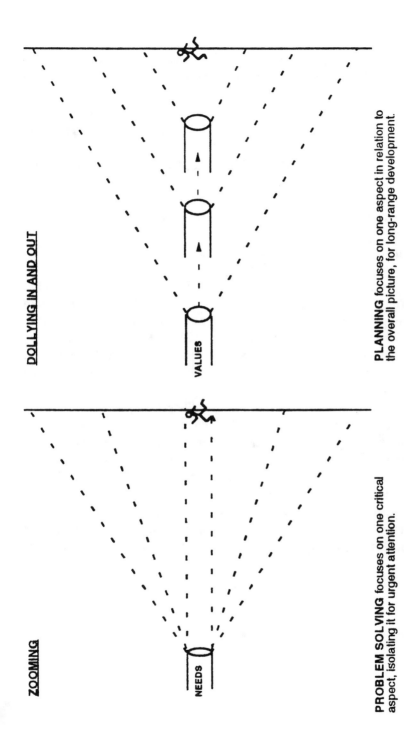

Figure III.1. Camera techniques illustrate the planning focus and the problem-solving focus. (Explanation of camera techniques courtesy of M. Jacques Béique, Radio Canada, Montreal.)

277

The other technique, zooming, changes the camera's focus to isolate the particular. This technique is used when the action itself is the story—it could take place anywhere. This is the problem-solving focus, necessary when the issue is crisis action. Figure III.1 illustrates the two techniques.

I propose that, although both planning and problem solving are important administrative skills, they are not the same skills and they do not serve the same purposes. Moreover, planning is not happenstance choice, disjointed incrementalism, or satisficing, although each of those ways of making choices has its proper place in our repertoire. We find it easy to accept, also, that "the best laid plans . . . gang aft agley" and that we should not be blinded by stated goals. Given all of those contingent realities, I propose that planning is a way of thinking and that, if it becomes a habit of thinking, then it becomes a "body knowledge skill," such as Zuboff (1988) describes. Then it becomes as natural as walking or using good manners or driving a car. If planning is a habit of thinking, it will not be necessary to construct a detailed plan for every activity or event. But for planning to become a habit of thinking, the overall picture of what goes into a plan must be imbedded in the mind, and the particular thinking processes needed to plan productively must be learned.

Section III describes the Values-Based Planning System proposed and provides directed practice for each of the thinking processes needed to construct a plan—a conceptual model of an educational activity, event, program, or project. The section starts with a discussion of logic in Chapter 8. This chapter reviews the classic forms of logic, deductive and inductive, and discusses how they relate to planning. Other forms of logic that enter into planning are then considered. Chapters 9 and 10 present the four stages of the Values-Based Planning Model: the meaning of success, value cost analysis, alternatives analysis, and action analysis.

CHAPTER 8

Logic and Planning

BASES OF RATIONAL THINKING

MOST educators would not consider themselves philosophers, nor would they be apt to assert a philosophical system. However, it is important to think philosophically, for thinking clearly and coherently is a second major contribution that philosophy makes to educators. Reasoning for educational choice and direction should be valid and logically consistent. Our profession's most fundamental proposition, its basis of action, is that we "do *this* in order to accomplish *that*." Reasons in support of such a proposition should be logically related to the major idea proposed, the purpose of the proposal. Beliefs about "how" should be logically related to "why." Although we do not want to allow ourselves to be boxed in by particular propositions, good practice demands that we be able to demonstrate the logic of relationships, to support our beliefs on some reasonable basis. Philosophical logic tells us how to determine if logical relationships exist.

Beliefs, Reasons, and Conclusions

In Chapter 3, some of the basic ideas of four philosophical systems that have had considerable impact on Western education systems were presented briefly. By looking at the different propositions made in those four systems (and perhaps others as well), we could become more conscious of our own beliefs and use them more productively to direct our planning and action.

The concerns that philosophy addresses are inescapably the concerns of education; indeed they are its heart and soul. The questions "What is reality?" or "What is real?", lead to what can be learned, what education should focus on, and what the curriculum should include or cover. *What is knowledge* leads to what "knowing" means. Does it mean remembering, being able to repeat or recite; understanding and appreciating; living and acting, experiencing fully; or being able to initiate, create, and invent. [These are the four "meanings of learning" presented in Figure 4.7 and in Burns (1993)]. The questions "How do we learn?" and "What is the source of knowledge?" determine the kinds of exercises, experiences, activities students engage in; the technologies and methodologies teachers use; and the structure of the education system itself.

The fact that people answer those philosophical (or basic) questions differently leads to different proposals about education. As we become more aware of the different answers to the philosophical questions, clear thinking for educational choice becomes more probable. Recognizing different possible answers makes it easier to see the relationships between a particular proposal, a particular answer, and the primary values involved.

If it is proposed that students should learn about city management by participating in city council meetings, we are considering one possible answer to the questions "What is the source of knowledge?" and "How do we learn?" If one parent group tells us, "Japanese students spend 85% of their time on math and language, and we should, too," and another says, "All students should be involved in the creative arts," we are hearing answers to the questions, "What is real?" and "What should be learned?" This process of considering proposals in terms of which set of beliefs and values is operating allows us to make better, more rational judgments about the broad implications of proposals and the conclusions we may reach. That is, the value of an action proposal, an activity, will be judged on the basis of a more fundamental value – the beliefs we have espoused about what education is or should be.

The process of thinking back to primary values, beliefs, ideas, or, indeed, to policies and principles is a basic thought process of rational judgment, a tool for rational planning and decision making. The mandate to give good reasons for a proposal or activity, to answer "why," is one of the important concerns of philosophy. Good reasons are understood to be logically related to some fundamental value. We may say students should participate in city council meetings because, through that experience, they will learn the reality of city management, learn what it is really like to be involved in the action, the real problems of the city. To those who believe that experience is the best teacher, our reasoning is sound – the project would be judged a rational choice. (The key words *experience, reality, really,* and *action* show which primary values are being espoused.)

An argument might come from the idealist who might say that students have to get the real picture, the idea of how the city is managed, and they can't get that from a few council meetings. They have to learn the structure of the system and the laws and policies within which the city operates. To get that understanding of the reality of city management, they would have to study the system. So the idealist might say that the pragmatist's reasoning is not valid.

School leaders can be more successful if they recognize that the debate is not solely at the level of means, it is also at the level of primary values – what it really means to know, to learn – to experience versus to have a clear idea of something. The school leader should be able to recognize the source of the reasoning (the kind of beliefs from which the proposal originates) and the validity of the reasons presented (whether the reasons actually relate to and support or offer real evidence for the conclusion that has been drawn – the proposal).

Rationality, Validity, and Logic

When philosophers, organizational theorists, or just plain folks talk about clear thinking, they use the terms *rational/rationality, valid/validity,* and *logic/logical.* Since the early 1950s, educators' attention has been directed at rational decisions, and the term has come to have two meanings. For one group of proponents, "rational" means statistically sound, or supported by valid research or empirical evidence. In a broader interpretation for day-to-day action, rational means experientially sound, or based on a fund of reflectively examined experience.

In either case, the judgment *rational* is based on the validity and logic of reasons given for a choice. The rational thinker, Ennis tells us, has seven "proficiencies," nine "tendencies," and "good judgment." Among the seven proficiencies is, "Offering well-organized and well-formulated *lines of reasoning*" (1981, 142, emphasis added). This emphasis on line of reasoning, plus other proficiencies such as generalizing and conceiving and stating assumptions are concerned with logic, the science of proof or evidence, as John Stuart Mill defines it.

In common use, one might hear, "S/he has a *valid* claim to the land." The speaker would be asserting that the evidence is both legal and sufficient to make a true case for ownership. Or someone might say, "That is a *valid* argument," meaning that it is logical and relevant to the proposal, perhaps even sufficient to prove the case. A valid *conclusion* implies proof; a valid *argument* implies relevance.

When we dispute an argument, we generally dispute it on a specific basis—that it is not logical or is not relevant or that it is not enough to prove anything. Perhaps all of us are becoming more sophisticated about rules of evidence or the science of proof because of the current spate of true cop shows and law court novels in which dramatic tension hinges on the distinction between relevant and sufficient evidence. Fingerprints on the gun are circumstantial (relevant) evidence but not, by themselves, sufficient to prove guilt. So the DA tells the investigating officer, "You can't make a *valid* case on that alone" (a case that will *prove* guilt).

Logic, defined formally as the science of proof, is the study of reasoning as it functions to provide evidence that some conclusion, inference, or proposition is valid. Logical thought, less formally, is any pattern of ideas or reasoning that provides an integrated and coherent presentation to support, clarify, or explain some belief, idea, action, or proposal. It is a line of thinking in which the thread of connecting ideas is clear, the statements made are both necessary and sufficient to justify the whole or to make it clear. When one writes an article or paper, the outline presents that line of thinking, the structured set of points, or reasons to be presented to support the thesis.

A valid conclusion is one that has been properly supported by logic, by clear and sufficient evidence. A rational decision or plan is one that presents a valid conclusion based on thoughtful examination of evidence and supported by sound reasoning. In other words, a rational decision proposes a sensible plan of action, given the facts of the situation and the circumstances in which the plan must be implemented.

Logic, Truth, and Morality

The way by which philosophy examines beliefs and assumptions is through the processes of logical thought. Thus, the second way in which philosophy can provide educational leaders with tools for planning is that it teaches systems of logical thought.

As a caveat, it must be recognized that logic does not require either truth or morality. Logic can be a tool for deception or for evil; however, our social and professional mandate as educators is that we start from a position of truth (at least, insofar as we know it at any point in time) and morality and apply logic so as to act in a manner consistent with the values from which we started. Logical and demonstrable unity of ethical values and action is the best protection against evil.

FORMS OF LOGIC AND LOGIC MAPS

In its general sense, logic is a line of thinking in which the thread of connecting ideas is clear, statements made are relevant, or the response is proper to issues being raised. As such, there are a number of patterns of thinking called "logic." Forms that are relevant to planning will be identified here and discussed in the following sections.

The classic forms of logic defined in philosophy are deductive and inductive reasoning, the science of proof and evidence, as John Stuart Mill says. They teach the patterns of reasoning from which valid conclusions may be drawn. They teach that good reasoning can be judged on its form alone, that it is concerned with conclusions that must be drawn or may be drawn from the reasons as presented, not from assumptions about the meaning of those reasons. They emphasize, too, that good reasoning does not guarantee either truth or morality.

Analytic philosophy proposes forms of logic not concerned with proof or evidence, but with clarifying meaning or concepts. There are many patterns for logical analysis of action, as well as of meaning. Flowcharts, networks, and computer programs are based on analysis of precedence and dependency and are serial or linear in nature. Analysis of sets and subsets (or of systems, subsystems, and supra-systems) is a characteristic of systems analysis and of all organizing.

A third set of patterns of logical thinking is concerned with "wholes": imaging (creating a mental image of a whole), prediction, and inference. Predicting probabilities is basic to decision tree analysis, imagining alternative courses of action, and envisioning an arena for choice.

Each of these patterns of logic will be discussed in the following sections in terms of how they can be useful tools for planning and action. Their relevance to a planning system will be evident in particular steps of the system presented in Chapters 9 and 10. In order to make a habit of rational thinking, we must have a mental "map" firmly imbedded in our minds. We have many such thinking maps—mathematical, linguistic, behavioral. We know automatically, for example, that $3 \times 6 = 36$ is not correct and that "into black the the ran house dog" is not a sentence (although we could easily create a sentence out of those words). We know, too, that the child's "I runned home," though incorrect in terms of formal grammar, is not faulty thinking. It is evidence of higher order thinking, a logical application of a grammatical map. These maps have been firmly fixed in our minds from childhood.

The Logic of Deductive Reasoning and Evidence

The two classic patterns of logic, deductive and inductive reasoning, the science of proof and evidence, were formulated as modes of reasoning in philosophy. All patterns of logical thinking owe some allegiance to the classic formats mapped by philosophers and the clarification of valid and invalid reasoning that results from the line of reasoning followed. Therefore, this format will be discussed first.

If the reasoning provides absolute proof that the conclusion is valid and inescapable, the logic form is called deductive. If the reasoning does not provide absolute proof but presents relevant evidence to support a conclusion, the logic form is called inductive. Obviously, some inductive reasonings are stronger than others. It is for this reason that research studies often require a control group. Results from a study including both treatment and control groups provide stronger evidence in support of a conclusion than do results from a case study, for example. Just as obviously, an exploratory study can provide insights that may be overlooked in a controlled study because it is not designed to prove something, but to find out what is going on. The map (format) of inductive reasoning derives from deductive logic.

The classic map is called a syllogism, and, in its basic form, it is made up of three statements: two premises and a conclusion. A premise is a statement of truth: fact, principle, belief, or policy presented as reasons for reaching some conclusion. (In most discussions, there may be several premises and many irrelevant statements as well. Also, the statements may be presented in reverse order, with the conclusion as the topic sentence of a paragraph, for example. But the pattern exists, nevertheless.) Figure 8.1 presents the example of a deductive syllogism often cited and the common graphic illustration of the logic represented (P, Q, and X can stand for any specific words).

Classic Syllogism

1st premise (P1) (P is Q)	P Q All men are human	
2nd premise (P2) (X is P)	X P Aristotle is a man	
Conclusion (C) (-->X is also Q)	X Q Aristotle is human	

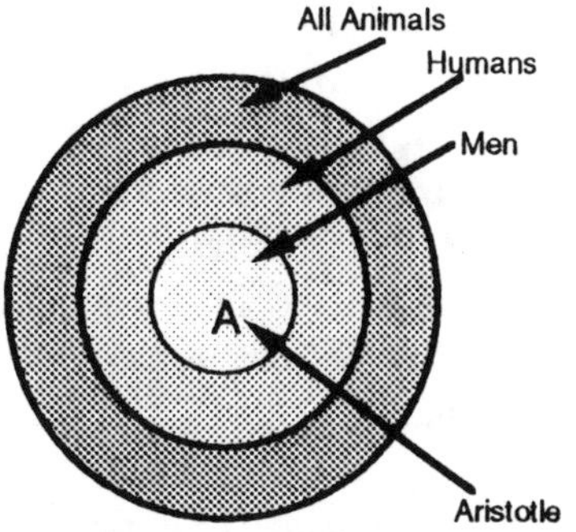

Figure 8.1. *A classic example of a deductive syllogism often cited and the graphic illustration of the logic represented.*

Such a syllogism is set up to determine (or prove) the validity of the third statement, the conclusion, not of the first. The third statement, the conclusion, started life as a hypothesis or a belief. To characterize the statement "Aristotle is human" as a hypothesis or belief is silly, of course. But suppose that we replace "Aristotle" with "Bigfoot" or with "the Wild Boy of Aveyron"[20] or with "Maryann." There certainly have been arguments as to whether this mysterious Bigfoot is human or is an animal. Also, in his day, it was proposed that the Wild Boy was, at best, an animal with human physiology. Bringing "Maryann" into the picture raises the question of "sufficient" reasoning. To be both valid and true requires that the first premise be made more inclusive: "All *people* are human."

For the "Aristotle" syllogism, the hypothesis to be proven carries the expanded implications, "Aristotle is a man, not an ape or some other type of animal." Therefore, the largest circle is "animals," and "humans" can be represented as a smaller circle inside the large class "animals." Other classes of animals might also be represented. "Men," being one class of humans, are included totally within the "human" circle. Aristotle, being a man, must therefore also be human. Thus, deductive logic is the logic of inclusion or classification — a primary logic of science.

The first premise in formal logic or in the sciences is a statement of accepted, proven, or assumed truth. In the sciences, it may be a state-

---

[20]The story of the capture and nurturing of the Wild Boy of Aveyron is told in Jones and Gerard (1967, 5 – 8).

ment related to a "class" of things, as in a taxonomy. For example, all insects are invertebrate and have segmented bodies. The hypothesis to be tested, then, is "a spider is an insect." The aim of deductive logic is to confirm the hypothesis, to demonstrate or prove that the conclusion is valid, that the relationships stated in "P1," the general premise, have been maintained in the specific case, the conclusion. IF all men are human and IF Aristotle is a man, clearly "A" is human. The conclusion is inevitable, given P1 and P2. A spider does not have a segmented body; therefore, it is not a true insect.

The syllogism (the logical argument form) provides a basis for assessing the reasonableness of proposals (since every proposal expresses beliefs or conclusions) and arguments presented in support of the proposals. Knowing the form, the map, as instinctively as we know word order for a sentence gives us an incredible tool for clear thinking.

Valid and Invalid Patterns of Reasoning

Discussions of the logic of a deductive syllogism present four patterns of thinking: two are accepted as valid because they lead to a valid conclusion consistent with the facts presented. Two forms or patterns are accepted as invalid because they lead to a nonlogical conclusion, one that is not proven by the facts as stated. Of course, the question of truth is a separate matter from logic. Truth depends on the truth of the premises, the beliefs and reasons presented, not on the logic of reasoning. The four patterns applied to the examples given are presented in Figure 8.2.

It is clear from these very obvious examples that you cannot always rely on a conclusion to be either reasonable (Bigfoot is human) or true (Maryann is not human). It all depends on how reasonable (valid) the line of argument is and on whether the statements are true, relevant, and sufficient to take the case to court as the DA would say.

Generalizations and Stereotypes

One important reason for understanding deductive logic is that, improperly applied, it can easily lead to stereotypes. Although it is possible to make a true statement as a conclusion, a hypothesis that could be supported, even though the reasoning is not valid, it is very easy to

Form 1—Valid line of reasoning: Affirm the antecedent. "X is P":

	P	Q
1st premise: All "Ps" are "Q".		
2nd premise: "X" is "P".		
Conclusion: —>"X" is "Q."		

P Q	P Q	P Q
All men are human (Definition)	All men are human (Definition)	All men are human (Definition)
X P	X P	X P
Aristotle is a man (Valid, True?)	Bigfoot is a man (Valid, True?)	Maryann is a man (Valid, True?)
X Q	X Q	X Q
Aristotle is human (Logical, True?)	Bigfoot is human (Logical, True?)	Maryann is human (Logical, True?)

Form 2—Invalid line of reasoning: Affirm the consequent. "X is Q":

	P	Q
1st premise: All "Ps" are "Q"		
2nd premise: "X" is "Q"		
Conclusion: —>"X" is "P"		

P Q	P Q	P Q
All men are human (Definition)	All men are human (Definition)	All men are human (Definition)
X Q	X Q	X Q
Aristotle is human (Valid, True?)	Bigfoot is human (Valid, True?)	Maryann is human (Valid, True?)
X P	X P	X P
Aristotle is a man (True; not Valid)	Bigfoot is a man (True? not Valid)	Maryann is a man (not True; not Valid)

Form 3—Invalid line of reasoning: Deny the antecedent. "X is not P"

	P	Q
1st premise: All "Ps" are "Q"		
2nd premise: "X" is not "P"	X	not P
Conclusion: —>"X" is not "Q"		

P Q	P Q	P Q
All men are human (Definition)	All men are human (Definition)	All men are human (Definition)
X not P	X not P	X not P
Aristotle is not a man (Valid, True?)	Bigfoot is not a man (Valid, True?)	Maryann is not a man (Valid, True?)
X not Q	X not Q	X not Q
Aristotle is not human (not True/Valid)	Bigfoot is not human (True? Invalid)	Maryann is not human (not True/Valid)

Form 4—Valid line of reasoning: Deny the consequent. "X is not Q"

	P	Q
1st premise: All "Ps" are "Q"		
2nd premise: "X" is not "Q"	X	not P
Conclusion: —>"X" is not "P"		

P Q	P Q	P Q
All men are human (Definition)	All men are human (Definition)	All men are human (Definition)
not Q	X not Q	X not Q
Aristotle is not human (Valid, True?)	Bigfoot is not human (Valid, True?)	Maryann is not human (Valid, True?)
X not P	X not P	X not P
Aristotle is not a man	Bigfoot is not a man	Maryann is not a man
(Not true, but valid conclusion)	(Questionable, but valid)	(True, and valid, but not based on truth)
		That is, true statement, but not based on the arguments given

Figure 8.2. Formats of deductive reasoning applied to the examples "Aristotle is human," "Bigfoot is human," and "Maryann is human." The truth and validity of the conclusion lie in the truth of the premises and whether, in fact, the premises (arguments/reasons given) "prove the case."

overlook illogical reasoning when we know (or believe) that the conclusion is true. Because the examples given in Figures 8.1 and 8.2 are so clear and straightforward, it may seem that these are not "real" questions for educators, that all of this is just semantics. There is no harm done with "Maryann is human," or "Maryann is not a man," both of which are true, but not supported by true statements. But the conclusions drawn on the basis of questionable "facts" in Figure 8.3 are not so harmless.

The broad generalizations that provide the first premise for deductive reasoning may easily become stereotypes when we are discussing educational issues. Stereotypes have been created on the basis of inadequate inductive reasoning (A is a troublemaker, and B is a troublemaker. They are from Z area. All students from Z area are troublemakers.) Once formed, however, a stereotype creates expectations that may be hard to eradicate. Figure 8.3 presents two examples of reasoning from generalizations so broad as to be stereotypes, to illustrate their weaknesses.

Two Examples of Valid Reasoning that May Become Stereotypes

Form 1--Valid line of reasoning: Affirm the antecedent, "X is P":

	P Q	P Q
1st premise: All "Ps" are "Q".	Students from "Z" area are troublemakers (Stated as if true)	Athletes are poor students (Commonly stated as true)
2nd premise: "X" is "P."	X P Tom/Sally is from "Z" (Stated as true)	X P Lena/John is an Athlete (Stated as true)
Conclusion: ---->"X" is "Q."	X Q Tom/Sally is a troublemaker (Valid argument, but true?)	X Q Lena/John is a poor student (Valid argument, but true?)

Form 4--Valid line of reasoning: Deny the consequent: "X is not Q"

	P Q	P Q
1st premise: All "Ps" are "Q"	Students from "Z" area are troublemakers (Stated as if true)	Athletes are poor students (Commonly stated as true)
2nd premise: "X" is not "Q"	X is not Q Tom/Sally is not a troublemaker (Valid reasoning, is it true?)	X is not Q Lena/John is not a poor student (Valid reasoning, but is it true?)
Conclusion: ---->"X" is not "P"	X is not P Tom/Sally is not from "Z" area (Valid reasoning, is it true?)	X is not P Lena/John is not an Athlete (Valid reasoning, but is it true?)

Figure 8.3. Deductive reasoning improperly applied is often the basis of stereotypes. Statements made may reflect generalizations with little or no basis in fact. Truth of conclusions lies in the truth of the premises. Validity lies in whether the arguments or reasons given (premises) are sufficient to "prove the case."

It is easy to recognize the similarity in form between stereotypes and established general categories from the hard sciences. We know very well, of course, that generalizations are suspect. We avoid such words as *all* and *every* when we are discussing students' abilities, behaviors, and attitudes, but, in spite of our greater understanding of and appreciation for differences, generalizations sometimes color our thinking. It is good to recognize the ''line of thinking'' that is inherent in stereotypes.

The validity of lines of reasoning is often illustrated graphically. Figure 8.4 gives a graphic illustration of three of the ''arguments'' presented in Figures 8.2 and 8.3 as examples of valid and invalid reasoning.

It is clear in this illustration that, if Aristotle is inside the circle of ''men,'' he is also inside the circle of ''humans.'' Therefore, Form 1, affirming ''P'' (Aristotle is a man) leads to a valid conclusion. On the other hand, if Bigfoot is not inside the circle of ''humans,'' clearly he is not inside the circle of ''men.'' Form 4, denying ''Q'' (Bigfoot is not human) also leads to a valid conclusion, Bigfoot is not a man. The questions remain, however, whether the statements made are true and, therefore, whether the conclusion is true.

The cases of troublemakers and athletes are even more subject to questions about truth. We can easily see that even if Tom/Sally is from ''Z,'' the truth of the first premise is not established. S/he may not be a troublemaker. Since we simply would not accept the first premise as being 100% true, we would not make the assumption that Tom/Sally is inevitably a troublemaker. We also recognize easily that, even though Lena/John is an athlete, s/he is not necessarily a poor student. However, as we know all too well, similar conclusions are often accepted on exactly such reasons as these.

Exercise 8.1 lists some statements commonly made that may have come from invalid reasoning. Identify stereotypes from which they may have originated.

The Power of Positive Generalizations

By thinking through a few examples of the forms of reasoning such as those that have been presented, we can become better able to recognize the pitfalls of poor logic. We can recognize how easy it is to ''turn the logic around'' (deny the antecedent ''P'' or assert or confirm the

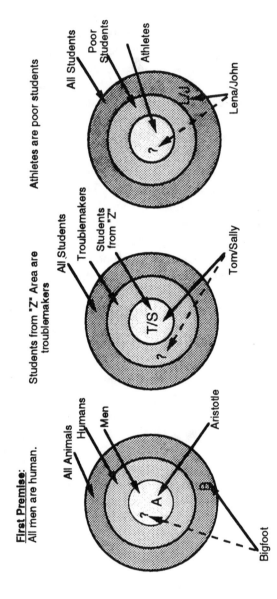

Figure 8.4. *Graphic illustration of reasoning presented in Figures 8.2 and 8.3. 1) Aristotle is a man, therefore human (valid argument and not something we would dispute). 2) Bigfoot is not human, therefore not a man (valid argument, but the question remains, is it true?). 3) T/S is from "Z," therefore a troublemaker (valid argument, perhaps true, perhaps stereotyping). 4) L/J is not a poor student, therefore not an athlete (valid argument, perhaps true, perhaps stereotyping).*

Types of Statements One Might Hear	Stereotypes or Generalizations Implied
Example:	
A. Mr./Mrs. T. is not a good leader, because s/he is not person-oriented.	Good leaders have to be person-oriented.
1. Mary/Pat may not do well in school; s/he is a latch-key child.	_____
2. Frank should try harder in the sciences, it will be important for his future.	_____
3. Mr./Mrs. G. can't evaluate me; s/he never taught my subject.	_____
4. Our students' parents probably won't come to the open house.	_____
5. You have to entertain the students in classes these days.	_____
6. Tommy is a cry-baby.	_____
7. Mr./Mrs. J. is not a very dedicated teacher; s/he doesn't help out in our club program.	_____
8. You don't need to take calculus, Mary.	_____
9. William should take the tech-voc option; his father is a mechanic, isn't he?	_____
10. Mr. F. would probably be a stronger principal than Mrs. C.	_____

Exercise 8.1. Identify a possible stereotype or generalization that is implied in each of the statements.

consequent "Q") and come to an invalid conclusion. The forms of logic also make it clear that, although generalization and classification of species may be the power base of the hard sciences, generalizations about people can easily lead to thinking in stereotypes.

However, the very fact that we recognize the power of generalizations to lead us toward stereotypes and negative attitudes, expectations, and choices, should suggest that positive generalizations (goals and objectives) can be powerful tools for planning for education. We might well propose that every educational stereotype implies an important goal or objective.

Stereotype: Girls are not good in math and sciences.
Goal/Aim: Girls in our school will do well in, and enjoy math and sciences.
Stereotype: Teachers today are not motivated.
Goal/Aim: Teachers in our school will enjoy and be enthusiastic about their work.
Stereotype: The arts are a waste of school time.
Goal/Aim: Our integrated arts and academic program will support holistic learning.

To turn a stereotype or a problem "inside out" and state the goal or objective that is at its heart is a step in logical inference. This step might be looked upon as the logic of extremes, a form of logical analysis, or clarification of meaning. The stereotype or problem identified is the negative pole of some continuum. How might we describe the opposite, most positive situation we could imagine? What would be the most desirable situation or state? With a continuum in mind, we can comprehend the direction toward which we wish to move.

Instead of the descriptive or defining statement, "All men are human," relevant to the logic of deduction and proof, a statement of positive generalization, of goals and objectives, would be prescriptive. It might say, "All of our 'men' (students, teachers, administrators) will treat each other humanely." It can be assumed that for every negative state or situation there is an opposing positive state. Thus, for the negative "vandalism," there is the positive "respect for property." For the negative "dropouts," there is the positive "lifelong learning." For the negatives "alienation" and "apathy," there are the positives "involvement" and "interest."

Setting goals is not simply backing away from an undesirable situation. Setting goals implies that planners will "ac-cen-tu-ate the positive . . . latch on to the affirmative" as the song says. This is the process of facing forward. It is not enough for effective leadership to back away from the negative—less violence, better achievement. Planning emphasizes and aims for the positive extreme—respect for people, enjoyment of learning.

Direction, stating clearly where we want to go from here, is an essential factor in planning and leadership. It is put into the context of creating a plan in Chapter 9 the section, Step One: Goals and Objectives. Exercise 8.2 lists stereotypes or problems that may appear in a school

Problem or Stereotype	Goal or Objective
Example: The teachers are stressed out.	— Teachers in our school will be happy and at ease. — Teachers in our school will enjoy their work.
1. There is too much violence in our school.	_____
2. Students will cheat.	_____
3. Administrators don't give us enough support.	_____
4. Parents don't know what their children are doing.	_____
5. Students create trouble in the mall.	_____
6. The curriculum doesn't meet the needs of our students.	_____
7. There's not enough emphasis on (arts, PE, math, language, ??)	_____
8. Students don't take part in extracurricular activities.	_____
9. We don't have high enough standards.	_____

Exercise 8.2. State a positive goal or objective that may be inferred from the negative problems and stereotypes listed. (Turn the negative statement "inside out" to set a goal that a school or system would want to aim for.)

setting; state the positive pole of the continuum implied, the end toward which action could be oriented.

Analytic and Holistic Reasoning

Logic as a science has always been associated with proof and evidence. As Fitzgibbons says, "[It is] the branch of philosophy that is concerned with identifying how well certain reasons function as evidence for particular beliefs" (1981, 53). Thus, formal logic teaches that we can learn to "see" a picture of any situation described by the reasons given. As we learn to distinguish between what an idea includes and what it excludes, we can judge whether the reasons given to support a claim are appropriate and sufficient.

However, proving a point is not the only situation in which clear, coherent thinking is important for anyone and especially for educational leaders. Other patterns of thinking that rely on clear thinking have developed to serve other purposes. There are forms of logical analysis that are not concerned with truth, reality, and goodness, that are not concerned with "proof" but, instead, are concerned with clarifying language or concepts with the questions of meaning (Ozmon and Craver, 1990, 270). These are, again, questions of what an idea includes and excludes, but for purposes of description and full understanding, rather than proof.

Serial or Linear Logic

Several forms of logical analysis are important for planning. Serial or linear sequencing of tasks or steps is one such pattern that has had great impact on education. Serial analysis is based on order, precedence, and dependency of actions or events. This logic is used to develop flow-charts, networks, and computer programs. Other modes of logical analysis are related to sets and subsets, such as identification of fields of study and their content areas, the structure of attendance areas (sometimes "gerrymandered" to establish politically acceptable subsets), and the hierarchy of goals created in management by objectives. Some applications of these forms of logical analysis will be presented in Chapters 11 and 12.

In the past few decades, many questions have been raised about whether the emphasis on linear thinking has inhibited other forms of thinking. Hart defined logic as "deliberate progression from fact or observation A or B and then to C, D, E, and more." He suggested that logic is more useful for description than for discovery. He cited the fact that scientists often make discoveries by accident, but when they report the discovery, they describe the process of discovery in the "tight, sequential word structures or word systems [of] conventional logic" (1983, 49, 51).

This is no doubt true; processes of thinking can only be described in words. Since words are, by their very nature, particular to single acts or things, we tend to describe action in serial steps. We think out the steps by which a task may be accomplished or a result achieved in order to lead our students through the process to the desired end (or our readers in a scientific report). We hope that the pattern of steps, the process, will become what Zuboff (1988) called "sentient knowledge," or "body knowledge," imbedded in habit. Our continual effort in education is to improve activities by describing them in steps and testing the effectiveness of learning that students achieve from following the described steps. There is no doubt that these efforts have reinforced serial, or sequential, thinking.

Hall presented much the same argument as Hart. He said that Westerners have been taught by schools and the media to think "in a linear, step-by-step, compartmentalized way" and have lost the capacity to think comprehensively. He described a "polychronic" mode of administration in the Middle East and Latin America where work is scheduled by the activity, not by the component tasks as in an assembly line, or in grade-level sequencing of academic content. He proposed that this "polychronic" mode permits the individual worker to accommodate the task to their own process, while the "monochronic" mode of Western administration requires the workers to accommodate themselves to a prescribed process. Hall argued that the poly-mode emphasizes outcome, while the mono-mode emphasizes procedure (1977, 11–12, 17).

It is an interesting fact that the Indian system of higher education, and British and European systems as well, traditionally did not follow the step-by-step course and credit system structure of North America. They were structured on the basis of "reading in a field," with completion based on submission of a major piece of work. More recently, the credit system has been adopted in many areas outside of North America. It will be interesting to see if the credit system (which has much in common with assembly line and piecework concepts) will spread mono-mode processes widely, both in education and in production, or whether current reactions against piecework learning will move our learning systems toward a more holistic mode.

It is well documented by neurology that we use only a small portion of our brain capacity, that when severe trauma has occurred to one side of the brain, the other may compensate (Restak, 1984, 255–257). Moreover, controlled studies of the brain have demonstrated that there is an analytic mode of thinking and a holistic mode of thinking. There are students who know the right answer and are only confused by step-by-step processes. Just as a basketball player *sees* the line from the ball to the basket without thinking about movements or steps, some people *think* in this direct line.

The instances that are easiest to recognize are of those savants whose abilities in numerology, music, and memory astound and humble us; however, this holistic mode of knowing, as opposed to thinking, may be more widespread than we realize. How else does one explain the child of four who comes running and holds up an inflated ball, shaking with intensity, saying "This ball is not empty, because, if it was empty, it would be flat"? Everyone has that capacity, to some degree, though it is not a capacity that we, as yet, know much about developing or training.

Sacks (1985, 181–182) describes "Rebecca" who tested 60 or less on standard IQ tests. But the tests, says Dr. Sacks,

> had given me no hint of her positive powers, her ability to perceive the real world—the world of nature, and perhaps of the imagination—as a coherent, intelligible, poetic whole: her ability to see this, think this.
> . . . [The tests] had given me no intimation of her inner world, which clearly was composed and coherent, and approached as something other than a set of problems or tasks.

Hart, Hall, and many others (March, 1984; Papert, 1980; Whitehead, 1966; and Zuboff, 1988) are all reminding us that there is more to this great human mind than step-by-step, linear, or sequential thinking. If Hart, Hall, and others are right, it may be that linear, or sequential, thinking has been emphasized in schools, because, in order to accommodate the large numbers of students, schools have had to be organized as places where teaching takes place. Teaching, as research has demonstrated, is largely comprised of the teacher giving information, much of which is describing and reporting. As Hart says, serial logic is the form scientists use to report a discovery, and it is inevitably sequential in nature.

We educators are, indeed, experienced and successful in sequential, step-by-step thinking, and that skill has played a large role in the development of North American life. We have all heard of people with innate mathematics intuition who may be able to tell us instantly, without "thinking" (without the *process* of logical thinking described by Dewey), that the square root of 214,369 is 463. When we teach square root, however, we must teach the steps by which it can be computed by those of us who have more ordinary abilities.

It is often true that students are urged to follow patterned processes. For example, they may be discouraged from guessing an answer in math (estimating) and are taught that their work will be assessed on process, as well as product. Equally, should a student reply, "Well, because it's right," when asked, "Why do we say 'They are' instead of 'They is'?" the answer is not usually accepted. When a student takes a great leap of imagination and asks, "Could that be why . . . ?" they may be ridiculed, ignored, or asked to make a special report. They quickly learn that guessing (estimating), relying on their learned habits or customs, and taking intuitive leaps are not highly favored.

Students may be demonstrating how well-trained they are in serial or linear logic when they ask, "How many pages does this paper have to be?" or "How many references do I have to have?" Many students feel quite threatened by an assignment to "develop a project applying some of the principles we have been studying." As everyone who has done a doctoral or masters research project knows, setting up the question for study is a major hurdle in the process. The question is holistic in nature; it is "the study in a nutshell," and to see this "whole" clearly requires a logic quite different from the serial, linear, or step-by-step logic we have more practice in.

Although extremely critical of overemphasis on serial, or analytical, logic, Hall himself accepts the fact that "without this capacity (of linear thinking), culture and the education institutions it has spawned could not have evolved. *It was once said that science is the process that makes it possible to make the average man brilliant"* (1977, 202, emphasis added).

Thus, linear or serial thinking is a major accomplishment of education systems and is not to be discarded; however, if schools were organized as places where *learning* is the focus, processes and experiences might very well be quite different. As a place where learning is the emphasis, we might encourage what March calls "playful" thinking. We might, as he proposes, "treat *goals as hypotheses,* treat *intuition as real,* treat *experience as a theory"* (1984, 232, emphasis in original). Some newer methods in elementary schools such as whole language learning are putting more emphasis on developing or creating. Can we incorporate these emphases without losing that capacity to "make the average man brilliant" that has emanated from science and teaching the "how to" of skills and processes?

Wholes, Analysis, and Logic

A second general set of forms of logical thinking is presented in analytic philosophy. Analytic philosophy is based on the assumption that all language deals with "wholes"; wholes do not have to be constructed by abstract reasoning. The logic of analysis is not concerned with proof or with establishing grand general systems of thought, but with clarifying ideas or concepts (Ozmon and Craver, 1990, 270). It is concerned with understanding meaning, and it approaches meaning through analysis and the search for "objective or existing equivalents" [Wittgenstein (1968) cited by Ozmon and Craver (1990), 292].

Analytic philosophers such as Moore (1959), Wittgenstein (1968), and Ayer (1952) say that it is not important to create great answers to the questions of reality, knowing, and being. They are concerned with meaning within context. They propose that, although we use the language of "universal ideas," the important task of philosophers is not to create one grand system of universals, but to understand the meanings attributed to ideas or words in the context in which they are used. Ozmon and Craver tell us, "Wittgenstein believed that in actuality words have no true meaning given to them by some independent power. They have the meanings people give them" (1990, 282).

Words represent ideas, concepts, or things. Words can represent things that could be observed empirically (red, cold, hit, daisy, spider), more abstract ideas such as interpretations of action and relationships (democracy, bureaucracy, leadership), or normative ideas (good, well, proper, rational). Regardless of how empirically verifiable an idea the word may express, it means different things to different people.

Since there is a common core of meaning to most ideas, we tend to believe that everyone knows the color *red* or the feeling *cold*. But we know very well, for example, that *cold* is relative to activity, acclimatization, and cultural experience. Even *red* would not be identified at precisely the same shade by different people—to say nothing of the difficulties we have in pinning down *democracy* or *leadership*.

Holistic logic and analytic logic have both had major impact on education and educational leadership. Analyzing and structuring tasks is one of the key components of scientific management and functionalist paradigms. Although we have rebelled against many of the developments from scientific management, there are many conveniences we would be reluctant to give up. Fragmentation and isolation may have resulted from specialization, but few of us would choose to go back to the days when we were expected to teach all subject fields.

Behavioral objectives seem to miss the point of education, but parents and students have demanded clearer definition of expectations held and the bases of evaluation. Uniform salary schedules based on levels of training and experience frustrate educators at times because they do not give adequate recognition to dedication, talent, and effort. Yet we do not wish to return to the 1920s when job security and salaries were vulnerable to any whim.

The orientation toward research in education and administration has also swung between holistic and analytic perspectives. Research has moved from task analysis in scientific management to case studies and from behavioral surveys and experiments in the social sciences to thick description and emphasis on the essence of situations in ethnography and phenomenology. The current move toward authentic testing is a move toward a holistic view of learning, away from the additive or analytic bases of standardized tests.

The differences in school environment between an elementary and a secondary school in Quebec reported by Ahola-Sidaway (1986) also reflect the two orientations. She characterized the environment of the elementary school as *Gemeinschaft,* having a family culture and a holistic approach to learning. In the secondary school, she found a *Gesellschaft* culture, individualistic, with the focus on specific skills and areas of learning and with less sense of belonging.

The logic of logical analysis requires that a base of analysis be established. We could analyze the meaning of *red,* for example, on the basis of uses in advertising, on its uses in different cultures (from weddings to death), or on variations in shade from light to dark or tone from orange to purple. Analysis requires that all specific elements be identified on the same base. Thus, each element, each particular cited, must "touch base" so to speak, "base" being the common relationship to the whole. If we are naming *shades* of red, we do not include in the list examples of tones. If we are comparing the *structure* of the education systems of Kenya and North America, we do not confuse the analysis with *content.* We could, of course, consider the content at different levels, that is, use more than one base of analysis. For a logical analysis, however, the base or bases used should be clear.

Analysis of Goals and Objectives

In education, the aspirations we have for our students are global in nature, and we think about them in global terms. Value terms express the desired "wholes" of achievement, skills, behaviors, attitudes, and understandings. But these global aspirations "mean" different levels of learning, different ways of knowing, and different means of learning under specific circumstances.

In every general idea about what we hope students will accomplish or in what we propose to do, there are at least two components that must be defined in the context of the situation. If we say "understand fundamental rights," both *understand* and *fundamental rights* need to be defined in more specific terms for particular groups of students. If we say "be able to solve word problems," both *be able to solve* and *word problems* differ for different age or ability levels of students. If we say "put on a field day," the activities that a field day should include and the activities needed to "put it on" must both be planned in advance.

It does not matter whether we are supervising a Ph.D. research report or are working with educationally handicapped fourth-grade students. In every case, we have as one general, holistic aspiration that our students will "use language well." But both *use language* and *well* have different meanings for the two groups. So we subconsciously "think out" (analyze) what these two important components of the "whole" mean for the group we are dealing with.

Our expectations for the specifics of vocabulary, complexity of sentences, and development of ideas define use of language in the proper context of our group on some universal range. The differential "pass/fail" or "good, better, best" expectations define "well" in a more limited context, within the group itself.

In planning for education, defining the content of a desired learning, a goal, is the process of clarifying goals and objectives called for in every planning system. The general skill *use language* is broken down into the specific skills considered important for the group.

Moreover, these same words have very different meanings for different professional groups, as well as for particular learning groups. One can readily visualize quite different sets of specific skills that would be proposed by grammarians versus proponents of whole-language learning. Although we all know what we mean by "use language," we do not all mean the same thing, nor should we.

The skills needed to be a skate dancer are quite different from those needed to be a hockey skater, but "good, better, best" is relevant to both. In addition to the specifics of content, the level of achievement expected, the meaning of *use well* is specified in clarifying goals and objectives. *Well* is made specific in terms of records kept or tests and measures used and in terms of standards set for the group. Thus, clarifying goals proceeds in two directions:

Toward--MEASURES/TESTS and STANDARDS SET

Toward--SUBSETS OF MEANING

in terms of SKILLS, CONTENT

ABILITIES, ATTITUDES

INTERESTS, BEHAVIORS

These are the two components of learning or achievement, upon which we base professional judgment. These are the two directions of clarification that must be addressed for effective practice. They may be done subconsciously or by thoughtful reflection, or they may be expressed consciously and explicitly as in a plan.

These two directions of analysis are the basis of writing behavioral objectives; however, our orientation is that the two directions by which goals and objectives are clarified should not be subsumed into one statement as in behavioral objectives. Our orientation is that goals and objectives should make explicit the values held in holistic terms. The level at which success is to be judged is the standard of success for the particular group at that particular time; it is not the goal. We propose that measures to be used and standards set for success should be specified separately, as in the map illustrated previously.

Goal analysis and clarification is a critical component of effective planning. It is presented in Figure 9.5, Stage One, The Meaning of Success. The rationale for maintaining the two directions of analysis separately is developed further in the discussion that follows that figure. Briefly, it is proposed that maintaining the two as separate directions of analysis aids planners to maintain a balance between the vision of the whole expressed in the goal and the reality of possible achievement expressed in the standard.

It is not enough for educational leaders to dismiss statements of visionary ideal outcomes as ''motherhood and apple pie'' statements, but neither is it enough to speak of outcomes only in the narrow focus of measurable quantities. To hit the target effectively, educators must "keep their eye on the sight line," the vision, the goal, and their "elbows firmly grounded on the sandbag," realistic standards.

Analysis of Strategies

A second point in planning at which logical analysis is an important step is at the stage of action planning. Just as a goal includes at least two components that must be clarified, so, too, does every action strategy proposal. "Put on a field day"; "show the movie XYZ"; "study Chapter 6"; "visit the museum"; "present a spring concert." All of these require analysis of tasks needed to make the activity or event possible and analysis of activities that may be included in the event itself.

Does "study Chapter 6" imply answering a set of questions—they must be prepared. Does it envision that the students will generate questions or hypotheses about social change, causes, etc.? Then it requires training in these types of thinking and planned feedback.

In the planning system presented in the next two chapters, simple formats for task analysis are presented in Figures 10.11, and 10.12. In task analysis, as in goal analysis, the equation of whole and parts is aimed for. *Equation* is a fundamental principle of logical analysis. The logic is complete only to the degree that the whole equals the parts or, more importantly, to the degree that the parts realistically capture and express the essence of the whole.

Limitations of Logical Analysis for Educational Planning

The limitations of logical analysis for educational planning are those that have been stressed by Hart, Hall, March, and others. The primary limitation is that logical analysis may create a "box" that the planner does not escape from. Thus we might analyze "4" by describing it as "1 + 1 + 1 + 1," as "2 × 2," as "3 + 1," or as "2 + 2." Having analyzed it thus, we could easily have failed to consider that "4" is also "6 − 2," or "1,748 − 1,744," or "200 ÷ 50," or any number of other possible descriptions. We might well have created the "tight word system" of which Hall speaks.

Analysis of an education system in the mid-twentieth century focused on the structure of authority for decision making (board, central administration, school administration, teacher). More recent analyses have directed attention to other bases of analysis such as power (Beneviste, 1989; Hamilton, 1991), culture (Carlson, 1991), behavioral approach (Inbar, 1991), and value systems (Campbell-Evans, 1991; Giroux and Purpel, 1983; Hodgkinson, 1983). Increasingly, the school organization is examined from different perspectives.

Such analyses point out the limitations for a holistic understanding of education imposed by the structural emphasis that dominated for several decades. However, no analysis is holistic, no analysis presents the whole. An analysis of influence groups and constituencies adds to our understanding but is no more the whole of an education system than a structural description. A consideration of *Gemeinschaft* and *Gesellschaft* cultures adds depth to understanding but does not negate the importance of recognizing power groups. It is important to recognize styles of leadership or of followership that affect the system, but styles of behavior are not the only component of an organization's culture. All complement each other.

There has always been the tension between thinking in wholes and analyzing as productive modes of studying behavior. This has been evidenced in gestalt versus behavioral psychology, in behavioral ratings of teaching effectiveness versus classroom culture studies. It is expressed in such aphorisms as, ''The whole is greater than the sum of its parts,'' and ''Man is what he eats.'' The arts and humanities look at life and reality in more holistic terms, and the sciences and basic knowledge studies through more analytical processes.

It is easier to draw a map to scientific or analytic thought than to creation and invention. We speak of ''teaching'' the scientific method, but of ''letting creativity flower'' or ''nourishing'' creativity. To develop plans that will ''nourish'' our values, both holistic vision and analytic precision are important. Kaufman and Herman (1991) move from mission and mission analysis (the large view) to tasks and task analysis (the specific view). (See Figure 6.2 for an example of their presentation.)

In Chapters 9 and 10, the Values-Based Planning System is presented, which emphasizes the goal as a holistic value and describes analytical steps that take place at various stages of planning.

Probability Reasoning

To this point, deductive and inductive reasoning and holistic and analytic reasoning have been discussed. It was indicated that there are logic maps or lines of thought that guide these types of reasoning toward consistency, validity, and rationality. A third major type of reasoning that governs planning, choice, and action for education is probability reasoning.

Both deductive and probability reasoning have the characteristics of propositions; they propose relationships between two things. In the classic deductive syllogism described earlier, the first premise assumes a relationship—"IF man, THEN human"—or states a rule or policy—"All principals are over thirty." Inductive reasoning seeks to find a common base of relationship that can be assumed and carried over to new examples: "Cigarette smokers are _____," "Junior high school students are _____."

Deductive propositions describe absolutes and are all-inclusive. Their service is classification and identification. As stated earlier, human behavior, the stuff of education, is not as easy to classify. We might be prepared to assert that "all artists are creative" because we are defining *artists*. We are setting up a criterion for discriminating persons whose work is creative from those whom we would not admit into the company of artists. Such a proposition implies that there is an established (or agreed) set of criteria pertaining to each of the two members of the relationship (criteria for artists and criteria for creativity). However, most of our assertions about behavior are much more limited in generality. Even laws, though categorical in nature, do not say, "All violence is _____"; they say there is such a thing as justifiable homicide, and there are degrees of culpability.

Every criterion of human behavior that has been described is variable; there are no absolutes. Probability reasoning is a means of dealing with this fact. The propositions of probability reasoning are predictive, not descriptive. A probability proposition may take several forms and deal with several different kinds of predictions. Pyke (1970) identified two approaches to forecasting: extrapolative and exploratory. Extrapolative projection derives from historical data and essentially proposes incremental change. Exploratory projection is a radar-like approach. It tunes into signals of emerging trends coming from the environment and assesses them for probable relevance, importance, and utility. However, both are reacting to some external signal, historical or emerging.

Friedmann (1973) spoke of a type of projection that imagines. "Future-casting," he said, is the domain of Utopian thought, the domain of hope, faith, and values. To think in this domain, probability is assumed to be 100% because it is concerned with the best of all possible worlds, the most ideal outcome.

One technique used for "future-casting" is brainstorming, but even brainstorming has to ask the right question. In a management seminar, Ackoff told about a planning session held for Bell Telephone in the days when all phones still had rotary dials. For several sessions, participants wrestled with the questions, "How could we make the telephone better?" and "How could we give better service and still keep costs within reason?" These are action questions, what Friedmann might call the domain of the "near future" or of "planning thought," and these questions produced uninspired proposals.

Finally, the question was changed, "What would you like the telephone to be able to do for you?" This question generated excitement and ideas that were not possible at that time but are common features of the telephone today: touch-tone dialing, screening out unwanted calls, taking messages, and letting you know if another call is coming in. These "imaginings" directed much of Bell's research and development for decades.

Future-casting is probability reasoning with all restrictions removed. The answers then have to be "back-hauled" into the realm of the possible and then hauled further back into the realm of the probable: "Of this, how much can we do right now?" In planning, this is the relationship between the goal, the bank of alternatives, and the action choice. The goal is future vision, the various alternatives are possible means to that vision, and the action choice is the most probable or most feasible means at the moment.

The form of probability reasoning that is most common is concerned with action choice. March (1988) proposed two focuses of probability logic that are concerned with action choice in organizations. One form he identified as "consequential logic [for which] a person is 'in touch with reality' and asks, What are my alternatives? What are the probable consequences of those alternatives?" He opposed that with what he called an "obligatory logic [for which] a person is 'in touch with self' and asks, What kind of situation is this? . . . What does a person such as I do in a situation such as this?" (p. 62). Consequential logic, as March identified it, is concerned with objective, external, or extrinsic consequences. "If we take this action, how will it affect our overall budget, how will concerned parties react, how likely is it to be successful, etc.?" These are the questions that decision tree analysis, or any formal system of choice analysis, addresses.

By obligatory logic, March was referring to the logic of norms or social mandates and the ethics or morality involved. What does a teacher do in "a situation such as this"? a parent? a counselor? an administrator? In an important way, obligatory logic could be seen as related to consequential logic. It deals with internal realities, the ways in which one relates expectations, ethics, and moral imperatives to choice. It is concerned with what might be seen as intrinsic consequences. Fulfilling or not fulfilling the obligations one feels as a teacher, parent, or administrator has important consequences for one's self-respect and satisfaction.

The questions of obligation, morality, and ethics come to play in all choice, but they are less commonly specified in a formal way in choice models. The matrix model proposed in Figures 10.8 and 10.9 suggests that attitudes, customs, and interests can and should be made factors in the formal analysis for any important choice in education.

IF ↔ THEN Format in Planning

Probabilities imply IF ↔ THEN relationships, both as predictions of probable outcomes and as predictions of probable contingencies or impact relationships. Probability logic for planning is grounded in this map.

We seldom question a statement like, "You want to get into a good college, so you had better do well in math," or "You have to do well in math to get a good job." We seldom phrase it in the IF ↔ THEN format. Most of the statements we commonly hear about education, most of the statements of what we educators and the public believe about education, imply cause ↔ effect relationships, but they are not made in the IF ↔ THEN format. They take several common forms:

- All (boys/girls/leaders/administrators) should _____.
- There is too much (or too little) _____.
- Students/teachers/administrators/parents don't _____.
- We are going to do/have/start _____.
- We will do A/B/C because/so that _____.

Any statement of what we are going to do as teachers or administrators, of what we are going to require students to do, or of what should be different or better assumes some cause/effect proposition. Consider the following statements:

- We should take the students to a Shakespeare play.
- For the next unit, you will do a project on a South American country.
- We will present a panel on cooperative learning.
- The ninth grade is preparing a program on jazz.
- The class should know more about how a court really works.
- We could have a three-day retreat in April.
- There is so much vandalism lately.
- We should require more writing and public speaking.
- Each child will have his/her own plants to raise.

All of these assertions contain IF ↔ THEN propositions within them; they all propose, or imply, that some action will, or should, take place to bring about some desired result; however, it is not clear what result the speaker anticipates. Nearly every assertion could act either as the IF (means) clause or as the THEN (effect) clause. (As a means statement: "IF we take the students to a Shakespeare play, THEN _____"; as an effect clause: "IF we organize _____, THEN we could take the students to a Shakespeare play.") Thus, an assertion could mean many different things to different people. One assertion potentially creates a thousand propositions.

The first step in using probability logic as a tool, then, is to change an assertion into an IF ↔ THEN statement, into a clear statement of the cause ↔ effect relationship proposed, or into several such statements. Figure 8.5 presents an example of the logic for step one, changing an assertion into propositions.

The example suggests only a few of the possible IF ↔ THEN propositions that could be made from the belief assertion. The question for planning is, "Which is the desired outcome we wish to plan for?" If the value (desired outcome) is less vandalism, we are thinking of vandalism as the consequent, and there might be many more possible strategies (IFs) than the three presented here. If we are thinking of one of the other values suggested in "less vandalism as a means, or antecedent," we could certainly suggest many other potential strategies for creating a good school climate, for reducing costs, or for reducing fear among students. The issue for any plan is, "What do we expect it to accomplish?"

The same exercise could be applied to any of the assertions given as examples above or to any statement one often hears the public make about education. Logic Exercise 8.3 suggests practice in this step.

BELIEF:	THERE IS SO MUCH MORE VANDALISM THESE DAYS
FORMAT:	Possible cause/effect propositions:
If P / Q* "BELIEF" as the <u>Antecedent</u> (the <u>Means</u> to a valued outcome)	IF there were less vandalism (1) THEN students would be less afraid of each other
	IF there were less vandalism (2) THEN repair costs would be lower
	IF there were less vandalism (3) THEN there would be a better climate at school
If P / Q "BELIEF" as the <u>Consequent</u> (the desired <u>end</u>– Valued <u>outcome</u>)	IF we had more counsellors in school (4) THEN there would be less vandalism
	IF parents had more control over their children (5) THEN there would be less vandalism
	IF we had better rapport with the community (6) THEN there would be less vandalism

Figure 8.5. Planning logic, step one. Transferring normative statements (philosophical or belief statements) into IF ↔ THEN statements. Every normative statement can be thought of as the antecedent (IF) or as the consequent (THEN).

It is important to recognize that statements imply propositions and that the statement can imply many different actions to different people. It is certainly not good practice to challenge every statement made, of course, but this step is one of the mental maps that are useful for planning. Mentally taking this step gives direction to thinking and can give direction to discussion as well. Indeed, taking this first step may be enough to recognize how easy it is to get off track in our thinking and planning.

We can easily recognize that, even if there is a better climate, vandalism may not be reduced, but, on the other hand, vandalism might be reduced. The probability question is, ''What are the chances of success with this strategy?'' There are no rules or formulas for creating the outcomes we consider most important. It is not quite, ''You can't get

Translate normative statements (philosophical or belief statements) into IF→THEN statements. Every normative statement can be thought of as the antecedent (IF) or as the consequent (THEN). Refer to Figure 8.5, and give three possible consequents (part 1) and three possible antecedents (part 2).

BELIEF:	**Students Today Are Not Well Educated**	**The Dropout Rate Is Too High**	**Teachers Should Participate More In Educational Decisions**
FORMAT Format	Example #1	Example #2	Example #3
If P/Q "belief" as the Antecedent. (The Means to a valued outcome)	IF students were well educated, THEN they would ____	IF the dropout rate were low, THEN ____	IF teachers participated in educational decisions, THEN ____
	THEN ____	THEN ____	THEN ____
	THEN ____	THEN ____	THEN ____

Exercise 8.3. Planning logic, step one.

BELIEF:	Students Today Are Not Well Educated	The Dropout Rate Is Too High	Teachers Should Participate More In Educational Decisions
FORMAT Format	Example #1	Example #2	Example #3
If P/Q "belief" as the Consequent. (The desired end, valued outcome).			
	IF schools/parents/the system did more ___	IF schools/parents/the system did more ___	IF schools/parents/the system did more ___
	THEN students would be better educated	THEN students would be better educated	THEN students would be better educated
	IF schools/parents/the system did more ___	IF schools/parents/the system did more ___	IF schools/parents/the system did more ___
	THEN students would be better educated	THEN students would be better educated	THEN students would be better educated
	IF schools/parents/the system did more ___	IF schools/parents/the system did more ___	IF schools/parents/the system did more ___
	THEN students would be better educated	THEN students would be better educated	THEN students would be better educated

Exercise 8.3. (continued). Planning logic, step one.

310

Planning logic is hypothetical in nature. It begins with the Consequent, the "THEN" or desired outcome, and creates a bank of optional methods for achieving that outcome.

Consequent as the goal:	Our Students Will Be Well Educated →	Our Parents Will Support the School →	Our Teachers Will Enjoy Working in Our School →
Antecedent as proposed action:	IF →	IF →	IF →
FORMAT Format	Example #1	Example #2	Example #3
→ IF → Option #1	IF →	IF →	IF →
→ IF → Option #2	IF →	IF →	IF →
→ IF → Option #3	IF →	IF →	IF →

Exercise 8.4. Planning logic, step two.

there from here''; it is more that ''The road is not straight and narrow.'' In one sense, thinking out the logic of IF↔THEN relationships is ''reality therapy.'' It helps bring us down to earth, so we do not expect too much from any one project or program and so we may keep an open mind to unexpected or serendipitous effects. It helps us be more rational in planning and choice. Exercise 8.4 gives further practice in this phase of probability analysis, creating a set of alternatives.

LOGIC AND PLANNING

Developing skill in analyzing the cause↔effect logic of beliefs and proposals is important in several ways:

(1) It encourages us to create a pool of IF↔THEN propositions out of any assertion, belief, or proposed program. This provides a pool of alternative strategies and brings us to better understanding of different points of view.

(2) It requires us to determine what assumptions are being made in this particular case. That is, out of all of the possible propositions that might be imbedded in an assertion, which one is important here?

(3) The IF↔THEN format forces conscious clarification of both means and ends and of the relationship between them that is being proposed.

(4) Restating assertions or beliefs in the IF↔THEN format and estimating the probabilities of success enable us to recognize easily that any program or activity we may plan will only contribute to an objective. All of the valued outcomes we work toward are so complex that no single program will guarantee success. We see that reality at once through the IF↔THEN format. It makes clear that we are hypothesizing, using our best judgment to predict what may be a successful approach.

All of these aspects are important for education. The skills of using probability logic are not the only tools needed for successful planning, but logic is an important skill. It helps keep values and action in tune with each other. After internalizing how probability logic may be tested, the brain takes a shortcut. It ''flips'' any statement into cause/effect statements and tests them quickly in both directions. This map joins the other subconscious processes of thinking that we use constantly. Like typing or tennis, after it is learned, our body, in this case, our brain, knows and uses the process unconsciously. But, like any other skill, it takes conscious practice to learn.

We have proposed that deductive logic, analytical logic, and probability or propositional logic are not the same. Deductive logic starts with an asserted unitary class (insects have segmented bodies; women administrators are humanistic; boys do not like poetry), an absolute or "word system," and applies a systematic test to determine whether a specific case, or example, is a member of that system: a spider is/is not an insect; Alice is/is not a humanist; Tom does/does not like poetry. It tests for validity of reasoning and truth of conclusions that may be drawn. The deductive logic of philosophy is "proving," or demonstrating, the correctness of an assertion about a specific case by testing it against a generally accepted truth.

Probability logic starts with the idea of an activity or program and asks, "How likely is this activity or program to achieve what we hope for?" There is no built-in system of testing the logic of probabilities, because it deals with the future, the untestable. Creating the set of propositions, the alternative strategies by which an outcome might be achieved, can be seen as factoring, or analyzing, an idea.

The Goal Is the Consequent

In philosophical logic, the first premise includes both the IF (antecedent) and the THEN (consequent). In education the antecedent is usually a means statement (IF we do _____; IF they know _____; IF there is _____). The consequent is usually an aim or a valued/desired outcome (THEN they will understand; THEN they will be able _____; THEN we can _____). When probability logic is applied to a plan, the first statement must be a statement of desired outcome, the value, the goal, not the means.

A great deal of educational planning does start with the means, of course, and uses analytic logic to list the steps needed for that activity. (We are going to try _____, so we will have to do A, B, C, D, etc.) However, to create a plan that incorporates values and places a particular activity properly into the whole of education's purposes, the particular value aimed at is the first premise. That is, in planning, the consequent (the result predicted or hoped for) is logically the first premise and becomes the first statement. There is nothing unusual about this order of thinking; we always decide where we are going before we decide whether to fly, drive, or walk. In educational planning, we should apply the same principle we apply in life: choose the destination first; then consider the alternative means. Thus, the logic of planning proceeds as in Figure 8.6.

A plan is hypothetical in nature; it predicts the most probable and feasible means to achieve a desired end. The aims, the goals, of education are quite constant and quite universal. We want all students to be able to read well (a value we hold), to be good citizens, to have healthy minds in healthy bodies, to be individuals but able to live in harmony with a group, to appreciate the arts, and to accept and enjoy people of all cultures. What *reading well* means will differ from age ten to age sixteen. What being a good citizen means may differ from one community to another or from one period of time to another. So we define our aims and goals through a set of objectives in light of the particular setting and circumstances.

Possible alternative strategies, means, or technologies are judged in terms of how likely they are to achieve the intended goal and how feasible

GOAL:	THEN.....OUR TEACHERS WILL BE ABLE TO WORK WELL WITH INTEGRATED STUDENTS	.....OUR STUDENTS WILL WORK WELL IN TEAMS
FORMAT Format	Example #1	Example #2
--------▷ IF-----▷Option #1	IF----▷	IF---▷
	There is a program of training in diagnosis and remediation provided	We institute Cooperative Learning in all classes
--------▷ IF-----▷Option #2	IF --▷	IF---▷
	There are trained special aides in the classroom with the teacher at all times	Their course marks depend on group productivity, not on individual productivity
--------▷ IF-----▷Option #3	IF---▷	IF---▷
	Teacher/pupil ratios are set at a maximum of 10 to 1	They are encouraged to help each other on all work (including tests)

Figure 8.6. Planning logic is hypothetical in nature. It begins with the consequent, the "THEN" or desired outcome, and creates a bank of optional methods for achieving that outcome.

they are. Thus, planning requires four "deep levels" or general stages in the development of its total logic. Figure 8.7 presents the four stages of planning logic.

(*1*) Stage One, belief level: the meaning of success. State the broad general goal or aim, and define it in a set of objectives relevant to the particular setting.

(*2*) Stage Two, organization level: values cost perspective. Clarify the priority of that goal in terms of the overall set of goals for the group (class, school, system). Values cost perspective is the allowable cost, the amount of money, time, effort, etc., that can be afforded for achieving that value.

(*3*) Stage Three, probability level: alternatives analysis. Generate a set of possible means or strategies for achieving the goal, and assess them on the basis of probability of success and feasibility.

(*4*) Stage Four, operation level: action analysis. Choose one option and plan the activities and allocation of resources needed to implement it successfully.

Realistically, How Does Planning Proceed?

Most of the time educational planning in real life does not proceed in the four stages of logic as outlined. Indeed, there is a psychological logic that naturally directs our thinking. The natural place to start is with an action proposal: Let's do _____. However, plans will have a higher success rate if the logic is checked. So the real thinking process often follows the following steps:

(*1*) Stage Four: Propose an activity.

(*2*) Stage One: What do we really want to achieve with this activity?

(*3*) Stage Three: What are some other possible activities or strategies we might consider that could also achieve the desired result?

(*4*) Stage Two: What is the priority—the value cost—what can be afforded in time, effort, and in loss to other activities (opportunity cost)?

(*5*) Stage Three again: Which alternative is likely to give us best results at least cost?

(*6*) Stage Four again: What all has to be done to make this a success?

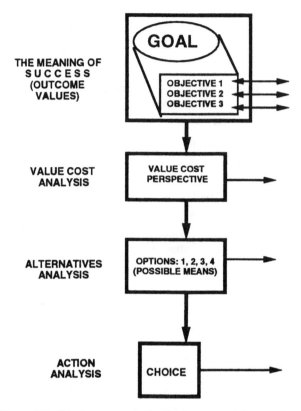

Figure 8.7. The four stages in the development of planning logic.

Quality education is defined in the values acted upon. To keep the eye on values and quality, the logic must be checked. The value must be up front, but checking the logic is more important than following it step-by-step. Chapters 9 and 10 present the planning system in the four stages of logic, as if thinking were to proceed in the pattern of logic.

SUMMARY

As has been stressed by theorists in the past several decades, rationality in planning and decision making is generally assumed to be desirable. Counter arguments have been presented in more recent years, and these have introduced new bases for planning and choice. Those positions should be kept in mind through Chapters 9 and 10 in which the Values-

Based Planning System is presented. In particular, it is important to think about where one might wish to draw the line between rationality and nonrationality, or the "playfulness" that March proposes. In the meantime, we assume for the purposes of further discussion that rationality in planning and decision making is good, at least up to some point.

Rationality in planning and choice is based on logical thought. It was proposed that there are three bases of logical thinking that are essential to planning for quality education: 1) the classical logic forms of deductive and inductive reasoning; 2) analytical reasoning and the logic of wholes; and 3) probability reasoning, forecasting, and predicting.

All of these patterns of logic are necessary to planning. Each form of logic, each type of logical thought is used, consciously or unconsciously, in creating any plan. The first step proposed for planning is usually to state the goals and objectives. This step requires consideration of the obligatory logic that March speaks of and projective logic, the logic of wishful thinking, of "the best of all possible worlds." It also requires analytical logic to clarify the meaning of goals and objectives. When the planners create a set of possible alternatives for action, they are concerned with consequences, cause/effect relationships, and probabilities of success and feasibility. To draw up a schedule of activities for implementation and operation, analytical logic and serial logic are relevant.

Applications of these several forms of logic are developed more specifically in the planning system presented in Chapters 9 and 10. Their uses are also evident in many of the specific planning tools that are described in Chapters 11 and 12.

CHAPTER 9

Stage One: The Meaning of Success

The goal is the mustard seed, and the plant, and the leaf, and the mustard, and the seed, and the plant, and . . .

THE VALUES-BASED PLANNING SYSTEM

MOST educators are experienced and successful at planning activities, projects, and programs. This is the "dolly in" position of planning, planning the short-term events and activities that support the whole. To provide unity, coherence, and direction to the whole of an education system requires dollying out as well, placing the specific activity or project in the perspective of the overall values held for education.

The Values-Based Planning System presented here focuses on the thinking processes necessary to maintain the perspective of the whole — in the particular. Figure 9.1 presents the "storyboard" for the whole planning process. Each of the elements, or pieces, of the storyboard will be discussed in the following chapters in detail, and practice exercises will be presented. Before looking at the whole or the parts, however, some premises upon which the system is based are restated here:

(*1*) The goal is the whole. It is like the title of a book. It is the heart of the plan and of a vision for the future. It tells you where you are going and is the basis for checking the validity of all proposed elements.

(*2*) To think holistically, the "whole" must be known, the goal must be made evident. The goal images the whole as a whole. Without such an image, holistic thinking is not possible.

(*3*) However, it is not necessary to start a plan with the goal. A proposed activity is a natural starting point. The necessary "goal check" is the logic check, "IF we do this, THEN what are we trying to accomplish?" Or, simply, why are we thinking of doing this? (See Figure 8.5 and Logic Exercise 8.3, Chapter 8.)

(*4*) Planning requires the use of many levels of thinking skills: memory,

319

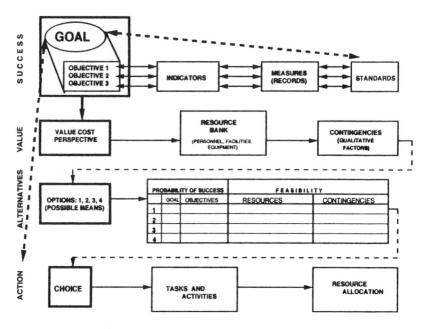

Figure 9.1. *The storyboard for systematic planning, placing the emphasis on values. (If you land on* action, *go back to* success.)

analysis, synthesis, inference, judgment, and prediction. Each skill is used for some particular aspect of planning.

(5) A plan that is prepared and presented in the storyboard format is easy to refer to, to remember, and to change. The visual storyboard keynotes the critical elements and the relationships of those elements to each other.

(6) After the separate skills are identified and practiced, it will not be necessary to complete the entire storyboard except for very major projects. The "body knowledge" held in the brain will use the separate processes as automatically as the body uses the skills needed for dancing or running a snowblower.

Several examples of completed storyboards for values-based plans that have been submitted by area educators are included in Appendix D.

The Source of the Goal

If the first step in developing any plan is always said to be to clarify the goals, the educational planner's natural inclination is to ask, "What goals?" or "Whose goals?" Practically everything discussed so far, particularly in Chapters 1 through 7, has aimed at identifying the many possible filters through which goals for education can come to the planning table. These filters are the patterns that develop in peoples' values and beliefs about education from their culture, experience, and study and from all of the community and environmental forces that shape them.

The parents of each third-grade child may be like the person who says, "I don't know anything about art, but I know what I like." They may not know anything about philosophies of education, but they know what they want for their child. Figure 9.2 illustrates the parents' view of the school system's organizational chart.

What they (and we) want, what we think is a good education, has been learned from all of those voices out of our culture, experience, study, and living. Although community groups have many common patterns of beliefs and interests, for each parent, *want* is very particular, focused on benefits for their own child. Beliefs about what will benefit their child most come from the deep structures of thinking and feeling, culture, world view, and life experiences. The orientation that can make

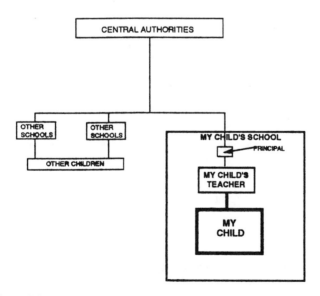

Figure 9.2. A parent's view of the school system's organizational chart.

educators' choices and plans for education richer and more truly choices is recognizing and understanding the different patterns of beliefs and values brought to our school or to our system.

This has been the purpose of Sections I and II, to offer tools or techniques for recognizing and choosing among the patterns that have shaped some of the important ideas about education and about planning and choice for education. Figure 9.3 illustrates the source of the goal, the filters through which ideas, hopes, and visions of the future come to the planning table.

Line of Thought

Overall, planning maintains a coherent line of thought. On the storyboard in Figure 9.1, the line of thought is represented by the flow of arrows. Although line of thought should be clear in a plan, building a plan does not necessarily move following this line. Line of thought is the organizing principle for the completed plan—completed, one should be able to read the plan for coherence, unity, and consistency, just as one would be able to read a blueprint for feasibility and coherence.

In planning, the line of thought moves from general to specific, from the whole to the particular in two directions. Figure 9.4 illustrates the movement from general (goal) to specific.

The broad, general value (qualitative in nature) stated in the goal gets translated into a quantified standard of success from left to right. It gets translated from success (the general, or abstract) at Stage One into action program (the specific) at Stage Four.

However, our natural thought pattern is more often from the particular to the general. We pick up pieces of information, habits, and experiences, and they coalesce into whole abilities, skills, or knowledge, often without our being conscious of the pattern formation, the generalization. It is important to remember, therefore, that not only *can* thinking move in either direction, it *must*. As in the logic exercises in Chapter 8, the line of thinking in a plan should be clear and easy to read in either direction.

It is not critical where on the rational planning model one begins to think about a project, but all of the elements must be developed for a plan to have a reasonable probability of accomplishing what you want it to accomplish. If one starts with action, proposing a particular event, an innovation, or a project, it is still critical to think through all of the

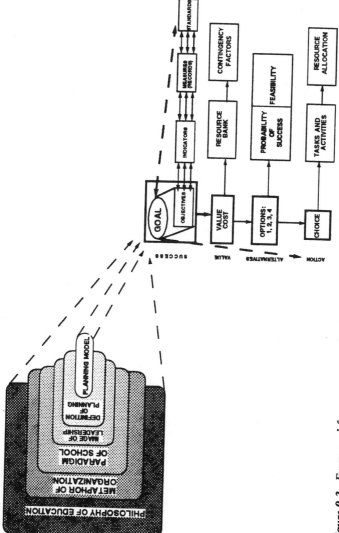

Figure 9.3. *Every goal for every system, program, project, unit, event, or activity derives from and reflects our most profound and holistic values and beliefs.*

323

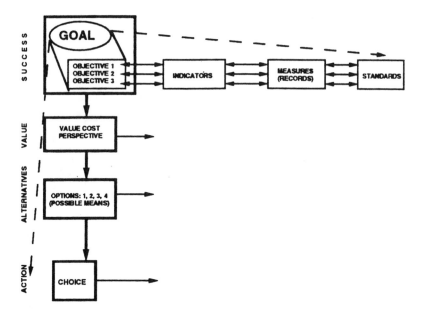

Figure 9.4. Planning moves from abstract to concrete or from general to specific in two directions—toward standards of success and toward action.

elements of a rational plan, to consider the implications for the whole school or system, and to consider possible alternative, perhaps more feasible, programs that might achieve the goal.

What is very natural for us all, but what educators should not do, is to propose a possible course of action and enthusiastically make action plans to carry it out. This style can lead to "weathervane" activity, turning from novelty, to novelty, whichever way the wind blows, without considering the goals and objectives, the implications, and alternative possibilities.

The primary elements of the planning process are the four levels or stages keynoted by the first box in each line. These are presented as Stage One, Success; Stage Two, Value Cost; Stage Three, Alternatives; and Stage Four, Action. The four key boxes—Goal, Value Cost Perspective, Options, and Choice—are the triggers for four thought processes central to planning: synthesis, estimation, projection, and judgment. Other thought processes such as analysis and inference are also employed in the overall process. Is it any wonder that Bologna (1980) found that the first three reasons given by managers for resisting planning are 1) it is too time-consuming; 2) there is too much work involved; and 3) there is a deficiency of knowledge (p. 29). However, everything is easy when you know how to do it. The following sections explain how to create each unit of a plan, each element for the storyboard.

STAGE ONE: PLANNING FOR SUCCESS

The success stage of the planning model requires clear goals and objectives, and it requires that measures and standards upon which success will be judged should be specified. Figure 9.5 presents the elements included in Stage One, Success: goal, objectives, indicators, measures, and standards. Each of those elements will be discussed in the following sections.

Although we have repeatedly said that, in all probability, a planning sequence begins with an idea for action, all of the elements of a rational planning model should be considered when the future is at stake. The goal is the focus for the whole; therefore, like most presentations in the literature on planning, the discussion begins with goals and objectives, the description of success.

If an idea for action is presented, the first step should be to ask ''Why?'' The answers to that question express the values held and are the real goals participants have in mind.

Step One: Goal and Objectives

From Chapter 8 logic exercises, you know how to leap backwards (dolly out) from action proposal to goal, to get a perspective on the educational purpose of the activity proposed. Suppose someone has

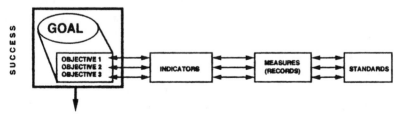

Figure 9.5. *Stage One of the plan: clarifying the meaning of success (what* success *means for this group at this particular moment in time).*

proposed a two-week winter camp-out for ninth graders or a state/provincewide competition in problem-solving skills for fifth graders. There may be many reasons given for these proposed activities, many probable outcomes. The broad, general outcome to be aimed for is the goal.

There is considerable difference in how planning might proceed if the goal chosen is to be able to survive in the mountains in winter versus to be able to use survival skills effectively. The broader goal allows more flexibility in planning, indeed, encourages greater creativity or inventiveness in developing alternatives in Stage Three, Action. Similarly, "to be skillful in solving word problems" could lead in an entirely different direction from "to be able to perform well under competition."

Suppose someone proposes that a parent volunteer program be developed. There are a number of good reasons why such a program might be helpful, but the program should be shaped by the present reason for being. If the goal, the *raison d'être*, were for parents and teachers to understand and appreciate each other more, the program might be very different than if the goal were to provide inexpensive support for teachers of special students. Or suppose a systematic program of supervision were to be proposed. Would the real goal be better teaching or better learning? Would these goals lead to different programs? Upon whom would attention be focused if the goal is better teaching or if the goal is better learning?

Specifying the goals and objectives of any project in terms of values is the key to planning for the quality of educational result we desire. The goal statement of a project is the statement of purpose, of the quality result desired, the statement of the whole. It expresses the value the whole will have for the people concerned if the project is successful. The goal is the kernel from which both the plan and the project develop, and it is also the tuning fork against which is tested every objective, every activity, every alternative, and every standard. How well is this objective, this standard, this activity, this alternative attuned to the result desired?

Having arrived at a clear statement of the result to be achieved, the goal, the plan can be developed smoothly and rationally. Moreover, implementation and operation can adapt readily to unforeseen circumstances; direction is clear, and the end result desired is clear. Activities can be easily checked against the goal to keep the project headed in the desired direction. Knowledge of destination allows us to make sensible choices of routes.

Thus, the goal is the synthesizing agent for the plan and the project; maintaining a constant "goal check" (destination check) keeps particular activities in perspective but also reinforces openness to possible change of the goal itself. Keeping an eye on the goal as the situation develops should notify us when the goal itself should be modified. The goal is the lens through which the project is kept in focus with the broader system and with the larger perspective of the profession.

Three Questions about Goals and Objectives

At this point, there are three questions about goals and objectives that should be considered; each will be dealt with in the next few pages.

(*1*) How does it happen that the terms *goals* and *objectives* are used with opposite meanings in organizational literature? The answer to this question will help put any organizational planning system into perspective.

(*2*) Aside from the philosophical bias already exposed, why should objectives and goals express values and not behaviors? How does the expression of objectives as values affect the administration of a plan, a project, a program, or a system?

(*3*) There are rules for writing behavioral objectives. What rules might be developed for writing values-based goals and objectives?

Confusing meanings of *goals* and *objectives* abound. In organizational literature, the terms *goals* and *objectives* are sometimes used interchangeably; at other times, they are used precisely but with opposite meanings. Kaufman, for example, defines goals as statements of broad general aims and objectives as statements of more narrow, specific aims (1972, 144). Immegart and Pilecki (1973, 158) define them as does Kaufman. On the other hand, Manning uses the terms with exactly the opposite meanings: *objectives* takes on the broad sense and *goals* the specific, immediate sense (1970, 16). Alioto and Jungherr use objectives for all levels of abstraction or generality (1971, 53−54).

Common usage, it is clear, accepts the first pattern. It seems reasonable and useful to follow common sense meanings of words in the behavioral sciences, at the same time defining and using the terms precisely. Therefore, goals are defined as broad, general values held, stated as the desired results or outcomes of an activity or operation. Objectives are defined as specific valued elements or aspects of a given goal, also stated as desired results or outcomes.

If a given goal is that students will be well educated academically, the objectives tell what *well educated academically* means or includes – well educated in math, in the use of language, or in the history of human beings and of one's country. The goal means or includes different aspects in different systems, in different areas of a community, or at different levels of age or ability. But the goal is appropriate broadly and generally. For students to be socially responsible is a universally accepted educational goal, but *socially responsible* has different meanings from one culture to another, from one community to another, from one school to another, and from one time to another.

Objectives state the "pieces of meaning" of a goal appropriate to the specific situation where the project or program or system is found. If a given goal is that students will appreciate good music, the objectives tell what *will appreciate* means (understand, recognize, listen to) and what *good music* means or includes. The goal means or includes different aspects of the whole in different systems, in different areas of a community, and at different age or ability levels. But the value, the desired outcome, the goal, is appropriate universally.

That is to say, simply, there is no universal meaning for universal values; the meaning of values is specific to the context (community, culture, society). Objectives make clear what each universal value goal means – the set of things that are parts of the value held where the planning happens to be taking place.

There seems to be a simple and logical reason why the terms *goals* and *objectives* are used with opposite meanings. There are two considerations that must be addressed in planning: the scope and the range within which the plan is being developed, that is, the parameters of the plan. There are three general scopes of organizational planning: system, program, and project. If planning is systematic, all projects fit rationally into program plans, and all programs fit rationally into the system plan. It is by means of goals and objectives that such coherence of direction is created.

This is the very simple and logical reason why the terms *goals* and *objectives* are used with opposite meanings. So we return to our camera analogy. A desired result may be "narrow and specific" (an objective) in the context of the system, but "broad and general" (a goal) in the context of a program. Figure 9.6 illustrates this understandable confusion, and demonstrates how planning maintains its holistic focus even as it moves closer to the particular operational level.

System goals are broad statements. They are concerned with all sectors, all levels, and all departments within the system. System objectives identify the important aspects of a particular goal to be focused on specifically for the whole system. For example, for all students to be competent in math might be a system goal. Objectives might be related to the various groups of math students. Programs that grow out of that system goal would include math programs for each grade level, for remedial, for gifted, etc., systemwide. Each system objective, therefore, becomes a program goal. In turn, that program goal becomes the overall statement of results desired for the program—that particular piece of the system.

Equally, a set of program objectives describes or details the important elements of the program goal, and, of course, each program objective can become a project goal. The scope continues to narrow to units, to lessons. Every result desired and aimed for can be seen as broad and general or as narrow and specific, depending on the scope of the operation or event being planned. Figure 9.7 gives an example of the relationship of goal to objective to goal as you move from program to project. It is through the relationship between goals and objectives that particular projects, units, departments, or programs establish or enhance the system, the organization. The unity of purpose of our education systems, thus, depends upon being sure that our goals and objectives express clearly the values we hold.

When moving from goal to objectives in planning, in general, it is wisest to consider any project as aiming to accomplish one primary goal, one broad, general outcome, even though every program or project is bound to affect many different skills, knowledge, understandings, and attitudes. It is always important to try to see the big picture. Thus, several "goals" may be proposed such as students "will respect other students," "will be courteous to visitors at school," "will treat service personnel with courtesy," "will be good representatives of the school when they are at the mall," and "will be considerate of school neighbors."

It is readily apparent that the planners could dolly out to "students

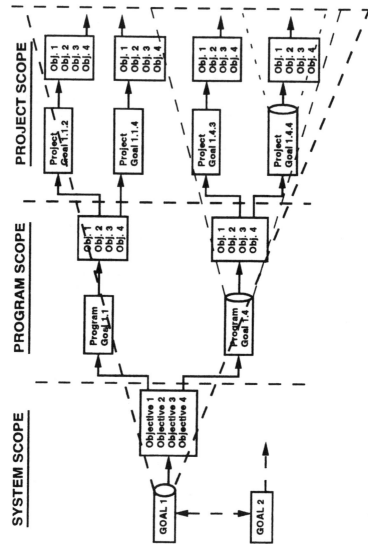

Figure 9.6. *"Goal" or "objective" depends on scope. The integral relationship of goals and objectives keeps the whole system in perspective.*

330

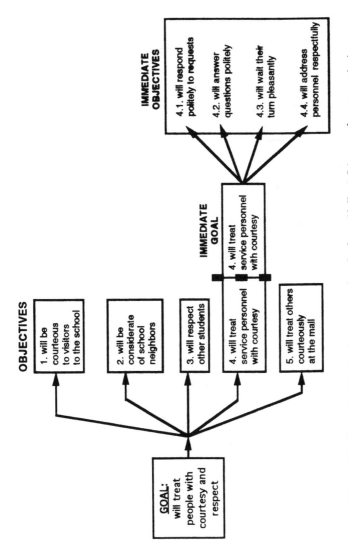

Figure 9.7. Example: objective becomes goal as the focus "dollys in" (moves closer to action).

331

will be considerate of, or respectful toward, others," or dolly in by selecting one of the proposals as the goal for this project. If "will treat service personnel with courtesy" is chosen, then more specific objectives will be defined. Perhaps they may include, "will respond politely to requests made by service personnel," "will answer questions pleasantly," "will wait their turn at service counters," "will address personnel properly," etc. Figure 9.8 illustrates the two perspectives in terms of scope and range.

Concerning values-based objectives or behavioral objectives, much has been said in educational and organizational literature. It has been asserted that objectives should be stated in terms of specific behaviors desired, with the level at which they should be performed clearly specified [see, for example, Ansoff (1970), Armstrong (1968), Burkhart (1974), and Mager (1962)]. A good case has been made on the bases of clarity, objectivity, and fairness to the persons concerned. Indeed, the use of behavioral objectives has made a tremendous contribution to curriculum and program development by clarifying the bases of judgment about achievement. As well, behavioral objectives have contributed to labor contracts by clarifying bases of contract decisions.

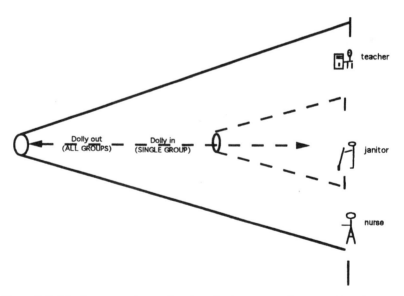

Figure 9.8. The focus may change, but the value is constant: "treat people with respect and courtesy."

In planning for quality education, however, goals and objectives should be stated qualitatively, not quantitatively; they should be value-based, not behavior-based. Behaviors are clues to whether our objectives and goals, our values, have been achieved, but behaviors are not our objectives. Criticisms leveled at behavioral objectives have always been of the "yes, but. . ." variety. Behavioral objectives always leave us with the uneasy knowledge that, like the correlation of IQ and achievement, they are not appropriate to the specific case.

If we say, for example, that "all fourth graders will be reading at the 4.0 level on the _____ reading test," we have to say to ourselves, "yes, but that is the minimum level we want, or there are exceptions, of course." We really want fourth graders to be reading well (for their ability, background, etc.). It is this recognition and the growing uneasiness fostered by too much emphasis on standardized testing that have led to such recent developments as criterion-referenced testing, alternative testing, and authentic testing. Perhaps unfortunately, an assumption is developing that these more qualitatively based forms of testing should themselves be standardized on a state or national level in some way (Madaus and Kellaghan, 1993; Worthen, 1993).

It is impossible to state a behavioral objective appropriate to all members of any group without expressing it at a level that the lowest member of the group can attain. The reason this is true is that such objectives, focused on particular groups (fourth graders, ninth graders, science students, etc.), are program or project objectives. They are the criteria by which we judge the success of our program, not the criteria by which we judge the success of individual students.

It might be appropriate to write behavioral objectives for each student, "J. J. will be reading at the 4.0 level"; "R. S. will be reading at the 3.6 level"; "T. F. will be reading at the 6.2 level." Teachers do that intuitively when they say to themselves, "J. J. is doing well this year, s/he is at 4.0; I'm really proud of R. S., s/he is at 4.0, too; T. F. is slipping, s/he is only at 5.7. All in all, though, 'we' are doing *well.*" The objective is reading well, and professional judgment tells us what that means in individual cases. Well is not "motherhood and apple pie"; it is the appropriate base for professional judgment.

The planning difficulty inherent in behavioral objectives is that they include in the statement of objective five different elements. Cunningham includes an additional element, the time constraint, as "by the end of fourth grade" (1982, 71):

(*1*) End result valued	— Reading (*well* is assumed)	Goal
(*2*) Behavioral indicator	— Performance on a test or — performance in class	Indicator
(*3*) Instrument/ measure	— Specific test or Set of judgments	Measure
(*4*) Standard: "success" for students	— 4.0, or 85%, etc.	Student Standard
(*5*) Standard: "success" for program	— All students; 75% of the students, etc.	Program Standard

In the planning model I propose, those five elements are presented separately. It is the standard of success and the type of measurement used that must be particular to the level of the students, but the overall goals and objectives are appropriate to all. If our goals and objectives are value-based, stated qualitatively, we can spend our planning time where it is useful, on the questions, "What test (or type of record) shall we use and what shall we set as the standards for this group?" We can focus on determining what standards and measures are appropriate for each particular group. We can direct our planning attention to the individual differences between particular groups.

When I propose to students or colleagues the argument that objectives should be stated as values, and indicators and standards as behaviors, they often ask if that is not just semantic nit-picking. This is a reasonable question. The fact is that we must rely on observations of behaviors to make professional judgments. And pupils and parents have the right to know which behaviors form the bases of our judgments.

In the past, educators have often made value judgments without identifying the behavioral bases of those judgments (good citizen, creative work, respectful, understands concepts, appreciates good literature). We do owe it to ourselves and to our students to state *behavioral* indicators, to make clear what it is that we will look at to make the judgments we are required to make.

I find myself coming back, however, to the simple fact that behaviors are not our objectives. It has not been so long ago that standing to recite was seen as an indicator of good citizenship or of respect. The goals of good citizenship and respect are still among us but not the behavioral indicators used in the early twentieth century. Objectives stated as values encourage us to consider individual differences in our plans and in our evaluations; standards set behaviorally encourage us to be realistic, equitable, and adaptable to changing circumstances.

There is a second confusion that often enters into behavioral objectives and causes educational problems. A statement such as the following may be found in program objectives: "All students will submit 300 words of written composition per week." Aside from the obvious fallacy of assuming that any particular number of words might result in good writing skills, this is a means statement. It is one possible means to the end of "writing well," but it is only one possible means and should be judged along with others in Stage Three, Alternatives. If means or technologies have slipped into our goals and objectives statements, it is easy to begin to think of them as ends in themselves. This leads us to attributing a wide range of values to particular means. As a result, we may become frustrated and discouraged when all values are not achieved.

If the objective is to carpet the classroom floors, reasons given (values held) may be to create a homelike atmosphere, to make the children feel comfortable, to save maintenance time and money, to teach the children proper care of facilities, or whatever. Those answers express the real goals and objectives, the values held. Carpeting the floors may be a good means for achieving any or all of these values, but there may be other, better means that should be considered. Actions that educators may take and actions that may be required of students are means to desired ends, and desired ends are qualitative in nature. Eisner (1992a) says there are no "silver bullets"; means that look like objectives take on the aura of silver bullets.

Administratively, then, goals and objectives stated as values free us to use our planning time productively and to review progress more appropriately. Yes, we got the floors carpeted, but did this accomplish the hoped for result? Goals and objectives are quite general and do remain relatively constant over time, though their behavioral "meaning" may change. Indicators, measures, and standards, and means, options, alternatives, or strategies change to meet changing circumstances.

Rules for Writing Values-Based Goals and Objectives

Behavioral objectivists have formulated careful rules for writing good objectives. In the previous pages, I have taken issue with most of those rules. I have implied that there are specific criteria for judging "good" values-based goals and objectives statements. I will try to make the rules I propose for writing values-based objectives clear by expressing them in two ways. First, I will state the rules and give types of words and phrases that should and should not be used in goal or objectives statements. Second, Table 9.1 gives some specific examples related to each rule.

The rules proposed for writing values-based goals and objectives statements are as follows:

(*1*) Rule 1: Goals and objectives should express attitudes, beliefs, and achievements that are valued, because they are the ends or results aimed for. They should not be stated as behaviors because behaviors are only clues to, or indicators of, the attitudes, beliefs, and achievements valued.

(*2*) Rule 2: Goals and objectives should express values qualitatively, not quantitatively. Values expressed qualitatively are constants. They are general and generalizable. Values are the basic criteria by which we judge a broad range of specific cases. They form the body of knowledge basic to our professional expertise. We are not able to measure such values as responsibility and creativity, but our professional training should enable us to make educated judgments about whether students (or teachers or administrators) are or are not responsible and creative. We can, we must, and we do make judgments. We make them on the basis of our values and use behaviors as clues. Growth professionally implies growing in the ability to make good judgments.

Goals and objectives stated quantitatively are always specific to narrow ranges of cases. To aim for no more than three absences per pupil completely overrides professional judgment of sufficient cause. Degrees, percentages, and ratios are the tools we employ to set standards, not goals. Seventy-five percent of our class, with no more than three absences each, may be a rational standard for a group. It allows for normal distribution of variable causes and reminds us that only very rarely can we look for 100%. *All* and *every* pound people into standard molds; such a mental set contradicts our credo of concern for individual differences and individual potentials.

(*3*) Rule 2a: Never use words such as *improve, increase, develop,*

Table 9.1. Examples Illustrating the Rules for Writing Good Values-Based Goal and Objective Statements.

Right	Wrong
Rule 1: Goals and objectives should state attitudes, beliefs, and achievements valued, not behaviors.	
Values-based:	Behavior-based:
• Students will enjoy good books (an attitude and value we aim for).	• Students will read two unassigned library books per term (a behavioral clue; it may evidence different attitudes).
• Students will be able to express their ideas creatively.	• Students will write one Haiku poem (a behavioral clue).
• Students will respect each other (an attitude we value).	• Students will not interrupt others (a behavioral rule, a clue; may evidence fear, etc.)
Rule 2: Goals and objectives should express values qualitatively not quantitatively.	
Value (expressed qualitatively):	Standard (expressed quantitatively):
• Students will understand percentage.	• Students will get 60% or more on the percentage test.
• Students will be responsible citizens.	• Students will have no more than two office reports.
• Teachers will keep abreast of professional developments.	• Teachers will attend one professional course per year; attend three professional workshops, etc.
Rule 2a: Never use words that imply premeasurement on some quantitative scale (increase, more, less, better).	
No premeasurement implied:	Premeasurement implied:
• Teachers will enjoy their work.	• Teachers will be more satisfied with their work.
• Students will have good job skills.	• Students will be better trained for jobs.
Rule 3: Values-based goals and objectives should be written in terms of product (result), not process (means).	
Product terms:	Process terms:
• Students will be happy in school.	• We will provide students with a pleasant atmosphere.
• Parents will understand the school program and codes.	• We will present seminars for parents on school programs and codes.
Rule 3a: Verbs should be appropriate to product, not process.	
Product verbs:	Process verbs:
• Students will have good math skills.	• We will provide students with appropriate math tools.
• Students will be good citizens in the community.	• Teach students community citizenship.

337

more, less, or *better* in goals and objectives statements. This rule flies in the face of everything we are accustomed to, but it is a critical mental set. Such words are quantitative, nondefinite, but quantitative nevertheless. Moreover, they imply prejudgment. To aim for "greater" respect for property implies that the group has already been assessed on this value and found wanting.

The fact that we may have formed an opinion about the degree of respect for property residing in the minds and the behaviors of students is not sufficient basis for judgment. Our opinions should trigger investigation, not judgment. Words such as those listed above imply that measures have been made or that a point on some scale has been established. They generally do not reveal the instrument or method used for premeasurement. Therefore, they place no constraints on the instrument or means of post-measurement and provide no valid basis of comparison for judgment regarding change: more, better, etc.

The standard sets the level of expectation for the particular group or time. Thus, 65% may be "better" than the 58% achieved last year. This perspective implies that trends will be tracked, and that is indeed a perspective we adhere to.

(4) Rule 3: Goals and objectives should be written in terms of the product, result, or outcome to be achieved by the learners, not their means of achieving, not the work they will do to learn. Neither should they be written in terms of what the teachers will do to enable students to learn (show, discuss, develop). These are means, not outcomes. Product is the desired result. Process is the means or method of accomplishing.

(5) Rule 3a: Verbs should be appropriate to end products (results), not to processes. Product verbs are will know, will understand, will be able, and will appreciate, and process verbs are will teach, will encourage, will develop, will require, will begin, and will provide.

We have repeatedly said that qualitative goals and objectives are the keys to the quality of learning and the quality of life in our education systems. *Remember:* Even if the impetus for beginning to plan is a proposal for action, it is extremely important to back away from that proposal and examine it through the lens of the camera, that is, through the value held, the goal.

Many sets of goal or objective statements include all three types of goals and objectives discussed: values-based goals or objectives, process objectives, and behavioral objectives. The set known as America's Education Goals for 2000 is an example. Exercise 9.1 identifies the type of goal statement(s) included in each proposition and asks you to rewrite them all as separate, individual values-based objectives.

Step Two: Planning for Evaluation

In planning an educational project or program, the objectives set provide direction to the plan for overall strategy and implementation activities. The objectives also direct the plan for evaluation of the project

---

We have discussed three types of goals or objectives statements: behavioral objectives, process objectives, and values-based objectives. Former United States President, George Bush, and the governors prepared a list of six education goals for the year 2000. Some of the statements include more than one objective.

State separate possible values-based objectives *focused on students as clients* that would be relevant for each.

GOAL STATEMENT	TYPE OF STATEMENT	POSSIBLE VALUES-BASED OBJECTIVES
Every American chlid must start school prepared to learn, sound in body, and sound in mind.	three values-based	
The high school graduation rate in the U.S. must increase to no less than 90%.	behavioral objective	
All students in grades four, eight, and twelve will be tested for progress in critical subjects.	process objective	
American students must rank first in the world in achievement in mathematics and science.	behavioral objective	
Every adult must be a skilled, literate worker and citizen, able to compete in a global economy.	four values-based objectives	
Every school must be drug-free and offer a disciplined environment conducive to learning.	one values-based (school) two process objectives (school)	

Exercise 9.1. Types of objectives statements.

and for judging success. Indicators, measures, and standards are the tools for planning a means of evaluation of success. The next section will discuss indicators and measures; following that, setting standards will be discussed.

Indicators and Measures

It is useful in planning to think of indicators and measures together. Indicators name what we are going to look at, or look for, to judge success. Measures are the specific tools we are going to use to gather data on that indicator. They are data-gathering instruments such as tests and records, and they are designed so we may make fair judgments. Standards set the pass/fail level for any particular project, program, or group.

In this respect, we differ from behavioral objectivists who propose that the standard is an inherent element of the objective. We treat objectives as constant values, and indicators, measures, and standards as variable and particular to groups and circumstances. We propose that, for effective planning these three elements should be stated separately and separate from the objective. Stating the four elements separately enables us to test each element against its context: objectives in the context of professional, social, and cultural values; and indicators, measures, and standards in the context of the purpose of assessment and the group for whom the project or program is being planned.

The distinction between indicators and measures is between generality and specificity. Indicators are general types of behaviors, items, or facts we will take note of; measures are the particular notations we will make about those observations and the ways in which we design those notations and establish scales from them.

It is almost universally asserted that we cannot "measure" most of the learning results we care about in education. Yet, just as universally we rank students on everything from use of mathematics functions to physical dexterity to verbal skills to reading appreciation, creativity, responsibility, courtesy, respect for property, organization, and insight. Some of those rankings are determined on the basis of carefully designed, even standardized, tests. Others are determined on the basis of written records kept over time. Still others are determined on the basis of "records" kept mentally and circulated in staff lounges.

So to say that we cannot measure simply means that we do not have, and never will have, scalar measures that even approximate those applied to physical properties. However, Western education systems and the Western societies in which they exist demand that educators rank, or rate, students on a great variety of factors.

Measures: When we think of educational measures, we may think first of standardized tests. They have been developed to the highest degree of scalar stability of all the measures we may use; however, the past decade has produced an increasingly vocal challenge to the use of standardized tests. The challenges voiced include the following:

- They do not test what is learned.
- They do not test what it is important to learn.
- They do not provide useful information for teaching or improving curricula.
- They provide only quite general information about individual students who are the real concern of teachers in the school.
- They subvert education itself, in that they induce teaching to the test, to the particularized bits of knowledge called for by test items.

As Abruscato says, "Teachers need less information about percentile rankings and more information about students' performance. . . . [They need] information to create learning experiences to help students go even further" (1993, 475). The issue has become comparability of results across schools and systems versus formation or development of students' abilities and skills. This is an issue that has not been resolved, not within the profession, the education systems, or in the minds of the parents or national leaders.

Indicators: In every educational activity, we make judgments about the success of individual students and about our own success, that is, the success of the activity itself. The "things" we look at to make those judgments are the indicators of success, the clues to learning or to desired attitudes and understandings. Most of those indicators, or clues, are quite standard. Those we use consistently include performance on tests; behavior around the school (in class, on the playground, in the halls, in the cafeteria); written work; homework completed; absences and tardiness; care of books and equipment; class discussions; exercises, workbooks, projects, reports; office referrals; and friendship patterns.

All of these and many more specific things that we take note of become the bases of our judgments. We keep formal and systematic records of some of these, so we are very conscious of them. We accept them as reasonable bases for judgment about academic success, citizenship, attitudes, abilities, etc. Indeed, we do not think of them as clues, or indicators. We think of them as measures because subconsciously, or consciously, we have established a "scale" for them. Others are less consciously noted and less consciously rated.

It is our business to make judgments about learning results, and it seems useful to direct our efforts toward being more conscious of and more specific about the bases of judgments that we educators generally accept. It seems useful to put our energy to work toward refining those subconscious or subjective scales that we may use.

What, then, are the characteristics of the measures we commonly accept? What do they have in common that makes them reasonably acceptable as measures? First, many of the bases of our judgments are things that are repeated over time and for which records are kept. This enables us to get a count for things such as absences, homework completed, detentions, correctness of work done on assignments, and participation in various activities. Given the record over time, we think of the count in one of two ways. We may set absolute points for various degrees of acceptability, or we may establish a trend scale, interpreting change over time as favorable or unfavorable. We then read that scale as a measure of some educational skill, ability, attitude, or learning.

Thus, when we interpret the record of homework completed as "responsibility," we have done several things. We have thought of homework completed as a fair indicator of responsibility, we have made a systematic record for all students, we have established a scale for "reading" the record, and we have read each student's record on the same scale. In other words, we have systematized, or standardized, our judgments insofar as it is possible. We have approached a measure.

The second type of measure we accept is a judgment on a one-time activity, such as a science project, a story, a history report, a wood project, or a book report. For these, we establish (subjectively or consciously) a set of indicators of "goodness" — neatness, organization, thoroughness, and technique. We may make separate judgments on each factor, in which case, we are creating something that approximates the "count" scale of the first type. Students themselves often press for that approach by asking how many points for each aspect. In this case, however, the scale is based on a summation of separate judgments. Again, by systematizing judgments, we have approached measurement.

The third type of measure we accept is a holistic judgment of a single work, or skill. The indicator in this case is the artistic or creative merit of the whole, the impact of the whole as a whole. The scale is established on the basis of a population of such works that includes primarily the work of students but holds, as a shadowy ultimate range, the work of artists in the field. This type of measure is applied most commonly in the arts, music, sports, composition, and drama, for example. It is also quite possibly the scale applied to academic abilities when we speak of such qualities as insight, perception, and understanding.

There are four characteristics that make both the second and third type of measures described as generally acceptable. First, thought has been given to establishing both the indicators (the indicators of goodness) and the possible values of each beforehand. Second, there is an effort to judge the work of individual students on the same scale. Third, the particular work of all students is generally judged at a common point in time. That is, a reading on achievements is taken under as nearly equivalent circumstances as possible. Fourth, a written record of judgments is made. It is these four characteristics that make professional judgments reasonably acceptable as surrogates to measures. Whether work or behavior is judged by the teacher in the classroom or by some "expert," the judgments made are, indeed, surrogates to measures.

I believe that the thoughtful exercise of professional judgment is essential to quality education. I also believe that reflective practice implies that we consistently bend our efforts to knowing more surely what the clues are to success, upon which we base those judgments. I believe, thirdly, that making reflective judgments systematically is the closest we can get in education to measures. The reasonable exercise of reflective judgment is our business.

Even beyond all of the emphasis placed here on measurement, I believe that the practice of continually reflecting on and endeavoring to improve the bases of judgment will enhance our teaching or our administrative skills. A brief example may be of interest.

A young college physical education teacher in the master's program was working on the indicators box for his plan of a volleyball competition project. One objective he had stated was, "Students will be able to control the ball." I poked and prodded him with questions such as, "How do you know if a student has control of the ball?" and "What *indicates* to you that a student can control the ball?" and "What do you look at or look for?" and "OK, you have decided that Student A controls the ball better than B. How do you know?" and "How do *you* control the ball?"

He struggled with, "Well, I watch them," and "I see where the ball goes," and "I can just tell." Suddenly, that flash of comprehension all teachers thrive on came, "I look at their finger position on the ball." Then he said, "You know, I can *teach* ball control better now. That is what makes the difference."

This little cameo tells us something else about indicators, too. There are indicators by which we may judge outcome of learning, and there are indicators by which we may judge and enhance learning itself. "Where the ball goes" is the result the team wants, the *test* of successful learning (or of accidental result), but finger position is the indicator of learning. We cannot always reach the learning indicator, but that is what we should aim to be clear about.

Thus, the thinking process that is required, the probing reflection into what we mean by *success,* and on what bases we will judge whether we have achieved it, is not an exercise of filling in boxes in a plan. It is not even an exercise of planning a project. It is the exercise of thinking clearly about what we hope to achieve as a result of our efforts and of how we will know whether we have achieved it. If we are very sure about what the purpose of our project is, we could change any part of the activities and still head in the right direction.

Because of challenges to the earlier reliance on standardized tests, there have been serious efforts to refine the bases of evaluating student performance, which teachers have commonly used at the classroom level. These developing modes of alternative testing include portfolios of student work, exhibitions, presentations, and projects, or research and service activities. There are a number of recent articles and books describing and reporting on the development of these new modes of alternative testing. See, for example, the reports of Abruscato (1993) on a portfolio project, McDonald (1993) on an exhibition, Madaus and Kellaghan (1993) on the British experience with alternative assessment, and Worthen (1993) on a review of the critical issues involved in alternative forms of assessment.

All of these reports of alternative testing modes propose that the issues of validity, reliability, and equity should be addressed by systematizing the processes of assessing the work presented. The bases of assessment are to be specified and efforts made to provide rating reliability checks by including more than one rater in the process. However, these issues are addressed at the school level, not at the macro level. They are addressed on the basis of school and system objectives, indicators, measures, and standards. Their purpose is to provide information to teachers about the learning of individual students first, and second about the effectiveness of the educational program of that system or that school in terms of learning expected there, and at that time.

Whether these alternative modes of testing will survive against the voices for national curricula and national standards remains to be seen. The call for data that may be compared across schools and systems is a strong one. Parents hope to choose the school where their children will have the "best chance"; corporations hope to locate in areas where the schools provide a large pool of well-educated young adults; nations hope to gain competitive advantage by producing a populace that can meet the demands of industries of the future. But from our perspective, from the perspective of planning at the local level, these newer modes of assessment are moving in the right direction. No local planning for education can take place without setting local expectations and local systems of assessing results.

What such projects have in common is that they propose that we must make the effort to invent methods for assessing skills and abilities other than the knowledge and reasoning skills that are the primary focus of standardized tests. They intend to assess such skills as organizing materials, presentation, planning and carrying out a project, developing ideas, arguing a thesis, and self-assessment.

The new assessment directions have specified the things raters will look at as bases of assessment and have structured systems of rating the separate elements, or the whole, to provide information upon which to strengthen individual learning and to strengthen the learning activities included in curricula. Moreover, some evidence suggests that the process of engaging in alternative testing projects is in itself a learning experience for teachers (Madaus and Kellaghan, 1993). I propose that the process of planning for evaluation described here would provide a similarly productive learning experience.

Indicators and Measures on the Storyboard

One of the primary reasons for using the storyboard format for building a plan is to make the ideas behind the project easy to read at a glance and easy to implement; therefore, every element of the plan should be kept as simple as possible. Few words should be used—only the key words that will get the idea across quickly and simply. For example, do not use complete sentences, and use only those adjectives or adverbs that express key values. The heart of a planning idea is verb expressing value + value word + object:

Valuing Verb	Value Level	Object
understand		math functions
respect		rights of others
be able to originate		new ideas
appreciate	good	literature
behave	responsibly	in community

Complex, involved plans do not get implemented. Make sure that implementation will cost as little time and energy as is reasonably possible. This rule is particularly true in planning for evaluation of the project. No educator has time to collect and interpret masses of data. Therefore, on the storyboard for a plan, only one indicator and one measure should be specified for each objective. One could specify several, of course, but teachers have none too much time on their hands in the best of circumstances. Adding tedious data collection to a project may be the proverbial last straw.

There are two criteria for good indicators and the measures or records that follow from them: 1) they should provide reasonably good information about the particular objective, and 2) they should be as simple as possible to keep records of. Thus, in-depth interviews with parents might tell us a great deal about how well they understand the school's programs. However, under most circumstances, neither teachers nor administrators have the time for conducting such interviews or for analyzing them. They are not feasible.

Keeping some kind of record of trash collected might tell us something about the success of our "Keep the school clean" project.

> *More than one-third of cigarette*
> *packages swept up in the*
> *Forum were either smuggled*
> *Canadian or copycat brands.*
> —The Montreal Gazette, *April 14, 1993*

But could we devise a simpler and equally useful indicator? The measure designed should incorporate the four characteristics identified above. 1) Thought should be given ahead of time to establishing both the indicators of "goodness" and the possible scales (ranges of goodness) for each measure. 2) There should be an effort to judge all students on the same scale. 3) The work of all students should be judged at a common point in time. That is, a reading on achievements, skills, or attitudes should be taken for all students under the same basic conditions. 4) A written record of judgments should be made. Table 9.2 gives examples of indicators and measures that may be informative and feasible, and of some that may be too complex or impractical.

How do you pick a good indicator, then? You have to turn your "mind's eye" back to specific times when you have made a particular judgment. Then "run the tape" in your mind to "see" again what it was that you saw or heard that caused you to know how the student was thinking or feeling or learning. Sometimes, you have to "run the tape" a number of times to focus in on the exact thing that indicated success or failure, right or wrong, as the volleyball coach ran the tape of his hundreds of observations of students in action before he saw the key.

Zuboff (1988) has coined the word *informating*. He uses this term to describe the capability of new technologies to study the processes people use in doing tasks. Such technologies are capable of recording the number of seconds between stimulus and reaction; the tendency to move right or left, up or down on a keyboard; the strength used in keystrokes or use of tools; and differences between morning and afternoon or between before break and after. That is, the technology records and analyzes the way the individual performs the job. *Informating* implies that the individual's actions are providing informational data about his/her own tendencies and that information is used to design or modify tools and processes.

Reflective thinking is much the same process. One reflects back on events and pinpoints key aspects that will help them refine their projects, programs, and activities. Often enough, the real clues are very subtle, and we have to seek them out, but it is worth the effort. The choice of indicators of *success* and of the systems, methods, tools, and records that will be used for collecting data about those indicators has great impact on teaching and learning.

Nothing succeeds like success.

We might call it the principle of directed attention. Reinforcement theory is based on that principle that if desired behavior is noted and acknowledged it is likely to increase. In a feedback study conducted with

Table 9.2. *Examples of Indicators and Measures That May Be Informative and Feasible and of Those That May Be Too Complex or Impractical.*

Objective	Indicator (*more meaningful for learning*)	Measure/Record (*more feasible or Informative*)	Indicator (*less meaningful for learning*)	Measure/Record (*expensive or less Informative*)
S's will be able to control the ball	Finger position on the ball	Weekly judgment of s's finger control	Where the ball goes	Daily record of successful ball placement (less informative re: learning)
S's will address personnel respectfully	Surveys—or observations	Monthly/quarterly surveys or recorded observations by staff	Complaints	Recorded complaints—or recorded observations of discourtesy (less information re: learning)
Artistic creativity	Teacher's judgments	Weekly/monthly recorded judgments; recorded judgments on completed works	Experts' judgments	Experts' judgments on exhibited work (more expensive)
Parent involvement	Parent initiated contact with school	Record over time of contacts made with parents	Attendance at PTA/Home and School meetings	Record of attendance (less informative)
Innovative teaching	Discussions with teachers re: new ideas	Record of planned and scheduled discussions	Observations of teaching	Recorded observations over time (more expensive, if informative)

elementary principals in California in 1968, it was found that ideal feedback was more effective in producing positive change than actual feedback. Ideal feedback consisted of giving the principals information about what their teachers considered ideal behavior; actual feedback gave principals information about their teachers' ratings of their actual behavior. In this study, the group of principals who received actual only feedback showed the lowest percentage of positive change. On many items, they showed negative change, away from the behavior considered by their teachers to be ideal. Knowing what the teachers wanted or expected was the most effective impetus for positive change (Burns, 1977).

The principle of directed attention is the same principle upon which shopping malls are created—direct attention over and over again to the things you might want and you are more apt to buy. It is the principle, also, upon which processes are taught—direct the attention to each step in its order, and the process will be learned (internalized).

Watzlawick, Weakland, and Fisch (1974) expressed the same principle conversely. They concluded from years of therapeutic counseling that the more one criticizes the behavior of another, the more that behavior is reinforced and intensified. Attention directed to undesirable behavior produces an action↔reaction chain, the push-me↔pull-you effect. The parent who scolded the child for not being on time for dinner, for not taking out the garbage, or for not cleaning the room increased the probability that tomorrow the same behavior would be repeated.

There were a number of studies of boys in school done in the 1960s that suggest they increase aggressive behavior in a classroom to the degree that they get rewarded by attention, even though the attention is negative (Cohen, 1961; Maccoby, 1966, 1974). The principle of directed attention says that, if we take note of failure, failure will increase, but *if we take note of success, success will increase.*

The important implication of reinforcement theory and other related propositions and studies is that serious, reflective attention to behavioral clues of success will pay off positively. It is this proposition that is the basis of the success analysis proposed here.

Step Three: Standards

The final step in planning for success is to set standards for the project or program. Standards are based on the measures/records used for data collection. The line of thinking extends directly from objective to indicator to measure to standard. This line of thinking can generally be traced by following the key words across the line. If "finger position" is the indicator, the standard is set in terms of percentage of students judged to be using correct/good "finger control" over some period of time. For example, "70% will have good finger control by the third week."

For a project or program plan, *success* means project or program success. Evaluation aims at evaluation of the program (perhaps through examining student success, of course), but the issue is, did our program or project work? That is, did our approach, our strategy, and our activities achieve the results we hoped for? Therefore, standards are set in terms of the project. How well did the group—students, teachers, parents—do as a whole? The data we collect are most often on the behavior or activities of individuals, so program data are the summation of successes of individuals.

If, for example, pass/fail for students on an assignment is 75%, the program question is, "What percentage of students can we reasonably expect to pass in this class?" The standard of success for the program, thus, involves two considerations: the standard of success for individual participants and the percentage of individuals that may reasonably be expected to reach that level. You might say that this is the only time that a "double standard" is good. Standard of success for a program must express two standards: that for individuals and that for the group as a whole.

Teachers, pressured by parents, school systems, and society, have internalized the mandate that no one fails. The program standard they first set is often, "100% will achieve 85% success," or some equally idealistic result. When pressed, they acknowledge that they would not like to call their program or project a failure if one student achieves only 84% success. But, in general, teachers set very high, even unrealistic standards of success for their teaching programs and for any special projects they are involved in.

It is easy enough to reach those high standards, too. You can not only "teach to the test," you can "rate to the standard." A cost/benefit study was recently conducted in two elementary schools in the Montreal area. Standards were set by the principals for grades 2 and 6 academic subjects without informing the teachers. Standards set for grade 6 English language arts were 75% at level 2 ("Developing") in School A and 90%

at level 3 ("Fluent") in School B. Actual rates of success achieved based on term reports to parents were 76.25% at level 2 in School A, and 93.5% at level 3 in School B.

Although the teachers did not know that standards expected had been set for the study, similar levels of expectations are held in all schools in that board. The actual rates of success reflect board expectations and the expectations of parents in the community (Burns, Patterson, and LaFrance, 1993).

What has happened over the past five decades is that our "normal curve" has simply moved up the percentage scale and has crowded the whole population into a tighter and tighter range. If there are four levels and only two are used, marks or grades are basically meaningless. That danger to the profession has grown with the growing cry for accountability that has demanded of teachers that "all our students should be above average." [See the National Center for Education Statistics (1987) for the Lake Woebegone effect. See also, Breinin (1987, 1992) for the teacher's perspective on developing pressures of accountability.]

Teachers cannot correct this situation themselves. They cannot shoulder the burden of ranking students alone. Perhaps the very idea of ranking students and of measuring achievement is outdated. Ranking or rating has served three primary purposes over the years. It has kept (or has been intended to keep) students' noses to the grindstone, to keep them working productively. But maybe the school of the twenty-first century will not be a place where young people work, but where they live for some part of the day. So perhaps ratings and rankings as a tool for encouraging work have outlived their usefulness.

A second purpose of school records, grades, scores, and rankings was to inform parents and the community about what their tax money was paying for. Was their tax money earning a good return? As parents grew more convinced of the relationship between continued schooling and lifetime earning, they focused their concern on the key to continued schooling—good marks. They no longer thought of school marks as assessments, but as tickets to success, and they wanted the right tickets for their own child. So for parents, too, perhaps marks as descriptions of levels of achievement have outlived their usefulness.

A third purpose of ratings has been to inform the receiving institutions (colleges, universities, businesses) about what they are receiving. With the capabilities of technology rapidly increasing, it may be simpler for each receiving institution to design screening instruments particular to their own requirements. So perhaps as a tool for screening, school records have outlived their usefulness.

None of those "perhapses" is very pleasant to contemplate for educators, but it is clear that a ranking system that distributes between one and two is not very informative. National, societal, and parental demands pressure the schools into such a range. National testing and national curricula are part of that pressure system.

Setting reasonable and appropriate standards of success is as important as being clear about goals and objectives. All educators recognize the child who has given up because expectations were unreasonable. It is equally unreasonable to set expectations of success for a class group, a school, or a school system beyond the capacity to achieve them. In the Goals 2000 statements, some standards are expressed, and some of them may be unrealistically high. In Exercise 9.2, use the values-based objectives statements you created in Exercise 9.1, and set reasonable standards of success for your own school or system.

MEANWHILE, BACK IN THE SCHOOL

The next century may be very different from the one we have grown up in. We may be using very new systems of assessment, though the forms used for those systems have been around for centuries. New technologies may be developed to determine much more than correct answers, correct spelling, use of passive verbs, and run-on sentences. Conceivably, technology will take much of the chore out of assessment.

However, inventing and organizing learning experiences that will be productive for particular students are still the realms of the teacher. And still teachers, or educators, want to know how well their activities, units, projects, and programs achieve the results they hoped for. Still (perhaps increasingly), it is important to think clearly about indicators, measures, and standards. The educator's job is still to affect the individual student at particular points in time and to try to determine the degree to which efforts have moved that individual in desirable directions.

It is still necessary for educators to design the best programs and activities possible and to assess success in terms they have set. At the same time, it is necessary to look for unexpected effects and to reflect on them in terms of new methods and new directions. Reflective practice may be the best way to keep ahead of standardization and technology.

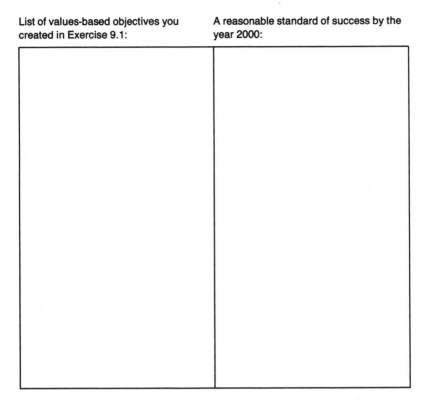

List of values-based objectives you created in Exercise 9.1:	A reasonable standard of success by the year 2000:

Exercise 9.2. Setting reasonable standards of success for Goals 2000. Assume: "By the year 2000 _____ will be achieved."

Table 9.3 gives examples of clear lines of thought from objectives to standards. These examples were taken from plans developed by students over the past several years.

It should be possible to trace the line of thought directly from objective to indicator to measure to standard. If the objective is "understanding," but the measure is "number of activities completed," the line of thought is not clear. It should be possible to read the success line either from objective to standard or backwards from standard to objective and recognize the coherence of thought in both directions.

Key words should make it easy to recognize that success is to be evaluated in terms of the desired outcome (the value) expressed in the objective. If the value is to treat others as equals, the indicator should be behavior toward others in some more general sense than tolerating

Table 9.3. *Examples of "Line of Thought": Objective → Indicator → Measure → Standard.*

Objective*	Indicator	Measure	Standard
Line of thought is appropriate:			
There will be sufficient space* for PE and athletics.	Requests for, and allocations of space in the PE facilities	Ratio of allocations to requests	85% of requests are satisfied.
Parents will have a sense of commitment to and pride about the school.	Communications from parents	Record of nature of communications re: school and/or student	70% of parent initiated communications will reflect positive involvement.
Special students will have good gross and fine motor control skills.	Success with shop projects	Weekly record of progress on shop projects	70% of the students will handle shop projects satisfactorily.
Students will be able to complete income tax forms properly.	Exercises on completion of tax forms	Record of success on income tax exercises	65% of tax form exercises will be completed without error.
Students will participate in school sponsored activities.	Count of participants in activities	Record of participation over time	Average of 50% of students participating in 25% of school activities.
Parents will tutor students.	Time spent in school tutoring students	Record of parent tutoring hours	Average of 40 hours per week
Students will enjoy reading.	Library sign-out of reading material	Record of library signouts by student	50% of the students will sign out three books per month.
Teachers will understand the theory of "learning styles."	Observations of teacher's reactions to learning differences	Record of variety of approaches to learning allowed by teacher	In 50% of their program, teachers will use approaches that meet individual learning styles of their students.
Students will perform different types of music well.	Performance on different styles of music	Instructor's record of performance	75% will perform at least two styles of music well.

Table 9.3. (continued).

Objective*	Indicator	Measure	Standard
Students will read well orally.	Oral reading interviews	Record of oral reading—monthly	50% of students will read well 80% of the sessions.
Students will appreciate their local environment.	Participation in community projects	Record of voluntary participation	50% of students are actively involved in at least one project.
Teachers will trust in and believe in their professional association.	Assistance sought from association by teachers	Record of teacher initiated requests	70% of association issues initiated by teachers
Remediation students will make up areas in which they have displayed weakness.	Standardized test	Records of results compared over time	65% of students show acceptable progress.
Line of thought is not clear: Students will treat others as equals.	Students' tolerance of others' views (weak indicator of "treat others as equals")	Teachers report on participation in class discussions.	All students speak openly about their cultures (poorly defined standard of success for a program).
Students will be able to listen attentively and with understanding.	Students will understand what they hear (more properly an objective).	Students will be asked to report what is said (a weak indicator, not a measure).	Progress will be monitored and specific areas of difficulty noted for feedback (more properly a measure).
Students will share common and similar goals on stage.	Negotiating (not clearly expressed: by students re: ?)	Teacher's judgment of student's goal-oriented discussion (more clearly, "role negotiations")	60% successfully negotiated role or scenario interpretations

*Each objective is from the plan of an individual student; they are not a "set of objectives" for one plan.

355

views. The standard set, students speak openly, suggests that the objective is perhaps that students will *feel* respected by others. (The target population is the potential "discriminatee," not the discriminator.) Through "proofing the line of thought" by reading for key words, it is easy to clarify and confirm the true value aimed for and to establish a system of evaluation that will maintain the focus on the value.

Chapter 10 will discuss value cost/worth perspective, resource bank, and considerations. Value cost perspective, again, views the particular project goal in the focus of the whole of the commitments of a unit and assesses the project in terms of opportunity cost.

Value Cost, Choice, and Action

CHAPTER 10 presents three major levels of the line of thought being developed for the planning system proposed—Stage Two: Value Cost; Stage Three: Alternatives; and Stage Four: Action. Each of these lines of analysis arises directly from the goal. That is, the "keynote" concept, which initiates each line of analysis, should be thought of, first, as it relates to the project or program as a whole. The line of thought does not flow from standards ↔ value cost, as might appear from Figure 9.1, the storyboard for the plan; it flows from goal ↔ value cost, or, in reality, from the meaning of success as a whole to value cost.

Each of the lines of analysis should be thought of as a unit, as if it were a developed section of a manuscript. In a manuscript outline, one would see the continuity of development from subsections to a following major unit, but one would expect the line of thought to flow from major unit to major unit. The planning system proposed here is based in that same organizing framework. Each keynote box or concept can be thought of as a major section heading, with the analysis units following as subsections.

The first section of Chapter 10 presents the idea of a value cost perspective and describes the process of value cost analysis. The second section presents the idea of options and describes the process of options analysis or alternatives analysis. The last section presents some ideas related to action analysis. Action is the realm we are most familiar with and most experienced in. The ideas presented here are oriented toward keeping action in harmony with values.

STAGE TWO: ESTIMATING ORGANIZATIONAL VALUE COST

This section presents the rationale for estimating a value cost in terms of resource use for any project, prior to developing it fully. The process

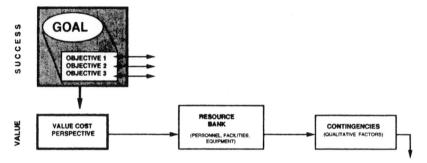

Figure 10.1. *Stage Two of planning: estimating the value cost of the project.*

of estimating this value cost, specifying the resources that can be made available and identifying the other factors that must be considered, are described. Figure 10.1 presents the model of Stage Two: Value Cost.

Value Cost Perspective

Up to this point, some time has been spent making clear what important results it is hoped the project will achieve, but educators are notorious idealists. We know how important it is for our students and ourselves to grow in many ways. The demands on educators grow constantly because hopes for the future grow, and the skills, knowledge, attitudes, and behaviors needed to fit productively into that future grow. School is the place dedicated to leading young people into the future, whatever it may be like.

Because the publics of education are so diverse and their circumstances are even more diverse, educators' responses and their efforts to fulfill the mandate give rise to hundreds of potentially productive programs. Every new project makes demands on time and effort, and every new project raises the question of opportunity cost. If we undertake this project, what loses out? Where can the time be found for this project?

The reality of resource allocation is not money; it is time and energy. How much time and energy can the group afford to spend on any one project, on any one piece of the whole? That is the question of value cost perspective. Even if one educator dedicates fifty hours a week (well over contract agreements) to the profession, how much ''flex time'' do they have? What is true for the individual educator is, of course, true for the group, for the school, for the system. "We all hang together, or we all hang separately."

> *For the strength of the Pack is the Wolf,*
> *and the strength of the Wolf is the Pack.*
> —Rudyard Kipling

Most planning systems propose that you deal with this issue of multiple demands by ranking priorities. Since many of the demands on time and effort are mandated, a large portion of the pool of resource time in a system is frequently overlooked in the process of ranking. In fact, the "basics" absorb a very large portion of time, so setting priorities on new projects often becomes a question of "squeezing blood from a turnip." Figure 10.2 illustrates the situation educators face in hoping to implement a new project and the incredible professional demands made on educators' time and effort. One could add to the picture that the educator also has a personal life with its own demands. Far too often, new projects get started based on the assumption that "professionals" will be willing to put forth the effort. We have all heard an administrator say proudly, "I can get *my* teachers to give the extra time needed." Although that is generally true, it is not necessarily rational, not necessarily fair and reasonable given the total picture.

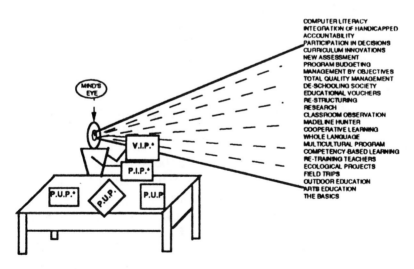

Figure 10.2. *Value cost perspective: life is a zero-sum game. Can you afford a V.I.P.* (Very Important Project), a P.I.P.* (Pretty Important Project), or a P.U.P.* (Potentially Useful Project)?*

I propose that looking at project proposals in terms of setting priorities on them makes the assumption that something can be added. Setting priorities seldom includes all of those programs already in process as alternatives among the priorities. It seldom faces the prospect of eliminating something.

I propose that the only rational perspective is that life is a zero-sum game; there is a finite number of hours available for educational projects and programs. I propose that resources available for the school or the system should be thought of as a "bank" upon which all programs and projects draw.

Thus, if we have twenty members of staff and if they all dedicate forty hours a week to the school, we have a "bank" of 800 resource hours per week upon which *all* programs must draw. A department of four would have a "bank" of 160 resource hours per week. Every new proposal then should estimate the percent of total resources the school or the department can afford for that particular project.

The Meaning of Value Cost and Value Worth

We do not customarily make percentage estimates of the "worth" of a learning outcome; however, we do apportion time differentially, depending on how important a particular outcome is and on where the students are in their skills and abilities. The allotments of time say something about the real value, the real worth or importance of various learning outcomes. Table 10.1 presents the required allocation of time in an English-language and a French-language school in Quebec, grades 2 and 6.

All schools and school systems do some similar allocation. In the late 1960s, California passed a law placing physical education on a par with English and mathematics. All students were required to have the same number of minutes per day in each of those three subject areas. The value, the worth, of physical education had been enhanced by Kennedy's attention to physical fitness. The amount of time allocated is an indicator of the "value worth" placed on particular learning outcomes.

For programs, time is allocated by holistic judgment, made using the primary desired outcome as the basis of judgment. Thus, time is allocated on a judgment of the importance of language skills, or of physical fitness, not on the basis of how many hours or minutes it takes to read stories, write compositions, do pushups, or play basketball. Time al-

Table 10.1. Allocation of Time in an English-Language and a French-Language Elementary School in Quebec.

| | English-Language School | | | | French-Language School | | | |
| | Grade 2 | | Grade 6 | | Grade 2 | | Grade 6 | |
	Students' Hr/Week	% of Week	Students' Hr/Week	% of Week	Students' Hr/Week	% of Week	Students' Hr/Week	% of Week
English language arts	7.5	31.8	5.0	21.3			2.0	8.6
French language arts	5.0	21.3	7.5	31.8	7.0	29.9	7.0	29.9
Mathematics	5.0	21.3	5.0	21.3	5.0	21.3	5.0	21.3
Social sciences	1.5	6.3	1.5	6.3	1.5	6.3	1.5	6.3
Natural sciences	1.5	6.3	1.5	6.3	1.5	6.3	1.5	6.3
Art	.5	2.1	.5	2.1	1.0	4.2	1.0	4.2
Music	.5	2.1	.5	2.1	1.0	4.2	1.0	4.2
Physical education	1.0	4.2	1.0	4.2	1.0	4.2	1.0	4.2
Moral and religious studies	1.0	4.2	1.0	4.2	1.0	4.2	1.0	4.2
Other					4.5	19.1	2.5	10.6
TOTAL	23.5		23.5		23.5		23.5	

Source: Burns, M. L. Based on Appendices A and B, in "A Test of the Cost Benefit Model in Two Elementary Schools," *The International Journal of Educational Management* (1993).

locations are not made by a summative process. They are indicators of value worth, holistic judgments based on the goal and objectives of a program.

Thus, we come back yet again to the camera image as a means of gaining perspective. The goal of a program or of a proposed project is viewed and judged against the whole. Value cost perspective is the portion of time and effort the system, school, or unit can afford to allocate to that particular desired outcome, that goal.

An estimate of value cost should be made before a program is designed, to gain perspective on the importance, or worth, of this particular goal in light of all goals, all mandates. Value worth is related to the desired outcomes, the goal and objectives, as they may fit into the whole of the commitments of a unit, not to the activities of a proposed program. Choice of strategy (option) and allocation of resources must live within the value worth determined for the whole, the goal and objectives. To specify the activities before looking at the proposed program in perspective of the commitments of the whole school tends to inflate the project. The danger in building a program before setting a value worth (a limit to value cost) on it is, to paraphrase a common saying, to permit resource demands to expand to fill the dream available.

I propose, then, that estimating the probable value cost of a project in terms of the pool, or bank, of resources available is the second major stage in the line of thinking of a plan. This step is not the same thing as doing a "situation audit," as is proposed in many planning models, although an audit might produce a similar result. Value cost perspective proposes that you take a running leap and guess (estimate) the percentage of total resource hours the whole unit can afford to spend on this project. You realize that you are still in the dolly out position, looking at the end results you hope to achieve from the activity proposal you first put forward. You have not yet decided whether the gains you might make are worth any effort at all, let alone how much effort. Of course, you really have decided; the question now is how much effort.

Making a Realistic Estimate

It is relatively easy to consider language arts or natural sciences in the perspective of the whole elementary school resource pool. This is partly because they have always been scheduled to run in a standard pattern throughout the year. (Scheduling patterns may change dramatically with the increasing use of technologies, but we are still operating in the class period syndrome.) The practice of estimating the worth of language arts as at least a third of the elementary program has been well established, but how do we estimate the "worth," the percentage of resource time we can set aside for a multiculturalism program, an ecological awareness program, an interschool music competition, a student newspaper, or a parent volunteer program? None of these fits neatly into one of the "basics"; they may involve only one or two staff members, or they may involve all. They may be concentrated in a block of time, or they may run throughout the year. How can such variable programs be looked at in the perspective of the whole?

To take one example, you might be considering a project that would take place in a four-week block of time. Thus, you have already limited the resource "bank" for the project to a maximum of 11% (four weeks out of thirty-six). Suppose further that only four teachers out of a staff of twenty would be involved. Now you are down to a value cost perspective maximum of 2.2% of the whole pool of resource time (20% of 11%). But even further, you estimate that your four teachers will spend only about ten hours of their forty-hour professional week on this particular project (two hours per day for four weeks). Thus, the value cost perspective, or estimated cost in resource time, is only about .55% of the total teacher pool, or 160 teacher work hours, based on a forty-hour work week. To show the basis of this estimate more clearly, the following is the line of thinking involved:

$$20 \text{ tchrs} \times 40 \text{ hr/wk} \times 36 \text{ wk} = 28{,}800 \text{ hr/yr} \qquad 100.0\%$$
$$20 \text{ tchrs} \times 40 \text{ hr/wk} \times 4 \text{ wk} = 3200 \text{ hr/yr} \qquad 11.0\%$$
$$4 \text{ tchrs} \times 40 \text{ hr/wk} \times 4 \text{ wk} = 640 \text{ hr/yr} \qquad 2.2\%$$
$$4 \text{ tchrs} \times 5 \text{ hr/wk} \times 4 \text{ wk} = 80 \text{ hr/yr} \qquad .27\%$$
$$4 \text{ tchrs} \times 10 \text{ hr/wk} \times 4 \text{ wk} = 160 \text{ hr/yr} \qquad .55\%$$

Only one number will be entered in the value cost perspective box — one percentage estimate. Goal, value cost perspective, options, and choice are the keystones of the project plan. They stand alone at the head of each line of analysis, and they are the "touch bases" of the project. Thinking and checking progress always come back to these four keystones. They are intended to be expressed in flashcard simplicity, so anyone can pick them out immediately and check where we are.

Therefore, the single number .55% is the entry in the value cost perspective box. The value cost perspective is estimated in terms of the whole unit because nothing takes place in isolation in a school or in a department. Value cost perspective assumes an opportunity cost consideration. If time is spent on one activity it cannot be spent on another. When one or two teachers overcommit themselves to special interest projects, demands may increase on others. This needs to be put in perspective. Since educators may not be accustomed to estimating time allocations for projects, an example of the steps to work out a value cost estimate for an environmental awareness program is presented in Table 10.2.

Following the steps in Table 10.2, the worksheet, is not estimating of course. It is a mathematical analysis of time available. Most educators, when first asked to make such an estimate, think in terms of the students' future or of the potential world or community impact of a successful worldwide program. Thus, ecological awareness may be thought of in global impact terms as having a value worth of 25%. Value cost perspective, however, must be estimated within the constraints of time and resources available, the allowable cost.

Ten percent of teacher time on a forty-hour week would be four hours per week per teacher. No system can afford to allocate that large a block of resource time to a special project outside of the required program. If the estimate of time needed were a total of four teacher-hours per week (one teacher × four hours or four teachers × one hour each), the value cost assigned would be 1% for a staff of ten, or .5% for a staff of twenty. For special projects supplementing the regular program, an estimate of .5% to 2.0% is the general range of allowable time.

The alternative, of course, is to restructure the entire program on thematic issues such as ecological awareness, multicultural appreciation, world peace, justice and equity, and community service. Such restructuring might result in five two-and-a-half-week blocks of time, with two cycles of thematic programs and eleven weeks for added themes. Each thematic program then would have to incorporate each of the subject matter, or skill, areas of the traditional program. Such a structure could be pictured as a matrix, as shown in Figure 10.3.

There are many other possible matrices that might be developed. Other themes would suggest themselves, and blocks might be scheduled on varying cycles. It would be possible to structure themes on a daily basis, but that would bring the program back to the fragmented approach to learning of the traditional system. It seems reasonable to suggest that

Table 10.2. Values Cost Perspective Example. Estimating a Realistic "Cost Value" (Allocation of Time and Resources to a Project) and Creating the Resource Bank.

Values Cost Perspective Worksheet

Determine:	Bank of resource hours for all personnel, in total:
Assume:	Secondary school students = 1000 *Bank:*
	T:P ratio 1:25 Teachers = 40 × 25 hrs/wk (1000 hrs)
	Principal, 2 vice principals = 3 × 50 hrs/wk (150 hrs)
	Secretary, custodian, nurse, librarian = 6 × 40 hrs/wk (240 hrs)
Project:	Environmental Awareness Program
Estimate:	Resource time that can be allocated to this project: % of total hours available for all school programs (as of the basic 1000 teacher hours in this case)
Consensus:	A very important project.

Estimating a "Value Cost": A resource commitment that is realistic in terms of the total of all school programs and commitments:

Estimated Value Cost = % of Time to Be Committed	× Total Hours Available	Estimated Program Hours per Week	÷ Number of Persons	Estimated Program Hours per Week per Person
1st Estimate	25%	1000 hr tchr time	250 tch hr/wk	40 tchrs	6.25 hr/wk/tchr or 1.25 hr/da/ tch
2nd Estimate	5%	1000 hr tchr time	50 tch hr/wk	40 tchrs	1.25 hr/wk/tchr or .25 hr/da/ tch
3rd Estimate	2%	1000 hr tchr time	20 tch hr/wk	40 tchrs	.50 hr/wk/ tchr or 5 hr/wk/4 tchrs

Agreed: Value Cost perspective chosen = 2%
Determine the Resource Bank: including all personnel at 2%

			Bank:	÷	Equivalent
Teacher time	1000 hr	2%	20 hr/wk	40 tchrs	.5 hr/wk/tchr
Admin time	150 hr	2%	3.0 hr/wk	3 admin	1.0 hr/wk/adm
Support persons	240 hr	2%	4.8 hr/wk	6 support	.8 hr/wk/spt

365

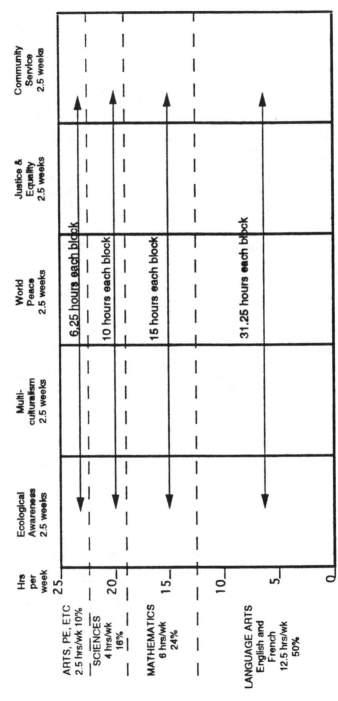

Figure 10.3. *Thematic matrix of program scheduling. Based on two cycles of five themes, two and a half weeks each, incorporating skill and knowledge areas in each block in proportions similar to those reported for the English-language school in Table 10.1.*

student interest might be higher if learning focused on themes or issues, with skills and knowledge as products of work activities. Such a program structure would require more generalist knowledge and skills on the part of teachers and would be resource costly, at least in the beginning. Other limitations to such an approach would also be clear.

Contingencies – Qualitative Factors

Beyond the actual resource time that could be made available, there are many other factors to be considered that will affect the success of any project or program. These are qualitative factors such as the attitudes, customs, policies, interest, and feelings of all those who may be affected. French pictured the formal, or ''overt,'' factors as only the ''tip of the iceberg'' in considering programs. Nonformal, or ''covert,'' factors, he proposed, form the larger mass of concerns lying below the surface of organizational life (1978, 16). Figure 10.4 presents his image of the relationship of overt to covert factors that must be considered in making educational decisions.

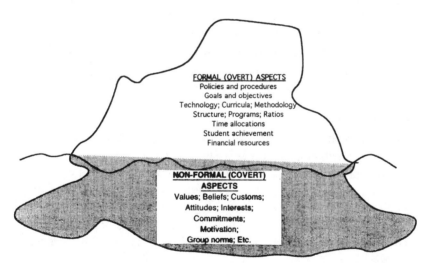

FORMAL (OVERT) ASPECTS
Policies and procedures
Goals and objectives
Technology; Curricula; Methodology
Structure; Programs; Ratios
Time allocations
Student achievement
Financial resources

NON-FORMAL (COVERT)
ASPECTS
Values; Beliefs; Customs;
Attitudes; Interests;
Commitments;
Motivation;
Group norms; Etc.

Figure 10.4. *Organizational iceberg. Value cost factors include both formal (overt) and nonformal (covert) aspects. (Source: p. 19, W. L. French and C. M. Bell, Jr. in* Organization Development. *© 1990, Prentice-Hall, Inc. Adapted by permission of Prentice-Hall, Inc., Englewood Cliffs, NJ.)*

French includes among overt or formal factors some that are not numerical in nature in the way resource hours are. For example, he includes among overt factors such formal organizational factors as policies, curricula, and methodologies. Although such formal factors are overt because they have been made explicit, they are not quantifiable in the same way resource time is. We propose two categories for the value analysis, quantitative factors or resources, and qualitative factors or contingencies. Qualitative factors form a "bank" of contingencies equal in importance to the resource bank. Contingencies, those deep qualifiers of human behavior, are vitally important in education. The success of educational programs, as well as the failures, may be more a result of the mass of the iceberg below the surface than of the resource time available.

Such other factors may affect a program negatively, of course, but they can be very strong positive agents for some projects; therefore, they should not be thought of as constraints. If the teacher's attitude toward a proposed program is very positive, attitude is certainly a resource, a source of energy and renewal. If attitudes are negative, they could be viewed as a constraint. Management terminology leads us to think that only money is a resource and that affective factors are constraints. In fact, personnel time, which we analyze as a resource, is a resource only if you have enough time. If not, time is a constraint. Therefore, the management terms *resources* and *constraints* are not particularly helpful in making educational decisions.

In reality, qualitative factors are contingencies, factors to be considered because they affect all education in one way or another. Hopefully, they may be harnessed in support of the planned project; however, attitude should *not* be assessed only in cases where it is negative. Planners should not make the assumption that attitude or any other affective factor is a constraint. The same might be said of community customs; parent, teacher, and student attitudes; and values held. Contingencies, those other factors that cannot be easily quantified, affect all projects to some degree, some positively and others negatively. Figure 10.5 illustrates how resources and contingencies would be entered on the storyboard.

Contingencies may affect any program and must be identified in value cost analysis. They will be assessed for positive or negative impact on each proposed option in Stage Three: Alternatives Analysis.

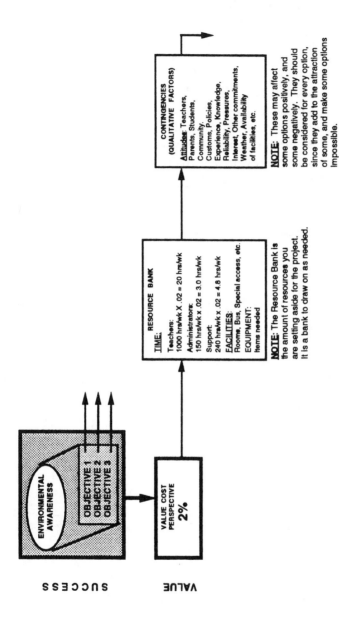

Figure 10.5. Value cost perspective analysis: resource bank and contingencies (qualitative factors) to be considered.

369

STAGE THREE: ALTERNATIVES ANALYSIS

Again, the line of thinking to build a plan moves back to a keynote box, options. Again, the reference point of the keynote is the focus, goal. Figure 10.6 presents the alternatives analysis line of the storyboard.

Alternatives analysis includes three steps: 1) creating the pool of options, 2) predicting for each their probability of success toward achieving the goals and objectives intended, and 3) predicting the feasibility of each option, given the resources available and the situations or contingencies. The two processes of thinking required are brainstorming (or "imaging"), step one, and predicting, steps two and three.

Step One: Creating a Pool of Options

The Best of All Possible Worlds

Brainstorming is future-casting, or imaging, the possible. Hall says,

Even the most pedestrian of planning is impossible without some capacity to image creatively. Yet there is no common word or phrase in English for the capacity to image realistically and dynamically, to mentally plan and rearrange the furniture. The poet, the artist, the writer, the sculptor, the architect, the designer, the hostess, the cook, the seamstress, and the

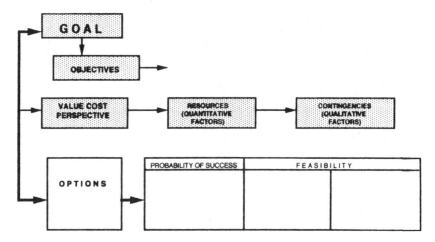

Figure 10.6. Stage Three of planning: alternatives analysis.

carpenter must all be able to image creatively. . . . Yet how little is made
of this extraordinary capacity in everyday life! (1977, 187, emphasis
added)

Creating a set of possible strategies or means returns the planner to
the logic of planning (Figures 8.5 and 8.6 and Exercise 8.4). Brainstorming, whether it is done by an individual or by a group, is the art of
probing the impossible, the imaginary world of "what if." It pushes
aside all realities and deals only with images of what would be ideal, if
only _____. To be most creative, the assumption must be that there are
no limitations, no constraints. All things are possible in the best of all
possible worlds being imagined. In a seminar, Ackoff related the story
of the invention of the *idea* of the touchtone telephone in a brainstorming
session many years before it became a reality.

As a process, brainstorming is probably most productive in a group,
since one idea leaps onto the shoulders of another to build a pyramid of
ideas, any one of which may become the pivot for action. As is well
known, in brainstorming no idea is rejected out of hand; debate and
discussion are not allowed.

In creating the bank of options, one has already been proposed – the
action plan first suggested is the first option. It is important to generate
at least three more alternatives, however. Because we have habits of
thinking from experience, our first alternatives are apt to be quite
traditional. Although there is nothing wrong with choosing and implementing a traditional program and doing it well, the excitement in
planning comes when someone, or the group, has generated an entirely
new possibility. An example may illustrate.

Many of our master's students at McGill are teachers or have been
teachers, so they think first of planning curriculum. One history teacher
wanted to create a curriculum plan for Canadian history. (Canadian
history is not as integral a part of national life or culture as is American
history in the United States, and he wanted to stimulate the students'
interest.) His first options were projects, student presentations, and
guest speakers.

When forced to the fourth option, he suddenly said, "You know, the
parents and grandparents of my students have lived in this Montreal area
for most of their lives. They have stories to tell about how it was in the
early days. I could have the students interview their family members and
their parents' friends, and they could write their own history." While

that is certainly not a unique idea, it was a new way of looking at history for him. He had not thought of history as a story of real peoples' lives. The fourth option is hardest to come by and is generally most creative. It is not always chosen, even then, but it opens a new window on the world. Brainstorming is another of those processes of thinking that gets little exercise in education settings. Planning is an activity where our powers of imaging can be most productive.

Cautions

It would be easy at this point of planning to slip into the practice of listing as alternatives some activities that might form a part of an action plan, rather than creating alternative strategies. Alternate strategies implies alternate whole programs, not elements or activities to be included in a program. The intent is that only one option will be chosen for implementation; the others will be eliminated. The other options will not form a part of the project that is developed. Thus, again at the keynote step, creating a bank of options, the thinking is holistic, not analytical. We have decided where to build the house, and we are now mentally imagining possible ways to arrange the living space, as Hall might say. Will our overall design, our design strategy, be open spaces or traditional rooms? Do we want rustic, lodge style, contemporary, or modernistic? Strategies (alternatives or options) are principles of design that affect all subsequent choices.

The thought pattern is, ''We *could* do this *or* that, not we *can* do this *and* this,'' not, ''We *will* do this *and* this.'' Moreover, the thought pattern is not, ''We can do A to achieve Objective #1, and B to achieve Objective #2, and C to achieve Objective #3.'' If the goal is understanding the need for healthful living for all, what are possible strategies for developing a program that could achieve that understanding? The program could be a community service program, a research program, a science fair program, or a project to write and produce a play. Any one of those approaches could be the basis for designing a program focused on healthful living. Each option/alternative is a possible design principle, a possible strategy.

The second caution is, again, to be brief. All boxes on the storyboard should be presented in telegraphic style, but that is particularly true of the four keynote boxes, goal, value cost perspective, options, and choice. Figure 10.7 presents several examples of the bank of options created for different educational plans. In most cases, it is clear that the options considered would lead to very different programs, that they are not pieces of or steps in some larger strategy or program.

Step Two: Matrix Analysis

Assessing the options is the process of thinking that goes on for every choice we make, large or small, personal or professional, in helping one student understand, in creating a board transportation system, or in spending ten dollars or ten million dollars. The complexity of the process varies greatly, but the process is the same. In its common elements, all choice requires predicting the probability of success of the various options we have (the probability of achieving what we hope for) and the feasibility (whether the option can be handled within the resources and contingencies that exist.)

For most of our choices, that process takes place in a flash of thought. We are not even aware of the fact of having considered options, but we always do. Even at the point of a gun, there is always the flash of "beg, grab something, run, or give in." Each option is judged against, "Would it work?" and "Can I do it?" For most of our choice situations, it is essential that we permit choice to be made by such a "flash thought" process.

That is particularly true for educators dealing always with action-based situations involving other people. Educators, in practice, do not have the luxury of the scientist, to sit and weigh alternatives and to test them under varying conditions. We must act instinctively and hope that intelligent use of experience (gut feeling), pays off productively. For projects and programs of any scope, however, it is important to undertake the process of choice systematically and with some deliberation. Tools to make choice systematic have been developed by behavioral scientists.

Behavioral theorists are people who "informate," as Zuboff would say, on their own processes and their own experience. They reflect and analyze and attempt to make explicit those processes that some people excel in. They try through science "to make the average man brilliant" (Hall, 1976, 202).

Decision theorists have developed powerful tools for enabling complex choices to be made systematically and on rational bases. The best

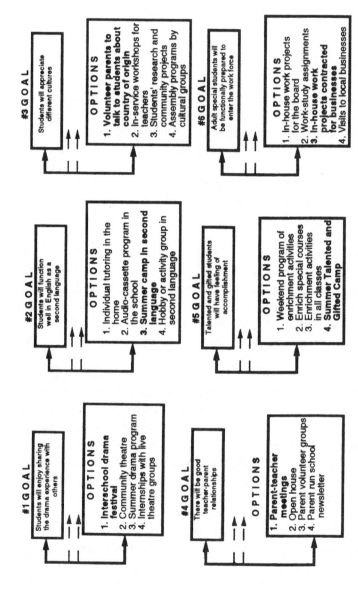

#1 GOAL

Students will enjoy sharing the drama experience with others

OPTIONS

1. Interschool drama festival
2. Community theatre
3. Summer drama program
4. Internships with live theatre groups

#2 GOAL

Students will function well in English as a second language

OPTIONS

1. Individual tutoring in the home
2. Audio-cassette program in the school
3. **Summer camp in second language**
4. Hobby or activity group in second language

#3 GOAL

Students will appreciate different cultures

OPTIONS

1. **Volunteer parents to talk to students about country of origin**
2. In-service workshops for teachers
3. Students' research and community projects
4. Assembly programs by cultural groups

#4 GOAL

There will be good teacher-parent relationships

OPTIONS

1. **Parent-teacher meetings**
2. Open house
3. Parent volunteer groups
4. Parent run school newsletter

#5 GOAL

Talented and gifted students will have feeling of accomplishment

OPTIONS

1. Weekend program of enrichment activities
2. Enrich special courses
3. Enrichment activities in all classes
4. **Summer Talented and Gifted Camp**

#6 GOAL

Adult special students will be functionally prepared to enter the work force

OPTIONS

1. In-house work projects for the board
2. Work-study assignments
3. **In-house work projects contracted for businesses**
4. Visits to local businesses

Figure 10.7. Examples of alternative strategies (optional means) developed for local school projects (the chosen option is in bold).

374

known process of rational decision making is the decision tree. A second process commonly used is matrix analysis. Both are based in the process of probability estimation, and both address the issues of probability of success and the possible impact of contingency factors. They differ in the specific questions they address and in the manner of presenting data for the choice process.

Decision tree analysis is most useful for mega projects, such as those intended to be national in scope, or for major building projects. It was discussed in Chapter 6, and a further description of the process will be presented in Chapter 12. In the planning system presented here, it is proposed that matrix analysis be used for step two of alternatives analysis. Figure 10.8 presents the elements of step two that are included in the assessment of options.

Advantages of Matrix Analysis

Matrix analysis of alternatives or optional programs has several advantages over decision tree analysis, especially for projects and programs planned at the school or school system level. Some of those advantages are the following:

(*1*) A matrix analysis can be completed quite simply without using a computer program.

(*2*) Probability and feasibility estimates for each option are entered into the matrix under each criterion heading (goal, objective, personnel time, community attitudes, etc.) so the estimates for each alternative can be easily compared. This permits easy reassessment for one option weighed against another on each criterion. A change or rating (estimate) in one cell does not necessarily affect other cells. Each criterion produces a separate priority ranking across the options. Option #2 could be rated more effective on Objective #1 than Option #4, but the reverse could be true on Objective #3.

(*3*) A simple scale can be developed to suit the purpose. Three commonly used ranges are +5 to −5, +10 to −10, and 0 to +10.

(*4*) Specific criteria (as weather, parental consent) can be given added weight if desired. A rating of −5 with a weight of 3 would total −15.

(*5*) The sum of points allocated gives the overall priority.

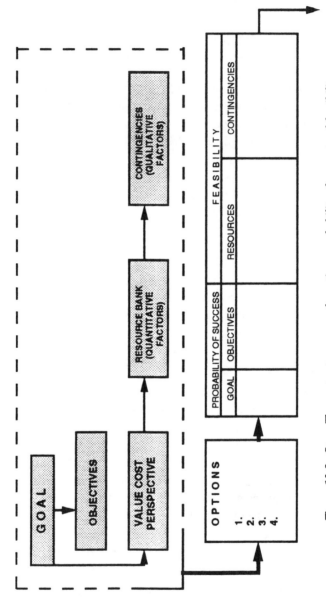

Figure 10.8. Stage Three, step two, assess the options: probability of success and feasibility.

(6) If the option that received the highest overall rating cannot be implemented for some reason, a second option is clearly identified. The matrix makes clear possible directions for modification and further development.

To make a reasonable choice among the bank of options created in step one, each should be rated by testing it with the following four questions:

(1) What is the probability that Option 1 (or 2, 3, 4) will achieve the intended goal?

(2) What is the probability that Option 1 (2, 3, 4) will achieve Objective #1, Objective #2, etc.?

(3) How feasible is Option 1 (2, 3, 4) given the resources allocated to the project?

(4) How feasible is Option 1 (2, 3, 4) given the contingencies? (Or how positively or negatively will a contingency affect this project?)

The worksheet for carrying out this matrix analysis is presented in Figure 10.9. Each of the questions to be considered will be discussed in the following pages.

Rating Probabilities

In creating a bank of options or alternative strategies, the aim was to invent possibilities. The orientation was "no restrictions, no limitations—if it were possible, what would be the best, or most interesting strategy?" It is important to start from that perspective, because that is the way new ideas are generated. That impossibly exciting idea may not be realistic today, but if it is really good, someday it will happen—it is a vision for the future.

However, reality must play its role. The present question is, "Which of these options is most realistic?" The two questions that must be answered to determine which option to implement are always, "Will it accomplish what we hope?" "Can it be done, given the realities of the day?" If we cannot expect to implement our ideal program, what is the closest thing to it? Thus, we should not look at small progress as satisficing or as disjointed incrementalism. We should be "managing logical incrementalism," as proposed by Quinn (1980). By creating a bank of possibilities and then looking at their probabilities rationally, we

Project Name:

Value Cost
Perspective
Ratio:

ALTERNATIVES STRATEGIES ANALYSIS WORKSHEET

Probability of Success

	Project Goal	Objective #1	Objective #2	Objective #3	Objective #4	Sum Probability
Option # 1						
Option # 2						
Option # 3						
Option # 4						

FEASIBILITY

Resources: Personnel, Facilities, Equipment, Supplies

Contingencies (Qualitative Factors)

Sum Feasibility

CHOICE (sum P & F)

Figure 10.9. Assess each option in terms of the probability that it will achieve the goals and objectives and in terms of its feasibility: 1) within the resources available and 2) given the contingencies (the qualitative factors).

have added potential flexibility to the planning process. We have set the stage for slow but steady progress in the direction we want to go.

Rating Probability of Success

To assess the overall probability that a strategy, an option, will be successful, a rating should be applied to the goal and to each objective separately. One method or technique will be more effective in achieving one result than another. No program is ever equally effective in accomplishing all objectives set for it. It is important to recognize this fact in planning and to weigh the several objectives separately. Part of the question in choosing one option is, if something has to give, which objective can we afford to let go or put less emphasis on? Something always has to give; it is critical for planners to face that fact in the planning process, so the orientation of probability, of hypothesis making, is maintained. Perfection is not the realm of the planner; progress is.

The data below illustrate the variation for ratings assigned to chosen goal options presented in Figure 10.7. (Ranges differ because the examples included in Figure 10.7 were selected from plans created by different educators.)

	Chosen	Range	G	O1	O2	O3	O4
Goal #1	Option 1	0 − 10	10	9	6	8	7
Goal #2	Option 3	−5 − +5	4	−2	3	5	3
Goal #3	Option 1	0 − 10	9	7	9	10	5
Goal #4	Option 4	0 − 10	8	9	8	7	1
Goal #5	Option 4	0 − 10	8	4	9	9	7
Goal #6	Option 3	−3 − +3	+2	−1	+1	+2	+2

Thus, for the proposed talented and gifted students program (#5), the planning group judged that a summer camp would be only minimally successful in helping the students "O1: feel less pressure from the parents to compete" (rated 4), but would be very successful (9) in helping the students "O3: feel that their work is realistic and worthwhile."

Similarly in project #4, the committee rated the probability that parent-teacher meetings would produce "O1: effective communication between parents and teachers'' high (9), even though they also rated ''O4: parents' involvement in school programs'' low (1).

Rating Feasibility

Whether a program might achieve desired results is only one question that has to be answered. The second question, equally important, is can it be done here and now? Feasibility addresses the question, ''Can this proposed project succeed given the reality of the situation?'' Reality has two aspects in planning programs or projects—the quantitative aspects (resources that can be allocated) and qualitative aspects (contingency factors that describe the situation as it is where the project will be implemented). There are a number of factors relevant to both resources and contingencies, and each should be rated separately for its probable impact on every option.

Resources: The four main categories of resources are personnel time, facilities, equipment, and supplies. The details of quantities available in each category have been specified in the resource bank, Stage Two. How well will 2% (or .55%) of staff time satisfy the requirements of Option 1, 2, 3, 4? How well will the space that can be made available meet the needs of each different program that might be developed or, similarly, equipment and supplies? Again, the predictions will vary from one option to another. The same amount of resource time will enable one type of program to be handled well but will not be enough for another.

Contingencies: Individual tutoring in the home (Option 1, Goal 2 in the English as a Second Language Program, Figure 10.7) was rated low feasibility overall on resources available, as was the chosen option, summer camp. Both were also rated high on probability of success on all objectives. The difference became evident when contingency factors were rated. Pupil, teacher, and family interest weighed heavily in favor of the summer camp. Pupil self-concept and social development also entered the analysis as contingency factors—possible effects not related to the intended outcome of English as a second language. They also were rated positive as they would affect the feasibility of the summer camp option. Home tutoring rated low feasibility on those two factors.

The Total Score: The outcome of the complete matrix analysis is a total summed rating for each option. It is expected that the option receiving the highest total score should be chosen. But it is important to remember that numbers do not make decisions; people do. The purpose of the analysis is not to find out the score for any option; the purpose is to clarify thinking and to consider rationally the factors that may help make a program successful or that may cause it to be less successful than you had hoped. None of the options will result in failure. Some may be more easily successful than others. The three steps of analysis to this point are aimed at picking the option most likely to succeed and easiest to implement (least costly in resources and in frustration and conflict).

What happens then if the numbers say choose one option, and your instincts (or your personal interest) say another? One of two things is at work. You may say, "Well, the numbers say Option #2, but we really can't do that because. . . ." The "because" is a contingency you forgot to enter into the matrix. It should be entered, and all options reconsidered. If necessary, cancel that option from consideration on the basis of that one contingency. The keynote is values, and an option that cannot be implemented because it conflicts with an important value should not be implemented, regardless of numbers.

Numbers Do Not Make Decisions: A real example illustrates the use of matrix analysis for a project in Montreal and the fact that decisions are based in values, not in numbers. The city planned to build a convention center to attract major international conventions to Montreal. Fourteen possible locations in the city were identified, and the criteria for choice were developed. Some of the criteria were objective, and some were contingency factors to be considered. A matrix was developed, using a black dot to indicate an unfavorable rating on a criterion. Part of the matrix, printed in *The Gazette* (1977) is reproduced in Figure 10.10.

The site finally chosen for construction received more "black dots" than any of the others being considered. A major criterion had not been included in the matrix. A very important consideration was that the center was seen as critical to a general development program—a program intended to revitalize and strengthen the Old Montreal area. Numbers should not be permitted to override experienced judgment and important values, but that does not suggest that the matrix analysis is a waste of time. Analysis clarifies thinking; it calls to the surface the critical values that must be considered and additional actions that may be necessary to make the project succeed.

The second thing that may happen is that the group may say, "Well, we wanted to try #1, but looking at the whole picture, we really can't do it right now. Maybe later. We will have to prepare the groundwork." In

CRITERIA	E	F	G	H	I
Pedestrian access by surface	Limited choice Unpleasant	Limited choice Unpleasant	No advantage ●	Varied choice Unpleasant surroundings	Varied choice Unpleasant surroundings
Underground shopping	No advangage ●	Limited choice, Pleasant appearance	No advantage ●	Varied choice Pleasant surroundings	Varied choice Pleasant surroundings
Access by Metro	No advantage ●	Access indirect 1 or 2 lines	Access direct- 1 line	Access direct- 1 line	Access indirect- 1 line
Circulation	Needs work	Few difficulties	Difficult ●	Difficult ●	Difficult ●
Proximity of Hotels (10 min.)	3715 rooms	3715 rooms	1815 rooms ●	5761 rooms	3141 rooms
Proximity of Ste. Catherine St.	700'	700'	1600'	1500'	2100' ●
Proximity of Old Montreal	6 min	5 min	2 min	8 min or direct by Metro	Direct by Metro
Proximity of shopping complexes climate protected	Direct to Desjardins 7min-PVM	Direct to Desjardins 8min-PVM	4min Desjardins 8min-PVM ●	Direct to Place Ville Marie	Direct to Place Ville Marie
Cost of land in millions ($)	1,744	2,667 (1/2 utilization)	1,174	3,204 ●	1,724
Estimate in millions ($)	437 (to demolish)	332 (non demolish)	1,449 (to demolish) ●	3,121 (to demolish) ●	650 (to demolish)
Ownership	Principally Dorchinvest	Govt. of Canada	CTCUM & Govt. of Quebec	Principally Bell Canada	Principally CN & Govt. of Quebec

Part of a chart prepared by consultants to the provincial government which rates 14 possible sites for a convention centre. The site chosen last week--designated "G" at the top of the chart--chalked up more black marks than any other.

Figure 10.10. Example of the use of Matrix Options Analysis, illustrating a possible result when criteria for choice may have differing "weights" or values. [Source: The Gazette, *Montreal. Thursday, December 1, 1977, p. 2. Story by K. Sindeyer. Reprinted by permission of* The Gazette, *Montreal, QC (translated by M. Burns).]*

this case, the time, frustration, and stress of trying to implement something that is beyond the moment are saved, but the idea is not lost.

To ask the question, "Are these predictions 'accurate'?" is not relevant. Did the raters take the task seriously, and did they have enough experience to do a fair job? Those are fair questions. But the most important questions are, "Did the rating produce a result that the people affected can live with comfortably and productively?" and even more important, "Did the process itself help to create a better project?"

In the past fifteen years, education groups have developed more than 150 project plans using the planning system described here. Of those, more than 100 are known to have implemented the alternative chosen by matrix analysis. In fourteen known cases, the option receiving the second highest rating was implemented. Overall rating totals are often only a few points apart, so "first and second" have little real meaning. In several instances, the leading planner has said, "Well, I really wanted to go with Option #1, but, realistically, #3 is probably best for now."

Having reached the point that the values upon which the project will be based are clear and are thoroughly imbedded in the general rationale for the project, a choice can be made. The three stages of planning described to this point are the foundation for a potentially successful project. Stage Four in developing a project plan grounded in values is action analysis. This is the stage of planning most familiar to educators. It will be described briefly in the next section.

STAGE FOUR: ACTION ANALYSIS

The great end of life is not knowledge, but action.
— Thomas Henry Huxley

Knowledge and values are the ground upon which educators stand, but action is the daily life of the educator. Educational action is inevitably propositional in nature; every choice and every action has an end, aim, or purpose. Stages One through Three in the system proposed here offer tools for laying the groundwork for effective action. This section discusses two steps basic to action planning: task analysis and resource allocation. The third step, scheduling the actual sequence of activities is entirely dependent on context. Figure 10.11 presents Stage Four, planning the action.

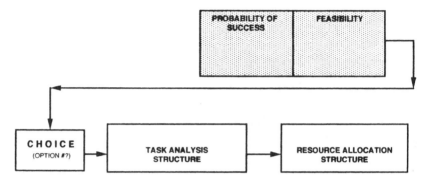

Figure 10.11. Stage Four: planning the action – plan to implement and operate.

There are a number of planning tools used for organizing the tasks or activities of a project. They include flow charts, Gantt charts, networks, and task matrix analyses such as the Responsibility, Authority, Communication (RAC) matrix used by Canadian Pacific Consulting Services in SPEC® processes. These tools will be discussed in Chapters 11 and 12, which present planning tools and management systems. However, all of these tools are organizing tools. Analysis of tasks either accompanies the process of organizing, or precedes it. It is useful to prepare a Task Analysis Structure and a parallel Resource Allocation Structure before organizing and scheduling the work group activities. The emphasis is again on getting the whole picture clear before scheduling particular tasks.

Task Analysis Structure

In its simplest form, a Task Analysis Structure is just a list of things that have to be done. In many cases, that simple list is adequate. Often, however, the size of a project or the need to involve groups from different departments, schools, or sectors of the community makes it important to structure that task list so work can be organized effectively.

One of the basic propositions of the SPEC® system is, "Structure absorbs complexity." That is, structuring ideas makes it possible to think clearly. A structured task list organizes the tasks on the basis of some categories or types of tasks. There are common types of activities in most education projects. Figure 10.12 presents an example of a task analysis

TASK ANALYSIS STRUCTURE
(LIST ACTIVITIES OR TASKS BY TYPE)

ACTIVITY NO.	TYPE	# TIMES TO BE DONE
A	TEACHING ACTIVITIES	
1.	CLASS SESSIONS	12
2.	FIELD TRIPS	2
3.	MEETINGS WITH PARENTS	1
4.	ETC.	
B	ADMINISTRATIVE ACTIVITIES	
1.	MEETING WITH TEACHERS	1
2.	ASSEMBLY WITH STUDENTS	1
C	COMMUNICATION ACTIVITIES	
1.	PREPARE PERMISSION FORM	1
2.	COLLATE PERMITS/ NON-PERMITS	2
3.	CALLS TO FIELD TRIP SITES	8
4.	PREPARE ADVERTISING	1
D	EVALUATION ACTIVITIES	
	ETC.	
E	SUPPORT ACTIVITIES	
F	OTHER ACTIVITIES	

Figure 10.12. *Task analysis structure. List of activities needed to make the project a success, with number of times the activity must take place. Note: Task analysis is the "big picture" of staff load, preparing to determine actual hours of work needed — the basis for allocating resources and scheduling.*

structure based on kinds of activities common to many educational projects.

In preparing a task analysis, there should be no attempt to place activities in a time sequence. A task analysis is not a schedule; it is an analysis of the activities and tasks that must not be overlooked. The tasks should be identified by categories, because they will be allocated to people on the basis of the type of activity, not on the basis of timing. The activities listed in the task analysis can be numbered within each category, so other activities can be added and so the reference can be carried over to resource allocation, which is the breakdown of time to be allotted to each task.

Step Two: Resource Allocation

Task analysis and resource allocation are parallel tools in planning for implementation of a project. Resource allocation determines how many units (hours) of the resource bank the various activities and tasks will actually require. Resource allocation is the test of whether the value cost perspective estimate and the resource bank were realistic.

In major construction projects in the business world, contracts mandate the resource bank (the contracted estimate established). The contract is the "bottom line" for a corporate project.

We are not suggesting that education projects should be bound by such restrictive clauses. However, we are suggesting that there is a bottom line to the energy, capacity, and commitment of professional resources. Careful planning can conserve those professional resources; inadequate planning puts the burden of cost on people. Figure 10.13 illustrates resource allocation as it would be carried forward from task analysis (Figure 10.12).

Each activity should be analyzed for the resources needed (specific personnel, facilities, and equipment) and for the total hours each would be required. If the numbering system created for task analysis is carried forward, it is easy to refer from one analysis to the other. The total number of hours allocated for each staff group should not exceed the hours reserved in the resource bank. It is in this way that the bottom line of demands on professional time can be kept in perspective (Figure 10.14).

RESOURCE ALLOCATION WORKSHEET

(FROM FIGURE 10.12)

ACTIVITY NO.	# HRS EACH	ACTIVITY AND TYPE OF RESOURCE NEEDED	# EACH	# TIMES	HOURS ALLOCATED STAFF Tc	Ad	Sp	Os	OTHER
A.1	1 hr	Class sessions		12					
		Teachers	1	12	12				
		Overhead	1	12					12
		Film projector	1	2					2
		Volunteer parents	4	1				4	
.2	8 hr	Field trip—20 students		2					
		Teachers	2		32				
		Volunteer parents	4					64	
		Bus driver	1					16	
		Bus	1						16
		Lunches	26						52
.3		Etc.							
B.1									
.2									
C.1									
.2									
.3									
.4									
		TOTAL HRS* ALLOCATED			44			84	

Figure 10.13. Resource allocation structure. Resources and hours needed for each activity. Note: Totals should not exceed resource bank. Tc = Teacher; Ad = Administrator; Sp = Support; Os = Other staff; Other = equipment, facilities.

387

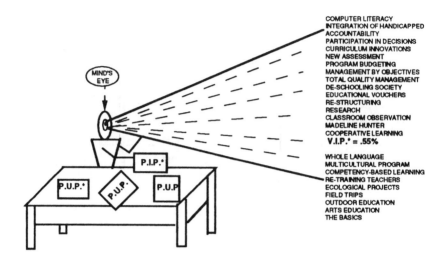

COMPUTER LITERACY
INTEGRATION OF HANDICAPPED
ACCOUNTABILITY
PARTICIPATION IN DECISIONS
CURRICULUM INNOVATIONS
NEW ASSESSMENT
PROGRAM BUDGETING
MANAGEMENT BY OBJECTIVES
TOTAL QUALITY MANAGEMENT
DE-SCHOOLING SOCIETY
EDUCATIONAL VOUCHERS
RE-STRUCTURING
RESEARCH
CLASSROOM OBSERVATION
MADELINE HUNTER
COOPERATIVE LEARNING
V.I.P.* = .55%

WHOLE LANGUAGE
MULTICULTURAL PROGRAM
COMPETENCY-BASED LEARNING
RE-TRAINING TEACHERS
ECOLOGICAL PROJECTS
FIELD TRIPS
OUTDOOR EDUCATION
ARTS EDUCATION
THE BASICS

Figure 10.14. A V.I.P.* (Very Important Project) in perspective.

MAJOR DIFFERENCES OF THE VALUES-BASED PLANNING SYSTEM PROPOSED

There are basic differences between the planning system developed in Section II and other systems proposed in the literature. The differences lie both in the general approach to planning and in specific steps proposed.

Differences in General Approach

Differences in the general approach to planning can be summarized as follows:

(*1*) The emphasis is primarily on values as expressed in intended outcomes, goals and objectives, and in cost—both resource cost and professional, or human cost.

(*2*) Emphasis is always on the hypothetical nature of planning. A plan proposes and presents an integrated set of hypothesized action ↔ outcome relationships. Hypotheses are educated guesses, subject to test. Careful planning is a process of self-educating for the planners, so that better "guesses" can be made, but hypotheses are always open to change as new evidence is revealed. It is this psychological mind-set that is basic to planning.

(*3*) The camera metaphor and the keynote boxes at the head of each stage in the planning storyboard emphasize maintaining a perspective of the whole. Each of the keynote steps describes how to maintain the holistic perspective while, at the same time, focusing on the specific project at hand.

(*4*) It is assumed and is emphasized that the reality of planning is not in the logic of serial steps. Planning almost universally starts with action. The planning system presented here proposes that planners should dolly out and place the proposed project in the perspective of professional values (the goal) and organizational resources and contingencies. To the degree that this clarification tak s place, implementation of plans will be less costly in professional and human terms, as well as in resource time.

Differences in Specific Steps

Specific steps in the system proposed also differ from much of the literature on planning:

(*1*) The emphasis is on a practical approach to planning. How to carry out each step is illustrated and described in practical terms.

(*2*) It is proposed that goals and objectives should be stated in value terms, not in behavioral terms. Goals and objectives are treated as constants, relatively universal and unchanging. Indicators, measures, and standards are treated as variables, separate from goals and objectives and specific to the situation.

(*3*) Value cost perspective is unique to the system proposed here. It proposes that the probable cost in resource terms of any project should be estimated and set aside as a bank of resources to draw on before a project is designed. That estimate places the purpose of a project into the perspective of the whole set of purposes of the education system.

(*4*) The system recognizes that an action proposal has initiated the planning cycle. It then proposes that alternative project ideas should be generated as possible means to the same end. Each alternative should be tested systematically for probability of success and feasibility. The matrix approach used for analysis is considered simpler and more useful for most education projects than decision tree analysis.

(5) Task analysis and resource allocation are specified as additional tools to maintain the professional and organizational limitations established by the goal and value analyses.

CONCLUSION

To make the education system better is the rallying cry of present-day educators and the public. To make it better, we must be clear about what *better* means to our community and about the values upon which change should be based. And we must have tools for translating values into action. The Values-Based Planning System proposed is founded in that proposition, and each step proposed is designed to reinforce that perspective.

TOOLS USEFUL FOR
SPECIFIC PURPOSES

SECTIONS I, II, and III have moved from broad general perspectives on planning and education to the very specific Values-Based Model of Planning. Within the Values-Based Model, techniques were presented for dealing productively with issues that arise at the four basic stages of planning: defining success, maintaining perspective (values cost), assessing alternatives for choice, and planning for implementation and action.

However, there are many other technologies, or tools, presented in the literature that are useful at those four stages. Section IV will review some of those tools most often proposed for use in education. Each of these tools has been developed to accomplish some planning purpose, and each is based on some reasonable proposition.

The fact that a technique has had a cycle of popularity does not negate its underlying rationality, its underlying purpose. Creative administrators and educators planning for quality have modified or adapted such tools to make them as useful as possible under the fluid conditions of organizational life. They have looked to the heart of a technology, which is always a way of thinking about a planning issue. Planning leaders have recognized that every technology is a means to an end and, thus, have avoided the trap of making the technology itself the end product.

Planning tools are most useful when they have been internalized, when they have become the "common grammar" of planning. At that point, it is no longer necessary to "draw the little boxes," except for a major or very complex project. For that to come to be, of course, it is necessary to work through the technology very specifically for practice.

Chapter 11 will present tools related to goal setting and goal clarification such as Delphi Technique, needs assessment, behavioral objectives, and management by objectives. Techniques for seeking or inventing new directions are also available in the literature and are receiving increasing attention. Chapter 12 will present techniques of task and resource use analysis and will compare and contrast common budgeting systems as tools for planning for quality education.

There are many good discussions in the literature of all of the tools to be presented in Section IV; therefore, the general focus here will be on the "heart of the technology," the way of thinking that is basic to the tool, and on where it has been found to be useful. The detail of "how to do it" will be presented for some particular variations of common tools.

CHAPTER 11

Vision and Perspective

WHITHER EDUCATION

ONE of the most pervasive assumptions about the purpose of planning in education is that there is a need for change, an urgency to find a better way to do things. Realistically, every proposal for action must answer clearly the *how* questions: how to create and operate clinical supervision, site-based management, authentic testing, cooperative learning, parent councils, competency-based learning, or participative decision making. Educators and their constituents want to know how before they can "buy into" a proposal.

But every proposed new project, program, or approach carries with it reasons *why* the project should be implemented, where the project is heading, and what results are expected. Whether the reasons why are clearly stated or are only implied, these are the propositions about the direction the system, school, or department is or should be going. In "turbulent times" (as Drucker calls the present era), the questions of where public education is and should be going are very much in the public mind.

Every economist and every futurist for the past thirty years has pointed to the service sector as the base of future growth and strength and to the declining impact of extraction and manufacturing activities. Even within the extraction and manufacturing sectors of the economy, J. B. Quinn reported in a seminar in Montreal in May 1994, service activities (primarily cognitive and social in nature) account for as much as 90% of employment. The conclusion reached by Drucker (1980, 1992) and by Quinn (1994) is that the critical industrial asset for the future that is upon us today is a well-organized and creative intellect. It should be added that it must also be a moral and socially responsible intellect.

393

Meanwhile, our public, the parents and communities we serve, cry out for realistic job opportunities for their children and urge that their children be well prepared for this new world of work. This places the greatest growth opportunity squarely at the feet of the world's largest service sector—education.

If Drucker, Quinn, Naisbit, Toffler, and a host of others are correct (and who would deny the signs that are everywhere around us), the questions before us as educators are, "What does a 'well-organized, creative, and moral intellect' mean or require?" and "What kinds of experiences, knowledge, activities, and understandings will foster that intellect and moral strength for the largest number of our children?"

Some new form of education is rising out of the ashes of criticisms and complaints. What will it be like? What learnings will be relevant in the world in which work is the use of a "well-organized, creative intellect," not use of the hands and back? What kinds of social (or human) skills will be needed so that intellects can work together effectively and harmoniously? How will these interaction skills be different from those needed for cooperative physical work? Just as the telephone in the 1920s (and, indeed, the book in the seventeenth century) forced upon people new media through which to relate to each other, so, too, will the computer and video technology in the twenty-first century.

Perhaps we are back to Counts's question, *Dare the Schools Build a New Social Order?* (1932). Must the school serve the social and economic order that exists (ensure that a nation is strong economically, politically, or militarily) or is its role to create some other vision of the world? Given the multiple visions we are more and more aware of, what is that new social order to be? The planning tools that might help education find new directions are, again, particularly important.

DIRECTION-SETTING TOOLS

We have classified planning tools and technologies into three groups: holistic tools, process tools, and management systems tools. Another way of classifying all tools might be in relation to the two basic questions we continually address: where to go and how to get there. That is, some technologies can help us determine or clarify why we should go in certain directions or why we do go in those directions. Others help us plan how to get there, how to accomplish the results we consider important.

The holistic tools help us understand why educators do make particular kinds of decisions and do demonstrate patterns in their choices and actions. People do act in certain patterns of ways because they have learned patterns of thinking, feeling, and believing. They have learned what is the "right" or "good" way to think or feel or act from their own particular philosophical, cultural, religious, and social community experience. Learning to recognize the differences in patterns can help educators make more adaptive choices and can allow the patterns themselves to be used as bases for choosing direction for a system, school, or classroom.

Thus, we have said throughout Section II that the study of and continuous reflection on differing patterns of beliefs, values, and world views is the most important means by which educators can clarify and make thoughtful choices of direction—of aims, purposes, goals, and objectives.

Process Tools for Goal Seeking

Beyond the holistic tools that exert a powerful and pervasive influence on all goal choice, several process tools have been developed for the express purpose of determining direction or for developing consensus about the appropriate direction for a system. The Delphi Technique and needs assessment have received the most explicit descriptive analysis in the education literature. But other techniques such as the Nominal Group Technique (NGT—a variation of the Delphi Technique), task forces, Royal Commissions on Education, public forums, Gallup polls, and coalitions of interest groups or lobbying groups are all deliberate efforts to establish direction for education.

Each of these means, methods, tools, or techniques has a fairly well established operating technology, but all are based in the same principle. All seek or present opinions and beliefs from particular concerned groups, and all aim for some area of common or general agreement about what is good or is needed or what would be best for the next generation of students.

Delphi, Nominal Group, and Individual Needs Assessment

These three processes are similar in several respects. They are iterative surveys, and they seek opinions from a selected group of respondents. (Needs assessment takes two forms. Opinion survey as described here is the form most commonly employed. The more systematic form, based on measurement and pre- and post-data collection, will be described later.) Very briefly, the process of all three technologies involves the following general steps:

(*1*) A respondent group is selected, and commitment is obtained to participate through three rounds of questionnaires.

(*2*) An open-ended question is presented to the group, and participants are encouraged to give as full a response as possible. The question might be, ''What will young adults need to be successful and happy in the next decade?'' Or it might focus on the system, ''What should be the priorities for the education system in the coming decade?''

(*3*) Responses are analyzed qualitatively for patterns, and second round questions are formulated to elicit opinions about the implied directions.

(*4*) Responses from the second round of questions are again analyzed, and more precise questions are formulated. This third round often asks for ranking of proposed directions.

(*5*) The third set of responses is analyzed for final conclusions about consensus and for the direction options or strategies implied.

The Delphi technology was originated by Dalkey and Helmer in the 1950s and developed under the auspices of the RAND Corporation in the 1960s (Dalkey and Helmer, 1963). Most of the research and development of the technology occurred in the 1970s. A number of useful descriptions of the process can be found from that period. A very thorough review of the literature was presented by O'Brien at Banff Alberta (1980). Delbecq, Van de Ven, and Gustafson (1975) presented a clear description of how the process might be useful in education. They itemized ten steps (Table 4-1) and estimated a minimum time requirement of forty-four and a half days.

For these three technologies, the group of respondents is selected on some sampling proposition. Delphi and Nominal Group Technique usually address specialists or experts—in education, generally, or in some special field. Delphi, of course, received its name from the Delphi Oracle of Greek origin, so there is the implication that direction comes ''from the voice of the gods.'' Barnette, Danielson, and Algozzine (1978) call Delphi ''a debate between experts.''

Needs assessment (NA) often addresses relevant groups concerned. These might be parents, particularly if the NA concerns elementary, or educators if the issue is professional development. Other groups that might be addressed in a needs assessment could be consumers of the education product: corporate employers (if the question concerns work skills students need) or recipients of graduates from some level of the system — secondary, collegiate, or university (for better alignment of programs). The iterative process is considered useful for NA but is less commonly carried out, partly because it is more difficult to retain the necessary commitment from such groups of respondents.

Nominal Group Technique, like Delphi, generally addresses experts. Unlike Delphi, however, this technique brings the group together to work through the series of iterations in one or two days of sessions. It is called "nominal group" because it is a group in name only. The members are selected from different areas or sectors so as to be widely representative. They are deliberately chosen not to be a "working group" in order to minimize the possibility that responses will be affected by personal relationships or role pressures. Of course a major difficulty with NGT lies in time for analysis of responses and refinement of questionnaires between response and feedback cycles.

Each of these technologies is extremely time-consuming but can be very informative. If resources are available (a willing university researcher, for example), any one of the three could be well worth the effort. Each has its own limitations and offers its own advantages. Is it important to get information from experts or from practitioners? Is the long-term future or the immediate future the focus? Since one of the stated purposes is to arrive at consensus about direction, if the immediate future is the focus, needs assessment may have an advantage in terms of commitment. If those who participate will have to "live with the results," there may be an added incentive to think deeply and to reflect on important values.

Customarily, a primary purpose of Delphi (as well as of NGT and NA) is to build consensus, which leads to decisions about direction. However, Turoff (1970) developed a variation he called "Policy Delphi." He proposed that one important potential usefulness of the technology could be to develop and explore options. He said, "The Policy Delphi . . . seeks to generate the strongest possible *opposing* views on the potential resolutions of a major policy issue. . . . [A] policy issue is one for which there are no experts, only informed advocates and referees" (p. 84, emphasis added). He added, "The Policy Delphi also rests on the premise that the decision maker is not interested in having a group generate his decision" (p. 84).

A variation on the Delphi Technique closely related to Turoff's Policy Delphi was tried out for a class project in spring 1993 by a masters student at McGill. She divided her respondents into two groups. After the first response, one group was given the customary type of feedback and follow-up questionnaire: the most common responses, with a request for reaction and clarification. The second group was given "the most unusual responses," with a request for ideas those responses might trigger for new directions.

It had been hoped that the patterns of responses between the two groups would be quite different. Some interesting and innovative suggestions were made, but only a few differences resulted. A number of factors might have been involved. The two groups were being asked to describe an ideal teacher training program, and they were recent graduates of such a program. They had had no teaching experience, so did not have the perspective that actual teaching might have given them. Also, they all knew each other well, having gone through the program together, and they acknowledged that they had talked about their responses with each other.

Since the purpose of this project was for the student to learn the Delphi Technique, not to provide direction for the program, none of these limitations negated the value of the project. The fact that several interesting and different ideas did come out of the second group supports the possibility that Delphi might be used as a tool for promoting inventive, or innovative, thinking.

All three of these technologies (Delphi, NGT, and survey NA) rely on subjective sources of information. The focus of the information solicited is different, at least hypothetically. Delphi customarily is concerned with broad general directions and emphases and with the long term. It is intended to provide forecast information: future trends in society and work and predicted implications of those emerging trends for education. The focus of survey needs assessment is commonly more immediate and more specific. A survey NA often addresses needs within a particular sector of education, as technology, second languages, sciences, or math.

System Needs Assessment

A more quantitatively based technology of needs assessment is proposed in the literature to address system needs. It is not a survey methodology; in fact, it closely resembles a research model, in that it relies on objective data collected periodically. In this model, precise objectives and standards in the mode of behavioral objectives are set for each area of concern. The cycles of data collection employ the same instrument, and actual results are compared with expected results (standards) to determine discrepancies. Areas in which discrepancies are found (where need is observed) may be allocated more resources, provided with new programs, changed to a more effective time slot, etc., and the cycle continues. Post-data from the first round becomes pre-data for the second cycle.

Kaufman and English (1979), Patterson and Czajkowski (1976), and Cornell (1971) have described this system-oriented model of needs assessment. They propose it as a continuous examination and review of education programs. Such a model of needs assessment is an integral part of the PPBS (program, planning, budgeting systems) model. MBO (management by objectives) is also intended to incorporate this principle of cyclical analysis and review: statement of intention, review of results, and redefinition of objectives.

Delphi, Nominal Group Technique, and survey needs assessment are based on perceptions, opinions, predictions, and judgment. One of the important effects of such technologies is motivational. They can be effective instruments for renewal of commitment and are particularly useful in periods when societies are in stress. In this respect, they may offer some of the ''bonding'' effects sought through retreats and mission review.

System needs assessment, on the other hand, is more akin to management system tools such as PPBS and MBO. The primary aspect of all of these management systems is review and evaluation of results in terms of the quality of results expected. Both motivation and evaluation are oriented toward ensuring high-quality results, and planning tools that focus on developing goals and objectives may come from either base.

Time commitments of these goal planning tools differ also. Time commitments of Delphi and NGT are considerable, but they are concentrated into a particular period of time. Because of the bonding effect, members may extend their efforts beyond a normal range to complete such a project. The time commitment to any management system tool is continuous. Collation and analysis of data, plus thoughtful reflection on implications and possible strategies, is very heavily time-based. And the burden of this type of activity must necessarily fall to administrators.

Since the people of a school system call out for attention more demandingly than data, any system that requires a heavy commitment to data collection and analysis is vulnerable.

Certainly, data collection and analysis in the manner proposed cannot be handled by the teacher in a group learning situation. Anyone who has tested out the Flanders Interaction Analysis System or who has attempted to analyze quantitatively any participant observation data knows very well that the teacher cannot lead and record systematic data at the same time.

Technologies may make Zuboff's "informating" (1988) possible. Recording all classroom discussion and analysis on the basis of key words and phrases is technologically possible right now, but, in education, "data" are vulnerable in other ways as well. The whole concept of education is based on the reality of the individual—individual freedom to develop ideas and individual intellectual development. To educators, data are often seen as the mountain of sand that buries the individual. To be able to see meaning relevant to the individual and to allow for individuality of person through the mountain of data are skills critical to planners.

"Can't see the forest for the trees" is the common complaint against special interest groups or demanding parents who do not try to see their demand in perspective of the whole of education. The contrasting cry to educational planners and system administrators is, "Don't lose sight of the individual under the mountain of data."

Management by Objectives

The management systems tool that has been expressly designed to focus attention on intended direction is management by objectives (MBO). MBO proposes a hierarchy of objectives, with objectives of individuals being set in harmony with department objectives, which are expected to be in harmony with school objectives. In turn, those objectives are expected to support system objectives. The pattern in Figures 9.6 and 9.7 illustrate the ideal of integrated and harmonized objectives.

Ideally, too, the system proposes that objectives should be expressed in the model of behavioral objectives, with time limitations and mode and basis of measurement specified. Moreover, it is intended that yearly reviews examine the degree to which objectives have been achieved at each level. This is surely a mountain of sand. The Gantt chart (which will be discussed in Chapter 12 with other task structuring tools) is a common tool for maintaining records and determining success in such a system.

Peter Drucker (1955) is credited with inventing the phrase *management by objectives* and with describing its purpose and process. Odiorne (1965) was one of the first to describe in detail an application of MBO to education. During the 1960s and 1970s, many descriptions of applications and many discussions of benefits to be gained and of the difficulties that arise in application were presented in the literature.

The idea upon which management by objectives is based is not just good; it is such good common sense that it is inevitable. How else can any system of education work, other than with harmoniously integrated objectives? All else is anarchy. But it is through the idea of integrated objectives as the basis of professionalism that such harmony develops. To attempt to create a written, prescriptive taxonomy of the profession and to test individual success against each objective allows the system to devour the meaning.

When one commits oneself to the profession of education, one commits to professional purposes, aims, goals, and objectives. The underlying meaning of *professional* is that the individual is dedicated to these aims and objectives and exercises good judgment in fulfilling them; however, it is useful to remind oneself of those commitments and to recognize that both the system and the individual educator are committed to those ideals. Data collection is not the end or purpose of MBO (though it can consume the purpose). The renewal of commitment is the fundamental good upon which the concept of MBO is based, and that good, that concept, should not be discarded because the system is unwieldy.

Other Means of Initiating Direction

Many of the descriptions of specific methodologies or technologies for determining directions in education can be found in discussions of the more general topics of decision making, planning, and change strategies. A good overview of many of the technologies for identifying possible directions and for choosing direction (or setting mission, goal, or objective) is presented by McNamara and Chisolm (1988). They distinguish between identifying and choosing directions. Methodologies that they associate primarily with identifying possible directions include Delphi, Policy Delphi, trend analysis, cross-impact analysis, scenario writing, environmental scanning, and forecasting and prediction. Tools for choosing direction include DTA and matrix analysis.

Trend Analysis

Trend analysis attempts to predict a future state or condition from factual data about some particular factor. The factor to be tracked might be enrollment, for example. The analysis would attempt to predict enrollment for the next year or for a longer period of time. Figure 11.1 is an example of trend analysis applied by Jared to enrollment for the secondary schools of a suburban school board near Montreal. This example and other applications of effective use by Jared of trends as bases for determining direction are reported by Erjavec (1994).

In this analysis, the administrator was attempting to make accurate predictions of enrollments for each secondary school in his board, because in Quebec, the number of teachers that may be allocated to a school is determined by actual enrollment as of September 30 of any given year. Accurate prediction helps the board ensure an adequate pool

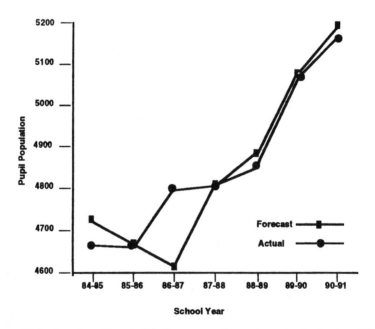

Figure 11.1. Enrollment forecast trend accuracy: forecast vs. actual secondary division of suburban school board. (Reproduced by permission of J. Jared and the school board.)

of teachers for assignment to the schools. During the period shown here, population trends in Quebec were very volatile. Many Anglophone families were leaving the province; ethnic groups were moving within the city as they gained a foothold economically, and the birth rate in French Catholic families was declining dramatically. Despite the volatility, it can be seen that trend analysis provided quite accurate predictions for most years. Jared used three sets of data to arrive at his forecast: numbers completing in elementary feeder schools, actual enrollment for the current year supplied by the principals of receiving schools, and forecasts made by the provincial ministry of education. He prepared individual trend graphs for each of the secondary schools in his division and was able to keep ahead of population fluctuations.

Societal factors that will have an impact on education systems are routinely tracked by government bodies and futurist groups. These include birth rates, postsecondary enrollments, employment trends by job sectors, aging of the population, literacy rates, health factors, immigration and emigration, crime and violence rates, and a host of other factors. One of the first such trend analyses was Durkheim's study of suicide first published in 1897. A sad present-day parallel is found in the studies of suicide rates among teenagers and within native and minority groups. All of these factors, and many more, have important implications for education systems. System needs analysis, described earlier, is an application of trend analysis, based on data internal to the system and tracked over time.

Cross-Impact Analysis

Cross-impact analysis deals with and attempts to relate two different estimates: 1) estimates of the probability of a certain event occurring or of a change taking place and 2) estimates of the possible impact of that event or change (if it does occur) on certain aspects of the education system. Suppose, then, that Quebec provincial demographers have been tracking immigration patterns and the choices of English or French schooling for their children. In addition, they have been tracking the declining birth rate within the Francophone population. The question arises, "What impact will these trends have on the strength and viability of French language and culture in the province?" One can easily see the matrix that develops (Figure 11.2).

In the 1970s, such an analysis was undertaken by provincial demographers. On the basis of trend data, it had been found that new im-

	PREDICTED CHANGE	Use of French in workplace	Use of French at school	French arts, theatre, etc.	Appreciation of French culture	TOTAL EFFECT/ IMPACT
Immigration Trend	* (+ or -)	** (+ or -)				
Emigration of English families						
Enrollment in French sector schools						
Birthrate in Francophone sector					ESTIMATED TOTAL EFFECT →	**

DECISION QUESTION: (reading from row to column, range = -5 to +5):

*Probable change: <u>decreasing dramatically</u> = (-5); <u>increasing dramatically</u> = (+5)

**Probable effect on this factor: <u>negative/ will reduce</u> = (-5); <u>positive/ will increase</u> = (+5)

Figure 11.2. Example of a simple matrix that might have been performed to predict the impact of various factors on French language and culture in Quebec.

404

migrants tended to choose English-language schooling for their children and to choose English as their language of work. Probability estimates suggested that those trends would remain high or would increase. Such estimates presented a bleak picture for French language, culture, and sense of identity. The "Language of Instruction" law (Bill 101) was passed, requiring all children of immigrants to undertake their schooling in French. Other laws were also passed to modify the impact of changes taking place. In the United States, in Florida, New York, and California, for example, similar concerns are initiating questions of "impact."

Although cross-impact analyses are not always formally spelled out, we do tend to think in terms of cross-factor impacts: the possible impact of a possible event. The concern educators often express about setting a precedent is evidence of this pattern of prediction.

Scenario Writing

Scenario writing is an offshoot of data-gathering prediction technologies such as Delphi, trend analysis, and cross-impact analysis. Scenarios are stories about the future, based on one or more sets of data and predictions. Often, a situation is set up in which several small groups (of three or four members) take the same data and write up separate accounts or stories about the future. They might be asked, for example, to write a scenario of what the school would be like in the year 2025 or of how learning will take place. Or they might be asked to write a story about what kinds of knowledge, skills, and attitudes the worker of 2025 would employ in work or of what living patterns would be like in that period. They could also be asked how the school or school system should be designed to meet those conditions. Given three or four different scenarios, the larger group could then discuss pros and cons and choose the scenario thought to be most useful or probable as a guide for action.

One experience I had in leading a large group through scenario writing was concerned with new directions for the nightly news program of a major Canadian broadcasting network. All of the factors that might come into play had been identified, and the group started to develop a plan for the program. It became evident that choice of one factor affected choices among other factors, and the large group soon began to get hopelessly bogged down in dealing with the multiple cross-impacts.

As session moderator, I decreed that the group would form small groups, and each group would write its own scenario, based on assigned "first choices." Each built its story by predicting impacts evolving from that first choice. When they returned to the large group, variations were easily discussed, and a choice of directions was made within a short time.

Such a technique could be used when curricula are being developed to address newly identified learning needs, or, for example, when whole language was first being implemented and a new reporting system had to be created to deal with this very different approach. The world after authentic testing, or after site-based management, are other instances when scenarios might help clarify implications of different choices. The 1990 competition for funding innovative schools sponsored by the New American Schools Development Corporation (NASDC) in the United States was an instance of scenario writing by school project groups.

As a planning course project, master's students at McGill have been asked to design a new type of school, starting with the premise "Our school is (a) (the) _____." Limitations were specified and included the following:

- The "school" itself (whether as a building or not) must complement the concept of the focus of the school.
- All traditional, mandated subject requirements must be met through the chosen focus. That is, math, language, science, history, etc., must be developed from the focus but must cover required content.
- Learning experiences cannot be programmed into class groups and systematic schedules.
- There are no limitations on resources: the best of all possible worlds exists.

Several very interesting scenarios were developed. For one student, "Our school" was the human body. The building was designed as a body, with particular types of inquiry taking place in the heart, brain, hands and arms, etc.

For a Cree student, "Our school" was the outdoors. Quebec history from past to present was traced in the movement of native peoples and the invading groups. Math and science were to be learned through the facts of life in the outdoors and through the necessities of survival. Map reading and trail skills were sources for geography. Writing (both in Cree and in French) arose from outdoor living experiences and from stories and myths.

Other scenarios developed included a space ship, a village, and a library. All were interesting and provided new ideas about ways to develop learning experiences.

Brainstorming

Brainstorming is most often used to create a pool of strategies or possible ways to achieve the ends desired, but it can also be used to generate ideas about new directions. One way brainstorming can help identify where to go is by creating a pool of trends—the "tips of the iceberg" that different participants see for the future. The question asked is, "What is going on 'out there' that may signal a change we must deal with in the future?" The basic rule of brainstorming must apply, of course. All ideas go up on the board; no debate, discussion, or development of ideas is permitted during the brainstorming session. This exercise generates a pool of possible events or changes that might subsequently be examined through a cross-impact matrix.

Brainstorming could also be used to generate the image of the "best educated person" of a future generation. What should that person know understand, experience, and be able to do? This technique is used in focus groups to design "the best possible _____." In a focus group at Concordia University, engineering students designed the "best possible" hand calculator for use in test-taking circumstances. It had a switch to change from numeric to alpha mode and had keys for preprogramming particular functions.

Idea leads to creation. One could propose that Buck Rogers led to space shuttles and that Dick Tracy's wrist radio generated the pocket pager and cellular telephones. If educators have a clear vision of the well-organized, creative, and moral intellect, they will create the means to help students develop in that direction.

Chapter 12 will discuss some of the useful tools for putting ideas to work to accomplish the results envisioned.

Planning for Effective Action

MUCH of the planning in education systems is focused directly on action. Courses, activities, and events get scheduled, and people are made responsible for the detailed plans for action. If the event is complex and costly or if it will affect large numbers of people, planning tools are commonly employed. Even when plans focus on small daily or weekly happenings, the thinking patterns upon which planning tools have been designed are commonplace.

Or, to say the same thing conversely, planning tools have derived from common, everyday patterns of logical thinking. They are not created out of whole cloth, and they are not dramatically different in concept from thinking that comes naturally. These patterns that we call tools are more complex, more precise, and they incorporate and interrelate more factors than one can easily hold in memory. But the basic thought line is one we use from childhood [see, again, Joel's "Life Cycle of a Walnut" (Figure 7.3)]. To study some tool from the literature is not to learn something "new"; it is to refine patterns already known and to examine ways to use the pattern more productively.

As stated throughout, the focus of the book is on the relatively common planning situations that educators are involved in. Projective planning for nations or world systems of education is not the stuff of life for most educators. The tools the people need are those that will help keep activities and events moving smoothly because they provide reminders, and they call attention to tasks that must be done, to contingencies that must be considered, and to questions that may be raised.

In this chapter, the planning tools that directly address questions of implementation of projects and action will be discussed: operational process tools and management systems tools.

OPERATIONAL PROCESS TOOLS

The planning tools that focus directly on action are those called process tools and management systems tools in Figure II.3. In Chapter 11, the process tools that provide means of identifying direction, the "where to go" questions of educational planning, were discussed. Included in that chapter was management by objectives (MBO), the management systems tool that offers technology for articulating and harmonizing goals and objectives throughout the system. In earlier chapters, too, some of the social dynamics process tools such as leadership styles, communication models, and the dynamics of participation were discussed. Moreover, each separate step of the Values-Based Planning System described in Chapters 9 and 10 is a process tool for planning, focused on a particular step in the logic of building a plan.

Figure 12.1 presents the types of process tools and the management systems tools that will be discussed in this chapter. There are many good descriptions in the literature of all of the tools to be discussed here. Each of them can be said to have "had its day" in the limelight, and the literature shows the pattern of rise and fall in popularity. The fact is that educators and the public continually seek new tools and new technologies that may enable them to achieve the results they value. To borrow Quinn's phrase, we are in a continual cycle of logical incrementalism—trying to move toward some new technology for greater gain, then trying to regain whatever valued outcomes we may have lost from the old, to achieve the best of both worlds, old and new.

But new technologies derive from older ones. PERT and CPM, popular in the 1950s and 1960s and derived from Gantt charts, were first developed during World War I. Site-based management reminds us of the small, independent rural schools of the early 1900s. Cooperative learning has much of the character of those same small rural schools where six or seven students represented six or seven grades.

We will examine three types of process tools: choice, task analysis, and resource allocation tools. The focus of resource allocation tools will be on four management systems budgeting tools. Particular emphasis will be on PPBS (program, planning, budgeting systems). Other management systems tools such as OD (organizational development) and TQM (total quality management) place the emphasis on different aspects of overall management planning.

Organizational development addresses primarily the personal and

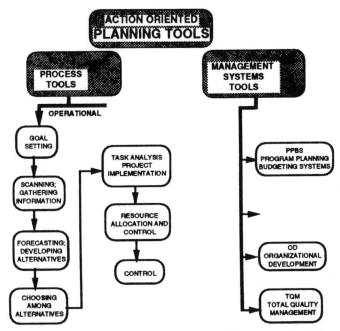

Figure 12.1. *Process tools and management systems tools that are particularly oriented toward action.*

interpersonal relationship aspects of organizational life and provides techniques for enhancing those relationships to improve work life and the climate of work for all. Organizational development encompasses a wide variety of specific technologies; nearly every change strategy, leadership technology, or intervention strategy has, at one time or another, been referred to under the rubric of organizational development. One of the earlier technologies, the T-group, received a great deal of attention in the 1960s. Such present-day technologies as stress management, role playing, and scenario building are considered OD interventions. In fact, surveys, needs analyses, Delphi, and many other tools and techniques are sometimes used for the purposes of organizational development.

Total quality management (TQM) focuses on quality in every aspect of the organization's life and affairs. In education, TQM would insist on high-quality relationships with students and parents, would be equally concerned with the quality of financial responsibility and of building maintenance, would expect high-quality professional knowledge and behavior, and would assume that the quality of administrative behavior toward teachers and the quality of teachers' behavior toward administrators are of equal importance to an effective school. TQM would concern itself with curriculum, testing, counseling, health services, bus service, cafeteria, teaching methods, and home and school relationships. Quality action in every aspect of the school's life is the orientation of TQM.

The literature on TQM and its implications for education are still current. Nearly every issue of management journals has interesting articles describing practice or proposing approaches. Organizational development has been longer established, and journals such as *The Journal of Applied Behavioral Sciences* are particularly focused on ways and means of developing better climate and relationships and of the impact of development technologies. Proper consideration of either TQM or OD alone could consume a full book. As planning tools, the perspective of each is the holistic system, and each focuses on one aspect of action: TQM on the quality of all action within the system and OD on the quality of personal and interpersonal action and behavior.

Choosing among Alternatives

DTA – Decision Tree Analysis

The best known decision making tool in the management literature is Decision Tree Analysis (DTA). In Figure 6.7, Cunningham's (1982) example of decision tree analysis for predicting success of alternative programs for exceptional children was presented. In the discussion following that figure, the complexity that such an analysis can generate was stressed, and it was suggested that DTA is most useful for choices that have global implications and for situations where it is worthwhile to tap computer facilities to handle complex analyses.

In this section, I would like to refer back to that example and explain the process of thinking that takes place to produce the computations at each point in the analysis. It is the process of thinking that is generalizable to a broad spectrum of choices, and this process of thinking is common knowledge. Educators at the local level will not often create a decision tree with precise statistical analyses. Most educators do not even want to try to understand the statistics involved. However, the mental process of predicting the probability and the desirability of possible outcomes based on predictable contingencies is a process that every educator uses constantly. It is the way educators try to estimate which technique will be more successful with which group. "If we do A or B with group P and Q, how well will it work (probability of success/failure), and is it worth the effort (cost)?" These two factors are the basis of the "util" of DTA.

DTA Computations

This section will describe the mathematical computation of the DTA example without going into statistical validation of the concept. [For descriptions of the Bayesian statistics upon which DTA is based, see, for example, Newman (1971) or Winkler (1972).] In order to present the pattern of analysis and computation involved, a portion of Cunningham's decision tree for exceptional children that was presented in Figure 6.7 is reproduced here as Figure 12.2.

As stated in Chapter 6, the situation Cunningham describes is really quite simple compared with many education decisions; however, the special education example is a good one for studying the *process* of DTA.

In the decision tree, squares represent decision points, circles represent outcome points, and lines indicate the path of decision analysis. To make the discussion easy to follow, I have labeled what might be considered columns as A, B, C, etc. We have labeled the far right column (the utility estimate, or "util" column) "A," because the mathematical computations move backwards from final estimated value of outcome to the first choice point.

Cunningham says, "The utility that an outcome has for a decision maker is its desirability or usefulness to the decision maker and is measured in 'utils.' ... [A] value of 1 is assigned to the most preferable outcome and a value of 0 to the least preferable outcome" (1982, 180). Remember that "util" or utility is the combination of high success and low cost.

Desirability, or utility, in this exercise is affected by cost (of screening and program), success (probability of successful learning by students), correct identification of students (probability that normal learners will be ID'd normal and exceptional learners will be ID'd exceptional), and cost of most favorable program. The possible outcomes are rated on subjective estimates of the interaction of those factors as follows:

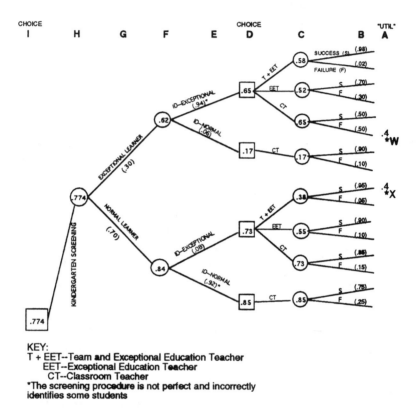

KEY:
T + EET--Team and Exceptional Education Teacher
EET--Exceptional Education Teacher
CT--Classroom Teacher
*The screening procedure is not perfect and incorrectly
identifies some students

Figure 12.2. *A portion of Cunningham's (1982) DTA for exceptional children showing Case W and Case X.*

414

Real Learner Population	Probability of Correct Screening	Real Cost, Based on Screening, Plus Program	Probability of Learning Outcome
Normal	normal vs. exceptional	low medium high	success vs. failure
Exceptional	exceptional vs. normal	low medium high	success vs. failure

Table 12.1 presents the best and worst case scenarios, and the two pathways "W" and "X" that will be described below. Refer back to Figure 6.7 to find the best case pathways, with "utils" of 1.

In Figure 6.7, four outcomes were starred, which we labeled W, X, Y, and Z. These four particular outcomes were chosen because they represent success and failure under different conditions. The computations for all four starred outcomes are presented in Figure 12.3, but I will describe the mathematics involved in following only one outcome, "W," which appears in the part of the DTA shown in Figure 12.2. The computations move from "util" (Column A) back to program choice and screening choice. Cunningham and others call this mathematical process of computing backwards to estimate the effect of successive factors on the final outcome "folding in."

Table 12.1. Selected Case Scenarios from the Decision Tree Analysis for Exceptional Learners, Developed by Cunningham (1982).

Learner	Screened	Placed In	Performance
Best Case (util = 1.0):			
Normal	Normal	Low-cost program	Success
Exceptional	Exceptional	Low-cost program	Success
Worst Case (util = 0):			
Normal	Exceptional	High-cost program	Failure
Exceptional	Exceptional	High-cost program	Failure
"W" Case (util = .4):			
Exceptional	Exceptional	Low-cost program	Failure
"X" Case (util = .4):			
Normal	Exceptional	High-cost program	Failure

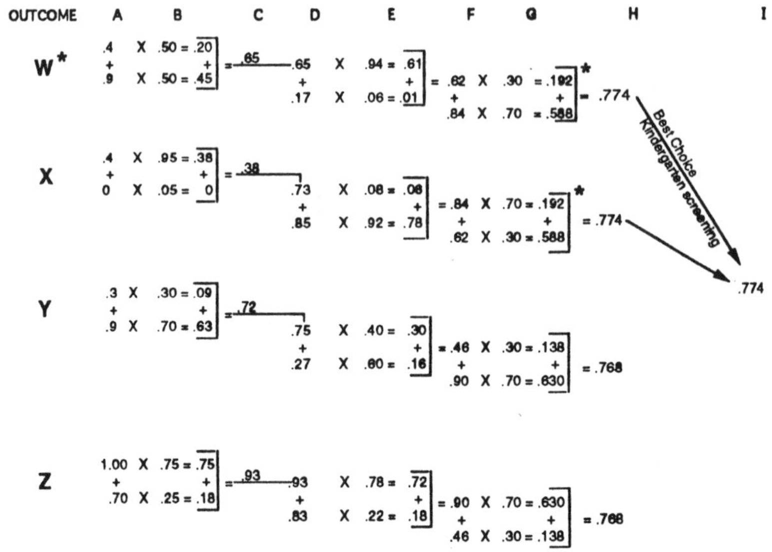

OUTCOME | A | B | C | D | E | F | G | H | I

W*
$.4 \times .50 = .20$
$+$
$.9 \times .50 = .45$ $= .65$ —— $.65 \times .94 = .61$
$+$
$.17 \times .06 = .01$ $= .82 \times .30 = .192$
$+$
$.84 \times .70 = .588$ $= .774$ *

X
$.4 \times .95 = .38$
$+$
$0 \times .05 = 0$ $= .38$ —— $.73 \times .08 = .06$
$+$
$.85 \times .92 = .78$ $= .84 \times .70 = .192$
$+$
$.62 \times .30 = .588$ $= .774$

Y
$.3 \times .30 = .09$
$+$
$.9 \times .70 = .63$ $= .72$ —— $.75 \times .40 = .30$
$+$
$.27 \times .60 = .16$ $= .46 \times .30 = .138$
$+$
$.90 \times .70 = .630$ $= .768$

Z
$1.00 \times .75 = .75$
$+$
$.70 \times .25 = .18$ $= .93$ —— $.93 \times .78 = .72$
$+$
$.83 \times .22 = .18$ $= .90 \times .70 = .630$
$+$
$.46 \times .30 = .138$ $= .768$

Best Choice Kindergarten screening

$.774$

*These are the same computations as are the basis of the DTA in Figures 6.7 and 12.2.
The order has been reversed to be able to read from left to right.

Figure 12.3. *Pathway for computing the steps ("folding back") in the DTA example to arrive at the "best choice" (based on cost and success) for the exceptional education program.*

Of course, the first step in the overall process of decision tree analysis is to draw the decision tree. In the example here, we begin with one set of assumptions (that the real student population is composed of 30% exceptional learners and 70% normal learners). The first decision point allows two possible actions: 1) prescreening at kindergarten or 2) no prescreening (identification of normal and exceptional to be based on recommendation of the classroom teacher).

The second decision point allows three alternative programs: 1) T + EET—teacher plus exceptional education teacher (high cost); 2) EET alone (medium cost); or 3) CT—classroom teacher alone (low cost). The issues are: 1) How well could normal and exceptional learners be identified correctly by special screening in kindergarten and 2) would it be worth the cost? (Would it add sufficiently to the success rate to make the cost of such screening worthwhile?)

Probabilities are estimated or computed. To check the computations on the decision tree, read from ''W'' (Column A on the right) to the left (Columns B, C, D, etc.). In Figure 12.3, computations have been reversed to flow from left to right (A to I), our more normal pattern of reading. Thus, as follows:

1.0 The util of "W"   success under CT of
     (Col A)   exceptional learner ID'd
                         exceptional   =   .4
1.1 The util of   failure under those
     (Col A)   conditions (see branch
                         above)   =   .9
1.2 The probable rate of success for each was
     predicted (see Column B)   =   .50
1.3 The predicted learning outcome (Column C) is
     computed: (.4 × .5) + (.9 × .5)   =   .65
2.0 The parallel predicted learning outcomes under
     Column C   = .58 and .52
3.0 The best choice of these three alternatives for
     exceptional learners ID'd exceptional is .65,
     which is folded back to "choice point D"   =   .65
4.0 The parallel "choice point D" for normal
     learners ID'd exceptional is .17   =   .17
4.1 The predicted decision outcome (Column F) is
     computed: (.65 × .94) + (.17 × .06)   =   .62
4.2 The parallel predicted decision outcome for
     normal learners ID'd normal (Column F) is .84   =   .84
5.0 The predicted decision outcome for
     kindergarten screening (Column H) is
     computed: (.62 × .30) + (.84 × .70)   =   .774

The same pattern of computations follows for all other "utils." The four examples of "utils," W, X, Y, and Z, were presented in Figure 12.3. As stated, few decisions made at the school level require the statistical analysis of DTA. However, it could be very useful in a number of cases to draw the tree with its branching alternatives. Exercises 12.1 and 12.2 suggest practice in thinking through the mathematics of a DTA. Exercise 12.3 proposes practice in analyzing the alternatives of a set of choices by creating the branches of a decision tree.

Matrix Analysis

A second tool used very frequently to analyze factors that will affect the success of a project being planned is matrix analysis (MA). Matrix

For practice in following the line of reasoning, compute one or two more of the "utils."

Exercise 12.1. Computing DTA mathematics.

Perhaps you do not agree with some of the "utils," the desirability factors assigned in the DTA example in Figure 6.7, Column A. For example, would you assign a 40% "utility factor" to the outcome we have labeled "W"? (Failure for "Exceptional Learner" identified "Exceptional" and placed in the Classroom Teacher program.) Remember, DTA is oriented toward the organization's utility, and utility is assessed on the interaction of cost and result (success/failure).

If you disagree with the utility factors assigned to the outcomes (Column A), change them and recompute the DTA to see whether you reach a different "Best Choice."

Exercise 12.2. Recompute pathways.

Create a decision tree that requires a choice between two options and that may be affected by two or three contingencies.

Exercise 12.3. Create a decision tree.

418

analysis was discussed briefly in Chapter 6, and a number of examples of how the tool is used in planning were presented. See Figures 2.10 and 2.11 for models of relationships analyzed, Figure 6.8 for determining goal priorities, Figure 10.3 for creating a program schedule, Figures 10.9 and 10.10 for alternatives or options analysis, and Figure 11.2 for impact analysis.

There are, of course, countless other specific questions for which matrix analysis can be useful. It can be a particularly enlightening process used as a group participation exercise. Participation should be set up in small groups of three or four. Each member is given the same matrix to complete individually. Then the small group works on a combined response to the same matrix, which can be recorded on a flip chart or an overhead transparency. These are shown to the large group for discussion. Two matrices that have stimulated thoughtful discussions when used in this manner are presented in Figure 12.4.

Other factors can be added to either axis to make the exercise most relevant to the group. Of course the most common tools of all for making decisions are executive command and democratic vote. However, tools such as DTA and MA, which permit ranges of opinion to be expressed, encourage more thoughtful consideration of issues and open up discussions to a wider range of issues and the ways various factors interact.

It should be remembered that neither DTA nor MA *prescribes* a decision. The decision is always made by people and does not have to be bound by the numbers. As in the analysis reported in *The Montreal Gazette* (Figure 10.10), the greatest usefulness of a systematic analysis may be that it brings out the subconscious values that are important factors. Though we necessarily make judgments and decisions constantly in education, it is obvious that they are not based solely on objective/factual data. For an exercise such as DTA or MA, data are collected, criteria for judgments are specified, and alternatives are assessed systematically and overtly. In this way, judgments approach "measurement" insofar as it is possible for human behaviors.

Task Analysis Tools

Task analysis is at the heart of getting programs, projects, activities, and events to run smoothly. The educator's worst nightmare is to arrive at the moment "GO" and suddenly realize that the tickets weren't

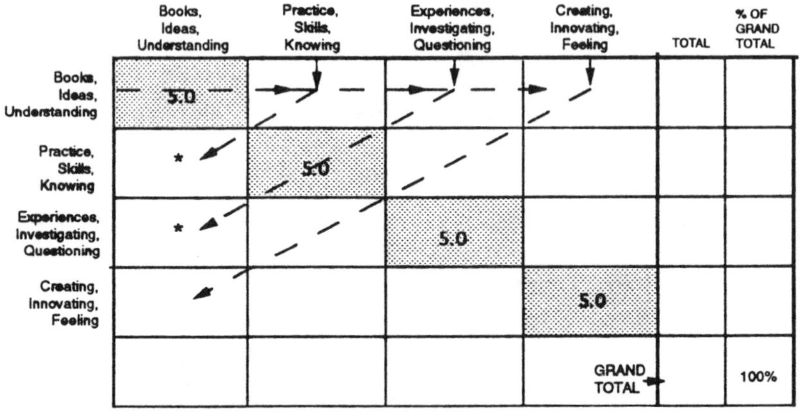

	Books, Ideas, Understanding	Practice, Skills, Knowing	Experiences, Investigating, Questioning	Creating, Innovating, Feeling	TOTAL	% OF GRAND TOTAL
Books, Ideas, Understanding	5.0					
Practice, Skills, Knowing	*	5.0				
Experiences, Investigating, Questioning	*		5.0			
Creating, Innovating, Feeling				5.0		
					GRAND TOTAL	100%

PLANNING QUESTION: Where should the greatest emphasis be placed in the educational program?
ANALYSIS QUESTION: How much more or less emphasis should be placed on
Books than Practice—on Books than Experiences—on Books than Creating
Practice than Experiences—on Practice than Creating
Experiences than Creating
* INVERSE SCORES: Note that scores in the lower left cells become inverses of those in the upper right cells.

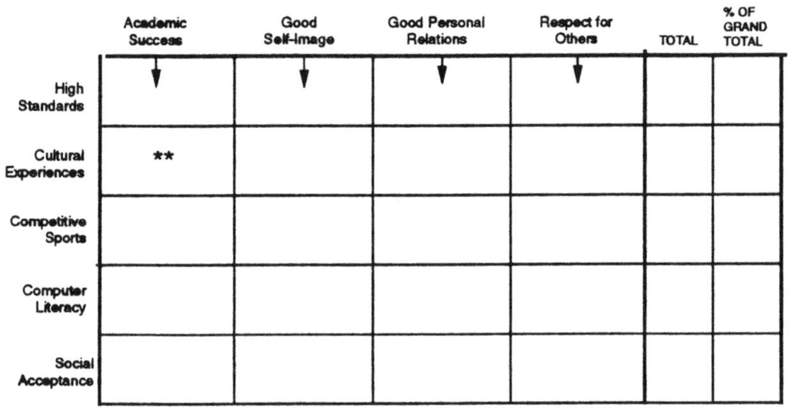

	Academic Success	Good Self-Image	Good Personal Relations	Respect for Others	TOTAL	% OF GRAND TOTAL
High Standards						
Cultural Experiences	**					
Competitive Sports						
Computer Literacy						
Social Acceptance						

PLANNING QUESTION: What do we need to strengthen most in our educational program?
ANALYSIS QUESTION: How much impact (positive or negative) do
High standards have on: Academic Success; on: Good Self-Image; on: Good Personal
Relations; on: Respect for others
Cultural experiences have on: Academic Success—etc.
Competitive Sports————etc.
** There are no inverse scores in this matrix.

Figure 12.4. Two examples of simple matrices that have stimulated thoughtful discussion in groups of educators.

printed, the wrong overheads are in the file, the books have been ordered out by someone else, or there is no one on tap who can run the PA system. The details will get you every time.

So educators have become famous "list makers." One of Montreal's best known women educators was known at the provincial ministry of education as "Sarah, la liste." She had every detail in hand and had her lists at hand. She was a very successful negotiator on behalf of the English-language cégep she was director general of.

Despite the fact that every educator can lay claim to considerable skill in task analysis, in making those lists of things to be done, structuring tasks is a separate skill. A "to do" list is generally the order of business for one person. It has somewhat the character of a flowchart, because tasks may be subconsciously ordered in terms of what has to be done first. A structured list is the tool for coordinating the activities of several working groups or individuals. It allows for delegation of tasks to separate groups or individuals without losing the coherence of the whole. A structured task analysis is preliminary to creating a network.

Structuring a task analysis requires organizing activities into related groups. The structure (the grouping of the sets of tasks) is generally built on the basis of major functions. For example, if a track and field day were being planned, the tasks would be organized under headings such as judging, registration, scheduling, food service, organizing prizes, etc. Each of these headings would encompass a list of relevant activities. The task analysis structure in Figure 10.12 suggests another common basis for grouping activities in education projects: teaching, administrative, communication, evaluation, support, etc.

A simple task list may be preliminary to setting priorities; it may assume that some items in the list are expendable. A structured task analysis assumes that every item is a piece of a whole, that every task is critical to the successful completion or operation of the whole. That is, a simple task list (analysis) describes "a day in the life of _____." A structured task analysis describes the project, program, or event in all of its elements.

The structured analysis may identify how many times a particular activity will be done and may estimate the amount of time each activity will take. Frequently, the analysis worksheet will also identify how many people will be involved in the activity. So "on-site registration" will take place one time, for a period of three hours and will require six people. These estimated data lead to three subsequent steps in project planning:

building a network (planning the coordination of tasks), resource allocation (as Figure 10.13), and scheduling activities.

In the values-based planning system presented in Chapters 9 and 10,
the task analysis led directly to the resource allocation component. These
two steps combine to provide a critical double check on whether it will
be possible to implement the project with the resources available. There
are far too many school systems in North America in serious financial
difficulty because of overextending their resources. They may not have
set limits on proposed activities before plans are made, or they may not
have constrained the plans to fit resources available. The concept of a
resource bank for a project helps maintain a realistic perspective for any
one project within the whole operation of the system.

Task Structuring Tools

Three types of task structuring tools will be discussed in this section:
Gantt charts, networks, and the RAC (responsibility, authority, communication) matrix.

Networks and Gantt Charts

In addition to leading to the resource allocation component of a plan,
the structured task analysis (called a work breakdown structure by
Canadian Pacific Consulting System) is the means of preparing to build
a network. A planning network is a technology for describing all of the
activities or tasks needed to complete a project in their relationship to
each other and to final completion. A completed network depicts the
separate flows of activity that compose the types of tasks identified under
the headings of the task structure and, also, the intersections (or junctions) of those separate flows of work into a coordinated operation.

The two network patterns most commonly described in the literature
are PERT (program evaluation review technique) and CPM (critical path
method).[21] There are now computer programs for building networks,
and they can save planners considerable time and frustration in drawing
and redrawing the ''boxes.'' However, because of the GIGO principle

[21]There are any number of good descriptions of how to prepare a PERT or a CPM network,
as well as of how and when they are most useful. See, for example, Holtz (1969), Banghart
(1969), Simons (1965), Horowitz (1967), Boulanger (1961), Michaels (1971), and AASA
(1979a).

(garbage in, garbage out), the network that the computer draws is only as good as the thinking that goes into it. And "network thinking" is not a skill that comes naturally to everyone.

Gantt Charts: Indeed, it may astonish many educators to learn that the first, preliminary tool for planning the integration of *time* and *tasks* was created during World War I (Banghart, 1969). That tool, the Gantt chart, was not a network. It was a simple bar chart on which the bar progressed along a scale of time (hours, days, weeks) and recorded the number of tasks completed as compared to the number planned. Such is the chart used to show the number of books a child has read this month/term/year or the number of candy bars each team or class has sold or the contributions of various sectors to United Way or the March of Dimes. This Gantt chart is such an ordinary part of our repertoire now, it hardly seems possible that there was a day when recording tasks over time was not done this way.

The history of Henry Gantt is interesting in itself, as is the history of many figures in the scientific management revolution—the Gilbreths, Lillian and Frank, for example, remembered now for the book and movie *Cheaper by the Dozen*. Gantt was of the scientific management era but had strong humanist instincts. He was a keen analyst and logical thinker, but a creative innovator as well.[22] At any rate, his Gantt chart blasted the United States' war effort planning into a higher realm of efficiency and soon became a standard tool for planning and control of production in industry. Figure 12.5 illustrates two examples of how a Gantt chart could be used to track progress against plan in a fifth-grade class.

Example #1 shows the use of a Gantt chart to track the progress of the class. This use can build a team or cooperative spirit in a class. It also can help the teacher check on whether his/her plan is realistic and whether assignments are properly geared to the level of the students. The use shown in Example #2 is intended to encourage individual effort on the part of each child. Each of the uses illustrated has advantages and disadvantages well-known to teachers.

[22]George (1968, 101 – 102) credits Gantt with four major contributions to management concepts: 1) "the idea of a straight-line chart to portray and measure activity by the amount of time needed to perform it"; 2) "the task and bonus plans [which] guaranteed a day wage for output less than standard, offered a bonus in addition to the day wage for achieving standard, and rewarded the worker for production above standard"; 3) "a policy of instructing workers rather than driving them . . . [and] the idea that management had a responsibility to teach workers"; and 4) "that emphasis be placed on service rather than on profits."

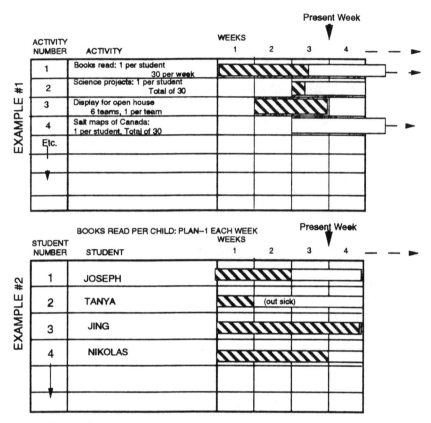

Figure 12.5. *Two examples of the use of Gantt charts in a fifth-grade class, showing progress against plan. Number of students = 30; plan* ☐ *; progress* ▧.

Gantt charts are simple tools, adaptable to many uses, and they have become common tools for educational planning, as unconsciously used as the structure of a sentence in language. Used as a tool for planning a project, a Gantt chart, Drucker says, "analyzes the steps necessary to obtain a final work result . . . by projecting backward, step by step from end result to actions, their timing and sequence. . . ." But, he adds, "The Gantt Chart tells us very little about the logic that is appropriate to given kinds of processes. It is, so to speak, the multiplication table of work design" (Drucker, 1974, 182).

PERT and CPM: By the 1950s, Gantt charts were not adequate to deal with the complex coordinating issues that arose in industrial and military planning. The U.S. Navy's Special Projects Office, responsible for the development of the Polaris missile produced the task structuring planning tool called PERT. PERT (planning evaluation review technique) structured tasks by focusing on "events," the completion of some task. On the PERT chart, events are signaled by nodes (circles named as an event) and are connected by arrows to create a network. Thus, the network is an integrated set of flowcharts, and it describes very precisely the operation of a project in terms of all necessary tasks and their relationship to each other.

The precise graphic, mathematical, and computerized nature of PERT provided for coordination of a project that integrated the work of "a huge, complicated, weapon system development program, being conducted at or beyond the state of the art in many areas, with activities proceeding concurrently in hundreds of industrial and scientific organizations in different areas" (Archibald and Villoria, 1968, 13). It was the need to keep abreast of these disparate pieces of an operation proceeding concurrently in different locations, but critically dependent on each other, that led to the invention of PERT.

At roughly the same time, a DuPont engineer and a Remington-Rand computer expert designed a computerized network modeling system called CPM (critical path method), which depicted graphically the dependencies between separate tasks of an operation. Thus, where the PERT node might have been titled "Approval by Head Office Confirmed," the CPM activity arrow might be titled "Get Approval of Head Office." The emphasis on tasks or activities, rather than on events (completions), focused responsibility for control of the activity on the individual department or unit. This model was seized upon in construction and process industries where a project was in the hands of one dominant organization (Archibald and Villoria, 1968, 15). Figure 12.6 shows the roughly parallel development of PERT and CPM, as depicted by Archibald and Villoria (1968) in their Figure 1.

In education, PERT network technology is probably better known than CPM, although the conditions might suggest the use of CPM: 1) projects are generally well defined; 2) usually, operation is confined to one dominant organization; 3) the uncertainties are minimal; and 4) the project is generally restricted to one geographic area (Archibald and Villoria, 1968, 14). These conditions are more compatible with education than are the Polaris missile conditions. At present, there is less

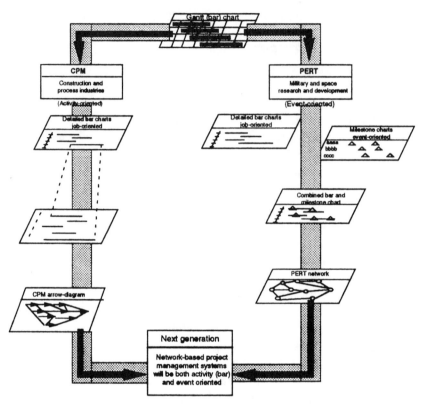

Figure 12.6. *Evolution of the network plan. [Adapted from Figure 1, p. 15 in Archibald, R. D. and R. L. Villoria.* Network-Based Management Systems (PERT/CPM). © *1968. John Wiley and Sons, Inc. New York, NY. Reprinted by permission of John Wiley and Sons, Inc.]*

distinction between PERT and CPM; the features have become some-what interchangeable. Figure 12.7 depicts the format of a simple PERT network and lists the conventions used in building it.

It is important to realize that networks are not schedules. That is, they do not customarily proceed on the identification of calendar dates, although certain deadline dates (milestones) are probably noted. The number of days for an activity is an estimated allocation of working days for completion of a task. PERT protocol computes that network allocation from three estimates: most optimistic (a), most pessimistic (b), and most probable (m). A weighted average (t_e) of these three estimates is computed using the formula (most probable m is given more weight):

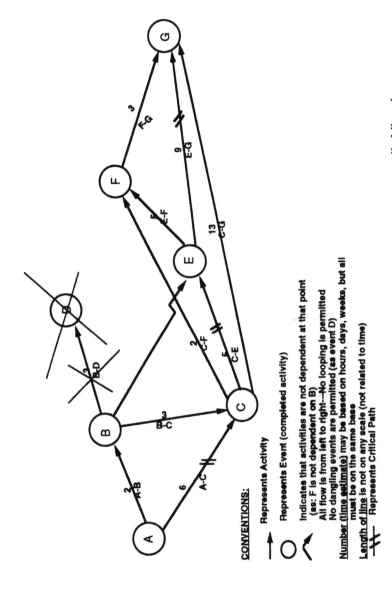

CONVENTIONS:

↑   Represents Activity

○   Represents Event (completed activity)

❮   Indicates that activities are not dependent at that point
       (as: F is not dependent on B)
       All flow is from left to right—No looping is permitted
       No dangling events are permitted (as event D)

Number (time estimate) may be based on hours, days, weeks, but all
       must be on the same base

Length of line is not on any scale (not related to time)

⫻   Represents Critical Path

Figure 12.7. Simple PERT network illustrating conventions generally followed.

427

$$t_e = \frac{a + 4m + b}{6}$$

For a discussion of the probability statistics upon which PERT computations are based, see those references cited earlier.

The "critical path" is based on the total number of working days allocated to all events along the pathway, which identifies the line of completed events that has no "slack time." That is, each activity *must* be completed within the allocated time, or the project as a whole will suffer.

Two of the important principles upon which all networks are built are 1) precedence-dependence and 2) junction. Events or activities are ordered in terms of whether they precede or are dependent on each other. In education, this ordering is partially a matter of personal interpretation. Must "invitations to the professional day" await "confirmation of speakers"? That depends on how specific the invitations might be. Junctions (points at which various sets of activities must be completed before further action can begin), too, are less absolute than in space programs or military affairs.

SPECNET®: The distinctions between network technologies has blurred since the 1960s. Every operational management team has developed its own modification, but the essential elements remain the same:

- graphic format that employs arrows to show progress toward completion and nodes (circles or boxes) to show points at which tasks intersect
- precise and complete detail of activities (tasks) or events (completions)
- time estimates for each activity, with some sort of "flag" to highlight critical time junctions
- indicator of the "critical path" (the line of junctions that allows for no lag in time if the project as a whole is to be completed on time)

Canadian Pacific's model, the SPECNET is an example. The format it uses gives managers important information not customarily found on PERT and CPM networks. Figure 12.8 illustrates the SPECNET node and the conventions employed.

The particular characteristics of SPECNET node include

- The nodes are named as activities (not as completed events as in PERT).

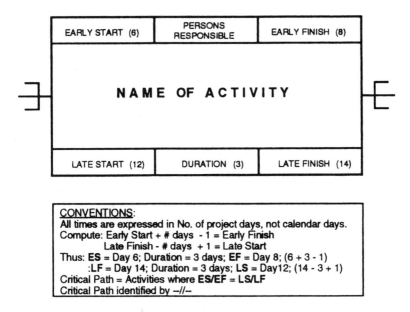

Figure 12.8. SPECNET® node. Critical information is placed on the node. It employs simple conventions for estimating start and finish times and for determining critical path. [SPEC is a registered trademark of CPCS Ltd., and SPECNET is copyrighted. Reproduced by permission of Canadian Pacific Ltd. Systems Services, Montreal, QC, Canada (1985).]

- The number of days estimated for the activity is shown on each node. (A single time estimate is made by the person or group responsible for the activity. Early and late issues are dealt with separately.)
- Early start-early finish and late start-late finish are shown on the node for each activity.
- The person responsible is identified on the node.

Figure 12.9 gives an example of a simple SPECNET.
The SPECNET itself also has some distinguishing characteristics:

- Activities going on concurrently are maintained in vertical columns.
- All of the activities in any one column (as A, C, D) are being or can be done concurrently. All in Column A start (early start – ES) on Day 1; all in C start (ES) on Day 12; all in D start (ES) on Day 26; etc.
- Early start-early finish is computed beginning with the node named

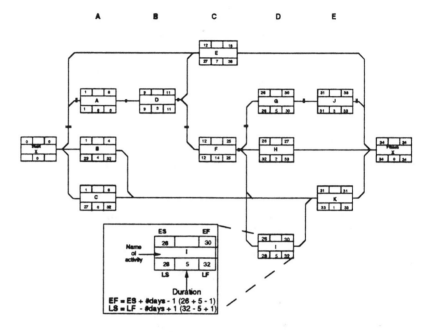

Figure 12.9. Sample SPECNET®, showing early start-early finish, late start-late finish, and critical path. [Reproduced by permission of Canadian Pacific Ltd. Systems Services, Montreal, QC, Canada (1985).]

"start." Early finish = early start + days duration − one day (because finish day becomes start day for the next activity and should not be counted twice). Late start-late finish is computed beginning with the node named "finish" and computed backwards. Late start = late finish − days duration + one day).

- Thus, the critical path is easily identified: Whenever ES-EF and LS-LF are the same, the activity is on the critical path.
- The length of the line between activities (as from C to K) does not indicate time; the line signifies dependent on. Thus, the line signifies that K cannot begin until C, F, and I have been completed.

A network can be a helpful tool when planning any fairly complicated educational event such as a national debate contest, a professional retreat for all teachers on a board, a drive to gain support for some social cause, a new curriculum development, or a wilderness campout. It can also be helpful for routine tasks that are repeated but that, each time, involve coordinating the work of different groups of people. Examples include scheduling courses, scheduling busing routes, producing computerized report cards, or planning cafeteria service. Any activity or event requiring many logistical details to be completed so the work will proceed as planned can benefit from the analysis of tasks and junction (coordination) points that a network requires. Exercise 12.4 suggests that you create a SPECNET for a professional workshop.

A special note: Post-It™ notes are extremely useful in building any network. Invariably, planners will want to change the order of some

---

Use SPEC type nodes for the activites.

Include time estimates: early/late start/finish, flow lines (arrows), critical path.

Include all of the activities listed below. You may add activities, but you must use all of those listed. (They may have different meanings to different people.)

Assume:

- The workshop will last for three days.
- It will be at a location that requires an overnight stay.
- It will be for personnel from at least three boards.

Activities that must be included:

Form committees	Get funding
Choose location	List teachers
Choose animators	Choose topics
Invite animators	Arrange accommodations
Send out info	Assign rooms for sessions
Advertise	Arrange transportation
Arrange meals	Fix time limits
Arrange parking	Schedule dates
Schedule program	Arrange printing
Set fees	Set up accounting
Arrange AV	Divide participants into groups
Form subcommittees	Arrange session handouts
Previsit to site	Schedule confirmation dates
Arrange honorariums	Arrange entertainment
Design program	Organize badges, materials, etc.
Arrange favors	Organize coffee breaks

Set deadline date for registrations
Set up procedures for selecting participants
Arrange on-site registration
Confirm on-site arrangements
Organize greeters/hosts/hostesses

Exercise 12.4. Create a SPEC® network to plan for a professional workshop.

activities, and Post-It™ notes could have been invented for everyone who changes their mind frequently.

Flowcharts: Networks are sometimes called flowcharts because they delineate the flow of operation, which should be distinguished from flow of work in that it is system oriented. A network plans for the integration of the several relevant flows of work at critical junction points. Thus, the network is concerned with the overall project, while separate flowcharts may be relevant for each set of activities that feed into the whole somewhere along the network's paths. Table 12.2 compares flowcharts and networks on several relevant characteristics.

Flowchart thinking is pretty much a basic tool of all educators. Educators work alone for the most part and are responsible for all elements of most projects they are involved in (we estimate that close to 90% of the educator's planning effort is concerned with their own work), and activities take on a linear or serial relationship.

One of the values of making a list, creating a flowchart, or building a network is that it gets the details out of the planner's head and down on paper. That makes one less thing to worry about—you don't have to worry about forgetting. A second important value, particularly of a network, is that it puts the picture of the operation out where everyone can see it. Since a network is built when many groups are concurrently completing pieces of the action, it is useful to have the whole picture clearly detailed for everyone.

RAC (Responsibility, Authority, Communication) Matrix

The third type of task structuring tool focuses on relationships among units working on a project. The proposition made is that projects often fail because the lines of authority, responsibility, and communication are not clearly understood or are not followed properly. Units are not informed of decisions or are not consulted when their advice or approval is required for a decision or when a decision is made without proper authority.

The format used for this type of analysis by CPCS (Canadian Pacific Consulting Services) is called an RAC matrix. The emphasis of the RAC matrix is on making sure that everyone knows what is expected of them and making sure, as well, that no one treads on anyone else's toes—that each unit's areas of expertise and responsibility are respected. How often are innovations in education met with the cry, ''We should have been

Table 12.2. Comparison of Flowcharts and Networks.

Flowcharts	Networks
Use: repetitive, formalized procedures or processes which will be done many times, by many different people, but generally by one person or one group doing the complete sequence. *Examples:* assembling a bicycle; planning a lesson; solving a problem.	*Use:* Special events, projects and programs that are complex and require the cooperative efforts of several groups. *Examples:* intramural sports day; scheduling classes and students; music festival; professional convention
Nature: Linear or serial flow of work	*Nature:* Set of interrelated flows of work
Assumes: The whole is one chain of actions performed serially, one action at a time. Can be done by one person.	*Assumes:* The whole is a set of interrelated chains; that several things can be done at the same time (concurrently). Different groups are working on subsets of activities at the same time. Subsets are dependent on completion of other subsets.
Basis of analysis: Dependence/ independence of activities. Necessary order for steps to be done	*Basis of analysis:* Dependence/ independence of sets of activities. Which can be done at the same time? Where are dependency junctions? Which activity cannot be started until others completed by a different group?
Sequences: Order of actions, check or decision points, and revision cycles	*Sequences:* Sets of actions; order of actions within sets; junction points where dependencies are specified; and time constraints (critical path)
Shows: Logical order of activities and points where check-ups and revision should take place	*Shows:* Independence/dependence of subsets of activities being completed by different groups, and interdependence of groups
Primary purpose: Monitor process to be sure each step is done, and done to standard (checkpoints).	*Primary purpose:* Coordination of production when tasks are the responsibility of disparate groups. Control of deadlines, the critical path

told,'' or ''We were never consulted,'' or ''We could have told them that you need _____,'' or ''That really should be in our department''? Clear guidelines for responsibility, authority, and communication could prevent many misunderstandings.

This type of analysis has not received as much attention in the literature as networks have, but it may be more generally applicable in education than networks are. An RAC matrix does not address time; it

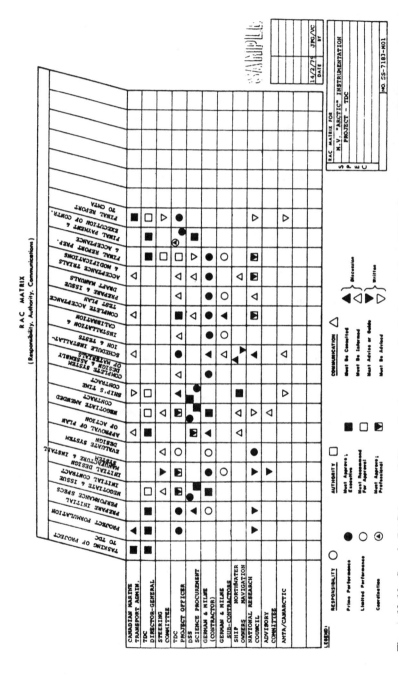

Figure 12.10. Sample RAC (responsibility, authority, communication) matrix from SPEC planning process. (SPEC is a registered trademark of CPCS Ltd., and SPEC processes are copyrighted. Reproduced by permission of Canadian Pacific Consulting Services.)

434

assumes that the time needed to accomplish a task will be determined by the responsible group or that a network or schedule will be developed separately.

The format of an RAC analysis is a simple matrix. Units, groups, or departments are listed down the vertical axis, and tasks (from the structured task analysis) are listed across the horizontal axis. CPCS proposed three responsibility roles, four authority roles, and four communication roles, and they created symbols to identify which roles each unit played for each task. Figure 12.10 gives a sample RAC matrix showing the format and the symbols used.

Many would insist that everyone knows who is responsible for projects in education or that responsibilities should be more open and flexible or that no one should take their position too seriously. However, in CPCS project-planning sessions, there were frequently rather heated discussions over who had prime performance responsibility for a particular task, who must approve, who must be advised, etc. It is easy to imagine equally heated discussions between teachers' association representatives, curriculum development groups, school board members, administrative and consultant representatives, and parent advocates.

An RAC matrix cannot be developed without the active participation of key players. Developing an RAC matrix for new projects or for innovations in the education program could generate heated debate, but the potential of such debate is clearer understanding of issues involved and of factors that might cause good projects to fail. This planning tool could be used productively for many of the changes being implemented in education today.

MANAGEMENT SYSTEMS TOOLS

Each of the management systems tools has a particular action focus, but all such tools address their action focus within the larger context of the system. Thus, MBO, as previously stated, focuses on goals and objectives but situates them within the system by emphasizing articulation and harmonization. The various budgeting systems (PPBS, ZBB, and line item) focus on enabling activities by providing resources but determine specific allocations in the context of the whole. Organizational development (OD) generally focuses on people's working relationships to improve the work climate for all. Total quality management (TQM) makes the proposition that the quality of work output, whether in service, relationships, or hardware, is directly related to the growth and vitality of the system.

Thus, all management systems tools look at the system's activities through a particular lens but are concerned in their overall perspective with the system, its purposes, operations, maintenance, growth, and vitality. One of the oldest system planning tools is the budget. However simple or complex, however limited or vast, the budget has always been a tool for empowering future action, a planning tool. In addition, a budget sets limits and provides a base of control and accountability. The next section will discuss the origin and development of four different budgeting systems and will draw some comparisons and contrasts among them.

Budgeting Systems

Planning and Accountability[23]

There are two dimensions to accountability in education: financial accountability and educational accountability. There is general agreement that the two dimensions should be maintained in close relation to each other, but there is little agreement on how to accomplish this. Discussions of accountability often confuse the two. They conclude that education is so complex there is little real possibility of establishing any manageable technology for accomplishing the task in terms of real learning, except on the macrolevel by relating costs per pupil to results on standardized achievement tests or to admissions to prestigious colleges and universities. Such correlations leave most educators with a "yes, but . . ." reaction.

In early nineteenth century North American school systems, the community had firm control over both dimensions. By far the largest percentage of North American school districts ran isolated one-teacher elementary schools, and each district had its own locally elected or appointed school board. As late as the 1940s, for example, one rural county in Nebraska had fifty-two such districts, with an average student

---

[23]This section is taken from Burns (1991), "Accountability for Educational Values; A School-Based Application of PPBS," presented at the *Canadian Association for Studies in Educational Administration Conference,* Kingston, Ontario, June 1991.

population of five. The fabric school was typical in Quebec; Quebec had over a thousand school boards/commissions in the 1950s, later amalgamated into regional boards.

The community provided money to run its own school, provided textbooks, set the length of the school year, and ran the life, both personal and professional, of the teacher. The community knew every word the teacher said, every learning activity required. The community knew which students were not "doing OK" and whether the reason was lack of ability on the part of the child or on the part of the teacher. On the basis of community values and judgments, teachers were hired or fired. In such a system, the two dimensions of accountability, financial and educational, were closely tied to each other. "Budget planning" focused on the cost of the teacher's salary, and financial records reflected this simplicity.

As towns, cities, and industrial centers grew, additional schools were needed. It became more difficult for the taxpaying community to keep track of how school moneys were being spent and also more difficult for taxpaying parents to control the personal and professional quality of the teachers now teaching their children. Boards handed over to agents, superintendents and principals, the responsibility for operational management.

Growth of the system was counted on the basis of numbers of teachers and classrooms and amounts of equipment and supplies needed. Community members readily understood that growth in numbers of students related to increasing costs of resources, so the budgeting system naturally enough reflected that focus. The tradition of the line budget based on costs categorized according to type of resources, function, and hierarchy was the result. The inherent assumption was made that cost of resources correlated with quality and that quality of learning would be reflected proportionally. The budget became the basic tool for control of quality of resources.

Boards and taxpayers, being cost-conscious, applied currently popular scientific management principles to the operation of schools. The family-style learning situation of rural schools, with all ages in one room together, was considered inefficient use of the teaching resource. Learning was broken up into one-year sized segments. One teacher could, thus, become more knowledgeable about particular "pieces" of subject matter or of the needs of particular age groups and could teach larger groups of pupils—a more cost-efficient use of resources, both human and physical. So age-graded groupings were created, a sort of assembly-line development of the educated child.

Responsibility for the success of the child now rested with a series of teachers, and the gap between financial and educational accountability widened. Financial planning continued to focus on recurring costs, primarily salaries as the largest operating cost and buildings as the largest capital cost. Still, some effort to relate fiscal costs to desired results was maintained. Few salary schedules existed, teachers' and administrators' salaries were reviewed annually, salaries differed from teacher to teacher, and there was little job security.

In the 1930s and 1940s, the growth of unions in the corporate world changed the economic picture for educators in spite of the fact that few teachers' unions existed. Teachers associations lobbied for, in some cases went on strike for, and secured job tenure, salaries more in line with private sector salaries, and standardized salary schedules. Salary advances were based on specified objective criteria and controlled by negotiated regulations and agreements, and firing a teacher became more and more difficult.

Thus, fiscal accountability, as it had been traditionally conceived in terms of costs of resources (particularly salaries), could no longer be easily related to educational accountability as it had been traditionally conceived in terms of personal (board and community) control over teaching/learning effectiveness. The board no longer had access to traditional rewards and penalties for teaching effectiveness, and it could no longer identify the source or cause of inadequate learning.

However, during the late 1940s and the 1950s, education was still North America's "favorite child." Education was viewed by parents as the highway to financial success and social status. Moreover, it was viewed by governments as food for the economy, by the corporate world as the source of a well-educated work force (the "human capital" theory was on the horizon), and by unions as the means to keep cheap labor out of the work force. These were four strong sectors of the public willing to pay for the education of North American youth.

At the same time, expectations for the school were increased with demands for social learning, emotional stability, health care, support for a variety of learning problems, and more years of required schooling. Bandwagons arose for and against technical-vocational education, basic skills, humanist education, streaming, BSCS, new math, PSCS, merit pay, clinical supervision, T-group organizational development, leadership training, language labs, summer schools, work release programs, and hundreds of other special programs, all without systematic assessments of their results or their costs. Unions questioned the principle of hierarchical salary formulas, and elementary teachers gained equality with secondary teachers.

So costs continued to grow, but an uneasiness about the effectiveness and efficiency of education systems grew also. Questions were raised about how effective schooling was for various socioeconomic and minority groups, about trends in achievement scores, and about streaming and other educational technologies. Coleman's massive study and others, such as the Chicago study and the Philadelphia study, fueled the growing unease. Communities began to refuse tax increases; small local school systems were amalgamated into cooperative boards, decreasing still further local parents' sense of control over their children's schooling.

However, given the system of the flow of students through grades, plus the function-based budgeting principles, it was impossible to assess effectiveness, except in the broadest sense and after the fact – the degree to which the students of a system had achieved success at specified points as indicated by standardized tests and were successful in obtaining prestigious jobs after graduation.

New Budgeting Systems Proposed

Program Planning Budgeting System: When U.S. President Lyndon Johnson instituted the Program Planning Budgeting System (PPBS) in all of the major civilian agencies of the federal government in 1965, the concepts caught fire in education. It seemed that education might be one of the most appropriate institutions in which the concept of budgeting (allocating resources) based on specified objectives could be applied. Education was a natural, organized as it is on the basis of programs offered to students: math, PE, languages, sciences, music, and vocational programs. The idea of determining the cost needs for and the effectiveness of various programs was intuitively appealing.

Systems analysis, program budgeting, and accountability were seen as means to resolve the two-headed problem: spiraling costs and questionable schooling effectiveness. After all, traditional economic theory proposes a correlation between costs of inputs and effectiveness of outputs. Theoretically, the relationship is one-to-one, but economists know that such a correlation is not a realistic probability. Figure 12.11 illustrates the theoretical proposition and various real correlational patterns.

It seemed eminently logical that, if desired ends (outputs/results) could be defined and measured, relationships between inputs and outputs could then be tracked, and resource allocations could be made based on better information. California passed a regulation requiring all school boards in the state to have some system of accountability in place. Books and articles on systems analysis for education and program budgeting were published [see, for example, Alioto and Jungherr (1971), Banghart (1969), Becher and Maclure (1982), Coleman (1972), Hartley (1968, 1969), Immegart and Pilecki (1973), and Popham (1972).

Many large urban school districts (Chicago, Philadelphia, Memphis, Baltimore, and Seattle, among others) implemented some form of program budgeting. Techniques such as modular scheduling and open grading for primary years were initiated to allocate varying amounts of time for various types of learning situations.

However, educators found that implementing the new concepts was an overwhelming task. North America's belief in universal education

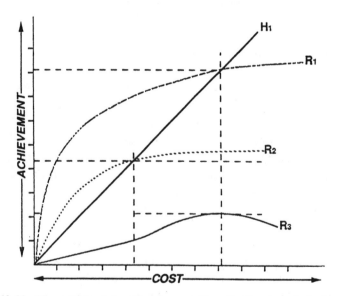

Figure 12.11. *Theoretical relationship of cost and benefit: H = hypothetical relationship, R₁,₂ = real relationships.*

had seemed to demand the application of the mass production systems of manufacturing—all students programmed into an equal number of minutes per day for a basic set of learning activities. When PPBS was attempted on a systemwide basis, a major problem arose immediately in efforts to define goals or desired results. There was little agreement within any system, and many specialist fields such as literature argued that setting standardized objectives was impossible and even detrimental to the true values of education. The relatively recent development of IEPs (individualized education packages) for special children is the technology that PPBS, at its extreme application, demands. Allocating resources on the basis of learning needs appeared to require specification of learning objectives and individualized programs well beyond the capacity of any universal system of education.

Zero-Based Budgeting: By the mid-1970s, those aspects of program budgeting that seemed possible had been modified to suit the situation, but, in many school systems, PPBS had, for all practical purposes, died. The next effort at bringing costs and effectiveness in line for schools was another new budgeting system proposed, zero-based budgeting (ZBB). ZBB also came to education from business and public administration. It focused attention on program or production units and required a total review of such units on a cyclical basis. (The cyclical reviews currently in place in many universities arise from the propositions of ZBB.)

The argument is that activities within units and units themselves develop without being sufficiently rationalized with the whole of the system, that they tend to grow beyond their usefulness, and that, once in place, they develop a strong root system that perpetuates them. A basic proposition of ZBB is that all units and all activities within a unit should be reviewed routinely to determine if they are fulfilling the needs of the unit or the system or if they satisfy a client demand. Thus, ZBB focuses on program or production units and activities and on need or demand.

Zero-based budgeting never received the attention in education that PPBS had received. It faced two major difficulties. First, the decision packages, or review packages, that are the major technology of the system require tremendous expenditure of resources. In a system in which large commitments of time beyond mandated requirements are already the norm, having to develop decision packages to justify activities and programs was viewed very unfavorably.

Beyond the amount of work required, the psychology of ZBB does not sit easily within the education system; the concept of zero in relation to education programs is not readily acceptable. In fact, where ZBB has been implemented, the reality of zero is seldom invoked. The idea of reviewing the system for elements/programs that have outlived their usefulness has merit but has met with little acceptance. For fuller discussions of zero-based budgeting, see, for example, American Association for School Administrators (AASA) (1979b), Granhof and Kinzel (1974), MacFarlane (1976), and Phyrr (1973).

Cost Unit or Cost Center Budgeting: A more recent approach to budgeting for education systems is called cost unit, cost center, or site-based budgeting. Cost center budgeting proposes that each school within a system and sometimes each department within a school should operate as a cost unit. As another offshoot of business practice, the school or department would rent facilities, pay salaries, buy supplies, etc., as if it were an entity. In some variations, central offices would act as purchasing agents or "sell" other services such as specialist-consultants, nursing services, and psychological testing. The unit would be accountable to central administration for its budget and for its results. Such a system might well employ internally any one of the three basic budgeting systems, line budget, PPBS, or ZBB. Tentative movements have been made in this direction, but, most frequently, the cost unit is not given full control over its expenditures, let alone budget planning and sources of financing.

Comparison of Budgeting Systems: All three of the major budgeting systems have been developed to address some of the problems inherent in attempting to resolve the effectiveness versus efficiency issues of resource use. All three have something to offer to education systems, and all three have problems in application. Table 12.3 presents a comparison of the three major budgeting systems, line budget, PPBS, and ZBB, based on a number of criteria.

The traditional line budget is simplest to implement because budget allocation decisions can be made by formula. Its focus is on inputs, and, while it allows for priorities, it faces difficulties in attempting to relate particular goals, aims, and outcomes to costs. Zero-based budgeting makes heavy resource demands in terms of developing decision packages—the in-depth reviews of programs and units. Such decision packages can, and often do, employ outcomes as part of the review package, but the focus is essentially on the process unit. Cost unit budgeting, to be successful, requires unit personnel who are well trained in budgeting

Table 12.3. Comparison of Budgeting Frameworks.

Characteristic	Traditional	ZBB	PPBS
Budget items	Resource units (purchased inputs)	Production units (schools, programs)	Output units (program goals, objectives)
Decisions based on	Cost and quality of resources	Demand/need for production unit	Cost and quality of desired end product
Budget decisions	Resource priorities	Process/product priorities	Result/outcome priorities
Assumes	High-quality resources = high-quality outcomes	Demand = need	Different types of outcomes require differing resources
Process of decision making	Formulas	Total review of demand and process	Tracking and analysis of success and costs
Budget allocations based on	Numbers of students last year + cost of living (COLA)	Proven level of need/demand	Cost/benefit results
Burden of "proof" on	Schools and unions	Administrator or unit head	Organization
Type of "proof" expected	Numbers of students COLA scales	Documented demand/need opinion surveys	Records of standards and achieved results

443

practices and who also have the ability to perceive relationships between costs and success. Figure 12.12 illustrates the basic focus of the three budgeting systems by relating them to the ''black box'' theory of education.

It is my view that the propositions incorporated into PPBS come the closest to being in harmony with the basic propositions of education. PPBS asks the program planner and the budget planner to work together to create the most effective and efficient educational package. It proposes that the focus should be on outputs, that is, on the results achieved, and that budget priorities should be established in terms of desired results.

I propose that the concepts of PPBS can best be applied at the school level, since it is at the school level where results can be most clearly related to community interests and needs. Where PPBS has not met with success, it is, at least in part, because the aim has been to establish systemwide standards, goals, and objectives. No system has universally homogenous communities, so no system should have only systemwide goals and standards.

It is at the school level that results make a difference to the community the school serves. Results at the school level may be measured by standardized tests, but expected results (standards) should be set differentially for different sectors or groups. Moreover, these should not be the only measures. Professional educators charged with the education of the children of a community should establish standards compatible with the community and create ways of assessing results in terms of those standards. The recent development of alternative assessment technologies is an important move in the direction of the individualized learning focus.

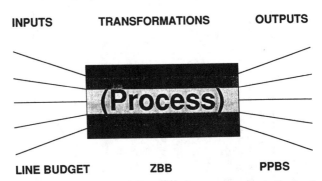

Figure 12.12. The 'black box' theory of education and the bases of budgeting systems.

Cost per Student per Hour as a Basis for Tracking Cost/Success: I have proposed (Burns, 1991) that cost per pupil hour is an effective measure of the cost of any program or of any unit within a program. A single program can be costed using this base, or programs can be compared on a uniform measure of cost. At the same time, success per pupil hour can be computed and tracked if expected standards of success have been set and measures of success specified (Burns, Patterson, and LaFrance, 1992, 1993).

Standards of success and measures to be used might be based on formal standardized tests, on carefully developed alternative testing or authentic testing programs, or on the basis of traditional teacher-made assessment practices and term reports. There are three important factors that should be addressed in every case: 1) the standards set should be appropriate to the community, the school, and the group of students concerned; 2) the issue of PPBS is success of the program in meeting the standards set and bringing about success for students, not just comparison of "our" students with those of some other community; and 3) tracking over time gives the most information about how successful programs are.

Whether the school has control of its budget or not, cost/success can be determined at the school level and can be tracked over time, and programs, technologies, and techniques can be modified to produce the success that educators and parents hope for. Students in the masters program in educational administration at McGill have, over the years, compared the cost/success results of two programs within their system and have found the process enlightening and productive. Appendix E reports a hypothetical example of determining success rate per dollar cost per student hour and two student-generated actual cost/success analyses.

During the academic year 1991–1992, the process of determining success rate per dollar cost per student hour was tested in two elementary schools in the Montreal region. The results have been reported by Burns, Patterson, and LaFrance (1992, 1993). In this study, standards were set for all programs at the second- and sixth-grade level in each school and were based on marks reported to parents on term reports. Since hours in the program differed across programs (language arts versus social sciences, for example), all costs per program hour and success per program hour were standardized to a sixty-minute hour, and a ratio of "dollar cost per unit of success, base 60" was computed for each program, Term 1 and Term 2. Table 12.4 reports the results of this study.

Table 12.4. Ratio of Cost to Success: Dollar Cost per Unit of Success Standardized at Base 60.

School A, Level Two			School B, Level Two		
	$ Cost/Unit Success, Base 60			$ Cost/Unit Success, Base 60	
Program	Term 1	Term 2	Program	Term 1	Term 2
Eng. L.A.	$3.06	$2.67			
Fr. 2ième	2.63	2.57	Franç. L.A.	$2.49	$2.46
Math	3.04	3.48	Mathémat.	2.85	2.85
Soc. Sci.	2.40	2.40	Sci. Hum.	2.43	2.48
Nat. Sci.	2.39	2.39	Sci. Nat.	2.48	2.31
Level Six			Level Six		
Eng. L.A.	3.48	3.29	Angl. 2ième	2.53	2.51
Lang. Fr.	2.45	2.35	Franç. L.A.	3.07	2.85
Math	2.70	3.40	Mathémat.	2.63	2.96
Soc. Sci.	2.87	3.90	Sci. Hum.	2.92	3.19
Nat. Sci.	4.79	3.53	Sci. Nat.	2.56	2.96

The results reveal several important facts:

(*1*) The cost per pupil per hour does not vary greatly across programs, and it is surprisingly low. Actual expenditure per pupil hour varied from a low of $3.62 to a high of $4.35 (Burns, Patterson, and LaFrance, 1993, Table IV, 25). In Quebec, this is considerably below minimum wage.

(*2*) The cost per unit of success on a base 60 hour is even lower, as can be seen in Table 12.4, and it does vary across programs.

(*3*) With the present technology, it is no longer necessary for all students to be programmed into standard blocks of learning time in every subject, but it is necessary to track costs and success over time to make more informed judgments about learning programs (Burns, Patterson, and LaFrance, 1993, 27).

The conclusions are inevitable: the cost of education on a global scale is high, but the cost per pupil per hour is low. Education may be the best bargain the public gets. Also, costing and tracking success over time (the propositions upon which PPBS is based) can be a most important tool for maintaining the focus on values and effective education.

Budgeting and Politics

The realistic fact is that budgeting, at whatever level, has both analytical (management) implications and political implications. Rational, analytical considerations that address questions of effectiveness and efficiency are paralleled by considerations of urgency, public demand, and negotiated priorities. Figure 12.13 illustrates the budgeting process that takes place at the provincial ministers' level in Quebec (Brown, 1989).

Provincial or state allocations for education compete with other public demands, transportation, health, security, communication, pensions, etc. Pressures are brought to bear to increase services in all competing sectors and, as well, by the taxpaying public to decrease expenditures. Elected or appointed public servants resolve those demands by negotiation, compromise, and best judgment.

If a planning tool such as PPBS can give education a strong argument for its real success per dollar cost, it may make education more competitive in the global negotiations for public support.

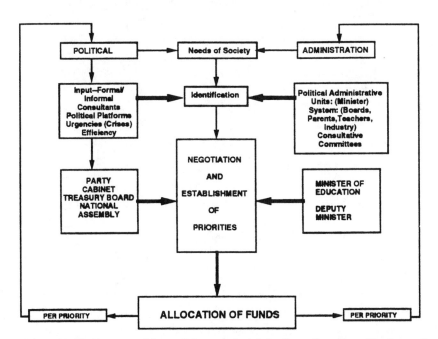

Figure 12.13. Process of determining provincial funding allocations, Province of Quebec (G. Brown, former Directeur des services aux Anglophones, Province du Québec, 1989).

CONCLUSION

Since action, effective action, is the *raison d'être* for all planning, it is worthwhile to learn where planning tools can be most useful and how to use them effectively. The tool should never become the end in itself. Having a beautiful PERT chart or SPECNET or hierarchy of objectives, or even a fine sounding mission statement, is not the purpose of examining these tools. The thinking processes that they describe in graphic detail are the real tools of planning, not the graphics themselves. A major value of the graphics is that they allow examination and reexamination of plans. One of the exciting contributions of computer technologies is that they permit relatively easy modification of such graphics; they help prevent fervent attatchment to one picture of life.

CHAPTER 13

A Final Word

A plan is the beginning of tomorrow.

TO end a book and send it on its way is almost as difficult as to "see" it at the beginning and carry out that idea. What, then, is it that I have intended to say; what have been the main ideas I have tried to stress?

First and foremost, all of my thinking about planning derives from the basic proposition that planning is an act of faith. To plan at all is to assert a belief in the possibility of a desired future. The nature of the future that is desired comes to us from our own context—our own set of values, beliefs, customs, and habits of thinking acting and feeling.

Since all planning, in reality, begins with a proposal for action, the desired outcome, that desired future state, is often assumed or understood, rather than prescribed in the formal, logistical terms of stated goals and objectives. Moreover, with the expanding human and technological world that is upon us, the "real" goals may be unknowable— the new, the experience of "trying out." They may be specified behaviors or attitudes, or they may be simply the possibility of opening a new window for everyone involved, including the planner.

Regardless, the business of planning is attempting to design, predict, and prepare for action that will achieve whatever desired ends may be envisioned. Therefore, models and systems of planning all propose that goals and objectives should be stated clearly in the plan. I have stressed throughout that the map to a good plan is a map of the logic, not necessarily the map of the order of steps in which a plan is prepared.

Although planning *begins* with an action idea or proposal, good planning suggests that it is critical to place that action into the perspective of values held (be they system values, professional values, or human values). This is the dollying out step in planning, the step that puts all action into the perspective of larger values.

The logic of planning does not require educators to think serially (to

449

follow prescribed steps in thinking); it does require them to think both holistically and analytically. The map of that combination of holistic and analytical thinking is the type of planning model found in the literature.

I propose that stating holistic, values-based goals and objectives will help maintain the duality of logic needed – holistic and analytical.

The Values-Based Planning System described in Chapters 9 and 10 proposes four keystones to maintaining the holistic perspective while undertaking four separate levels of analysis. Those keystones are goals, values cost, options, and choice. Analysis based on each of these keystones can enable planners to hypothesize outcomes with reasonable certainty. Through the four levels of analysis, every effort has been made to examine all factors involved: 1) the bases upon which "success" will be judged; 2) the allowable costs in resources, effort, and interests; 3) the impact of resources and human factors on several alternative options; and 4) the tasks and resources needed to accomplish the project.

Because of the central position of values in the planning system proposed, an important emphasis in the book is placed on the sources of beliefs and values that have had impact on Western education systems. Reasonably clear pictures of the different sets of beliefs and values that form the patterns of thinking in the Western world have been put forward as philosophical systems of thought and as research paradigms or world views of specific aspects of education.

Section II reviews briefly four systems of philosophical thought that have helped form modern Western education systems. It is generally proposed in the literature that research and practice have developed as traditions or paradigms that are founded in systems of philosophy. A number of influential paradigms that have developed as research traditions in the study of organizations, leadership, education, and participation are discussed in that section.

Since the propositions of philosophies and paradigms have entered into our subconscious, they may affect planning and choice as assumptions. It is a major proposition of the book that awareness of the several different systems of thought (philosophies and research traditions) can enable planners to address multiple interests and concerns more effectively. It is proposed that, just as sentence structure is a "tool" for communicating ideas, philosophies and paradigms, holistic views can be tools for clarifying the "what and how" of quality education and for leading education systems toward quality learning.

If the patterns of beliefs and values are known and if educators consider thoughtfully the human and organizational implications of those patterns, planning and choice can serve the community more effectively.

The aim of the book throughout has been to relate patterns of ideas and abstractions of general principles and propositions to the realities of practical planning, choice, and action. Present day educational leaders can learn much from the ideas developed by earlier leaders, scholars such as Barnard, Simon, Sergiovanni, Gage, Illich, Freire, etc. The better equipped today's leaders are to understand and use ideas and theories from many sources, the better they may be able to serve the demands and values of the real community within which they live and work. Then the system may move toward quality learning and living more smoothly.

Thus, it is proposed that ideas are the most useful and practical planning tools we have. They are the source of all visions of the future, of all planning, choice, and action. They are tools insofar as they are chosen and used consciously and appropriately to serve the values of the education community.

Models and propositions in the literature attempt to show or predict general relationships between abstract ideas and common issues or conditions. Models and propositions are the shape that planning tools take.

Carpenters or computer programmers are good if their knowledge of the tools of their trade is broad and if they are able to use those tools effectively for the purposes at hand. Equally, educational leaders are good and effective if they have a broad knowledge of the tools of their trade and are able to use them to serve the values, needs, and conditions of their community.

The ability to create "good" plans (REM—rational, effective, and moral) based in values held for the community is a leadership skill that can be developed through study and practice. It is hoped that this book has added to that skill through knowledge, understanding, application, and imagination.

Answers to Exercises Presented by Local Educators

A.1. Correct answers to Exercise 3.1, Facts and Inferences:
- No. 3 is False.
- No's 6, 11, 14, and 15 are True.
- All others are Inference—not enough information.

A.2. Intended interpretation of Exercise 3.3, Teach Time:
- Teacher A—Idealism
- Teacher B—Pragmatism
- Teacher C—Realism
- Teacher D—Existentialism
  The most common variation from this interpolation was that Teacher B represented Realism, and Teacher C, Pragmatism.

A.3. Example of a comparison made based on Exercise 3.6, Comparison of Two Education Proposals. This local educator compared Dewey's *Experience and Education* and Adler's *Paideia Proposal*.

Criterion	Experience and Education	Paideia Proposal
Education	"A continuous reconstruction of experience"	"Development of the skills for learning and personal growth"
Goals	To prepare the young for future responsibility and for success in life	To generate a true democracy through an enlightened electorate
Objectives for students	(1) Develop bodies of information and skills to transmit to new generation. (2) Understand and observe standards and rules of conduct.	(1) Continue to grow. (2) Meet the duties and responsibilites of citizenship. (3) Develop skills common to all types of work.

Criterion	Experience and Education	Paideia Proposal
	(3) Develop an attitude of mutual accommodation and adaptation.	
Learning process	• Observe surrounding conditions. • Know of similar situations in the past. • Make judgement of interaction between the two to form new ideas.	• Acquisition of organized knowledge • Development of intellectual (learning) skills • Enlarged understanding of ideas and values
Methods	• Determine individual experience. • Create stimulating environment (experience). • Encourage interaction between individual and environment.	• Didactic teaching • Coaching and supervised practice • Socratic method
Course of study	• Single course of study is not acceptable. • Nonspecific and experiential • Interaction with environment	• Same objectives and course of study for all • Highly specific and knowable • Interaction with representation
Teacher	Creator of environments which promote learning and growth	Transmitter of knowledge and cultural heritage
Mode	Scientific; criterion-referenced	Intellectual; norm-referenced

A.4. Answers to Exercise 5.4, Snack Bar Case:

The intervention that was implemented successfully in the school described was No. 5, Paint line-up lines on the patio floor. This suggestion was implemented after several other proposals had been tried unsuccessfully.

The proposals most frequently voted probably successful by students in educational administration at McGill University were the following, in order of frequency:

• No. 4 – Stagger lunch hour dismissals.
• No. 5 – Paint line-up lines on the patio floor.
• No. 2 – Have teacher monitors.

- No. 9 – Serve only sodas at the snack bar.

A number of the students added that their choice for the best intervention was whatever was simplest and least costly in time and effort.

A.5. Pattern of responses to Exercise 7.1, Decision Participation
Total items of decision making or planning listed: 405

Domain	Organizational Participation		Self-Participation	
		% O-O		% O-O
O-O	AI	10.0	SI	4.0
(Organizational/	AII	11.0	SII	16.0
Operational)	CI	10.0	SVI	8.0
	CII	20.0	SVII	20.0
	GII	44.0	SLI	52.0
		% P-O		% P-O
P-O	AI	10.7	SI	7.7
(Personal/	AII	15.4	SII	7.7
Operational)	CI	10.7	SVI	15.4
	CII	17.1	SVII	23.1
	GII	46.1	SLI	46.1
		% O-S		% O-S
O-S	AI	16.3	SI	28.6
(Organizational/	AII	13.4	SII	2.9
Strategic	CI	16.3	SVI	20.0
	CII	27.7	SVII	17.1
	GII	26.3	SLI	31.4
		% P-S		% P-S
P-S	AI	28.0	SI	
(Personal/	AII	15.5	SII	12.5
Strategic)	CI	1.0	SVI	12.5
	CII	15.0	SVII	12.5
	GII	40.5	SLI	62.5

Domain:
O-O: Development and evaluation (Organizational/Operational)
P-O: Techniques and use of materials (Personal/Operational)
O-S: Resource allocation (Organizational/Strategic)
P-S: Career development (Personal/Strategic)

Level of Organizational Participation:
AI – Admin. Solves problem and makes decision alone.

AII—Admin. Gets needed information from others; analyzes and makes decision alone.

CI—Admin. Shares problem with individuals; gets information and ideas; makes own decision.

CII—Admin. Shares problem with group; gets ideas and suggestions; makes own decision.

GII—Admin. Shares problem with group; group gets ideas and alternatives; group makes decision.

Level of Self-Participation (your own actions):

SI—(Self, Level One) You do not get involved; do not discuss it.

SII—(Self, Level Two) You decide not to get involved; but do discuss it with a few friends.

SVI—(Vote, Level One) Talk with colleagues, listen; attend faculty meeting, don't speak, do vote.

SVII—(Vote, Level Two) Attend meetings; give ideas to group; try to persuade others and vote.

SLI—(Leadership One) Take active role in meetings; express opinions; speak to leaders; give ideas and vote.

Examples of the Four Meanings of Learning (Exercise 4.6) Applied in Specific Subject Fields as Submitted by Workshop Participants

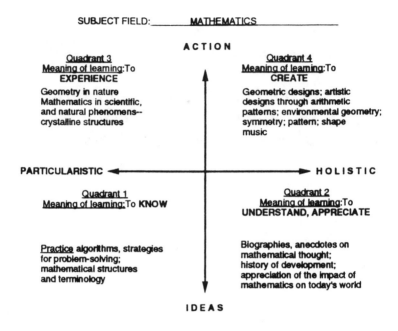

SUBJECT FIELD:_____ **MATHEMATICS**_____

ACTION

Quadrant 3
Meaning of learning:To
EXPERIENCE

Geometry in nature
Mathematics in scientific,
and natural phenomens--
crystalline structures

Quadrant 4
Meaning of learning:To
CREATE

Geometric designs; artistic
designs through arithmetic
patterns; environmental geometry;
symmetry; pattern; shape
music

PARTICULARISTIC ◄————————————► **HOLISTIC**

Quadrant 1
Meaning of learning:To **KNOW**

Quadrant 2
Meaning of learning:To
UNDERSTAND, APPRECIATE

Practice algorithms, strategies
for problem-solving;
mathematical structures
and terminology

Biographies, anecdotes on
mathematical thought;
history of development;
appreciation of the impact of
mathematics on today's world

IDEAS

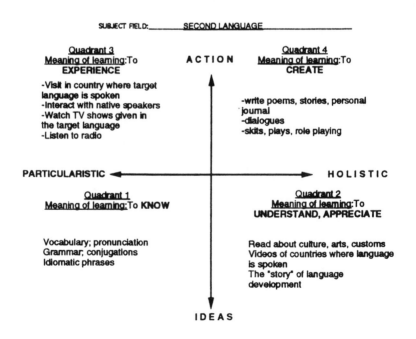

SUBJECT FIELD:_____ SECOND LANGUAGE_____

Quadrant 3
Meaning of learning:To
EXPERIENCE

ACTION

Quadrant 4
Meaning of learning:To
CREATE

-Visit in country where target
language is spoken
-Interact with native speakers
-Watch TV shows given in
the target language
-Listen to radio

-write poems, stories, personal
journal
-dialogues
-skits, plays, role playing

PARTICULARISTIC ◄————————————► **HOLISTIC**

Quadrant 1
Meaning of learning:To **KNOW**

Quadrant 2
Meaning of learning:To
UNDERSTAND, APPRECIATE

Vocabulary; pronunciation
Grammar; conjugations
Idiomatic phrases

Read about culture, arts, customs
Videos of countries where language
is spoken
The "story" of language
development

IDEAS

458

Examples of Strategic Options Analyses Submitted by Local Educators

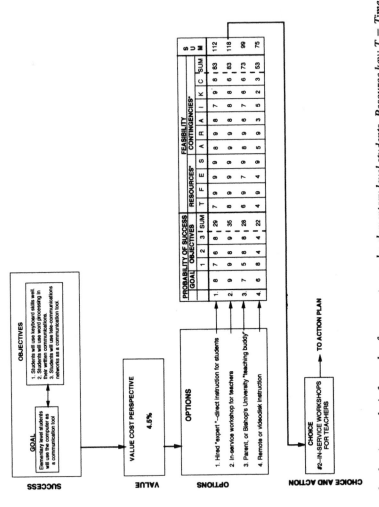

Figure C.1. Example of option analysis for a plan for computer use by elementary level students. *Resource key: T = Time; F = Facilities; E = Equipment; S = Supplies. Contingencies key: A = Attitudes of various groups; R = Reliability of equipment; A = Availability of facilities; K = Knowledge; C = Curricular commitments. (From a plan created by R. Orzechowski, June 20, 1994.)*

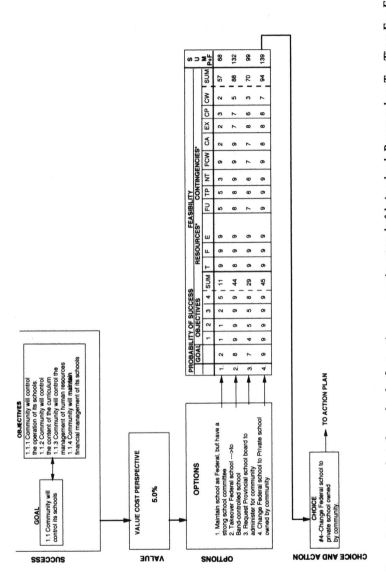

Figure C.2. Example of option analysis for a plan for first nations community control of their school. Resource key: T = Time; F = Facilities; E = Equipment. Contingencies key: FU = Funding; TP = Training programs; NT = Native teachers; FCW = Fluent curriculum writers; CA = Community attitude; EX = Experience; CP = Competencies; CW = Community will. (From a plan created by L. Simon, June 20, 1994.)

461

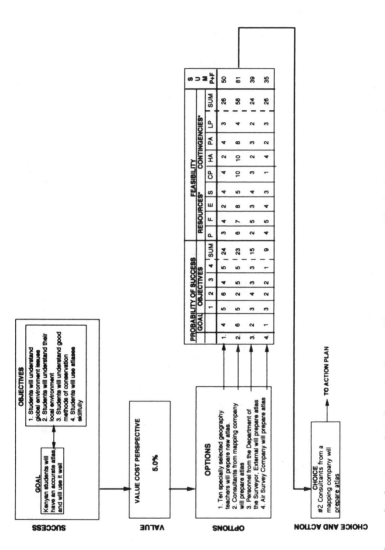

Figure C.3. Examnple of option analysis for a plan for providing an accurate, useful atlas for Kenyan students. Resource key: P = Personnel; F = Facilities; E = Equipment; S = Supplies. Contingencies key: CP = Commitment of participants; HA = Hierarchy acceptance; PA = Preferred approach; LP = Legal procedures. (From a plan created by M. Munowenyu, May 15, 1993.)

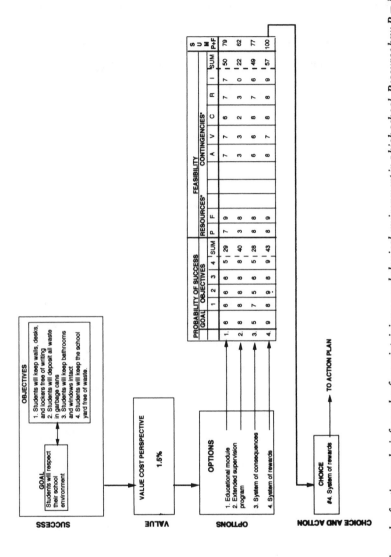

Figure C.4. Example of option analysis for a plan for maintaining a good physical environment in a high school. Resource key: P = Personnel; F = Facilities. Contingencies key: A = Attitudes; V = Values; C = Commitment; R = Reliability; I = Interest. (From a plan created by P. Moffa, May 15, 1994.)

Examples of Completed Storyboards for Project Plans Submitted by Local Educators

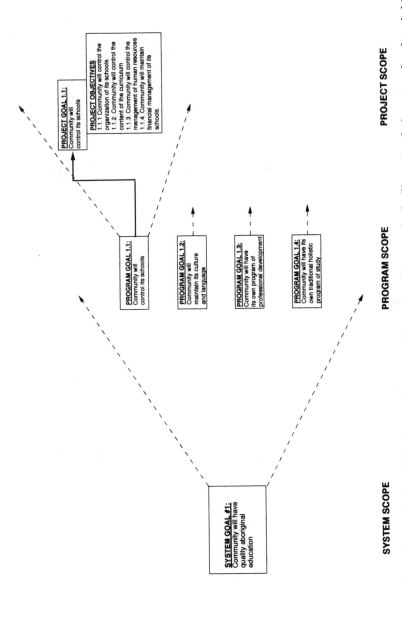

Figure D.1. *Origin of a plan for the first nations community to control its own schools. Illustrating the harmony of goals and objectives from system scope to program scope to project scope. (Based on the plan prepared by L. Simon, June 20, 1994.)*

465

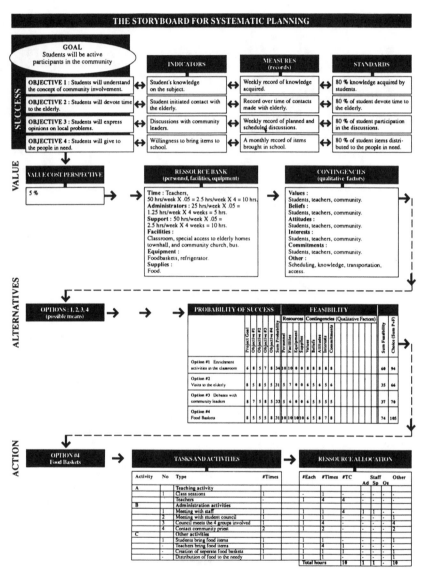

Figure D.2. *Storyboard for project plan: "Students will be active participants in the community."*

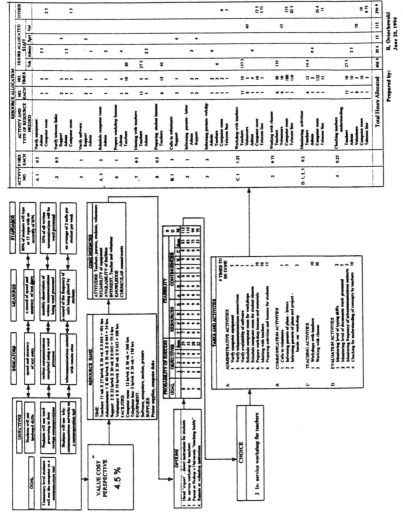

Figure D.3. Storyboard for project plan: "Elementary level students will use the computer as a communication tool."

467

Examples of Cost/Effectiveness Comparisons Submitted by Local Educators

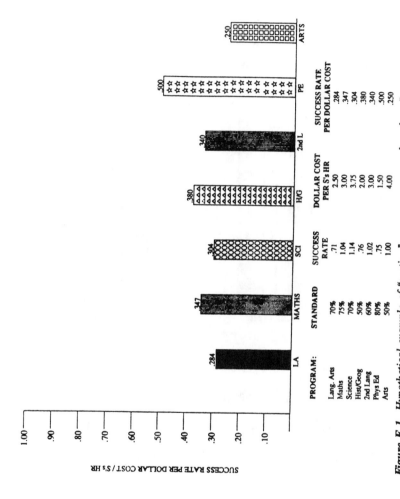

Figure E.1. Hypothetical example of "costing" program success, based on "success rate per dollar cost per student hour."

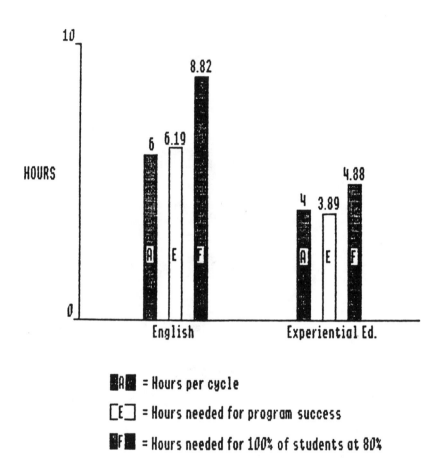

Figure E.2. *Example of "costing" program success comparing English and experiential education. Based on "hours needed for program success," and "hours needed for 100% of students at program standard (80%)."*

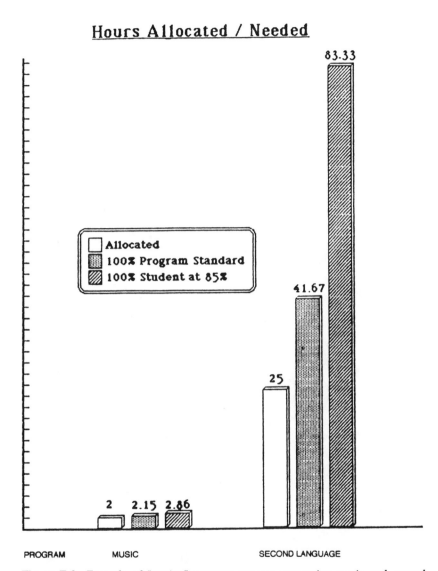

Hours Allocated / Needed

83.33

Allocated
100% Program Standard
100% Student at 85%

41.67

25

2   2.15 2.86

PROGRAM   MUSIC   SECOND LANGUAGE

Figure E.3. Example of "costing" program success comparing music and second language. Based on "hours needed for program success," and "hours needed for 100% of students at program standard (85%)."

471

AASA. 1979a. "Understanding PERT," in *Educational Management Tools for the Practicing School Administrator.* Arlington, VA: American Association of School Administrators, pp. 3–22.

AASA. 1979b. "Zero-Base Budgeting," in *Educational Management Tools for the Practicing School Administrator.* Arlington, VA: American Association of School Administrators, pp. 23–39.

Abell, D. F. and J. S. Hammond. 1979. *Strategic Market Planning.* Englewood Cliffs, NJ: Prentice Hall.

Abruscato, J. 1993. "Early Results and Tentative Implications from the Vermont Portfolio Project," *Phi Delta Kappan* (February):474–477.

Ackoff, R. L. 1970. *A Concept of Corporate Planning.* New York, NY: Wiley-Interscience.

Ackoff, R. L. 1978. *The Art of Problem Solving.* New York, NY: John Wiley & Sons.

Adams, D., ed. 1964. *Educational Planning.* Syracuse, NY: Center for Development Education.

Adams, D. 1991. "Planning Models and Paradigms," in *Educational Planning, Concepts, Strategies, Practices.* R. V. Carlson and G. Awkerman, eds., New York, NY: Longman, pp. 5–20.

Adams, H. 1988. "The Fate of Knowledge," in *Cultural Literacy and the Idea of General Education. Eighty-seventh Yearbook of the National Society for the Study of Education, Part II,* I. Westbury and A. C. Purves, eds., Chicago, IL: The University of Chicago Press, pp. 52–68.

Adler, J. J. 1982. *The Paideia Proposal.* New York, NY: Macmillan Publishing Co.

Ahola-Sidaway, J. 1978. "An Ethnographic Study of Student Life in a Small and Large High School," M.A. diss., McGill University, Montreal, QC.

Ahola-Sidaway, J. 1986. "Student Transition from Elementary School to High School," Ph.D. diss., McGill University, Montreal, QC.

Alioto, R. F. and J. J. Jungherr. 1971. *Operational PPBS for Education.* New York, NY: Harper and Row.

Alutto, J. A. and J. A. Belasco. 1972. "A Typology for Participation in Organizational Decision Making," *Administrative Science Quarterly,* 17:117–125.

Alutto, J. A. and J. A. Belasco. 1973. "Patterns of Teacher Participation in School System Decision-Making," *Educational Administration Quarterly,* 9(1).

473

Anderson, C. A. and M. J. Bowman. 1964. "Theoretical Considerations in Educational Planning," in *Educational Planning,* Don Adams, ed., Syracuse, NY: Center for Development Education, pp. 4–46.

Ansoff, H. I. 1968. *Corporate Strategy.* Hammondsworth, Middlesex, England: Penguin Books, Ltd.

Ansoff, H. I. 1970. *Strategic Planning to Strategic Management.* New York, NY: John Wiley & Sons.

Anthony, R. N. 1965. *Planning and Control Systems: A Framework for Analysis.* Cambridge, MA: Harvard University Graduate School of Business Administration.

Archibald, R. D. and R. L. Villoria. 1968. *Network-Based Management Systems (PERT/CPM).* New York, NY: John Wiley & Sons.

Argyris, C. 1957. *Personality and Organization.* New York, NY: Harper.

Argyris, C. 1978. *Management and Organizational Development: The Path from XA to YB.* New York, NY: McGraw-Hill.

Armstrong, R. D. 1968. *A Systematic Approach to Developing and Writing Behavioral Objectives.* Tucson, AZ: Educational Innovation Press.

Askey, R. 1992. "Review of Japanese Grade 7–9 Mathematics," *College Mathematics Journal,* 23:445–448.

Astley, W. G. and A. H. Van de Ven. 1983. "Central Perspectives and Debates in Organization Theory," *Administrative Science Quarterly,* 28(2):245–273.

Ayer, A. J. 1952. *Language, Truth and Logic.* New York, NY: Dover.

Bacharach, S. B. and S. Conley. 1986. "Education Reform: A Managerial Agenda," *Phi Delta Kappan,* 67(9):641–645.

Bacharach, S. B., P. Bamberger, S. C. Conley, and S. Bauer. 1990. "The Dimensionality of Decision Participation in Educational Organizations: The Value of a Multi-Domain Evaluative Approach," *Educational Administration Quarterly,* 26(2): 126–167.

Baig, E. C. 1987. "America's Most Admired Corporations," *Fortune,* (Jan.):18–31.

Bailey, M. 1992. "The Status of Strategic Planning in Quebec's CEGEPs," Ph.D. diss., McGill University, Montreal, QC.

Baker, D. P. 1993. "Compared to Japan, the U.S. Is a Low Achiever . . . Really," *Educational Researcher,* 22(3):18–20.

Baldridge, J. V. and T. Deal, eds. 1983. *The Dynamics of Organizational Change.* Berkeley, CA: McCutchan Publishing Corp.

Banghart, F. W. 1969. *Educational Systems Analysis.* New York, NY: The Macmillan Co.

Banghart, F. W. and A. Trull, Jr. 1973. *Educational Planning.* New York, NY: Macmillan Publishers.

Barker, J. A. 1992. *Future Edge. Discovering the New Paradigms of Success.* New York, NY: William Morrow and Co., Inc.

Barnard, C. I. 1938. *Functions of the Executive.* Cambridge, MA: Harvard University Press.

Barnard, C. I. 1940. "Comments on the Job of the Executive," *Harvard Business Review,* 18:295–308.

Barnard, C. I. 1948. "Dilemmas of Leadership in the Democratic Process," pp. 24–50, and "The Nature of Leadership." pp. 80 – 110, in *Organization and Management,* Cambridge MA: Harvard University Press.

Barnette, J. J., L. C. Danielson, and R. F. Algozzine. 1978. "Delphi Methodology: An Empirical Investigation," *Educational Research Quarterly,* 3(1):67 – 73.

Bateson, G. 1936. Naven, Cambridge: Cambridge University Press. Cited in Morgan, G. 1980. "Paradigms, Metaphors, and Puzzle Solving in Organization Theory," *Administrative Science Quarterly,* 25(4):605 – 621.

Batten, J. D. 1966. *Beyond Management by Objectives.* New York, NY: American Management Association.

Beach, R. H. and W. D. McInerney. 1986. "Educational Planning Models and School District Practice," *Planning and Changing,* 17(Fall):180 – 191.

Bean, J. P. and G. D. Kuh. 1983. "A Typology of Planning Problems," paper presented at the *Annual Meeting of the American Educational Research Association,* Montreal, QC, March, 27 pp.

Becher, T. and S. Maclure, eds. 1982. *Accountability in Education.* Windsor, Berkshire: Nelson Publishing Co, Ltd.

Belasco, J. A. and J. A. Alutto. 1972. "Decisional Participation and Teacher Satisfaction," *Educational Administration Quarterly,* 8(1):44 – 58.

Beneviste, G. 1989. *Mastering the Politics of Planning.* San Francisco, CA: Jossey-Bass Inc., Publishers.

Bertalanffy, L. von. 1968. *General Systems Theory.* New York, NY: George Braziller.

Blake, R. R. and J. S. Mouton. 1964. *The Managerial Grid.* Houston, TX: Gulf Publishing.

Blake, R. R. and J. S. Mouton. 1978. *The New Managerial Grid: Strategic New Insights into a Proven System for Increasing Organization Productivity and Individual Effectiveness.* Houston, TX: Gulf Publishing Co., Book Division.

Blankenship, L. V. and R. E. Miles. 1968. "Organizational Structure and Managerial Decision Making," *Administrative Science Quarterly,* 13(1):106 – 120.

Blau, P. M. and W. R. Scott. 1962. *Formal Organizations: A Comparative Approach.* San Francisco, CA: Chandler Publishing Co.

Bologna, J. 1980. "Why Managers Resist Planning," *Managerial Planning,* 28(4):23 – 25.

Boulanger, D. G. 1961. "Program Evaluation and Review Technique," in *Management Systems,* 2nd ed., P. B. Schoderbek, ed., New York, NY: John Wiley & Sons, pp. 451 – 457.

Boyan, N. J., ed. 1988. *Handbook of Research on Educational Administration.* New York, NY: Longman.

Boyd, W. L. 1990. "Balancing Control and Autonomy in School Reform: The Politics of *Perestroika,*" in *The Educational Reform Movement of the 1980s,* J. Murphy, ed., Berkeley, CA: McCutchan Publishing Corp., pp. 85 – 96.

Boyd, W. L. and H. J. Walberg, eds. 1990. *Choice in Education. Potential and Problems.* Berkeley, CA: McCutchan Publishing Corp.

Braybrooke, D. and C. E. Lindblom. 1963. *A Strategy of Decision. Policy Evaluation as a Social Process.* New York, NY: The Free Press of Glencoe.

Breinin, C. M. 1987. "A Complaint and a Prediction," *Phi Delta Kappan,* 69(1): 15 – 16.

Breinin, C. M. 1992. "Lamar and Me," *Phi Delta Kappan*, 73(10):759–767.

Brewin, C. E. and R. Sisson. 1971. "A Systems Approach to Planned Growth," in *Planned Change in Education. A Systems Approach*, D. S. Bushnell and D. Rappoport, eds., New York, NY: Harcourt Brace Jovanovich, pp. 183–187.

Bridges, E. M. 1967. "A Model for Shared Decision Making in the School Principalship," *Educational Administration Quarterly*, 3(1):49–61.

Bridges, E. M. 1970. "Administrative Man: Origin or Pawn in Decision Making," *Educational Administration Quarterly*, 6(1):7–25.

Brown, A. F. 1967. "Reactions to Leadership," *Educational Administration Quarterly*," 3(1):62–73.

Brown, G. 1989. "Model of the Process of Budget Decision Making at the Provincial Level," Course presentation. Montreal, QC, McGill University Department of Administration and Policy Studies in Education.

Brown, W. 1992. *Economic Services Notes*. Published by The Canadian Teachers' Federation. November/December.

Bryk, A. S., ed. 1983. *Stakeholder-Based Evaluation*. San Francisco, CA: Jossey-Bass.

Burke, Edmund. (1757–1827). "Intimations of Immortality," in *Auguries of Innocence*.

Burkhart, J. 1974. *Strategies for Political Participation*. Cambridge, MA: Winthrop.

Burns, M. L. 1977. "The Effects of Feedback and Commitment to Change on the Behavior of Elementary School Principals," *Journal of Applied Behavioral Sciences*, 13(2):159–166.

Burns, M. L. 1978a. "Planning, a Conceptual Process," paper presented at the *Northeastern Educational Research Association Conference*, Ellensburg, NY.

Burns, M. L. 1978b. "The Structure of Language in Educational Administration," paper presented at the *Northeastern Educational Research Association Conference*, Ellensburg, NY.

Burns, M. L. 1980. "Planning for Quality Education," paper presented at the *Canadian Education Association Short Course in Educational Leadership*, Banff, Alta., May.

Burns, M. L. 1985. "Report of the Study of Marketing Strategies Analysis," report submitted to corporate participants. Montreal: McGill University.

Burns, M. L. 1986. "Tri-Dimensional Strategic Planning Model," course presentation, McGill University.

Burns, M. L. 1988a. "Participative Leadership Made Easier with Consensor®, an Electronic Tool," *Educational Technology* (April):26–30.

Burns, M. L. 1988b. "Marketing Strategies in *Fortune* 200 Companies," Seminar presented to corporate representatives. Montreal, QC: Canadian Pacific Systems Services.

Burns, M. L. 1991. "Accountability for Educational Values; A School Based Application of PPBS," paper presented at the *Canadian Association for Studies in Educational Administration*, Kingston, Ontario, June.

Burns, M. L. 1992. "A Body of Knowledge and the Structure of Language in Educational Administration," paper presented at the *Canadian Association for Studies in Educational Administration*, Charlottetown, P.E.I.

Burns, M. L. 1993. "A Paradigm by Any Other Name," *International Journal of Educational Reform*, 2(3):249–255.

Burns, M. L., D. Patterson, and L. LaFrance. 1992. "Cost-Benefit Analysis: An Application in Two Elementary Schools," paper presented at the *Canadian Association for Studies in Educational Administration*, Charlottetown: PEI, June.

Burns, M. L., D. Patterson and L. LaFrance. 1993. "A Test of the Cost Benefit Model in Two Elementary Schools," *The International Journal of Educational Management*, 7(6):18−31.

Burrell, G. and G. Morgan. 1979. *Sociological Paradigms and Organizational Analysis.* London: Heinemann.

Bushnell, D. S. and D. Rappaport, eds. 1971. *Planned Change in Education. A Systems Approach.* New York, NY: Harcourt Brace Jovanovich.

C.P.C.S. (Canadian Pacific Ltd. Consulting Services). 1985. RAC Matrix., SPEC Process, Montreal, QC.

C.P.S.S. (Canadian Pacific Ltd. Systems Services). 1985. SPEC Planning Processes and Theatre, Montreal, QC.

Campbell-Evans, G. H. 1991. "Nature and Influence of Values in Principal Decision Making," *The Alberta Journal of Educational Research*, 37(2):167−178.

Carlson, D. 1960. "Planning," in *Modern Management Principles and Practices*, Paris: OECD, pp. 33−43.

Carlson, R. V. 1991. "Culture and Organizational Planning," in *Educational Planning. Concepts, Strategies, Practices*, R. V. Carlson and G. Awkerman, eds., White Plains, NY: Longman, pp. 49−64.

Carlson, R. V. and G. Awkerman, eds. 1991. *Educational Planning. Concepts, Strategies, Practices.* White Plains, NY: Longman.

Carnegie Foundation for the Advancement of Teaching. 1988. *Report Card on Reform: The Teachers Speak.* Princeton, NJ: Carnegie Foundation for the Advancement of Teaching.

Carnochan, W. B. 1993. *The Battleground of the Curriculum.* Stanford, CA: Stanford University Press. Cited in *The Stanford Observer*, September.

Carson, T. R. and D. J. Sumara, eds. 1992. *Collaborative Action Research: Proceedings of the Ninth Invitational Conference of the Canadian Association for Curriculum Studies, 1989.* Edmonton, Alta.: University of Alberta.

Carzo, R, Jr. and J. N. Yanouzas. 1967. *Formal Organization: A Systems Approach.* Homewood, IL: The Dorsey Press.

Cazden, C. 1988. *Classroom Discourse: The Language of Teaching and Learning.* Portsmouth, NH: Heinemann.

Chase, F. S. 1952. "The Teacher and Policy Making," *Administrators' Notebook*, (May).

Cibulka, J. G. 1974. "Measuring Formal Citizen Participation in Educational Programs," *The Generator.* American Educational Research Association, Division G Newsletter, 4(2):4−12.

Clark, D. L. 1981. "In Consideration of Goal-Free Planning. The Failure of Traditional Planning Systems in Education," *Educational Administration Quarterly*, 17(3): 42−60.

Clark, D. L. and E. G. Guba. 1967. "An Examination of Potential Change Roles in Education," in *Rational Planning in Curriculum and Instruction*, Washington, DC: National Education Center for the Study of Instruction, pp. 111−133.

Clavel, P. 1985. Model Illustrating the "Garbage Can" Concept of the Organization. Course submission, Montreal, QC: McGill University.

Cleland, D. I. and W. R. King, eds. 1968. *Systems Analysis and Project Management.* New York, NY: McGraw-Hill.

Cleland, D. I. and W. R. King, eds. 1969. *Systems, Organizations, Analysis, Management.* New York, NY: McGraw-Hill.

Clifford, G. J. 1988. "The Professional School and Its Publics," in *Contributing to Educational Change. Perspectives on Research and Practice,* P. W. Jackson, ed. Berkeley, CA: McCutchan Publishing Corp., pp. 1−26.

Cohen, Y. A. 1961. *Social Structure and Personality. A Casebook.* New York, NY: Holt, Rinehart, and Winston.

Coleman, P. 1972. *An Accountability Scheme for Manitoba.* Winnipeg, Manitoba: Manitoba Association of School Trustees.

Collingwood, R. G. 1946. *The Idea of History.* New York, NY: Oxford University Press. Cited in Shulman, L. S. 1990. *Research in Teaching and Learning. Vol 1. Paradigms and Programs.* New York, NY: Macmillan Publishing Co.

Collins, R. 1985. *Three Sociological Traditions.* New York, NY: Oxford University Press.

Commission royale d'enquête sur l'enseignement dans la province de Québec. A. M. Parent, Chair. 1963−1966. *Report,* 5 vol. Québec.

Conley, S. 1991. "Review of Research on Teacher Participation in School Decision Making," in *Review of Research in Education,* No. 17. G. Grant, ed., Washington, DC: American Educational Research Association, pp. 225−266.

Conway, J. A. 1984. "The Myth, Mystery, and Mastery of Participative Decision Making in Education," *Educational Administration Quarterly,* 20(3):11−40.

Cooke, R. A. and D. M. Rousseau. 1981. "Problems of Complex Systems: A Model of System Problem Solving Applied to Schools," *Educational Administration Quarterly,* 17(3):15−41.

Coombs, P. H. 1970. *What Is Educational Planning?* Paris: UNESCO.

Cornell, T. D. 1971. "A Systematic Approach to Needs Assessment," in *Educational Accountability through Evaluation,* Tucson, AZ: EPIC Evaluation Center, pp. 31−65.

Counts, G. S. 1932. *Dare the Schools Build a New Social Order?* New York, NY: The John Day Co.

Cunningham, J. B. 1993. *Action Research and Organizational Development.* New York, NY: Praeger.

Cunningham, W. G. 1982. *Systematic Planning for Educational Change.* Palo Alto, CA: Mayfield Publishing Co.

Dachler. H. P. and B. Wilpert. 1978. "Conceptual Dimensions and Boundaries of Participation in Organizations: A Critical Evaluation," *Administrative Science Quarterly,* 23:1−39.

Dalkey, N. C. 1969. *The Delphi Method: An Experimental Study of Group Opinion.* Santa Monica, CA: Rand Corp.

Dalkey, N. C. and O. Helmer. 1963. "An Experimental Application of the Delphi Method to the Use of Experts," *Management Science,* 9:458−467.

Davis, K. 1969. "The Role of Project Management in Scientific Manufacturing," in *Systems, Organizations, Analysis, Management: A Book of Readings,* D. I. Cleland and W. R. King, eds., New York, NY: McGraw-Hill, pp. 308−314.

Davis, R. C. 1935. *The Principles of Business Organization and Operation.* Columbus, OH: H. L. Hedrick.

Davis, R. C. 1940. *Industrial Organization and Management,* 2nd ed. New York, NY: Harper.

Davis, R. C. 1951. *The Fundamentals of Top Management.* New York, NY: Harper.

David, F. R. 1985. "How Do We Choose among Alternative Growth Strategies?" *Managerial Planning,* 33(4):14−17.

de Vasconcellos, F. 1982. "Strategic Planning: A New Approach," *Managerial Planning,* 30(5):12−20.

De Angelis, T. R. 1985. "A Rationale for Planning Excellence," *Managerial Planning,* 33(5):4−7, 10.

Delamont, S. 1992. *Fieldwork in Educational Settings: Methods, Pitfalls, and Perspectives.* London: Falmer Press.

Delbecq, A. L., A. H. Van de Ven, and D. H. Gustafson. 1975. *Group Techniques for Program Planning.* Dallas, TX: Scott Foresman, Inc.

Dewey, J. 1933. *How We Think.* Boston, MA: Heath.

Dill, W. R. 1964. "Decision Making," in *Behavioral Science and Educational Administration,* 63rd Yearbook, National Society for Studies in Education, Part II, D. E. Griffiths, ed., Chicago, IL: University of Chicago Press, pp. 199−222.

Doyle, D. P. 1990. "Teacher Choice: Does It Have a Future?" in *Choice in Education. Potential and Problems,* W. L. Boyd and H. J. Walberg, eds., Berkeley, CA: McCutchan Publishing Corp., pp. 95−120.

Doyle, M. and D. Straus. 1976. *The New Interaction Method. How to Make Meetings Work.* New York, NY: The Berkeley Publishing Group.

Driscoll, J. W. 1978. "Trust and Participation in Organizational Decision Making as Predictors of Satisfaction," *Academy of Management Journal,* 21(1):44−56.

Dror, Y. 1963. "The Planning Process: A Facet Design," *International Review of Administrative Sciences,* 29(1):44−58.

Drucker, P. F. 1955. *The Practice of Management.* London: Heinemann, Ltd.

Drucker, P. F. 1967. *The Effective Executive.* New York, NY: Harper and Row.

Drucker, P. F. 1974. *Management, Tasks, Responsibilities, Practices.* New York, NY: Harper and Row.

Drucker, P. F. 1976. "What Results Should You Expect? A User's Guide to MBO," *Public Administration Review* (January/February):12−19.

Drucker, P. F. 1980. *Managing in Turbulent Times.* New York, NY: Harper & Row, Publishers.

Drucker, P. F. 1992. *Managing for the Future: The 1990s and Beyond.* New York, NY: Truman Talley Books.

Duke, D. L., B. K. Showers, and M. Imber. 1980. "Teachers and Shared Decision Making: The Costs and Benefits of Involvement," *Educational Administration Quarterly,* 16(1):93−106.

Eisner, E. W. 1991. *The Enlightened Eye: Qualitative Inquiry and the Enhancement of Learning.* New York, NY: Macmillan Publishing Co.

Eisner, E. W. 1992a. "The Federal Reform of Schools: Looking for the Silver Bullet," *Phi Delta Kappan,* 73(9):722−723.

Eisner, E. W. 1992b. "The Misunderstood Role of the Arts in Human Development," *Phi Delta Kappan,* 73(8):591−595.

Elam, S. M. and A. M. Gallup. 1989. "The 21st Annual Gallup Poll of the Public's Attitudes toward the Public Schools," *Phi Delta Kappan,* 71(1):41 – 54.

Elliott, J. 1991. *Action Research for Educational Change.* Milton Keynes, England: Open University Press.

English, F. W. 1994. *Theory in Educational Administration.* New York, NY: Harper-Collins College Publishers.

Ennis, R. H. 1981. "Rational Thinking and Educational Practice," in *Philosophy and Education,* J. F. Soltis, ed., *Eightieth Yearbook of the National Society for the Study of Education, Part I,* pp. 143 – 183.

Erickson, F. 1986. "Qualitative Methods in Research on Teaching," in *Handbook of Research on Teaching,* 3rd ed., M. C. Wittrock, ed., New York, NY: Macmillan Publishing Co.

Erjavec, M. 1994. "A Case Study of the Financial Management System of the Secondary Division of a Quebec School Board," submitted in partial fulfillment of the requirements of an MA in Educational Administration, Montreal, QC: McGill University.

Estler, S. 1988. "Decision Making," in *Handbook of Research on Educational Administration,* a Project of the American Educational Research Association, N. J. Boyan, ed., New York, NY: Longman, pp. 305 – 319.

Etzioni, A. 1960. "Two Approaches to Organizational Analysis: A Critique and Suggestion," *Administrative Science Quarterly,* 5:257 – 278.

Fayol, H. 1949. *General and Industrial Management.* C. Storrs (trans.), London: Pitman.

Fiedler, F. E. 1967. *A Theory of Leadership Effectiveness.* New York, NY: McGraw-Hill.

Fiedler, F. E. and Chemers. 1974. *Leadership and Effective Management.* Glenview, IL: Scott, Foresman.

Fierhaller, D. 1979. "Planning in a Medium Sized Corporation," symposium presented at the *Planning Executives Institute International Conference,* Montreal, QC.

Filtgaard, R. E. and G. R. Hall. 1973. *A Statistical Search for Unusually Effective Schools.* Santa Monica, CA: Rand.

Firestone, W. A. 1977. "Participation and Influence in the Planning of Educational Change," *Journal of Applied Behavioral Science,* 13:167 – 187.

Firestone, W. A. 1980. "Continuity and Incrementalism after All: State Responses to the Excellence Movement," in *The Educational Reform Movement of the 1980s,* J. Murphy, ed., Berkeley, CA: McCutchan Publishing Corp., pp. 143 – 166.

Firestone, W. A. and H. D. Corbett. 1988. "Planned Organizational Change," in *Handbook of Research on Educational Administration,* a Project of the American Educational Research Association, N. J. Boyan, ed., New York, NY: Longman, pp. 321 – 340.

Firestone, W. A. and R. E. Herriott. 1982. "Two Images of Schools as Organizations: An Explication and Illustrative Empirical Test," *Educational Administration Quarterly,* 18(2):39 – 59.

Fitzgibbons, R. E. 1981. *Making Educational Decisions. An Introduction to Philosophy of Education.* New York, NY: Harcourt Brace Jovanovich, Inc.

Flesch, R. F. 1955. *Why Johnny Can't Read – And What You Can Do about It.* New York, NY: Harper.

Follett, M. P. 1924. *Creative Experience.* New York, NY: Longmans, Green and Co.

Follett, M. P. 1940. *Dynamic Administration: The Collected Papers of Mary Parker Follett.* H. C. Metcalf and L. Urwick, eds., New York, NY: Harper and Brothers.

Follett, M. P. 1949. "The Essentials of Leadership," in *Freedom and Coordination,* London: Management Publications Trust, Ltd., pp. 47–60. Reprinted in Merrill, ed., *Classics in Management.* New York, NY: American Management Association, pp. 323–336.

Freire, P. 1985. *The Politics of Education. Culture, Power, and Liberation.* South Hadley, MA: Bergin & Garvey Publishers, Inc.

French, W. L. 1978. "Management by Objectives," in *The Personnel Management Process,* Boston, MA: Houghton Mifflin Co., pp. 321–379.

French, W. L. and C. M. Bell, Jr. 1990. *Organization Development.* Englewood Cliffs, NJ: Prentice-Hall, Inc.

Freud, S. 1922. *A General Introduction to Psychoanalysis.* New York, NY: Liveright.

Friedman, A. L. 1977. *Industry and Labour: Class Struggle at Work and Monopoly Capitalism.* London: Macmillan.

Friedmann, J. 1966. *Regional Development: A Case Study of Venezuela.* Cambridge MA: MIT Press.

Friedmann, J. 1973. *Retracking America. A Theory of Transactive Planning.* Garden City, NY: Doubleday Publishers.

Friedmann, J. and W. Alonso, eds. 1964. *Regional Development and Planning: A Reader.* Cambridge MA: MIT Press

Frizell, B. 1972. *The Grand Defiance.* New York, NY: Dell Publishing Co.

Gage, N. L. 1963. "Paradigms for Research on Teaching," in *Handbook of Research on Teaching,* a project of the American Educational Research Association, N. L. Gage, ed., Chicago, IL: Rand McNally & Co., pp. 94–141.

Gage, N. L. 1972. *Teacher Effectiveness and Teacher Education: The Search for a Scientific Basis.* Palo Alto, CA: Pacific Books, Publishers.

Gage, N. L. 1978. *The Scientific Basis of the Art of Teaching.* New York, NY: Teachers College Press, Teachers College, Columbia University.

Gallup Poll. See Elam and Gallup. 1989.

Garman, N. B. and H. M. Hazi. 1988. "Teachers Ask: Is There Life after Madeline Hunter?" *Phi Delta Kappan,* 69(9):667–672.

Gazette, The. 1977. Montreal, QC (December 1):2.

Geerta, C. 1973. "Thick Description: Toward an Interpretive Theory of Culture," in *The Interpretation of Cultures,* New York, NY: Basic Books, pp. 3–30.

George, C. 1968. *The History of Management Thought.* Englewood Cliffs, NJ: Prentice-Hall, Inc.

Georgiou, P. 1973. "The Goal Paradigm and Notes towards a Counter Paradigm," *Administrative Science Quarterly,* 18:291–303.

Getzels, J. W. 1955. *The Use of Theory in Educational Administration.* Stanford, CA: Stanford University Press.

Getzels, J. W. 1959. "Administration as a Social Process" in *Administrative Theory,* D. E. Griffiths, ed., New York, NY: Appleton-Century-Crofts, pp. 150–165.

Getzels, J. W. 1968. *Educational Administration as a Social Process.* New York, NY: Harper and Row.

Getzels, J. W. and E. B. Guba. 1959. "Social Behavior and the Administrative Process," *The School Review*, 65:423–441.

Giroux, H. 1983. "Critical Theory and Rationality in Citizenship Education," in *The Hidden Curriculum and Moral Education. Deception or Discovery?* H. Giroux and D. Purpel, eds., Berkeley, CA: McCutchan Publishing Corp., pp. 321–360.

Giroux, H. A. 1992. "Educational Leadership and the Crisis of Democratic Government," *Educational Researcher*, (May):4–11.

Giroux, H. and D. Purpel, eds. 1983. *The Hidden Curriculum and Moral Education. Deception or Discovery?* Berkeley, CA: McCutchan Publishing Corp.

Goodnow, F. J. 1905. *The Principles of Administrative Law of the United States.* New York, NY: G. P. Putnam's Sons, pp. 6, 15.

Gouldner, A. 1954. *Patterns of Industrial Bureaucracy.* New York, NY: Free Press.

Gouldner, A. W. 1959. "Reciprocity and Autonomy in Functional Theory," in *For Sociology*, A. W. Gouldner, ed., 1973. Hammondsworth: Penguin, pp. 190–225.

Granhof, M. H. and D. A. Kinzel. 1974. "Zero-Base Budgeting: Modest Proposal of Reform," *The Federal Accountant* (December):45–62.

Greenberg, E. S. 1975. "The Consequences of Worker Participation: A Clarification of the Theoretical Literature," *Social Science Quarterly*, 56:191–209.

Greene, M. 1980. *Landscapes of Learning.* New York, NY: Teachers College Press.

Greene, M. 1983. "Curriculum and Consciousness," in *The Hidden Curriculum and Moral Education. Deception or Discovery?* H. Giroux and D. Purpel, eds., Berkeley, CA: McCutchan Publishing Corp., pp. 168–184.

Greene, M. 1988. *The Dialectic of Freedom.* New York, NY: Teachers College Press.

Greenfield, T. B. 1975. "Theory about Organization: A New Perspective and Its Implications for Schools," in *Administering Education: International Challenge*, M. G. Hughes, ed., London: Athlone, pp. 71–99.

Griffiths, D. E. 1959. *Administrative Theory.* New York, NY: Appleton-Century-Crofts, Inc.

Gross, B. M. 1964. "The Scientific Approach to Administration," in *Behavioral Science and Educational Administration*,, D. E. Griffiths, ed., *63rd Yearbook of the National Society for the Study of Education, Part II*, pp. 33–72.

Grove, A. S. 1985. *High Output Management.* New York, NY: Random House.

Grove, A. S. 1987. *One-on-One with Andy Grove: How to Manage Your Boss, Yourself, and Your Co-workers.* New York, NY: G. P. Putman's Sons.

Guba, E. G., ed. 1990. *The Paradigm Dialog.* Newbury Park, CA: Sage Publications.

Gulick, L. and L. H. Urwick, eds. 1937. *Papers on the Science of Administration.* New York, NY: Institute of Public Administration, Columbia University.

Habermas, J. 1972. *Knowledge and Human Interests.* London: Heinemann.

Hage, J. and M. Aiken. 1967. "Relationship of Centralization to Other Structural Properties," *Administrative Science Quarterly*, 12(1):72–92.

Hague, W. J. 1987. "Teaching Values in Canadian Schools," in *Contemporary Educational Issues: The Canadian Mosaic*, L. L. Stewin, S. McCann, and J. H. Stewart, eds., Toronto, Ont.: Copp Clark Pitman, pp. 241–251.

Hall, E. T. 1977. *Beyond Culture.* Garden City, NY: Anchor Books.

Halpin, A. W. 1966. *Theory and Research in Administration.* New York, NY: Macmillan.

Hamilton, A. 1788. *The Federalist*, 72: New York Packet, March 18.

Hamilton, D. N. 1991. "An Alternative to Rational Planing Models," in *Educational Planning. Concepts, Strategies, Practices*, R. V. Carlson and G. Awkerman, eds., White Plains, NY: Longman, pp. 21–47.

Haney, W. V. 1960. *Communication: Patterns and Incidents.* Homewood, IL: R. D. Irwin.

Haney, W. V. 1973. *Communication and Organizational Behavior.* 3rd ed. Homewood, IL: R. D. Irwin.

Hanson, E. M. 1979. *Educational Administration and Organizational Behavior.* Boston, MA: Allyn & Bacon.

Hart, L. A. 1983. *Human Brain and Human Learning.* New York, NY: Longman.

Hartley, H. J. 1968. *Educational PPB: A Systems Approach.* Englewood Cliffs, NJ: Prentice-Hall.

Hartley, H. J. 1969. "PPBS and Cost Effectiveness Analysis," *Educational Administration Quarterly*, 5(1):65–80.

Havelock, R. G. 1974. "The Planning of Alternatives," paper presented at the *6th Western Canada Educational Administrators' Conference*, Banff, Alta.

Hersey, P. and K. H. Blanchard. 1973. *LEAD: Leader Effectiveness and Adaptability Description Questionnaire.* La Jolla, CA: Center for Leadership Studies.

Hersey, P. and K. H. Blanchard. 1974. "So You Want to Know Your Leadership Style?" *Training and Development Journal* (February):22–37.

Hersey, P. and K. H. Blanchard. 1977. *Management of Organizational Behavior: Utilizing Human Resources.* Englewood Cliffs, NJ: Prentice-Hall.

Hills, R. J. 1967. *The Concept of System.* Eugene, OR: The Center for the Advanced Study of Educational Administration, University of Oregon.

Hodgkinson, C. 1970. "Organizational Influence on Value Systems," *Educational Administration Quarterly*, 6(3):46–55.

Hodgkinson, C. 1978. *Towards a Philosophy of Administration.* Oxford, Eng.: Basil Blackwell.

Hodgkinson, C. 1983. *The Philosophy of Leadership.* Oxford, Eng.: Basil Blackwell.

Hodgkinson, H. L. and L. R. Meath, eds. 1971. *Power and Authority.* San Francisco, CA: Jossey-Bass, Inc., Publishers.

Holmes, O. W. 1858. *The Autocrat of the Breakfast Table.* Boston: Phillips, Samson.

Holtz, J. H. 1969. "An Analysis of Major Scheduling Techniques in the Defense Systems Environment," in *Systems, Organizations, Analysis, Management*, D. I. Cleland and W. L. King, eds., New York, NY: McGraw-Hill Book Co., pp. 317–355.

Horowitz, J. 1967. "CPM and PERT—An Overview," in *Critical Path Scheduling*, New York, NY: The Ronald Press, pp. 3–13.

Hostrop, R. W. 1975. *Managing Education for Results.* CA: ETC Publications.

Hovland, C. I., I. L. Janis and H. H. Kelley. 1958. *Communication and Persuasion, Psychological Studies of Opinion Change.* New Haven, CT: Yale University Press.

Howland, G. 1896. *Practical Hints for Teachers of Public Schools.* New York, NY: D. Appleton and Co. Cited in F. W. English. 1994. *Theory in Educational Administration.* New York, NY: HarperCollins College Publishers.

Hoy, W. K. and C. G. Miskel. 1987. *Educational Administration: Theory, Research, and Practice.* 3rd ed. New York, NY: Random House.

Hughes, M. G., ed. 1975. *Administering Education: International Challenge.* London: Athlone.

Hull, C. L. 1966. *Principles of Behavior: An Introduction to Behavior Theory.* New York, NY: Appleton-Century-Crofts.

Illich, I. 1971. *Deschooling Society.* New York, NY: Harper & Row.

Immegart, G. L. and F. J. Pilecki. 1973. *An Introduction to Systems for the Educational Administrator.* Reading, MA: Addison-Wesley.

Inbar, D. E. 1991. "Improvisation and Organizational Planning," in *Educational Planning. Concepts, Strategies, Practices,* R. V. Carlson and G. Awkerman, eds., New York, NY: Longman, pp. 65−80.

Isherwood, G. B. and R. M. Taylor. 1978. "Participatory Decision Making via School Councils," *The High School Journal,* 61(6):255−270.

Jacobson, P., W. C. Reavis, and J. D. Logson. 1956. *The Effective Principal in Elementary and Secondary Schools,* second ed. Englewood Cliffs, NJ: Prentice-Hall.

Jacobson, S. L. and J. A. Conway, eds. 1990. *Educational Leadership in an Age of Reason.* New York, NY: Longman.

Johnston, A. P. and A. M. Liggett. 1991. "Linking Policy and Governance through Planning," in *Educational Planning, Concepts, Strategies, Practices,* R. V. Carlson and G. Awkerman, eds., New York, NY: Longman, pp. 109−123.

Johnstone, J. N. 1974. "Mathematical Models Developed for Use in Educational Planning: A Review," *Review of Educational Research,* 44(2):177−201.

Jones, E. E. and H. B. Gerard. 1967. "Case One. Wild Boy of Aveyron," in *Foundations of Social Psychology,* New York, NY: John Wiley & Sons, Inc., pp. 5−8.

Jucius, M. J. and W. E. Schlender. 1965. "Planning," in *Elements of Managerial Action,* Homewood, IL: Richard D. Irwin, Inc., pp. 46−62.

Jung, C. G. 1965. *Collected Works.* London: Routledge and Keegan Paul.

Kami, M. J. and W. F. Martz. 1979. *Corporate Planning Process Manual.* Lighthouse Point, FL: Corporate Planning Inc.

Katz, D. 1955. "Skills of an Effective Administrator," *Harvard Business Review,* 33(1):33−42.

Katz, D. and R. L. Kahn. 1966. *The Social Psychology of Organizations.* New York, NY: John Wiley & Sons..

Kaufman, R. 1972. *Educational System Planning.* Englewood Cliffs, NJ: Prentice-Hall, Inc.

Kaufman, R. 1988. *Planning Educational Systems: A Results Based Approach.* Lancaster, PA: Technomic Publishing Co., Inc.

Kaufman, R. 1991. "Asking the Right Questions: Types of Strategic Planning," in *Educational Planning. Concepts, Strategies, Practices,* R. V. Carlson and G. Awkerman, eds., New York, NY: Longman, pp. 177−200.

Kaufman, R. 1992. *Mapping Educational Success. Strategic Thinking and Planning for School Administrators. Successful Schools, Vol. 1.* F. W. English, series ed. Newbury Park, CA: Corwin Press.

Kaufman, R. A. and F. W. English. 1979. *Needs Assessment: Concept and Application.* Englewood Cliffs, NY: Educational Technology Publishers.

Kaufman, R. and J. Herman. 1991. *Strategic Planning in Education. Rethinking, Restructuring, Revitalizing.* Lancaster, PA: Technomic Publishing Co. Inc.

Kazmier, L. J. 1980. *Management. A Programmed Approach with Cases and Applications.* New York, NY: McGraw-Hill Book Co.

Kennedy, M. M. 1984. "How Evidence Alters Understanding and Decisions," *Educational Evaluation and Policy Analysis,* 6(3):207–226.

Kidder, T. 1981. *The Soul of a New Machine.* New York, NY: Avon Books.

Knezevich, S. J. 1969. *Administration of Public Education,* 2nd ed. New York, NY: Harper & Row.

Kuhn, A. 1963. *The Study of Society: A Unified Approach.* Homewood, IL: The Dorsey Press, Inc.

Kuhn, T. S. 1962. *The Structure of Scientific Revolutions.* Chicago, IL: University of Chicago Press.

Kuhn, T. S. 1970. *The Structure of Scientific Revolution,* 2nd ed. Chicago, IL: University of Chicago Press.

Lane, J. L. and H. J. Walberg, eds. 1987. *Effective School Leadership, Policy and Process.* Berkeley, CA: McCutchan Publishing Corp.

Lawrence, P. R. and J. W. Lorsch. 1967. *Organization and Environment.* Cambridge, MA: Harvard Graduate School of Business Administration.

Leithwood, K. A. and D. J. Montgomery. 1986. *The Principal Profile.* Toronto, Ont: Ontario Institute for Studies in Education Press.

Lewin, K., R. Lippitt, and R. K. White. 1939. "Patterns of Aggressive Behavior in Experimentally Created Social Climates," *Journal of Social Psychology* 10:271–299.

Lewis, J., Jr. 1986. *Achieving Excellence in Our Schools . . . by Taking Lessons from America's Best-Run Companies.* Westbury, NY: J. L. Wilkerson Publishing Co.

Likert, R. 1967. *The Human Organization: Its Management and Value.* New York, NY: McGraw-Hill Inc.

Lindblom, C. E. 1959. "The Science of Muddling Through," *Public Administration Review,* 19:79–88.

Litchfield, E. H. 1956. "Notes on a General Theory of Administration," *Administrative Science Quarterly,* 1(1):3–29.

Locke, E. and D. Schweiger. 1979. "Participation in Decision Making: One More Look," *Research in Organizational Behavior,* 1:265–339.

Love, J. M. 1985. "Knowledge Transfer and Utilization in Education," in *Review of Research in Education,* No. 12, E. W. Gordon, ed., Washington, DC: National Educational Research Association, pp. 337–386.

Lowin, A. 1968. "Participative Decision Making: A Model, Literature Critique, and Prescription for Research," *Organizational Behavior and Human Performance,* 3:68–106.

Lucas-Phillips, C. E. 1957. *Cockleshell Heroes.* London: Pan Books, Ltd.

Lynn, L. E., Jr. 1968. "Systems Analysis–Challenge to Military Management," in *Systems Analysis and Project Management,* D. I. Cleland and W. R. King, eds., New York, NY: McGraw Hill, pp. 216–231.

Maccoby, E. E. 1966. *The Development of Sex Differences*. Stanford, CA: Stanford University Press.

Maccoby, E. E.. 1974. *The Psychology of Sex Differences*. Stanford, CA: Stanford University Press.

MacFarlane, J. A. 1976. "Zero Base Budgeting in Action," *Certified Accountants Magazine*, 109(6):28−32.

Madaus, G. F. and T. Kellaghan. 1993. "The British Experience with 'Authentic' Testing," *Phi Delta Kappan* (February):458−469.

Maddock, T. 1990. "The Relevance of Philosophy to Educational Administration," *Educational Administration Quarterly*, 26(3):280−292.

Maeroff, G. L. 1988. "A Blueprint for Empowering Teachers," *Phi Delta Kappan* (March):473−477.

Mager, R. F. 1962. *Preparing Instructional Objectives*. Palo Alto, CA: Fearon.

Manning, W. G. 1970. *Toward a Breakthrough in Education. A Systems Approach to Educational Productivity*. Edmonton, Alta.: M & M Systems Research Ltd.

March, J. G. 1984. "The Technology of Foolishness," in *Organization Theory. Selected Readings*, 2nd ed., D. S. Pugh, ed., Hammondsworth, Middlesex, Eng. Penguin Books, pp. 224−237.

March, J. G. 1988. "Leadership and Power: Three Views," *The Stanford Magazine* (Spring):61−66.

March, J. G. and J. P. Olsen. 1976. *Ambiguity and Choice in Organizations*. Bergen: Universitetsforleget.

March, J. G. and J. P. Olsen. 1989. *Goals, No-Goals, and Own Goals: A Debate on Goal-Directed Behavior*. London: Unwin.

March, J. G. and H. A. Simon. 1958. *Organizations*. New York, NY: John Wiley & Sons.

Marcuse, H. 1964. *One Dimensional Man*. Boston, MA: Beacon Press.

Marshall, M. L. 1970. "Focus on Leadership in Group Decision Making," *Clearing House*, 8:41−44.

Marx, K. 1844. "Economic and Philosophical Manuscripts," in *Early Writings*, R. Livingstone and G. Benton (trans. 1975), Harmondsworth: Penguin, pp. 279−400. Cited in Morgan, Gareth. 1980. "Paradigms, Metaphors, and Puzzle Solving in Organization Theory," *Administrative Science Quarterly*, 25(4):605−621.

McDonald, J. P. 1993. "Three Pictures of an Exhibition: Warm, Cool, and Hard," *Phi Delta Kappan* (February):480−485.

McGregor, D. 1960. *The Human Side of Enterprise*. New York, NY: McGraw-Hill.

McManama, J. 1971. *Systems Analysis for Effective School Administration*. West Nyack, NY: Parker Publications Co.

McNamara, J. F. and G. B. Chisolm. 1988. "The Technical Tools of Decision Making," in *Handbook of Research on Educational Administration*, A Project of the American Educational Research Association, N. J. Boyan, ed., New York, NY: Longman, pp. 525−567.

Meath, L. R. 1971. "Administration and Leadership," in *Power and Authority*, H. L. Hodgkinson and L. R. Meath, eds., San Francisco, CA: Jossey-Bass, Inc. Publishers, pp. 39−53.

Melcher, A. J. 1976. "Participation: A Critical Review of Research Findings," *Human Resource Management,* 15(2):12−21.

Meyerson, M. and E. C. Banfield. 1955. *Politics, Planning and the Public Interest. The Cases of Public Housing in Chicago.* Glencoe, IL: The Free Press.

Michaels, A. J. 1971. "Establishing a PERT System," *Management Accounting* (October):26−32.

Michels, R. 1949. *Political Parties.* Glencoe, IL: Free Press.

Miklos, E., P. Bourgette, and S. Cowley. 1972. *Perspectives on Educational Planning.* Edmonton, Alta.: Human Resources Research Council.

Miller, D. R. 1969. "Policy Formulation and Policy Implementation in an Educational System," in *Strategies of Educational Planning,* R. H. P. Kraft, ed., Tallahassee, FL: Educational Systems Development Center, Florida State University.

Miller, J. 1980. "Decision Making and Organizational Effectiveness: Participation and Perceptions," *Sociology of Work and Occupations,* 7(1):55−99.

Miller, K. and P. R. Monge. 1986. "The Development and Test of a System of Organizational Participation and Allocation," in *Communication Yearbook 10,* M. M. McLaughlin, ed., Beverly Hills, CA: Sage Publications, pp. 431−469.

Miller, R. W. 1962. "How to Plan and Control with PERT," *Harvard Business Review* (March-April):104−115.

Mintzberg, H. 1973. *The Nature of Managerial Work.* New York, NY: Harper and Row.

Mintzberg, H. 1976. *Patterns in Strategy Formation.* Montreal, QC: McGill University.

Mintzberg, H. 1980. *The Nature of Managerial Work.* Englewood Cliffs, NJ: Prentice-Hall.

Mintzberg, H., D. Raisinghani and A. Thoret. 1976. "The Structure of 'Unstructured' Decision Process," *Administrative Science Quarterly,* 21(2):246−275.

Miskel, C., R. Fevurly and J. Stewart. 1979. "Organizational Structures and Processes, Perceived School Effectiveness, Loyalty, and Job Satisfaction," *Educational Administration Quarterly,* 15(3):97−118.

Mitchell, I. R. 1979. "Organizational Behavior," *Annual Review of Psychology,* 30:243−282.

Mitzel, H. E., ed. 1982. *Encyclopedia of Educational Research.* Sponsored by the American Educational Research Association, New York, NY: Free Press.

Mohrman, A. M., Jr., R. A. Cooke, and S. A. Mohrman. 1978. "Participation in Decision Making: A Multi-Dimensional Perspective," *Educational Administration Quarterly,* 14(1):13−29.

Moore, G. E. 1959. *Philosophical Papers.* New York, NY: Allen and Unwin.

Morgan, G. 1980. "Paradigms, Metaphors, and Puzzle Solving in Organization Theory," *Administrative Science Quarterly,* 25(4):605−621.

Murphy, J. 1990. "The Educational Reform Movement of the 1980s: A Comprehensive Analysis," in *The Educational Reform Movement of the 1980s,* J. Murphy, ed., Berkeley, CA: McCutchan Publishing Corp., pp. 3−56.

Murphy, J. 1991. *Restructuring Schools, Capturing and Assessing the Phenomena.* New York, NY: Teachers College Press.

Murphy, J., ed. 1990. *The Educational Reform Movement of the 1980s.* Berkeley, CA: McCutchan Publishing Corp.

National Center for Education Statistics. 1987. *The Condition of Education*. Washington, DC: U.S. Office of Education, U.S. Government Printing Office.

Naylor, T. H. and K. Neva. 1980. "Design of a Strategic Planning Process," *Managerial Planning*, 28(4):3–7.

Nelson, R. 1993. "Understanding Eskimo Science," *Audubon* (September/October):102–104, 106, 108–110.

Newberry, A. J. H. 1990. "Filters of Analysis: Bringing Meaning to Strategic Planning," *The Canadian School Executive*, 10(2):11–14.

Newman, J. W. 1971. *Management Applications of Decision Theory*. New York, NY: Harper and Row.

Newman, W. H. 1950. *Administrative Action*. Englewood Cliffs, NJ: Prentice Hall Inc.

NSSE. 1964. *Behavioral Science and Educational Administration. 63rd Yearbook of the National Society for the Study of Education*, D. E. Griffiths, ed., Chicago, IL.: University of Chicago Press.

NSSE 1972. *Philosophical Redirection of Educational Research. The 71st Yearbook of the National Society for the Study of Education, Part I*, L. G. Thomas, ed., Chicago, IL: The University of Chicago Press.

NSSE. 1981. *Philosophy and Education. The 80th Yearbook of the National Society for the Study of Education, Part I*, J. F. Soltis, ed., Chicago, IL: The University of Chicago Press.

NSSE. 1985. *Learning and Teaching: The Ways of Knowing. The 84th Yearbook of the National Society for the Study of Education, Part II*, E. Eisner, ed., Chicago, IL: The University of Chicago Press.

Nucci, L. P., ed. 1989. *Moral Development and Character Education, a Dialogue*. Berkeley, CA: McCutchan Publishing Corp.

Nystrand, M. and A. Gamoran. 1991. "Student Engagement: When Recitation becomes Conversation," in *Effective Teaching: Current Research*, H. C. Waxman and H. J. Walbert, eds., Berkeley, CA: McCutchan Publishing Corp., pp. 257–276.

Nystrand, M. and A. Gamoran. Instructional Discourse. Student Engagement and Literature Achievement. Research in the Teaching of English.

O Brien, P. 1980. "The Delphi Technique, a Review of Research," paper presented at the *Canadian Educational Administrators Conference*, Banff, Alberta.

Odiorne, G. S. 1965. *Management by Objectives*. Belmont, CA: Pitman Publishing Corp.

Odiorne, G. S. 1976. "MBO in State Government," *Public Administration Review* (January/February):28–33.

Ohmart, J. 1993. "Life Cycle of a Walnut," Chico, CA: Personal communication.

Olweus, D. 1978. *Aggression in the Schools: Bullies and Whipping Boys*. New York, NY: Halsted Press.

Ozmon, H. A. and S. M. Craver. 1990. *Philosophical Foundations of Education*, 4th ed. New York, NY: Macmillan Publishing Co.

Pajares, M. F. 1992. "Teachers' Beliefs and Educational Research: Cleaning Up a Messy Construct," *Review of Educational Research*, 62(3):307–332.

Pallozzi, D. P. 1981. "A Model for Community Participation in Local School District Decision Making," Ed.D. diss., Rutgers University.

Papert, S. 1980. *Mind-Storms. Children, Computers, and Powerful Ideas.* New York, NY: Basic Books Publishers, Inc.

Parent Commission Report. See: Commission royale d'enquête sur l'ensengnement dans la province de Québec.

Parsons, T. 1949. *The Structure of Social Action.* Glencoe, IL: Free Press.

Parsons, T. 1956. "Suggestions for a Sociological Approach to the Theory of Organizations," *Administrative Science Quarterly,* 1:63–85, 325–239.

Parsons, T. 1960. *Structure and Process in Modern Societies.* Glencoe, IL: Free Press.

Parsons, T. 1967. *Sociological Theory and Modern Society.* New York, NY: The Free Press.

Pateman, T. 1982. "Accountability, Values and Schooling," in *Accountability in Education,* T. Becher and S. Maclure, eds., Windsor, Berkshire: Nelson Publishing Co., Ltd., pp. 61–94.

Patterson, J. L. and T. J. Czajkowski. 1976. "District Needs Assessment. One Avenue to Program Improvement." *Phi Delta Kappan* (December):327–329.

Patton, M. Q. 1990. *Qualitative Evaluation and Research Methods,* second ed. Newbury Park, CA: Sage Publications.

Perry-Sheldon, B. and V. Anselmini-Allain. 1987. *Using Educational Research in the Classroom.* Bloomington, IN: Phi Delta Kappan Educational Foundation.

Peters, T. J. and R. H. Waterman, Jr. 1982. *In Search of Excellence.* New York, NY: Harper and Row.

Phyrr, P. A. 1973. *Zero Based Budgeting.* New York, NY: John Wiley & Sons.

Pinar, W. F. and W. M. Reynolds. 1992. *Understanding Curriculum as Phenomenological and Deconstructed Text.* New York, NY: Teachers College Press.

Popham, W. J. 1972. "California's Precedent Setting Teacher Evaluation Law," *Educational Researcher,* 1(7):13–15.

Porter, E. H. 1962. "The Parable of the Spindle," *Harvard Business Review,* 40(3):58–66. Cited in R. Carzo, Jr. and J. N. Yanouzas. 1967. *Formal Organization: A Systems Approach.* Homewood, IL: The Dorsey Press, pp. 329–334.

Posevec, E. J. and R. G. Carey. 1992. *Program Evaluation: Methods and Case Studies.* Englewood Cliffs, NJ: Prentice-Hall.

Postman, N. 1984. *The Disappearance of Childhood.* New York, NY: Dell Publishers.

Pyke, D. L. 1970. "Technological Forecasting. A Framework for Consideration," *Futures,* 2:327–331.

Quade, E. S. 1969. "Systems Analysis Techniques for Planning-Programming-Budgeting," in *Systems, Organizations, Analysis, Management,* D. I. Cleland and W. R. King, eds., New York, NY: McGraw-Hill, pp. 193–205.

Quinn, J. B. 1980. *Strategies for Change: Logical Incrementalism.* Homewood, IL: R. D. Irwin.

Quinn, J. B. 1994. Seminar presentation, Montreal, QC.

Raiffa, H. 1970. *Decision Tree Analysis: Introductory Lectures on Choices under Uncertainty.* Reading, MA: Addison-Wesley.

Reavis, C. and H. Griffith. 1992. *Restructuring Schools, Theory and Practice.* Lancaster, PA: Technomic Publishing Co. Inc.

Reddin, W. J. 1970. *Managerial Effectiveness.* New York, NY: McGraw-Hill.

Reddin, W. J. 1971. *Effective Management by Objectives: The 3-D Method of MBO.* New York, NY: McGraw-Hill.

Reid, K. , D. Hopkins, and P. Holly. 1987. *Towards the Effective School: The Problems and Some Solutions.* Oxford: Basil Blackwell.

Restak, R. 1984. *The Brain.* New York, NY: Bantam Books.

Rhine, R. W., ed. 1981. *Making Schools More Effective: New Directions from Follow-through.* New York, NY: Academic Press.

Robertson, E. 1992. "Is Dewey's Educational Vision Still Viable?" in *Review of Research in Education, #18,* G. Grant, ed., Washington, DC: American Educational Research Association, pp. 335–381.

Roethlisberger, F. and W. Dickson. 1939. *Management and the Worker.* Cambridge, MA: Harvard University Press.

Rosow, J. M., R. Zager, and Associates. 1989. *Allies in Educational Reform: How Teachers, Unions, and Administrators Can Join Forces for Better Schools.* San Francisco, CA: Jossey-Bass.

Rossi, P. H. and H. E. Freeman. 1993. *Evaluation: A Systematic Approach,* Fifth ed. Newbury Park, CA: Sage Publications.

Rutter, M., B. Maughan, P. Mortimore, and J. Ouston. 1979. *Fifteen Thousand Hours: Secondary Schools and Their Effects on Children.* Cambridge, MA: Harvard University Press.

Ryan, C. 1966. *The Last Battle.* New York, NY: Popular Library.

Sacks, O. 1985. *The Man Who Mistook His Wife for a Hat.* New York, NY: Harper Perennial.

Sargent, C. G. and E. L. Belisle. 1955. *Educational Administration: Cases and Concepts.* Boston, MA: Houghton Mifflin.

Saroyan-Farivar, A. 1989. "The Review Process in Formative Evaluation: The Role of Content Experts and Instructional Designers," Ph.D. diss., McGill University, Montreal, QC.

Sashkin, M. and H. J. Walberg, eds. 1993. *Educational Leadership and School Culture.* Berkeley, CA: McCutchan Publishing Corp.

Sawyer, G. C. 1983. *Corporate Planning as a Creative Process. Action Laid Out in Advance.* Oxford, OH: Planning Executives Institute.

Schmuck, R. and A. Blumberg. 1969. "Teacher Participation in Educational Decisions." *The National Association for Secondary School Principals Bulletin,* 53:89–105.

Schon, D. A. 1983. *The Reflective Practitioner: How Professionals Think in Action.* New York, NY: Basic Books.

Scott, J. F. and R. P. Lynton. 1952. *Three Management Studies.* London: Routledge & Kegan Paul.

Scott, W. R. 1978. "Theoretical Perspectives," in *Environments and Organizations: Theoretical and Empirical Perspectives,* M. W. Meyer and Assoc., eds., San Francisco, CA: Jossey-Bass.

Scott, W. R. 1981. *Organizations.* Englewood Cliffs, NJ: Prentice-Hall, Inc.

Seeley, D. S. 1980. "The Bankruptcy of Service Delivery," paper presented at the

Foundation Lunch Group: Panel on Children, at the Edwin Gould Foundation for Children, New York, NY, February.

Selznick, P. 1948. "Foundations of the Theory of Organizations," *American Sociological Review*, 13(1):25–35.

Sergiovanni, T. J. and F. D. Carver. 1980. *The New School Executive*. New York, NY: Harper & Row, Publishers.

Sergiovanni, T. J., M. Burlingame, F. D. Coombs, and P. W. Thurston. 1980. *Educational Governance and Administration*. Englewood Cliffs, NJ: Prentice-Hall Inc.

Sergiovanni, T. J., M. Burlingame, F. D. Coombs, and P. W. Thurston. 1992. *Educational Governance and Administration*, third ed. Englewood Cliffs, NJ: Prentice-Hall Inc.

Seyfarth, J. T. 1991. *Personnel Management for Effective Schools*. Boston, MA: Allyn and Bacon.

Sheathelm, H. H. 1991. "Common Elements in the Planning Process," in *Educational Planning, Concepts, Strategies, Practices*, R. V. Carlson and G. Awkerman, eds., New York, NY: Longman, pp. 267–277.

Shedd, J. B. 1988. "Collective Bargaining, School Reform and the Management of School Systems," *Educational Administration Quarterly*, 24(4):405–415.

Shulman, L. S. 1990. *Research in Teaching and Learning, Vol. 1, Paradigms and Programs*. A project of the American Educational Research Association. New York, NY: Macmillan Publishing Co.

Siann, G. M. Callaghan, P. Glissov, R. Lockhart, and L. Rawson. 1994. "Who Gets Bullied? The Effects of School, Gender, and Ethnic Group," *Educational Research*, 36(2):123–134.

Sickler, J. L. 1988. "Teachers in Charge: Empowering the Professionals," *Phi Delta Kappan* (January):354–356, 375–376.

Silverman, D. 1956. "The Theory of Organizations," *Administrative Science Quarterly*, 1(1).

Simon, H. A. 1944. "Decision-Making and Administrative Organization," *Public Administration Review*, 4:16–30.

Simon, H. A. 1945. *Administrative Behavior*. New York, NY: The Macmillan Co.

Simon, H. A. 1947. *Administrative Behavior: A Study of Decision-Making Processes in Administrative Organization*. New York, NY: Macmillan.

Simon, H. A. 1957. Models of Man: Social and Rational: Mathematical Essays. New York, NY: John Wiley & Sons.

Simon, H. A. 1960. *The New Science of Management Decision*. New York, NY: Harper & Row Publishers.

Simons, H. 1965. "PERT: How to Meet a Deadline," in W. J. Gephart and W. G. Hack, eds., *Educational Administration: Selected Readings*, New York, NY: Allyn & Bacon, Inc., pp. 277–285.

Slavin, R. 1987. "The Hunterization of America's Schools," *Instructor* (April):56–58.

Slavin, R. E. 1988. *Educational Psychology: Theory into Practice*, second ed. Englewood Cliffs, NJ: Prentice-Hall.

Smalter, D. J. 1969. "The Influence of Department of Defense Practices on Corporate

Planning," in *Systems, Organizations, Analysis, Management,* D. I. Cleland and W. R. King, eds., New York, NY: McGraw-Hill, pp. 140–162.

Southern States Cooperative. 1954. *Applying Research in Education: Report of a Conference held at the University of Chicago, July 19–23.* W. W. Savage, ed., Chicago, IL: University of Chicago Midwest Administration Center.

Squires, D. A., W. G. Huitt, and J. K. Segars. 1983. *Effective Schools and Classrooms: A Research-Based Perspective.* Alexandria, VA: Association for Supervision and Curriculum Development.

Starratt, R. J. 1991. "Building an Ethical School: A Theory for Practice in Educational Leadership," *Educational Administration Quarterly,* 27(2):185–202.

Steiner, G. A. 1969. "The Critical Role of Top Management in Long-Range Planning," in *Systems, Organizations, Analysis, Management,* D. I. Cleland and W. R. King, eds., New York, NY: McGraw-Hill Book Co.

Steiner, G. A. 1979a. "What Is Strategic Planning?" in *Strategic Planning: What Every Manager Must Know,* G. A. Steiner, ed., New York, NY: The Free Press, pp. 12–34.

Steiner, G. A., ed. 1979b. *Strategic Management and Strategic Planning. What Every Manager Must Know.* New York, NY: The Free Press.

Steller, A. W. 1988. *Effective Schools: Research and Promise.* Bloomington, IN: Phi Delta Kappan Educational Foundation.

Straughan, R. and J. Wrigley, eds. 1980. *Values and Evaluation in Education.* London: Harper and Row, Publishers.

Stufflebeam, D. L. 1967. "The Use and Abuse of Evaluation in Title III," *Theory into Practice,* 6:126–133.

Stufflebeam, D. L. 1971. *Educational Evaluation and Decision Making.* Written by PDK National Study Committee on Evaluation, Itaska, IL: Peacock.

Stufflebeam, D. L. and W. J. Webster. 1988. "Evaluation as an Administrative Function," in *Handbook of Research on Educational Administration,* a Project of the American Educational Research Association, N. J. Boyan, ed., New York, NY: Longman, pp. 569–601.

Sufrin, S. C. and G. S. Odiorne. 1985. "The New Strategic Planning Boom: Hope for the Future or a Bureaucratic Exercise?" *Managerial Planning,* 33(4):4–13.

Tagiuri, R. and L. Petrullo, eds. 1958. *Person Perception and Interpersonal Behavior.* Stanford, CA: Stanford University Press.

Tannenbaum, R. 1961. *Leadership in Organizations: A Behavioral Science Approach.* New York, NY: McGraw-Hill.

Tannenbaum, R. and F. Massarik. 1950. "Participation by Subordinates in the Managerial Decision-Making Process," *Bobbs Merrill Reprint Series in the Social Sciences.* Reprinted by permission of *The Canadian Journal of Economics and Political Science,* 16:408–418.

Tannenbaum, R. and W. H. Schmidt. 1973. "How to Choose a Leadership Pattern," *Harvard Business Review,* 51(3):162–171.

Tapscott, D. and A. Caston. 1993. *Paradigm Shift: The New Promise of Information Technology.* New York, NY: McGraw-Hill.

Taylor, F. W. 1911. *Shop Management.* New York, NY: Harper and Row, Publishers.

Taylor, F. W. 1913. *The Principles of Scientific Management.* New York, NY: Harper & Row, Publishers.

Taylor, R. L. and F. T. Helmer. 1978. "A Case Study of Information Gathering for Policy Decisions in Public Schools," *Journal of Educational Research,* 72(1):23–28.

Tead. O. 1945. *Democratic Administration.* New York, NY: Association Press.

Tead. O. 1951. *The Art of Administration.* New York, NY: McGraw-Hill.

The Montreal Gazette. December 1, 1977.

The Montreal Gazette. April 14, 1993.

Thomas, K. 1976. "Conflict and Conflict Management," in *Handbook of Industrial and Organizational Psychology,* M. D. Dunnette, ed., Chicago, IL: Rand McNally.

Thompson, J. D. 1967. *Organizations in Action.* New York, NY: McGraw-Hill Book Co.

Time. 1989. "Parent Power's First Big Test," *Time* (December): Education Section.

Tom, A. R. 1984. *Teaching as a Moral Craft.* New York, NY: Longman Inc.

Tregoe, B. B. and J. W. Zimmerman. 1980. *Top Management Strategy. What It Is and How to Make It Work.* New York, NY: Simon and Schuster.

Turoff, M. 1970. "The Decision of a Policy Delphi," *Technological Forecasting and Social Change,* 2:149–171.

Umstattd, J. G. 1953. *Secondary School Teaching.* Boston, MA: Ginn.

Urwick, H. ed. 1943. *The Elements of Administration.* New York, NY: Harper.

Venn, G. 1970. *Man, Education, and Manpower.* Washington, DC: The American Association of School Administrators.

Von Neuman, J. and O. Morgenstern. 1947. *Theory of Games and Economic Behavior.* Princeton, NJ: Princeton University Press.

Vroom, V. and P. Yetton. 1973. "A New Look at Managerial Decision-Making," *Organizational Dynamics,* 1(4):69–78.

Walberg, H. J. and J. W. Keefe, eds. 1986. *Rethinking Reform: The Principal's Dilemma.* Reston, VA: National Association of Secondary School Principals.

Watzlawick, P., J. H. Beavin, and D. D. Jackson. 1967. *Pragmatics of Human Communication; a Study of Interactional Patterns, Pathologies, and Paradoxes.* New York, NY: Norton.

Watzlawick, P., J. H. Weakland, and R. Fisch. 1974. *Change. Principles of Problem Formation and Problem Resolution.* New York, NY: W. W. Norton & Co., Inc.

Weber, M. 1947. *The Theory of Social and Economic Organizations,* A. M. Henderson (trans.), T. Parsons, ed., New York, NY: Free Press.

Weick, K. E. 1982. "Administering Education in Loosely Coupled Systems," *Phi Delta Kappan,* 63(10):673–676.

Weick, K. E. 1993. "The Collapse of Sensemaking in Organizations: The Mann Gulch Disaster," *Administrative Science Quarterly,* 38:4, 628–652.

Weiner, S. 1983. "Participation, Deadlines, and Choice," in *The Dynamics of Organizational Change,* J. V. Baldridge and T. Deal, eds., Berkeley, CA: McCutchan Publishing Corp., pp. 278–305.

Whitehead, A. N. 1966. *Modes of Thought.* New York, NY: The Free Press.

Wilson, W. 1877. "The Study of Administration," *Political Science Quarterly,* 2:997.

Winkler, R. L. 1972. *An Introduction to Bayesian Inference and Decision.* New York, NY: Holt, Rinehart, and Winston.

Winter, R. 1987. *Action Research and the Nature of Social Inquiry: Professional Innovation and Educational Work.* Aldershot, Hants, England: Avebury.

Wittgenstein, L. 1968. *Philosophical Investigations,* 3rd ed. Trans. by G. E. M. Anscombe, New York, NY: Macmillan.

Wolcott, H. F. 1973. *The Man in the Principal's Office.* New York, NY: Holt, Rinehart and Winston.

Wood, C. J. 1984. "Participatory Decision Making: Why Doesn't It Seem to Work?" *The Educational Forum,* 49(1):55 – 64.

Worth, W. H. 1988. "A Perspective on Educational Planning in Canada," *The Canadian Administrator,* 27(7):1 – 8.

Worthen, B. R. 1993. "Critical Issues That Will Determine the Future of Alternative Assessment," *Phi Delta Kappan,* 73(2):129 – 136.

Zager, R and M. P. Rosow, eds. 1982. *The Innovative Organization: Productivity Programs in Action.* New York, NY: Pergamon Press.

Zaleznik, A. 1965. "The Dynamics of Subordinacy," *Harvard Business Review,* 43(3):119 – 131.

Zuboff, S. 1988. *In the Age of the Smart Machine. The Future of Work and Power.* New York, NY: Basic Books.